D0984745

THE MINI-NUKE CONSPIRACY

The Mini-Nuke Conspiracy

MANDELA'S NUCLEAR NIGHTMARE

Peter Hounam and
Steve McQuillan

faber and faber
LONDON · BOSTON

First published in 1995
by Faber and Faber Limited
3 Queen Square London WC1N 3AU

Printed in England

Peter Hounam and Steve McQuillan are hereby identified as authors
of this work in accordance with Section 77
of the Copyright, Designs and Patents Act 1988

© Peter Hounam and Steve McQuillan, 1995

A CIP record for this book is available
from the British Library

ISBN 0–571–17790–5

10 9 8 7 6 5 4 3 2 1

For the people who cared enough to speak out.
And for our wives, Liz and Lorraine.

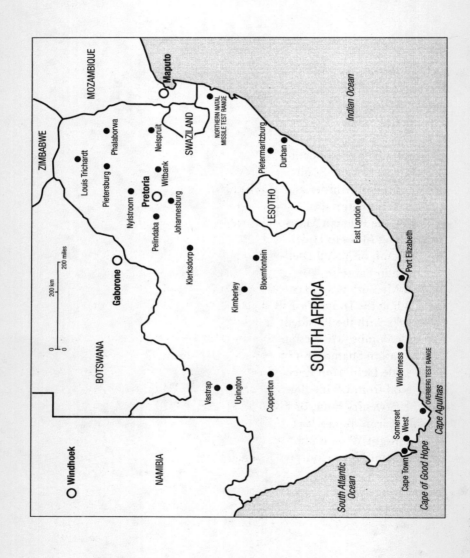

Contents

List of Illustrations

18 The Coventry Four pose with their wives in Pretoria, 1984 (courtesy Associated Press).
19 The mission control centre at South Africa's mini-'Cape Kennedy', a high-security missile testing range.
20 Artist's impression of South Africa's 'Hento' glide-bomb, designed to deliver a nuclear weapon.

Acknowledgements

We could not have completed this investigation without the help of many people.

Steve McQuillan was deputy editor of the *Weekend Star* in Johannesburg during the early months when an investigative team under his direction exposed the black market in red mercury and a related spate of murders. Reporters Janine Lazarus and Norman Chandler made a crucial contribution.

Channel 4 Television in Britain made a documentary on this subject for its *Dispatches* series, with Peter Hounam as researcher. It was directed by Gwynne Roberts and broadcast in February 1995. This documentary first alerted the British public to the possibility of a secret nuclear programme in South Africa.

Roberts also has made two other documentaries on red mercury for Channel 4. Through his determination, some of the truth surrounding the substance's notoriety has been explained.

Jacques Pauw, an investigative journalist with the South African Broadcasting Corporation, made a documentary about the red mercury trade in southern Africa, and showed how inextricably it was connected with a black market in nuclear materials.

Also in South Africa, Nick Badenhorst has made a lifetime's study of the country's nuclear developments. His story is told in Chapter 4, but he also contributed information to other parts of this book, and in particular to our understanding of the relevance of missile developments to the nuclear weapons programme.

The police team investigating the murders at the Brixton Murder and Robbery Unit in Johannesburg were helpful. Our thanks are particularly due to Lieutenant-Colonel Charles Landman, a cop of the old school.

Dr Frank Barnaby, a world authority on nuclear proliferation, is also one of the most knowledgeable scientists on red mercury and its development in the secret military plants of the former Soviet Union. He has given of his time and expertise unstintingly.

To all these people, and again to the scores of sources we pestered and grilled and who trusted us to protect them from any recriminations, thank you.

Peter Hounam and Steve McQuillan
Johannesburg
September 1995

Glossary

AAM	Anti-Apartheid Movement
Advena	Armscor's bomb-making plant, now part of Denel
AEB	Atomic Energy Board, which became part of the AEC in 1982
AEC	Atomic Energy Corporation, created in 1982
Aldermaston	Britain's atomic weapons plant
ANC	African National Congress
Apartheid	National Party policy of separate development of the races
Armscor	Armaments Corporation of South Africa Limited
AVF	Afrikaner Volksfront
AWB	Afrikaner Weerstandsbeweging
BBC	British Broadcasting Corporation
BKA	Boere Krisis Aksie
BOSS	Bureau of State Security, SA
BRA	Boere Republikienseleer
BVB	Boere Vryheidsbeweging
CCB	Civil Co-operation Bureau, covert Special Forces dirty-tricks operation
CIA	Central Intelligence Agency, US
CIS	Crime Intelligence Service, SA
CSIR	Council for Scientific and Industrial Research
Denel	Took over Armscor's manufacturing operations in 1992
Dexsa 94	Defence Exposition of South Africa, held in November 1994
DIA	Defense Intelligence Agency, US
Dimona	Site of Israel's nuclear weapons plant
DoE	Department of Energy, US
FBI	Federal Bureau of Investigation, US
FF	Freedom Front, political party led by General Constand Viljoen

FIS	Foreign Intelligence Service, successor to the KGB
G5	South Africa's 155-mm howitzer
G6	South Africa's 155-mm howitzer, self-propelled
GNU	Government of National Unity
Harwell	British Atomic Energy Research Establishment
HEU	Highly enriched uranium
Houwteq	Space rocket development company, a division of Denel
IAEA	International Atomic Energy Agency
ICBM	Intercontinental ballistic missile
IRS	Internal Revenue Service, US
ISC	International Signal & Control Corporation of Pennsylvania
Kentron Circle	Former name of Advena, the South African nuclear weapons plant
Kentron Irene	Missile manufacturer, part of Denel, formerly part of Armscor
Kentron South	Propellant manufacturer, later part of Somchem
KGB	Komitet Gosudarstvennoy Bezopasnosti, Soviet security service
Kiloton	Nuclear weapon's explosive power, equivalent to 1,000 tons of TNT
Koeberg	South Africa's only nuclear power station
LEU	Low enriched uranium
Megaton	Nuclear weapon's explosive power, equivalent of 1,000 kilotons
MI	Military Intelligence, wing of SANDF
MI6	Popular term for Britain's Secret Intelligence Service or SIS
Mossad	Israeli foreign intelligence service
MPLA	Popular Movement for the Liberation of Angola
MTCR	Missile Technology Control Regime, international missile agreement
NAM	Non-Aligned Movement
NATO	North Atlantic Treaty Organization
NIA	National Intelligence Agency, SA's new domestic intelligence service
NIS	National Intelligence Service, former name of SA's secret service
NPT	Treaty on the Non-Proliferation of Nuclear Weapons
NSA	National Security Agency, US

ORG	Oxford Research Group
Pelindaba	The AEC's National Nuclear Research Centre
Pelinduna	The AEB's heavy water/natural uranium reactor
R	Rand
Red mercury	Common name for liquidized mercury antimony oxide
RSA	Republic of South Africa
SA	South Africa
SAAF	South African Air Force
SABC	South African Broadcasting Corporation
SADF	South African Defence Force, succeeded by SANDF on 27 April 1994
Safari-1	Research reactor supplied to AEB by the United States
SANDF	South African National Defence Force
SAP	South African Police
SAPS	South African Police Service, post-apartheid name of SAP
Sasol	South Africa's oil-from-coal chemical company
SF	Special Forces, the SADF's specialized commando force
Shin Beth	Israel's internal security organization, also called Shabak
Somchem	Somerset West Chemicals, division of Denel, formerly of Armscor
UAE	United Arab Emirates
UN	United Nations
UNITA	National Union for the Total Independence of Angola
US	United States
USAF	United States Air Force
Valindaba	The uranium enrichment plant at Pelindaba
Vastrap	Nuclear test site on edge of the Kalahari desert north of Upington
Vekom	Volkseenheidskomitee (People's Unity Committee) (right-wing group)
VSC	Volkstaat Council
Y-Plant	Production plant for weapons-grade uranium at Valindaba
Z-Plant	LEU production plant, mainly serving Koeberg

Introduction

There is one inevitability about this book: its disclosures will be denied. The South African military cannot admit to what is uncovered here. They, after all, were the paymasters of the country's secret nuclear programmes.

Politicians too will express outrage or heap scorn on what is alleged, but many of them were behind the nuclear deception. Nor will foreign governments back this exposé. Without their covert help, cutting-edge weapon technologies in the Republic of South Africa would be less advanced.

Probably only a handful of decision-makers know the whole truth about South Africa's Mini-Nuke Conspiracy, but there are hundreds of dedicated people who know parts of the truth. Some worked round the clock to develop nuclear weapons believing they were essential for South Africa's security. Their achievements were brilliant testimony to what can be done when a nation's back is put to the wall.

To these physicists, theoreticians, technicians and engineers the bomb represented a brave new scientific frontier. To the government, it represented an instrument of policy – a policy based on the belief that South Africa, shunned by the international community for its practice of apartheid, could rely on no other nation to come to its aid in a time of crisis.

South Africa was alone, isolated from the society of nations. Or was it? Could the West really resist having resource-rich South Africa as a partner? Indeed they could not, as this book will show, including in the most important strategic area of all – that of nuclear weapons.

For Western intelligence agencies and military forces, it was business as usual. Their global strategies would not be disturbed by idealistic politicians. The global balance of power, including military movements in southern Africa, was more important to them than supporting the plight of black South Africans.

The South African military, with a little help from its friends, would deceive the world. It would build a nuclear arsenal to rank among the best. And it would come close to using that arsenal in its darkest hour.

Then came the political revolution in South Africa in the late 1980s. The country realized that the African National Congress, the most powerful black liberation movement, would one day govern the nation. Those who had their fingers on the nuclear trigger were determined to ensure that ANC leader Nelson Mandela did not get the bomb. But also they themselves did not want to give it up. Yet others wanted to use it to secure a better deal for whites.

That is how the Mini-Nuke Conspiracy entered its final stage. We heard how a renegade group, which most observers would place on the right of the political spectrum, had grabbed the means to wage their own private nuclear war amid South Africa's transition to democracy. Their precise relationship with elements of the military high command was a key factor. They threatened, and may still threaten, the country and the future of the free ballot in Africa.

Journalists sometimes get things wrong because they do not have the time to do proper research or they have too few witnesses to verify what they are trying to reveal. We believe that, because we have had ample time to check sources, to conduct proper research, and to interview scores of witnesses, we have done everything in our power to eliminate inconsistencies and inaccuracies. Research took more than a year in South Africa and many months in Europe, Russia and the United States before that.

Some may suggest disinformation and question the honesty of our informants. But to accept this would be to ignore the wide range and seniority of the sources who contributed to this investigation and the consistency of the accounts. Which mastermind could have orchestrated the dozens of people we interviewed at random?

The investigation in South Africa could not have been carried out even a year earlier. It is only because the country has now shaken off the yoke of apartheid and its bed-mate – repression – that the truth can slowly emerge. Even so, no one should be surprised that so many of our sources are anonymous. They may have been incautious, but they are not stupid. We have found no one quite like Mordechai Vanunu, the Israeli who in 1986 exposed his country's nuclear weapons programme and paid the penalty with an eighteen-year prison sentence. However, many of the people we contacted showed considerable courage in helping us to flesh out the truth.

The following is just a sample of what the some of the sources directly involved in the nuclear programme told us. These are not their real names.

Jeff, a scientist on the bomb programme: 'The bombs we made were smaller and more sophisticated than de Klerk has admitted. They were designed for a glide bomb and intercontinental ballistic missiles.'

Dion, a bomb programme-manager: 'The vaults were so full of nuclear warheads they had to bring in portable safes. The programme was originally for twenty-five, and we had enough enriched uranium to do that.'

Jake, a military sanctions-buster: 'The key project was to produce a "clean" neutron bomb with no fallout. It was called Project Shampoo, and the bomb was perfected by the late 1980s. It is the ultimate weapon of mass destruction. Britain, the United States, France and Italy were in on the project, and the Israelis also helped. There were at least two nuclear tests, and the Americans switched off their spy satellites for us.'

Jan, a senior military strategist for the former National Party government: 'We had silos across the country with medium-range missiles that could deliver a nuclear bomb on Lusaka or Dar es Salaam. There have been numerous nuclear detonations that were kept secret from the world as we tested our neutron bomb. Many of the bombs are now being hidden by a friendly country – probably Israel.'

Simon, a former Special Forces commando: 'We had tiny nuclear devices that could be fired from a hand-held weapon. I was told we used these in Angola.'

And these are some of their comments on the 'right-wing' nuclear bomb:

Jan: 'They've got G6s with nuclear shells in the Johannesburg area. They are regularly moved.'

Eugene: 'They've got up to twelve nuclear warheads stashed at farms across the northern Transvaal.'

Rick, a government agent who penetrated the right wing: 'I've seen part of a warhead and a long missile that was under heavy guard by the Right. So I have one confirmed, but information about four others.'

Hennie, a military agent: 'They've got it and they can use it and will use it if they are threatened. I'm told they have one of the "dirty" bombs and a Buccaneer to deliver it. One target I heard was Harare.'

Paul, a military intelligence agent: 'The right wing has nuclear weapons and poses a serious threat to South Africa. Ninety per cent of the people involved are military – serving and former. They say within five years they will retake the country.'

Asked to comment on the basic claims of this book, a high-ranking South African intelligence official, instructed to meet the authors on behalf of government, said: 'Possible, if not probable.'

This book tells the story of how South Africa found itself in such a mess.

1 The Body in the Boot

The police officer opened the official folder and flipped through a dozen or so pages before carefully spreading out the contents in his lap. There before us lay a series of grim crime-scene photographs.

A man's body had been horrendously disfigured, its arms and legs amputated and its buttocks sliced off. The killer's butchery had exposed part of the spinal column. Most strange of all, the torso and body parts had been smeared with a black, oily substance. They had all been unceremoniously dumped into the boot of a white BMW 728i. The car had been abandoned in Johannesburg – South Africa's largest metropolis and its capital of business and industry. From there it had been stolen and driven to Soweto, Johannesburg's sprawling dormitory township that is home for millions of black South Africans. Then the car thieves got the shock of their lives. They had apparently taken the vehicle to a quiet location near the Orlando soccer stadium to remove the radio and speakers. They opened the boot – and fled in horror.

Police had found the car, and its contents, on 9 November 1991, after a tip-off. It was the start of one of the biggest and most complex murder investigations in South African history – an investigation that would attempt to peel back the layers of national security and venture into the most sensitive areas of highly classified secrets.

The dead man was a forty-eight-year-old British sales executive called Alan Kidger. He had, by all accounts, a straightforward job with a chemical company. But even in the earliest stages this was clearly no ordinary case. Why was Kidger's body cut up and painted?

The case had first been handed to police in Soweto but it was quickly transferred to the Brixton Murder and Robbery Unit in Johannesburg, which boasted a 60 per cent success rate in solving serious crimes.

Brixton is one of eight special police squads dotted through South Africa's major urban centres to deal with the worst of crime. It has a reputation – not all of it good. During the 1980s the Brixton unit became notorious. Allegations concerning police torture were commonplace; rough-handed treatment was normal. Deaths in police custody generally were uneasily explained away. Looking at Brixton's past, it seemed almost natural that when disclosures about South Africa's military and police death squads emerged in 1989 and 1990 they eventually implicated a number of former detectives at Brixton, including two of its former commanding officers.

The man put in charge of investigating Kidger's death was Lieutenant-Colonel Charles Landman, a veteran detective with more than twenty years of police experience. He had worked in various posts across South Africa before arriving at Brixton with a reputation for 'getting his man' – not always by conventional means.

He leaned forward and jabbed his stubby right index finger into the file on his lap, seeking out the image of the carved-up body in the boot.

'Whoever did this has to be found,' Landman told us. 'We're not dealing with a normal killer here. No human being deserves to die in this manner.'

Landman leaned back into his chair, tapping his old wooden desk with the end of a pencil. Around him, on his desk, on side-tables and on the floor behind, were stacks of pale-blue folders, each one a case docket relating to some other murder or robbery. With such a workload, not many South Africans would have been surprised if the matter at hand had been left indefinitely, or forgotten amid the deluge of new cases flooding the offices at Brixton. But the body-in-the-boot case was not run-of-the-mill. It held a particular grisly fascination for police officers and journalists alike.

A post-mortem had established that Kidger had been slashed in the face and arm and killed by a huge blow to the head. There was virtually no blood left in his body, or in the boot of the car.

Landman reckoned he had been killed at an unknown location and the pieces of body had been loaded into the boot afterwards. Police forensic experts said the oily-black substance smeared on the body was an alkyd resin, used as an isolator in paints with a high lead content. Another analysis indicated a high percentage of mercury.

It seemed the substance might have something to do with Kidger's job. He was a paint technologist by training and worked for Thor SA (Pty) Ltd, which dealt in mercury compounds.

Landman believed Kidger had been involved in 'something big'. But, if he had been, where had his money gone? 'He wasn't poor, but there were by no means large amounts of money in his bank account.'

Kidger's Brazilian-born wife, Marlene, said that two days before the body was found the telephone had rung just after the couple had finished supper. She answered and passed the receiver to her husband, who arranged to meet someone. He then drove off in his car and she never saw him again.

Said Landman: 'Who would go to such extreme lengths, and why leave the body in the middle of the city? An advertisement? Was it a warning?'

Alan Kidger was born in an industrial area of Tyneside, in the north of England. After grammar school, he qualified as a paint technologist at Rutherford College. He left England in 1974 after successfully applying for a job at a Johannesburg paint company. There he met his first wife, an East German called Yeanni, ten years his senior.

Although he was putting down roots in Africa, Kidger returned to England every three years to see his family. They reported he was always cheerful, 'a real go-getter'. But his marriage wasn't going well. The couple were divorced in 1989, and Kidger then married Marlene, whom he had first met in Sao Paulo.

In 1976 Kidger had gone to work for Thor, based at Cato Ridge near the Indian Ocean port city of Durban in South Africa's Natal province. It was a fast-expanding subsidiary of a British-owned company based in Margate, Kent. His administrative talents were soon recognized, and he was eventually promoted to managing director of its plant that reprocessed mercury waste.

It was not an easy job, and Kidger was soon enmeshed in allegations from environmentalists that the mercury passing through the plant was slowly poisoning its workers. Later, Kidger got a new job as international sales director at Thor's offices in Alberton, on the southern outskirts of Johannesburg, but the allegations against Thor's safety procedures continued. In July 1992 a government inquiry into Thor heard allegations of mercury seeping into rivers from the Cato Ridge site. Several workers were seriously ill with mercury poisoning.

It was suggested that some workers had been deliberately poisoned by unknown saboteurs who 'spiked' breathing equipment with a massive dose of mercury. One worker said someone had tried to kill him by placing a white powder in his boots. He was later admitted to hospital, also with suspected mercury poisoning.

Desmond Cowley, chairman of Thor's parent company, Thor Chemical Holdings Ltd in the UK, said there had been 'a long list of events which we know were sabotage'. He then suggested Kidger might have been a victim of these saboteurs.

We heard from an intelligence agent that Thor had a close relationship with government. Three independent sources said Thor had been secretly linked to the Armaments Corporation of South Africa Ltd – better known as Armscor.

Jim Kidger is a brother in anguish. It's not knowing why his brother died that keeps him awake at night. He has pushed the authorities in Britain and South Africa to press harder to solve the murder, and was happy when the media finally showed they would not let the matter rest. At home in Cape Town it is difficult for him to come to terms with the horror and intrigue surrounding such an extraordinary death.

He said that at the mortuary, where he'd gone to identify his brother's mutilated body, a detective was in a discussion with an executive from Thor. Jim said they were speculating about the substance smeared over his brother's body. 'The Thor chap was talking about red mercury,' said Jim, 'a very expensive substance in which his company apparently had an interest at that time. From the conversation, it seemed Alan had been dealing with that aspect of the work as part of Thor's business plan.'

The Thor executive at the morgue that day was Dave Ramsey. He became sales director at Thor after Kidger's murder. Ramsey said that people had contacted Thor about red mercury, but the company had never made it.[1] He would not confirm that Alan Kidger had been looking at the chemical's potential. Asked why he had talked about red mercury at the mortuary, he told a reporter he wasn't prepared to continue the conversation and put the phone down. Said Jim Kidger: 'I believe my brother's death was connected to red mercury.'

Landman had also heard of the red mercury allegations, but at first he had not treated them seriously. He knew of stories that it was a hoax substance, connected with scams in Eastern Europe and the Middle East. His forensic experts could tell him nothing about it. But other people mentioned that Alan Kidger had talked about the chemical and was discussing it earnestly in phone calls.

Landman had also heard that Alan Kidger was trying to arrange a contract with Iraq, and he had unsubstantiated information that on the night of his death four men had been seen going into Thor's offices in Johannesburg in a great hurry and left with documents. This was intrigu-

[1] A Thor chemist produced a report for police working on another case in which she referred to red mercury's application in nuclear weapons and described the dangers of handling the substance. When contacted, she said the report had been speculative and based on what other people had said about the substance.

4

ing, but of no help in finding who had carried out the crime.

Other cases were piling up, but Landman resisted pressure to shelve the Kidger murder. Then on 16 July 1993 he had something else to think about. Five minutes before he left for work, a limpet mine ripped apart his white Ford Sapphire, parked outside his home in Florida on the western outskirts of Johannesburg. Warrant Officer Johan Bezuidenhout of the Bomb Disposal Unit said the saboteurs would have been able to set a time for the explosion of the MPM mine, which had been attached to the front of Landman's vehicle.

Was it just a warning, or did the bombers intend to kill him? It could have been connected to any number of police investigations in which Landman had been involved. But no one claimed responsibility, and there was a nagging concern that the explosion was connected to the body-in-the-boot case.

In mid-1994 there was yet a further development that would rocket the Kidger case into the headlines. Landman had spoken to a source in Europe who had sensational new information about the mystery killing. Apparently, in 1992 the source had warned Landman not to press ahead with his investigation until the arrival of the new democratic government that was expected following the unbanning of the ANC and the release from jail of Nelson Mandela two years earlier. 'You won't get anywhere under the old regime,' he had predicted correctly. 'There will be too much outside interference.'

He had promised to keep the police officer on the right track with a number of pointers, but urged Landman to do his own investigating to establish the accuracy of his claims. Having done this, Landman decided it was time to put the cat among the pigeons. Two months after the election, he made his move. In a tactic calculated to generate public interest in the case and flush out possible new leads – the case had been dormant for two and a half years – Landman delivered a bombshell. He accused Mossad, the Israeli secret service, of the Kidger murder.

In a front-page report in the Johannesburg-based *Weekend Star* newspaper on 25 June 1994, Landman said he believed Mossad – whose functions are primarily espionage, intelligence-gathering and covert operations in foreign countries – had killed Kidger because he was supplying Middle Eastern countries with high-tech chemicals that could be used in the manufacture of nuclear weapons. Disclosing the internationally sensational nature of his inquiry, he said he was convinced the Kidger death was connected to secret deals that could have become a threat to the international balance of power.

Police sources said later there was a strong possibility that the deals involved the export from South Africa of materials which could have been used to help Iraqi President Saddam Hussein build a nuclear bomb during or just after the Gulf War.

Landman told the *Weekend Star*: 'We believe Kidger was working for foreign governments, and the nature of that work had something to do with the production of arms that required high-tech chemicals. Alan Kidger was involved in supplying these chemicals to Middle Eastern countries. The chemicals are used in the production of nuclear weapons. The murder was a hit aimed at sending a clear message. It involved something only a government would be interested in.'

It was a sensational claim, and the Israeli embassy, predictably, kicked up a fuss. 'An imaginary story,' said the spokesman. 'I'm sure Mossad is not involved in any such activity.' But would he necessarily know about all the activities of Mossad? The response: 'No. Do you?' But he persisted: 'I can assure you Mossad has not been involved in killing anyone in South Africa.'

A week later, the pot was still boiling. The Israeli ambassador to South Africa, Dr Alon Liel, was angry with the newspaper for printing Landman's accusations and furious with the police for not going to him in the first place. He said he could only assume that, since nothing had been brought to his attention officially, there was 'nothing serious' behind the allegations. 'We categorically deny Mossad involvement in the death of Alan Kidger.'

Liel said that whenever there were arms sales to the Middle East, the 'prime suspect' of any subsequent wrongdoing was Mossad. 'It happens all over the world. Mysterious murder cases with international connotations are attributed to Mossad. Unfortunately, we are getting used to it. We have worked for the South African authorities in the past and we'll work for them in the future.'

It didn't end there. The allegations prompted South African defence minister Joe Modise to enter the fray, clumsily likening Israel's domestic policies to apartheid, and condemning its past links with the former South African government, its military and its weapons institutions. He promised to take action if the police charges were found to be true. Now it was becoming a diplomatic crisis. Liel hit back verbally, then called for a meeting with Foreign Ministry officials in Pretoria.

Matters were made worse when the Justice Department said that, if Mossad had killed in South Africa, it would attempt to extradite those responsible.

Foreign Affairs Minister Alfred Nzo stepped in to cool down the rapidly heating diplomatic incident. He said Modise had been referring specifically to the arms industry and that relationships between the two countries were on an even keel. Then Mandela stepped in, labelling Modise's words 'most unfortunate'.

Liel expressed his government's concern that the allegations against Mossad could make an impression on the South African public's perception of Israel broadly. 'This sort of thing can affect some people, even if it doesn't affect relations between the countries.'

The Department of Foreign Affairs promised consultations with the police. Safety and Security Minister Sydney Mufamadi later issued a statement saying he and Nzo had been apprised of the police investigation into the alleged involvement of Mossad in murders in South Africa. 'These investigations are now at a sensitive stage and are being conducted by a team of highly experienced SAPS detectives.'

Landman later said the source who had convinced him that Mossad was to blame came from within the Israeli government. He stood by his statement.

Investigations in Europe revealed that Mossad agents had infiltrated red mercury deals to sabotage them. An agent of South African Military Intelligence believed Landman was right to accuse Mossad. Speaking on condition of anonymity, he said Mossad had been involved before in killings that were related to red mercury transactions overseas.

Several people in a Belgian consortium wanting to buy red mercury were killed between 1986 and 1989, along with a West German scientist. 'There were four Belgians killed out of a group of seven. They were professors, chemical engineers, scientists. I think they were all murdered.' He said the killings were done by a specialist unit of the Mossad. The four- or five-man hit team operated across the world, led by a colonel.

Another South African intelligence agent was equally suspicious of Mossad. He said it was important to understand that the role of Mossad was to protect the state of Israel and its citizens from any threat, or *perceived* threat. In any case, he said, at least one senior agent at the Israeli embassy had left South Africa immediately after the Kidger killing, and he considered that suspicious.

If Landman was right and Mossad's role in the killing is subsequently proved, it will, apparently, not have been the first time this secret service has gone to such lengths to thwart Arab attempts to obtain nuclear weapons technology. In fact Mossad has been working hand in glove with the CIA in the United States and MI6 in Britain to curb Saddam's nuclear ambitions.

In 1979 an Israeli team of saboteurs broke into a warehouse in Toulon, France, where the 'beehive' cores of two nuclear reactors supplied by France and destined for Iraq were stored. Mossad agents tried to steal them, ran out of time, and blew them up instead. Both cores were heavily damaged, and it was thought that the raid would severely delay Iraq's nuclear plans.

A year later Professor Yahia El Meshad, the Egyptian-born head of Iraq's Atomic Energy Agency, was bludgeoned to death in his bedroom at the Hôtel Méridien near the Arc de Triomphe in Paris. His wallet and personal documents were untouched. The killer left a 'Do not disturb' sign on the bedroom door.

French police kept the murder secret for four days to give the French Foreign Ministry time to reassure the Iraqis that French intelligence had not been involved. Suspicion immediately fell on the Israelis, and, although they never admitted they were responsible, neither did they hide their satisfaction. A week later the call-girl with whom the professor had spent his last night was run down by a car and killed.

In Rome, bombs went off at the Italian company that agreed to sell Iraq a radio-chemistry laboratory, while back in France there was intimidation against engineers thought to be working in Iraq.

Then, on 7 June 1981, came one of Israel's most spectacular moves. Eight F16 bombers, each armed with two 1,000-kg bombs, took off with an escort of six F15 Eagle fighters to attack the Osiraq Research Reactor, just outside Baghdad. After one pass over the building, and despite the heavy concrete reinforcement, it was destroyed. There were suspicions that the success of the operation had also depended on saboteurs inside. French contractors were building the plant.

Of more immediate relevance was the death of maverick Canadian scientist Gerald Bull, who was said to be involved in secretly building a supergun for Iraq. Bull (sixty-two) was assassinated in March 1990 in Brussels. The scientist was struck by five bullets from an automatic pistol as he fumbled for his keys outside the entrance to his sixth-floor flat.

A television documentary into Bull's death made by the British Broadcasting Corporation (BBC) revealed that an Israeli defence official, a Mossad officer and two field agents said Tel Aviv had ordered his execution. The programme said Bull had been warned by the Israelis that they would be forced to act unless he severed ties with Baghdad.

*

Did Kidger ever get a similar warning? We may never know. However, a new witness who could shed light on what happened had emerged, and the police could thank the Kidger family for bringing him forward.

Jim Kidger revealed he had received a letter addressed to his brother's next-of-kin from a man in Birkenhead, England, less than a year after the killing. 'The letter intimated that this man had done business with my brother in mid-1991 and later the same year,' he said. 'He apparently wanted to finalize the business and pay out Alan's share of it. He needed power of attorney for insurance purposes.'

In March 1993 Jim Kidger had travelled to Liverpool to meet the man, John Allen, a highly qualified chemist whose speciality was 'purifying chemicals'. 'He said he had worked for the South African and British governments as a chemical specialist. He had apparently also lived and worked in a private capacity in Zambia, but had left in a hurry after an attempt was made on his life.'

Allen had smuggled chemicals out of Zambia using routes known to him while he was working for South Africa as a chemical specialist.[1]

At first, Allen had been wary of Jim Kidger: he explained there had been three other visitors all claiming to be relatives of the dead man, none of whom he had believed. One of them, he said, was 'definitely' a South African security agent. Allen had had this visitor checked out, and found that after their meeting he had returned to London, visited the South African embassy in Trafalgar Square and then, that same evening, boarded a flight to New York.

Asked how he could have anyone checked out, he implied he had security connections: 'Let's say I was a consultant on chemical matters.' He said he had used his contacts to get information on the man from the embassy.

Allen had married an Iranian woman called Seena while working for the British government, said Jim Kidger. 'He told me his wife's brother was a nuclear scientist working as a researcher for the University of New Mexico in the United States. Another of her relatives was a well-known Iranian political activist. Allen and his wife had met in Liverpool on a blind date arranged by a mutual friend, but had divorced in 1993.'

Allen had deliberately not disclosed details of his new wife's background, so, as a result of his new family connections with Iran, Allen

1 Sources with underworld connections in Zambia said there was a strong possibility of a link between such activities and smuggling operations from several African countries. Uranium, titanium and radium are believed to have been smuggled from Zaïre into Zambia.

said he was considered too great a risk and was asked to leave 'the service'. (Jim Kidger believed he meant MI5 or MI6, the British intelligence agencies.) This was exactly what Allen had hoped for. It allowed him to pursue his interest in refining chemicals.

Allen said he had left a lot of expensive chemicals behind in Zambia which he referred to as 'strategic material', said Jim Kidger. 'He wanted the chemicals to set up a legitimate business in Britain, refining chemicals to a high degree to sell to Middle Eastern countries. I asked what these chemicals would be used for. He said any chemical in its purest state would be used for medical research, printing money (which, according to Russian sources, is an application of red mercury) and making weapons. I asked him if it was for nuclear weapons, and he said "Yes."'

Allen disclosed he had contacted Alan Kidger to ask him to act as a consultant for his business after Allen fled Zambia, abandoning the chemicals. The idea was to have Kidger inspect the chemicals as they moved from Zambia, through Johannesburg and Durban, where the consignments would be repacked and shipped to Britain. He would have been paid a consultancy fee of about £80,000 ($124,000) to verify the first consignment.

In Britain they were to be refined and shipped through a Swiss company to the Middle East. Allen told Jim Kidger there were seventeen flasks of red mercury stored in a warehouse in Zambia. The stockpile apparently also included flasks of heavy water, used both in nuclear reactors and nuclear weapons, and tritium, used in thermonuclear devices.

Alan Kidger and Allen had then gone into business with two other international traders working in Zambia, Charles Hill and Ben Bruno, who had a warehouse in Kitwe. Bruno had apparently disappeared immediately after the Kidger death.

In March 1991 Hill, Kidger and Bruno had allegedly become directors of a company called Abbeywood Enterprises in Fallowfield, Manchester, which was formerly registered under the name Falconer. Allen had wanted no paperwork leading to him.

Jim Kidger's account of Allen's testimony then got even more interesting. 'He told me he had accompanied a truck driver in Britain with the first consignment of refined chemicals, worth £1.1 million [$1.7 million], headed for the Middle East – he didn't say which country. The impression I got was there were more consignments to follow.

'They were approaching Dover to take the ferry across to the Continent and the Middle East when they were hijacked by a gang of men with southern-English accents,' said Jim Kidger. The driver fled, but

Allen said he had been pulled out of the truck, beaten, and pushed into a car. However, he managed to throw himself out again. He was taken to hospital by people in a car travelling behind him.

He thought the attackers, who took the cargo, were part of British intelligence. They did not want the materials to go to the Middle East. These included titanium, mercury compounds and beryllium, used in nuclear weapons. As soon as Allen came out of hospital following the attack, he had tried to contact Alan Kidger and was then told of his death. He said he had immediately stopped the next consignment, which was worth £1.2 million ($1.9 million), and faced questioning from police, customs officials and the security services.

Said Jim Kidger: 'I asked him whether Alan was killed by the South African government or any other government. He shrugged his shoulders and said: "With a normal government, dispatch is clean and quick – a bullet in the head."'

'He then offered a comment that maybe the South African government found out that the channels being used to get the chemicals were the same ones they used, or would like to use, for their own ends. Then they may have approached Alan, either to stop it or to seek his help in using similar methods to get something for themselves or a third party. He said maybe at this stage Alan realized he was into something more than importing and verifying chemical consignments.'

Jim Kidger said he asked Allen about the telephone call made to his brother on the night he disappeared. Allen said the call 'could have been from London – MI6'. 'I asked why he said this, and he smiled and said it was only a possibility that the British government had got Alan to assist them. I asked in what, and Allen said there were things even he would not divulge.'

Allen said that if the full story were made public he believed the people most likely to be embarrassed were those in the South African government – 'and others' – because of their clandestine work over the years.

Jim Kidger's account of his meeting with Allen was a startling insight into what his brother had been doing just before he died. But had Allen been telling the truth? Jim Kidger believed he had, and that Allen had known his brother well. 'When we left his office in Liverpool, we went on this tortuous route to a coffee-shop. He said he had been shot at before and had his car tampered with. He was happy to say nothing until I questioned him. To me, all this lent him credibility.'

Later, the *Weekend Star* also tracked down Allen. 'I used to deal in a fairly murky world,' he told the newspaper's chief investigator on the murder, reporter Janine Lazarus. 'There have been a lot of attempts on my life. I am difficult to get hold of. But if you come here with the right contacts, I'll see you.'

Lazarus flew to Britain and met Allen at a hotel room in Bromborough, near Birkenhead. He told how he lived for two years in Zambia surrounded by armed guards, Dobermans and 'enough weapons to start a small war'.

Allen said he now ran a printing business called Mercury Printers and was semi-retired, but working in Zambia had been a 'profitable business'.

Allen was more than a little cagey with Lazarus and was less forthcoming than he had been with Jim Kidger. But he did refer to a bombing of his Liverpool home and to an attack on his Iranian ex-wife, shot four times in her arm while driving his car to a party. He said the shots were meant for him. 'Maybe I'd crossed somebody in business. I had some people in Zambia who would have preferred me not to be in business.'

Allen said he had worked in South Africa from 1981 to 1983 as an engineering inspector and subsequently returned to the country several times. He had never worked for the British government, he said. He had first met Alan Kidger in South Africa in 1986 while he was running his import/export businesses out of Zambia. 'Later he asked me for information on how to go about importing and exporting.'

He confirmed Kidger had asked about Iraq too. 'He asked if I had any way of getting into Iraq or had any contacts there.'

Allen said he didn't know what Kidger was involved in. Pressed for more information, he told Lazarus: 'It could be dangerous to know. If you do something for someone, you don't give them the third degree and ask them a lot of questions.'

He said that in Zambia it would have been 'most unusual' if any business had been '100 per cent legal'. 'You can transfer things with a minimum of paperwork or absolutely none at all. And you can transfer them anywhere. A police chief in Kitwe was getting something like £100 a month – if you want to buy a police chief or customs official, you can work it out for yourself. For a South African or Brit, it's like chicken feed. Unfortunately everyone has a price.'

He said Alan Kidger wanted to be a wheeler-dealer but he claimed not to know how.

Alan Kidger had probably become involved in something that was out of his depth. 'It was a very nasty way to go. It was obviously a message to someone. Who knows?'

Jim Kidger believed the same. 'Alan's death was an obvious signal to others to stop doing what he was involved in. Having seen Alan in the mortuary, it was obvious that it was a clinical dismembering of a body. My first thought was that there was international involvement in his death because of the smearing of his body with a mercury-rich compound. There is sensitivity over mercury compounds internationally.'

Landman also thought it would be worth meeting Allen. In July 1994, with three other detectives, the colonel went to Britain, but managed to get only a private off-the-record chat with Allen, after overcoming a number of bureaucratic hurdles with Scotland Yard, who seemed reluctant to help.

He then flew to Lyons, in France, to see Thor boss Desmond Cowley. Cowley had agreed to be interviewed, but when Landman arrived he apparently failed to show up. Landman had also planned interviews in Germany and the Far East – Kidger had travelled extensively to the Middle East, Hong Kong, China, Singapore, Thailand, Malaysia and Sri Lanka among other places – but once again there was mixed success. The murder inquiry was not going well.

The evidence pointed to Kidger's having secret dealings with the Middle East involving strategic chemicals. But Landman was little nearer pinning the blame on the group he had publicly blamed, Mossad.

Interviewed about Kidger's death, 'Rick', a South African intelligence agent, revealed another dimension, running parallel to, or connected with, the exporting of chemicals. Asked what he knew of the killing, this is what he told us.

'I believe he was killed by a foreign government, by the Israelis – Mossad.'

Why? 'Maybe they wanted to send a message to people.'

And what was that message? 'I'm led to believe he tried to export certain things.'

What were those items? 'A certain accelerator for a nuclear device.'

A nuclear trigger or an accelerator? 'I'm talking about a trigger.'

Are you talking about a mercury trigger? 'I'm talking about a trigger that's about this size' (he indicated the size of a fist).

An electronic trigger? 'An electronic trigger.'

Kidger was involved in chemicals. How would he have become involved in selling nuclear triggers? 'I don't know.'

But the brutality of the affair – he was chopped up in little pieces and then smeared with a substance … 'They wanted to send a message.'

That's very unlike Mossad. 'They wanted to send a message.'

Were these devices connected to Thor or Armscor and being sold offi-cially, or was Kidger involved in a private deal? 'I think he was involved in a private deal.'

Have you heard of attempts by the Israeli government to mop up sup-plies of red mercury that are being traded here? 'I think the Israeli gov-ernment is trying to.'

The relationship between Israel and South Africa had been cosy – especially on the armaments front. If the above is true, it would go a long way towards explaining what Jim Kidger had heard regarding a cover-up. He said that senior officials in the previous South African gov-ernment had actively discouraged the police investigation. 'The impres-sion I got … was that governments were involved, which was why the whole thing had become difficult.'

How right he was. A week later a senior police source told the *Weekend Star* he suspected the killing was linked either to the previous South African government or to agencies working for it. The source was reluctant to elaborate, but said the killing could have been committed with the knowledge or even partial consent of the South African govern-ment: 'We think so.'

Jim Kidger was also told by Allen that the murderer would never be brought to justice. 'He advised me to make as much of a stink as possi-ble, but warned that the South African government would block the case at every turn.'

This was just the start. The same police team would soon be investi-gating a second murder in which they suspected the victim had somehow been involved in supplying sensitive chemicals to the Middle East. And again the death would be linked to Mossad.

2 'They've Got the Bomb'

It was not the sort of thing you would expect. Here were the feared security police, politely identifying themselves as such in the offices of the *Weekend Star* in central Johannesburg. It's not that they hadn't been there before – they, like other intelligence services in South Africa, had been omnipresent in newsrooms across the country, filching snippets of political intrigue and background information on senior staff through their network of apartheid patriots or commercially minded informants. In the past, these were the people who helped plant pro-government stories, discredit opponents of apartheid, and harass proponents of democracy. But here we were witnessing something different, something alarming in its up-front honesty – in fact, something in liberal journalistic terms akin to a UFO sighting.

The two policemen seemed deeply troubled about something. It was September 1994 and almost four months since the newspaper had started running stories in increasing detail on the widespread killings in South Africa which slowly, inexorably, were leading journalists into the nuclear weapons arena.

They knew the *Weekend Star* coverage had been dealing with the issue of red mercury. And that was the point.

'Mr McQuillan,'[1] said the more senior police officer, 'please tell us as much as you can about red mercury.' He asked that the newspaper protect the officers' identities because they worked under cover and exposure could be dangerous. However, he did show his accreditation certificate and invited the newspaper to confirm his credentials by telephoning his superior officer at police headquarters. His story checked out. Now intrigued, the newspaper agreed to co-operate. 'But let's not talk here,' said the senior officer. 'Walls have ears.' Whose 'ears' he was talking about was not clear.

1 At the time, Steve McQuillan was deputy editor of the *Weekend Star* and orchestrating its investigation into the killings and red mercury. Later, he actively participated in the inquiries, establishing contact with a number of people within the country's security structures.

The meeting resumed at the Marshall's Inn, a downtown bar that offered inexpensive lunches and to which local office workers retired in legions at midday to escape their air-conditioned chores. Whatever was happening, it was apparent that even in a smoky environment of beer-enhanced joviality the two police officers were not comfortable. Maybe that was the fault of the now three journalists with them, for McQuillan had been joined by his co-author Peter Hounam and Gwynne Roberts, who at this time were both visiting South Africa on behalf of Channel 4 Television, which had commissioned a documentary on the South African killings and their links to nuclear weapons. The police were suspicious of two other men sitting nearby, so they stood up and without making a fuss quietly moved to another table, out of eavesdropping range.

The policemen, one moustached and in his thirties, the other clean-shaven, thin and in his twenties, ordered a round of drinks and surveyed the room.

The 'Moustache' was still jumpy as the discussion switched to the Crime Intelligence Service (CIS), which was born out of the notorious police Security Branch, whose brief had been to enforce the smooth running of the former apartheid state using any means at its disposal, including 'dirty tricks'.[1]

The CIS function remained national security. Looking to the British journalists, The Moustache said: 'It's roughly akin to your MI5. We are not the organization we used to be.' Then he shook his head and mumbled in his native Afrikaans: 'I never thought I would find myself dealing

[1] The CIS has since been disbanded. Under a new intelligence-gathering structure introduced in late 1994, its role was largely taken over by the National Investigation Services (NIS), operated by the South African Police Service (SAPS), and the National Intelligence Agency (NIA), operated by Civilian Intelligence (CI). CI was born from the old National Intelligence Services (NIS), the ANC's Department of Intelligence and Security, the Security Services of the Pan Africanist Congress and intelligence services from the black homeland states of Venda, Transkei and Bophuthatswana. CI's foreign arm is the South African Secret Service (SASS). Running parallel with the above is Military Intelligence (MI) of the South African National Defence Force (SANDF). CI, SAPS and the SANDF report to the National Intelligence Co-ordinating Committee, which in turn reports to the Cabinet. President Nelson Mandela now has ultimate responsibility for all intelligence-gathering and often is the exclusive recipient of sensitive information. A parliamentary committee, appointed by Mandela in association with the Speaker of the National Assembly, has oversight of all intelligence operations. The Minister of Justice, Dullah Omar, was delegated by Mandela to oversee the administration of all intelligence services, and Second Deputy President F. W. de Klerk is chairman of the Co-ordinating Committee on Security. De Klerk advises Cabinet on broad policy matters. However, this book deals with a period just before the new intelligence structures were announced, so in text the old acronyms apply.

like this with you Brits. As for dealing with journalists – it's unthinkable.'

The Moustache said a few days earlier he had received a 2 a.m. telephone call from a scientist who had been one of his paid informants years earlier: 'We got rid of the guy because we no longer needed him.' The man, who had worked on South Africa's nuclear weapons programme, had not been seen by the intelligence agents since. 'He was in a state,' said The Moustache. 'He said he had just heard something terrible. He told me an extreme right-wing organization had got a nuclear bomb, the size and shape of a baseball bat. Then he started to cry.

'He said it was hidden in the northern Cape and urged me to find out as much as possible about red mercury. He stressed I should do it urgently. Then he said: "Read Vortex – it's all in there!" I didn't know what he was talking about.'

There was an awkward silence. Could we really believe such an outrageous claim? Although the political Right in South Africa was clearly lamenting the demise of apartheid, people had already moved into the new South Africa with, all things considered, less of a problem from the Right than anyone had dared to expect. Just before the 27 April election there had been a spate of fatal bombings attributed to right-wing resistance, but these fell far short of the rightist-inspired civil war predicted by many, particularly foreign correspondents.

Besides which, it was somehow impossible to envisage that icon of the Right, Afrikaner Weerstandsbeweging leader Eugene Terre'Blanche, flanked by his army of white AWB farmers, striding into town on horseback with an arsenal of nuclear weapons and declaring a take-over. However, it would have been irresponsible to dismiss immediately what was now being said. Also, it chimed with the remarks of a colleague two days earlier. Norman Chandler, defence correspondent of the *Weekend Star*'s sister newspaper, *The Star*, had raised eyebrows after relating a similarly astonishing tale he had heard from a military contact. There wasn't enough to go on, but it was slated for further investigation.

Although the police appeared not to know, the word 'Vortex' more than likely referred to a best-selling novel by Larry Bond, which dealt with a right-wing take-over of South Africa orchestrated by extremist elements within Military Intelligence. The book sketched how Cabinet ministers were assassinated in a terror attack on a train and politicians sympathetic to the MI right-wingers were installed in the corridors of power. The South African military machine then slipped the leash and war subsequently raged across the subcontinent, ending in a chemical and nuclear confrontation with the superpowers.

We explained the book's plot to the policemen. Said The Moustache: 'That must be it then. I don't go along with this sort of thing. If what you're saying is true, then it seems someone is planning mass murder. That's a big conclusion to draw.' He did not say whether he had any other relevant inside information, but his colleague, 'Skinny', disclosed that his boss was a specialist on the right wing. Gathering intelligence in this political arena was his key area of responsibility.

In the light of the explanation of what 'Vortex' could mean, Skinny went off to telephone his colonel, who said he would see the two officers at eight that night.

The Moustache resumed his story. He indicated there had been strong support of the nuclear weapons programme from scientists on the Right. 'Did you know,' he asked, 'that Wally Grant is a right-winger?' Dr Wally L. Grant, whose right-wing views were widely known, was a brilliant scientist who had worked on the South African nuclear programme. He had jointly received the Hendrik Verwoerd Award with another prominent scientist, Dr Ampie Roux, for their development of the process behind South Africa's uranium enrichment programme. The programme, run under the wing of the Atomic Energy Board (AEB) – forerunner of the Atomic Energy Corporation (AEC) – would eventually enrich uranium to the levels required for South Africa's first atomic bombs. Nevertheless, there was no suggestion that this now retired, distinguished scientist or his colleague could in any way be involved in the nuclear ambitions of the Right.

The Moustache said his source worked at the AEC's National Nuclear Research Centre at Pelindaba, 35 km west of Pretoria. 'He said the red mercury was also hidden in the northern Cape and spoke about a Russian scientist who was working with the right-wingers.' Our inquiries had shown that red mercury was a product of the Russian military-industrial complex.

The police officer said he had met his source the day after the telephone call. 'He was crying like a baby. He showed me a Polaroid picture of what appeared to be a lead canister with a nuclear symbol on the side of it, photographed with a recent copy of the *Pretoria News*. He said the canister contained red mercury and was now in the hands of the right wing.'[1]

1 A Johannesburg commodities trader later told us he had organized the purchase by a well-known right-wing group of red mercury 20/20, known as 'twenties' and purported to be the basic product needed for nuclear weapons. The deal had gone through several years earlier. The material had come into South Africa from Namibia and been stored at two

The Moustache drew a diagram similar to the one on the canister. 'We arranged to meet again later that day, but he didn't show. We've been to his home, but it has been rented out for several months. We've got to find him. But I fear he could be dead.[1]

'I had heard a lot of rumours before about nuclear weapons. The guys involved are very dangerous extremists. I'm frightened of what they might do with a nuclear bomb.'

He paused, considering the implications of what he was saying, had a sip of beer and then pulled hard on his cigarette. 'This morning, I told my colonel what I had heard that night. He gave us full backing to start an investigation. This is very dangerous for this country. I hate these nuts.'

Despite the police officer's obvious dislike of journalists, he clearly wanted our help. He wanted to see two British television documentaries on red mercury, and asked us to arrange this. At that time, the video-tapes, along with a few news clippings, represented an overview of the total knowledge on the subject that was freely available in the West. The CIS had investigated red mercury several years earlier and concluded it was a hoax substance, said The Moustache. There had been no further investigation.

He said he hoped we would meet his commanding officer, suggesting we should pool information in an effort to get to the bottom of what was happening. It was a sticky situation for a journalist – and an equally sticky situation for police officers, we suspected. They could give away nothing that would compromise their covert intelligence-gathering, and we certainly could not give away anything that could compromise our sources.

Said The Moustache: 'This thing has to be publicized. It's probably the only way we're going to be able to stop it.' With some serious reservations about collaborating still on our minds, the meeting ended. The claims were far from established anyway, so there was no point worrying about anything yet. In any case, couldn't we see that this was all simply 'disinformation', an elaborate plot to get close to journalists investigating a string of sensitive murders? Couldn't we see that the prospect of the

military bases, one in Upington in the northern Cape and the other in Pretoria. It had been tested at a laboratory near Pretoria and was then taken by the right-wing group to an unknown destination. Upington is on the fringe of the Kalahari desert and close to a range where South Africa intended to test its prototype nuclear weapon in 1977.

[1] Months later the police managed to track him down. They said he had suffered a heart attack and died. At least one police officer was suspicious. 'All kinds of chemicals can bring on a heart attack,' he said. 'I believe he was murdered.'

right wing having a nuclear device was vaguely ridiculous? Absolutely. But there was another problem.

The issue Norman Chandler had discussed with us earlier concerned exactly the same scenario. His military source had told virtually the same story. Two nuclear devices had been hidden in the northern Transvaal and were outside the direct control of the military. Chandler had also been given a rough location. And now we had heard the police story. There had to be an investigation.

Walking back to the cars, The Moustache said: 'Look, man, I'm a right-winger myself. I wouldn't like to tell you some of the things I did in the past. I've got a bad history. But this nuclear thing I don't approve of. These guys have got to be eliminated – fast.'

The following day we met the police again, this time for lunch at a small Portuguese restaurant in central Pretoria, a well-known watering-hole for the Security Branch. We learned that there had been a high-level meeting early the same day about the 'Vortex' threat.

With us this time were The Moustache and his boss, The Col-onel. Although these intelligence officers operated in the shadows, they were well known there. The owner, a fervent Afrikaner, sat at our table briefly, as did one other visitor. The establishment was evidently a sort of safe house for the CIS. Much beer and schnapps were downed before a lukewarm meal was served very late in the afternoon.

The Colonel, a courteous, thoughtful and quiet man in his early fifties, with a great mop of silvery hair, said he had come from a meeting at which the crisis had been discussed. He could not introduce us to his bosses straight away, and in any case he first wanted his officers to see the British TV documentaries on red mercury. He promised to meet us again the following week, when we could talk in depth.

However he did confirm that he had information that right-wingers were trading in red mercury. It also emerged that, apart from the informant who had telephoned The Moustache, there were three other sources who supported the idea that the right wing had a nuclear weapon.

The Moustache said there were two groups on the Right with a reputation for grandiose schemes. 'There's Vekom, or the "Committee of Ten", which is an alliance of top people in the Afrikaner community, including leading intellectuals – among them a nuclear physicist involved in South Africa's nuclear bomb programme. Then there is the Boere Krisis Aksie, which numbers several thousand. Do not underestimate them. They contain the top commando and security people and are very well organized –

ruthless. Do not consider yourself safe from them. If their plans are threatened, they would have no hesitation in stopping you.'

The Moustache was being very open – much more than The Colonel, who made no attempt to silence him, however. 'Some of these guys are extremists,' The Moustache went on. 'They are fanatical about wanting the country ruled by the Afrikaner again. They hate blacks, and they hate the Brits – they are still fighting the Boer War.

'I'm an Afrikaner too, but I hate these guys. We stopped one right-wing group trying to mortar Mandela during the election. One cop got his left arm broken in seventeen places when one of them set about him with a baseball bat. Today, these people are even more angry. I'm frightened of what they would do if they had a nuclear bomb. They could set it off somewhere to demonstrate the threat they hold.'

We asked if the threat was iminent. 'I don't know,' replied The Moustache. 'We don't think it's short-term. They wouldn't make a move now. Maybe next year.'

There was a rapport developing as the conversation switched to dirty deeds of the past, including the activities of the military's Civil Co-operation Bureau and right-wing personnel who could be involved in the latest scare. We said approaches had also been made to our colleagues by the civilian National Intelligence Service. The police questioned whether it could have been people from MI. The Colonel revealed that MI agents had misrepresented themselves as NIS agents in one sensitive incident. 'You cannot trust MI in these affairs,' he warned.

The Colonel finally said he had to leave, but The Moustache stayed on. He disclosed that two years earlier one of his colleagues had received information from a paid informant at Thor, the company for whom Alan Kidger had worked. 'This informant alleged that Thor had been reprocessing red mercury obtained from America. They were dealing in highly specialized chemicals.' His colleague had written an intelligence report, but was ordered to take no further action and so had not been able to verify the story.

The Moustache said people employed by Thor had a close working relationship with people within the army's Special Forces – specialized military units trained to carry out difficult and dangerous tasks behind enemy lines. The Colonel was not telling him everything he knew, he said. 'That meeting this morning was with the top brass. All I know is that they came out and gave me the green light to keep going with you guys.'

Soon afterwards, we heard the security police had picked up another valuable snippet from their sources in the field. The Moustache had been told there was something very important under heavy guard at a farm north of Pietersburg in the northern Transvaal. He had seen heavy security around the perimeter.

We decided to call on another Pretoria source who had just attended a meeting of the right-wing BKA outside the city. The source said he was confident the Right would regain control of South Africa within two years. The meeting had been told the Right could 'retake the country without a shot being fired.'

Meanwhile, the *Weekend Star*'s reporter Janine Lazarus had come into contact with two enigmatic sources, Eddie and Peter,[1] who appeared to be connected to Israeli intelligence. One had telephoned and arranged to meet her on 7 September 1994, in Pretoria. This was her report to editors after the initial meeting:

'When I arrived, Eddie's colleague, Peter, told me Eddie was running late because "the environment was unfriendly". He said "some people" had got wind of the fact that Eddie was dealing with me and they were very upset. Apparently there are certain elements within the Israeli embassy who are aware of Eddie's dealings with me, but there are others who don't know anything about it.

'When Eddie eventually turned up close to 10 p.m. he was very jumpy. He kept asking me if I had been followed. In fact, he scolded me for not taking my security seriously enough.

'He expressed surprise at the fact that Steve [McQuillan] and I were "still walking the streets" and said that there were "many elements out there" who would rather see us otherwise.

'He referred to my flat … [a place he'd never visited] and said that all I had protecting me was a "puny little security gate". He also commented on the fact that Steve was going to become a father, and then he asked what security measures he had in place.

'During our somewhat stilted conversation, he repeatedly looked over his shoulder. He also left the table and walked outside the restaurant, returning a few minutes later.

'A bulletproof vest under his pullover stuck out obviously, and he was also armed. He kept a walkie-talkie on the seat next to him for the duration of our meeting.

'He said the *Weekend Star* was "barking up the wrong tree" in blaming Mossad. But we were "bang on target" with our coverage of the

1 Not their real names.

suspicious circumstances and about what he referred to as "the substance". He said there was a "mafia-type" operation running with the full consent of governments, albeit covertly. He mentioned the United States, France, Italy and "an Arab state". He also claimed the operation was going ahead with the full knowledge of the new SA government.

'He said we would never find red mercury in this country and that this investigation was much bigger than the *Weekend Star*. He said an Iraqi hitman was involved and he was extremely dangerous. He said a man called Malcolm[1] was on an Iraqi hit-list and "would not see Christmas". He knew we wanted to meet Malcolm. In fact he laughed at the idea. He said the man would never agree to an interview.'

Eddie had claimed to be from the Israeli embassy and representative of a faction that wanted to disclose secrets about something called the 'clean' bomb – a neutron device that could be detonated without any nuclear fallout. He claimed this was a bomb that was built using red mercury, and this was why people were dying. He said the weapon was linked to a secret project called Operation Shampoo. At a further meeting, he pulled out of a folder a number of documents, some of them in Hebrew, saying: 'It's all in here.' But he pulled the documents back before Lazarus, who speaks Hebrew, could examine them.

Another time she met Eddie in a Pretoria restaurant, on 18 October. It was four hours before he finally arrived. Said Lazarus: 'He was a great deal more agitated and aggressive than usual. Again, he was wearing his bullet-proof vest. His two-way radio was on the seat next to him, as it was the last time we met, and I saw at least one firearm in a holster on his waist.

'He left the café on countless occasions, checking for who knows what outside, and he aggressively asked me where Steve was and why he – Steve – had seen fit to let me see Eddie on my own. Then he changed his mind, warning that if I arrived at any meeting accompanied by anyone, he would cut ties with me.

'When I asked for proof as to who he was, he reacted so angrily that patrons in the café looked over their shoulders at us. He produced a small laminated card with a colour photograph of him and a logo in the top left-hand corner which I had never seen before. The date was current – 1994, with a Hebrew date next to it – and in Hebrew I read the words "Shin Beth".[2]

1 A Durban arms dealer, Malcolm Roelofsz.

2 Shin Beth, also called Shabak, is Israel's internal security police organization, similar to MI5 in Britain and the FBI in the United States. Operatives are stationed overseas if they are dealing with issues of terrorism that might harm Israeli citizens.

'He said it was becoming increasingly difficult to meet with him and that there were forces trying their very best to make life tough for him. He said he knew that there were five of us working on the investigation, and he also made reference to Gwynne Roberts and Peter Hounam and said he knew where they were staying in Johannesburg.

'When I asked him about Operation Shampoo, he laughed rather loudly and said: "The 'clean' bomb." I asked about the bomb programme, and he aggressively said he would bring me documents proving that South Africa still had its own programme, but he wouldn't say when I would be getting these documents. At this point, I was too intimidated to press him further. He also asked why Norman [Chandler] wasn't out in the field investigating the right-wing bomb threat.

'He told us to ignore Ambassador Liel [the Israeli ambassador] and said he was a lot of, and I quote, "piss and wind", but asked whether we were aware that pressure was being placed on the *Weekend Star* through the withholding of Jewish advertising because of its publication of police accusations against Mossad.

'He kept asking what I would do for him – or "for us", as he put it – in return for his help.

'He said the Iraqis were responsible for the "hits" – as he called them – in South Africa, and that they were done with South African government complicity. He also told us to look no further than the ANC, but refused to elaborate further. He would not let me take any notes, and he checked if I was carrying a tape-recorder before talking to me. Before he left, he said I had "big balls". Great compliment!'

Eddie had given Lazarus his identity, but it was difficult to check it without running the risk of compromising him. However, he correctly identified another Israeli intelligence agent who had been talking to us.

These encounters were suspicious indeed. The source's information was interesting, but that was as far as it went. Nothing could be confirmed. No papers were handed over. There was really no reason why we should trust anything he said, other than the fact that he clearly was well versed in the issues being investigated.

Two days later another meeting was arranged. Lazarus arrived for the 8 a.m. appointment ahead of time and had to wait until 12.45 p.m. before Peter arrived. 'All he said was that I had to be patient and wait,' said Lazarus.

'At around 4 p.m. Eddie arrived and asked why I looked so cross. I told him that all I seemed to do was to wait. He responded rather angrily – something about patience is a virtue and all that jazz. I have a feeling my resolve is being tested.

'We conversed in Hebrew, which, even if I say so myself, isn't bad since the last time I spoke Hebrew was at school. Not according to Eddie, however, who told me it wasn't good enough. Then he asked again what I could do in return for him. I smiled and answered: "Upgrade my Hebrew."

'He asked how big the team was that was investigating the right-wing bomb threat, and I replied that we were five. He then asked if part of the team was already out in the field. I asked where, and he replied: "The Cape, the northern Cape."

'He told me that from Monday (and I gathered he meant the project would span across a few days) I would be involved in meeting two people – one of whom is an official from the Israeli embassy here who is meeting me without the consent of his seniors. He wouldn't tell me who the other party was. He said that I would be shown documents on the "clean" bomb.

'When I asked if I could take notes, he told me not to push him. I said I did not have a photographic memory and requested that I be allowed to take notes. He said he would think about it.

'He disappeared again and returned around 9.30 p.m. He had a stiff Scotch and vaguely apologized for my looking tired. He told me to bear with him. He said it was becoming increasingly difficult to meet with me as the environment was becoming so unfriendly.'

Finally the encounters fizzled out, leaving Eddie's motives unresolved. Was he linked to South African security agents trying to find out what we were doing or to a sympathetic group from the Israeli embassy that was trying to set the record straight on Mossad, or was he engaging in a time-wasting exercise to slow down the pace of the newspaper investigation?

We had feared that our association with the security police was doomed to failure, and so it proved to be. Only weeks after our first meeting at Marshall's Inn, senior police officers ordered their men to end any contact with journalists investigating the nuclear issue and red mercury.

On top of this, sources told us police intelligence files were being shredded. Files on red mercury and Thor were 'already gone'. The original red mercury report by the police was inconclusive, so it was no great loss. But the Thor report, which was rumoured to show that Thor was reprocessing red mercury and supplying it to the military, would have been more useful. The report had supposedly been compiled in 1986 or 1987 and was based on information from an informant who had later claimed someone was trying to kill him.

The police investigation also looked as though it would not survive. Officers involved were threatened. 'I was told that if I asked further questions I would be killed,' said one. Later, the police investigation was officially halted after interference from the Defence Ministry, according to our sources. If there was a nuclear weapon outside of government control, it looked as though it would have to remain so.

After a string of encounters with the police and other sources in Pretoria and Johannesburg in the following weeks, it was clear that either there was a serious threat from the right wing or a disinformation campaign was running. But if it was disinformation, what was the purpose? It might artificially strengthen the right-wing hand in negotiations with the new government over a homeland, or 'Volkstaat', for Afrikaners, but that was risky. What if the media figured out the threat was bogus and blew the whistle before talks were concluded? Such a development would surely strengthen government resolve to ward off what in any case would be a largely unpopular undertaking.

And if the Right had the bomb and planned to threaten the government to achieve its goals, surely it would not want it known. Nuclear blackmail, or any other kind of blackmail, would never work once it became public. The rest of the world, let alone the now democratic South African government, could never be seen to give in to such a threat. The possibility was that Eddie was a genuine whistle-blower.

It was widely known that the military had within its ranks a host of powerful right-wing-inclined officers who had fought the creeping expansionist policies of the Soviet Union on a number of fronts. These people would not necessarily be happy to hand over South Africa to a black government that might later introduce the very Marxist policies they had for years challenged throughout southern Africa. The South African Defence Force had been all-powerful. The country's 'reds-under-the-beds' paranoia had ensured it received the money and political support it needed to become a mighty war machine.

If South Africa had secretly built nuclear weapons, these senior military figures might easily have been able to spirit some away to be controlled outside the SADF but in conjunction with other right-leaning generals still in uniform. It would have provided some kind of reassurance for the white-controlled military, a knowledge that if the incoming black government started to push around South Africa's whites it was in for a big shock.

Despite the logic, this was difficult to accept, particularly because South Africa supposedly no longer had nuclear weapons. The country had announced it had made only six nuclear devices, and had almost completed a seventh, but these had been secretly dismantled on orders issued by De Klerk soon after he took office in 1989. South Africa had become the first country in the world to build and then dismantle its nuclear arsenal, and was enjoying the moral rewards of this public-relations coup.

On the other hand it was impossible to dismiss everything we had encountered as disinformation. Why was red mercury such a big issue in South Africa?

3 The Trail of Murder and Mayhem

Wynand van Wyk (forty-four), referred to by South African police as 'the best chemical engineer in the country', was bludgeoned to death on 23 April 1993, after being lured to a room on the eighteenth floor of a Cape Town hotel for a bogus business meeting.

Lieutenant-Colonel Charles Landman believed the murder might be connected to the trade in red mercury. He and colleagues from the Peninsula Murder and Robbery Unit in Cape Town were now comparing notes. Did Kidger and Van Wyk have the same interests?

Van Wyk moved in upper management circles, according to his second wife, Sheila-Ann. He also had influential friends in government. Georg Meiring, the chief of the South African Defence Force, Roelf Meyer, Minister of Constitutional Development, Piet Badenhorst, Absa Bank chief, and Pietie du Plessis, the former Minister of Manpower, appeared in the pages of his diaries. Also, he had written a book, *Waardedemokrasie*, or 'Democracy of Value', which supported the National Party, then still the driving force in government. Copies had been sent to his friends in power.

Van Wyk had a taste for the good life – a Swiss bank account, a fancy mansion and top people as friends. His many black-bound diaries also neatly recorded his hectic social calendar: lunches, dinners, teas and even birthday parties, with names, telephone numbers and appointments all written methodically inside. Kidger and Van Wyk might have met in Cape Town. Kidger's name appeared on the page for 16 August 1990 – just over a year before his death. There was also an appointment arranged with the State President.

Van Wyk had worked as technical director of Chemical Holdings, an affiliate of the giant Anglo-American Corporation, for Armscor, the weapons manufacturer and procurement agency, for Sasol, the country's oil-from-coal industrial giant, and for the Atomic Energy Corporation. He did private consultation work and was a member of various national and international engineering institutes and technical committees. His own business was called Quality Technical Management.

Van Wyk travelled widely. His passport showed he had been on business to Saudi Arabia, Israel, Iran, Libya, Kuwait and Yemen, among other places. Like Kidger, he was believed to have been providing Arab governments with chemicals for military applications.

He had told his wife there would be 'lots of money coming in' when she asked him how they could possibly afford a new R700,000 ($180,000) home in Durbanville, one of Cape Town's most exclusive suburbs. But there were darker stories. Police said Van Wyk had told his wife he was on a hit list. She thought he was joking, but on 4 April 1993, three weeks before he was beaten to death, he told a friend 'something' had happened to him during a trip to Singapore. They arranged to have lunch, but Van Wyk was dead before he could keep the appointment.

His wife said her husband was involved in 'many, many different things' before she met him. 'He saw a lot of people, and there was a lot I didn't know. I can't believe he would have been involved in something devious for personal gain. Perhaps he knew something he shouldn't have.'

Also like Kidger, Van Wyk was last seen by his wife after receiving a mysterious message. He had been plagued by a series of strange telephone calls to his home and business. His wife said he had considered reporting the calls to the police, 'But what could we have told them?' She said her husband was very security-conscious. 'I just assumed that was part of his make-up. He was always concerned about locking doors.'

Between 17 and 19 March 1993, a man claiming to be a labour-relations expert who worked for the Namibian government called Van Wyk's office and said he wanted to set up a meeting with him. Van Wyk's receptionist said the man left a fictitious phone number. The caller mentioned a seminar on 'international certification of standards' at a hotel in Cape Town on 21 March. He thought her boss might be interested. When Van Wyk arrived at the seminar he discovered the seventeen-seat conference room had been booked, but no one was there. He told relatives that he thought he had been followed from the hotel to his Durbanville home that night.

On 22 April 1993, the day before he died, someone again telephoned Van Wyk at his office, but he was out, according to police. Warrant Officer Coenie Jooste of the Peninsula Murder and Robbery Unit said: 'Then a man calling himself Mr Frazer, who said he was from a packaging company, telephoned his wife and said he urgently needed to see her husband. He said the meeting would take only twenty minutes and that he would wait until midnight to see him.' Jooste said the caller, who could not pronounce the 'r' in Frazer properly, also called Van Wyk's receptionist and was aggressive. 'He told her he had been phoning all morning and couldn't get through,' said Jooste. Then there was another call to the receptionist, this time from a man called Selwyn, with an English accent, who told her he was calling on behalf of Frazer. He said he wanted to make a reservation at the Ritz Protea Hotel in Cape Town for a meeting.

Finally, Van Wyk was lured to a meeting in room 1803 on the eighteenth floor of the Ritz in the city's Seapoint suburb. His killer booked in under the name of Frazer at about noon. After filling in a hotel form with a false name, identity number, home and work telephone numbers and address, he took the lift to his room. He ordered from room service two whiskies, three small sodas, three Amstel beers and two toasted chicken mayonnaise sandwiches. 'We suspect there might have been another man in the room,' said Jooste.

Later a guest next door heard the sound of people arguing and what could have been a man's head being pounded against the floor. In the room opposite, other guests heard a terrible commotion. They phoned security and opened their room door. They saw a dark-skinned man with a black briefcase coming out of room 1803.

'You've just killed a man,' said one of the guests, as she caught a glimpse of a man lying face-down in a pool of blood. 'He's fine; don't worry about him,' the athletically built killer replied, closing the door. He then walked towards the fire escape and ran down eighteen flights of stairs, leaving blood stains.

A security guard stepped out of the hotel lift seconds after the killing to see Van Wyk's assailant disappearing down the fire escape. With his shoulders hunched and head down, he then walked briskly through the lobby, past the receptionist. A beige Volkswagen Golf then raced away. In room 1803, Van Wyk lay on his stomach next to the bed, bleeding to death. Like Kidger, Van Wyk was beaten about the head. He had splinters of wood in his face and cranium after being smashed repeatedly with what police believe was a pickaxe handle.

Since the murder, Sheila-Ann van Wyk has moved home, but her house has been broken into several times. 'I don't know why,' she said. 'I have also had a few strange visits. I feel under threat.'

Landman believed Van Wyk was murdered because of red mercury. The chemical specialist had meetings with a man known to have attempted to deal in this substance. The police officer believed Mossad may have killed Van Wyk as well as Kidger. Again Ambassador Liel was obliged to deny that the murder had anything to do with Israel: 'We totally and categorically deny any involvement.'

Arms dealer Don Juan Lange (forty-three) was the man with whom Van Wyk had attempted to deal, but he too was dead. Both men's diaries showed they had been holding meetings together, although the nature of their links was not known. By 2 July 1994, the *Weekend Star*, which was spearheading media coverage of the trail of death, was reporting that police suspected a red mercury connection.

Lange, a jet-setting and good-looking playboy entrepreneur, was found by his girlfriend, Phaedra du Plessis, with a plastic bag over his head at his luxury La Lucia townhouse in the port city of Durban. The bag was connected by pipe to a gas bottle on the floor next to the body. Dressed in a tracksuit, he had been lying on his back on the floor of a spare room, covered with a blanket, for at least six hours. The doors and windows of the house were all closed. No notes were found.

Du Plessis, who had been living with Lange for two months, said there had never been a gas bottle in the house.

Initially, police put the Lange case down to suicide. Soon, however, they were not so sure. Suspiciously, the bag was not tied around his neck. Police later said that as he lost consciousness he would have released his grip and air would have entered the bag, possibly reviving him.

There also appeared to be evidence of a head injury. Police intervened to prevent the body being cremated, insisting on a second post-mortem. His organs and a sample of blood were sent for analysis, along with the gas bottle.

Said Landman: 'We suspect Lange didn't commit suicide. The investigating officer says it appears he was murdered.' There was no trace of the bottled gas in his body.

One of Lange's associates told police that Lange knew of Israeli involvement in the Kidger murder. 'I was having dinner with Lange shortly after the Kidger murder and he told me the Israelis did it.' Now, the investigators were planning to go through Lange's notes, diaries and letters. 'We will be going back to the scene,' said a spokesman.

Lange too had travelled extensively, particularly in the Far East. He held false British and Philippine passports, the latter in the name of 'Langel', which was used for his trips to mainland China and South and Central America. South African, German and Hong Kong passports were also found. He had been involved in business in Asia for seventeen years, and had sold South African weapons, including high-tech equipment such as ground-to-air missiles and heavy artillery, around the world. He had particularly good connections in Singapore, having shuttled between the two countries for a number of years.

At the time of his death, the high-flying Lange – a black-belt karate expert – was managing director of Anglo World Resources, a company owned by the Dynasty group, which in turn was owned by the Tang family – one of Singapore's wealthiest. His diaries were filled with the names and telephone numbers of senior personnel in Armscor and the SADF with whom he had scheduled appointments.

But at least one of his arms deals had gone wrong. German businessman Franz Rothkop was upset with Lange, who, according to security sources, cheated a group of German businessmen out of $520,000 in 1991 in a failed helicopter deal.

Police said Lange knew Kidger and had done business with Van Wyk. Lange may have met Van Wyk in November 1991, the month Kidger died. Van Wyk's name appears twice that month in Lange's diary.

Police have his diaries stretching back as far as 1985. They record appointments at the South African embassy in Taiwan and Singapore, the Japanese Chamber of Commerce and Industries, the Hong Kong Development Council and numerous board meetings in Hong Kong. Days, even weeks, were blanked out during his visits to Beijing and Singapore. Then there were references to meetings with the SADF, the AEC, the ANC, the Department of Foreign Affairs and the Department of Trade and Industry. An entry on 10 May 1994 reads: 'Mr Nelson Mandela'. Perhaps Lange had attended the President's inauguration too.

A business associate said Lange, once married to former Miss South Africa Sandy McCrystal, had 'no reason to kill himself ... But he must have made a few enemies in his time.'

A compulsive workaholic who 'turned heads' when he walked into a room, Lange led a glamorous lifestyle. Living fast and expensively, he often dashed between Durban and Johannesburg for business meetings, driving his Volkswagen Golf VR6 at speeds of over 120 m.p.h., said an associate. He was not surprised to hear reports that Lange had been linked to the sale of arms, including a deal to send South Africa's G5 howitzer to Iraq: 'You always got the feeling that he would have been mixed up in some pretty shady stuff in his life, and that he was always looking over his shoulder.'

Lange had also known Gerald Bull, who helped the South Africans design the G5 howitzer, widely considered to one of the best artillery guns in the world.

The associate said Lange had told how two women had approached him with a proposal to handle a package obtained from a Russian ship that docked in the port city of Maputo, Mozambique's capital, on the Indian Ocean. Lange had said the package contained a substance called red mercury. 'Lange turned down the offer, but he said Kidger had somehow become involved in the deal. When Kidger was killed, Lange told me: "It's the Israelis. I know how they operate."'

The associate said that, days after the Kidger murder, ten plain-clothes agents of one of South Africa's security services raided Lange's Johannesburg apartment and asked questions about Kidger. 'They slapped him around a bit.' Police could find no record of such an incident.

The *Weekend Star* later disclosed that Lange had earlier been found by police in possession of the nuclear material caesium-137 only days after Alan Kidger's dismembered body had been discovered in November 1991.

On 13 November, in Alberton, on the southern outskirts of Johannesburg, Lange was shown wooden boxes in the boot of a car. There were no official markings and the lids were screwed shut. He insisted on testing the material before a deal could be done. The sellers said there were another 131 containers to be sold and they wanted R4.5 million ($1.2 million) in cash for the shipment, which, they said, came from another country.

Newspaper reports say that Lange had led police to two men who had offered to sell him a sealed lead container and another box. The first container, of caesium, could have killed five thousand people if opened, according to a spokesman for the AEC. The second contained enriched uranium. Lange said he had thought it was a legitimate business deal.

On 7 October 1994, BBC TV's *Newsnight* programme cast new light on the incident. It disclosed that Lange had told friends he was working for the Israelis and wanted to buy red mercury.

A South African commodities dealer and friend of Lange, Alda Croucamp, who normally dealt in T-shirts from the Far East, said Lange had asked her if she could obtain red mercury, so she put feelers out along her trading network. 'He said he had clients in Israel.'

A woman dealer friend told Croucamp that she knew someone who had red mercury to trade. Subsequently, Croucamp was offered red mercury by a man from Maputo.

Croucamp, her dealer friend, Lange and another person who controlled the red mercury had met in the lounge of the plush Carlton Hotel in central Johannesburg a few days before Kidger died, and three photographs of the red mercury for sale had been passed around.

'I put a meeting up between the buyer and seller who showed Don the consignment of goods he had,' said Croucamp. 'Don said it was the right stuff. Then the dealer from Maputo disappeared.'

Croucamp said the deal fell through and she couldn't find red mercury elsewhere, but she came across uranium and asked Lange if it was a possible alternative. Two men had obtained it at the Ponte Flats tower, a notorious centre for crime that overlooks the city of Johannesburg.

Lange agreed to buy and take possession of the uranium on 11 November – two days after Kidger's body had been found.

An affidavit from Croucamp said another meeting was arranged for 13 November at which a wooden crate containing an unspecified product was handed over to Lange. She said she never knew what was in it. On the following day she met yet another dealer who said he wanted R5 million ($1.4 million) for the product, a sum he had already received for four other containers he had sold.

Croucamp then had nothing more to do with the transaction, because Lange dealt directly with the trader involved.

Three other affidavits supported her version, but an affidavit by Lange told a different story, making no mention of red mercury. He said Croucamp had contacted him with an offer to sell uranium. He confirmed the Carlton meeting, but at the second meeting he spoke to the dealer on the phone and was told that a R100,000 ($28,000) deposit would be required. Lange refused to pay this until the product had been tested. It was then that the dealer threatened to kill him.

Said Lange: 'The next day Croucamp phoned me. She was hysterical and told me that these people wanted R4.5 million in cash for the goods. I refused to pay that much. Croucamp then supplied the phone numbers of her contact. I spoke to him and told him I wanted the certificate of origin of the product. He then told me he wanted the money or else I would be killed.' The caller said his body would be put in the boot of his car.

Details of the Kidger killing didn't emerge until that day, 14 November, when the evening television news said Kidger's body had been dumped into a car boot and left in Johannesburg. Lange panicked, according to Croucamp, and phoned in a state of great agitation. She said: 'Don asked if I had been watching the news, about the man being cut up and put into the boot of his car. Don believed Kidger must have become involved in the earlier deal involving red mercury that had fallen through for us, and that Mossad had killed him. Why did he phone? Why was he so nervous?' She said he asked if she knew what was involved in trading in red mercury, but she said she had no idea.

On 16 November police arrested the two men offering the nuclear materials. They were later charged with illegally trading in them and were convicted. They paid nominal fines. Lange was never prosecuted.

It was also discovered that in September 1991, two months before Kidger died, Lange made a drawing in his diary. It referred to 50/50, one of the versions of red mercury. The drawing looked like a map showing the smuggling routes for the material, and mentioned the cities of Zurich and Frankfurt.

Said Landman: 'Lange and Kidger knew each other between 1989 and 1991. They had frequent discussions regarding red mercury. We have ample evidence to prove that.' The evidence also indicated that each had tried to deal in red mercury. Lange had kept a news clipping on the Kidger death.

Lange had told one of his Johannesburg business associates, Hugo Grobler, that he feared he would be killed – the same fear Van Wyk had expressed. 'I'm telling you this as a friend,' said Lange. 'I might be eliminated one day, and that's all I'm saying to you.' Said Grobler: 'I asked him what he meant, and he switched to another subject. I got the impression that he was always on the run. He lived out of a suitcase and moved from hotel room to hotel room. He never wanted people to know where he was. When he was married to Sandy [McCrystal] they would be fetched by limousine at 2 a.m., taken to the airport, and flown to the Far East by private jet. He kept flaunting figures and always carried cash. She never knew where the vast amounts of money were coming from.'

Lange had confided that he had a high profile in arms dealing and had done business with the South African government and deals between China and South American countries. Lange also said he had been based in Hong Kong for the SADF. 'He told me he used to work under cover during the sanction era for arms trading.'

Grobler said he did not believe Lange had committed suicide: 'He was too much in love with life, the high life.' He also disclosed that two of Lange's passports had disappeared, along with a briefcase containing his personal documents.

Again, there were suspicions that Mossad had a hand in the killing. Again, the embattled Israeli ambassador vehemently denied that his country was involved.

In a statement to the *Weekend Star* on 9 July 1994, the police finally announced that they would reopen investigations into all suspicious deaths connected to the South African chemical and armaments industries. They now suspected an international conspiracy, having heard that a trail of bodies also stretched across Europe.

All the killings, some of which took place in the 1980s, involved materials that could be used in the manufacture of nuclear weapons and which appeared to have been destined for Middle Eastern countries. Estimates from police and intelligence sources put the possible South African murders alone at between fifteen and twenty. 'Investigations into other murders are just beginning,' said the police, 'and we are liaising with police forces in Europe.'

Soon after the announcement, police tentatively added to the list a mysterious double killing of two young men in Port Elizabeth, on the Indian Ocean. Police were looking at a possible connection between the murders of Scott Ayton (twenty-five) and Felix Coetzee (twenty-six) and their broader nuclear chemicals investigation.

The two young men had had their hands bound and their mouths sealed with masking tape and had been shot 'execution style', with a single bullet to the head, on 22 May 1994, while looking after the Ayton home. Both men had just started out in engineering careers, Coetzee for the Port Elizabeth-based chemical company Algorax and Ayton for Decca Contractors, a subsidiary of the UK-based Racal Electronics, which is involved in the manufacture of military equipment and trades with Middle Eastern countries. Said the detective investigating the case: 'Nothing was stolen; nothing was disturbed. They must have let the killer in through the front door. There were no signs of forced entry. There was something fishy here. There was no motive for murder and no leads. There just has to be a reason.'

Police were also looking at possible links between the Kidger/Van Wyk/Lange killings and the death of the British-born South African managing director of Wacker Chemicals, John Scott (forty-one), who originally was thought to have stabbed to death his wife, Andrea, and two daughters, Sarah (six) and Helene (two), before gassing himself in his car at their home in Randburg, Johannesburg, three weeks after Kidger's death in November 1991. It was one of the most brutal family murders police had seen. There were dozens of stab wounds on the bodies of the mother and her children. Some of the wounds appeared to have been made with precision, to puncture the heart. In some wounds the knife blade had gone right through the body.

Scott was believed to have butchered his family, then gassed himself in the front seat of his car by connecting a hose to the car's exhaust pipe. In a hastily written suicide note found on the kitchen table, he said he was 'sorry' but he could no longer carry on. Said the note: 'I made a big mistake five weeks ago and this was the only solution. I had everything, and I blew it because of ten minutes of irresponsibility.' He also left instructions on how to dispose of the family's R2 million ($545,000) estate.

Police were curious about those ten minutes. They were also interested in the fact he had just been on a business trip and was not the same man when he returned.

Five weeks earlier, Scott had visited other African countries with a German executive of Wacker Chemicals, a subsidiary of the German multinational Hoechst. According to his itinerary, he visited Wacker and Hoechst subsidiaries in Namibia, Zambia and Zimbabwe. His secretary, Cathy Duncan, said his behaviour after the trip changed dramatically: 'Every time I went into his office he was looking into space and biting his nails. He didn't seem to be concentrating on his work. He always seemed to be on the phone, and I couldn't understand why he was making all those calls.'

Like Van Wyk and Lange, fear gripped Scott too in his last days. He was due to fly to Germany on 16 November to submit an important report to Wacker's directors. On the 15th – the day after the full horror of Kidger's murder came through on the evening television news – he took fright.

Duncan said he came to her, stood in the corner of her office, near the door, and said he didn't know why he was going to Germany: 'I really don't want to go.'

Said Duncan: 'I was shocked. "Why not?" I asked. "What about all the work we have done?" I said they were expecting him. He said, "Oh, well, I suppose I'd better go."'

In Germany, Scott became unwell and visited a clinic in Munich. A report from a doctor there showed he was suffering from sweating and palpitations, and had a red face and pins and needles in his hands. But the doctor found nothing wrong medically. The symptoms suggested a panic attack. Scott cut short his trip and arrived home a week early. Three days later he and his entire family were dead.

Police believe Kidger was storing red mercury in Zambia and might have met Scott there. Said Landman: 'They were in Zambia at the same time. The information we gathered was that Kidger had a storage facility in Zambia. It wasn't anything to do with Thor.'

The detective said that from the pictures of Scott's body it was clear he had injuries to his hands which were not completely described in the post-mortem. 'He had these injuries, and yet he was the person who was supposed to have committed the murders.'

The police said Scott's blood had never been analysed, and it had not been established whether there were unexplained injuries on his body. 'We are searching for his diaries and interviewing people with close relationships to him,' said the police officer.

Scott had several bank accounts, three of them in places where banking secrecy prevailed – Switzerland, Liechtenstein and Jersey.

Bridget Meiring, who lived next door and discovered John Scott's body, said he was a nice person and obviously a family man who loved his children. 'He wasn't capable of such horrific murders.'

Daniël Jacobus du Preez was a wealthy man. He was a director of companies with offices in South Africa and New York and, according to his colleagues, an agent for a company in Russia. One of his passions was his love of cars – he had a fleet. At various times and sometimes together, he and his wife, Mina, had run a Lotus, a Rolls-Royce, a Ferrari, a BMW, a Nissan 4x4, a Porsche and a Mercedes-Benz. He also had a helicopter. He spoke excitedly to his colleagues about the money to be made in the red mercury trade.

Du Preez, who among other things ran an industrial cleaning company called Vac-Q-Tec, was killed in a mysterious road accident in October 1994, along with one of his managers, Okkert van Wyk, and his helicopter pilot, Graham Heath, while they were driving Mina du Preez's Mercedes-Benz 500E. The car had just been serviced.

Like Van Wyk and Lange before him, he had told his friends someone was trying to kill him. Earlier, his Daimler had spun off the road. He had told at least one business acquaintance that someone had tried to shoot him. Business acquaintances and friends added their voices to those of the AEC and Mintek, a mining research unit that boasted a high-tech Johannesburg laboratory, confirming that Du Preez had spoken about red mercury and taken samples for analysis.

Sources told the *Weekend Star* that as early as 1991 a man calling himself Kobus du Preez telephoned Mintek to ask technicians if they could analyse a red mercury sample. Coincidentally, one of the lab's technicians had become an expert on red mercury because of the numerous inquiries over the years. Du Preez arrived at the lab with what looked like a bar of lead which, according to the technician, he said was red mercury that he was selling for a London client to an Austrian buyer.

The technician, bearing in mind what was purportedly inside the bar, determined that its weight was too heavy for pure lead. In fact the bar was so heavy, said the technician, it had to contain uranium or something heavier. Pronouncing the bar's contents 'highly radioactive', the technician sent du Preez to the AEC.

An AEC spokesman told the *Weekend Star*'s reporter Anita Allen that Du Preez arrived in a white Rolls-Royce and asked for an analysis of the bar. The spokesman said the bar turned out to be lead. Du Preez left the bar with the AEC. The spokesman said the bar had been reanalysed and reweighed. 'It has been cut into three pieces and it is really only lead.'

In its disclosures of 27 August 1994, the newspaper established that Du Preez was well known to the AEC. He had a classified contract with the nuclear agency, on at least one occasion travelling overseas with an AEC official to look for US partners to finance options Du Preez held on uranium fields in the giant, semi-desert Karoo region of South Africa's Cape province.

Long before the *Weekend Star* had highlighted the subject of red mercury, Du Preez showed one of his friends a long, silvery, bar-shaped container which he had in the boot of his car and said: 'This is red mercury. We spend our lives doing deals, but this is where the real money is.'

Others, independently, said they had seen in a safe at Du Preez's Johannesburg home silver-coloured bars that he said contained red mercury.

A business partner and long-time friend, Daantjie van Vuuren, said he once met Du Preez in a restaurant in Johannesburg where other men were present and there was a lot of talk about red mercury. 'It was long ago and I can't remember the details. I didn't understand what they were talking about. It was all about making lots of money.'

He said Du Preez had a close relationship with the AEC and Mintek. 'It was very secret, and I can't say any more.' However, the AEC said they knew nothing of Du Preez, other than the occasion on which he brought the bar for analysis.

Official investigations indicated that no one was to blame for the death crash, but investigations by Allen and her newspaper revealed several inconsistencies and lapses involving the official inquiries.

Statements from eyewitnesses, emergency services personnel and the post-mortem report differed over the identification of bodies and their injuries. There was also confusion as to who was driving the car, which left the road on a bend without leaving any braking marks, making tracks on the gravel verge and grass for about 100 metres. It then leapt in the air, hitting the ground after 30 metres, then, taking off again, it hit a tree 10 metres beyond. It destroyed the tree without touching the ground and came to rest 20 metres away, on its roof.

Du Preez apparently had been flung from the driving-seat. But when the car had last been seen Heath had been driving. A witness, on the scene in seconds, said: 'There was liquid coming from the exhaust. As it fell on the grass it was so hot the grass was smouldering. I was first on the scene. Why did the police never question me?'

A South African intelligence agent later told us that the authorities knew Du Preez was murdered and the crash had been staged to look like an accident. He said a special heavy-plastic canister containing a toxic gas in a solidified state had been connected to the exhaust pipe of the car; when heated by the exhaust pipe, this gave off a highly toxic but undetectable gas, which was piped into the interior of the car. 'The car should have crashed and burned, but still you might have found traces of the canister,' said the agent. This sensational allegation could not be verified by other sources. However, photographs obtained of the vehicle after the crash show that the large exhaust system of the Mercedes was almost completely detached from the car when it was removed from the crash scene. In the breaker's yard, the exhaust pipe was found upright, detached and lying across the top of the wreck.

The last person to see Du Preez alive was his friend Deon Faul. 'I can't understand how he died that way. He was used to the road and, although he drove fast, he drove carefully.' Du Preez and his colleagues had left Faul at 7.45 p.m. and headed off for another business meeting at an oil refinery, but they never arrived. The crash occurred just after 9 p.m. Police said they had never managed to establish where Du Preez and his colleagues were in those one and a quarter hours before the crash.

Police promised that if new evidence came to light it would be conveyed to the state prosecutor or the attorney general. A spokesman said the case was 'curious' and its circumstances would be re-examined.

Mina du Preez, who took over her husband's business, doesn't know what to make of the stories about red mercury, a substance she insists was never mentioned to her by her husband.

According to a report in the Johannesburg-based newspaper the *Sunday Times* on 17 July 1994, a tip-off from the intelligence department of the ANC had helped police investigate the series of mysterious deaths. Quoting a well-placed source, it said the ANC's own intelligence wing gave police information linking the murders to illicit arms deals with the Middle East that might have attracted the wrath of Mossad.

The changed political climate in South Africa had given police the opportunity to bring their investigation into the open. However, the report said, there had been a concerted attempt by other government agencies to derail the investigation. The report said this had led to a campaign of 'disinformation', including claims that there were links between the dead men and the drug trade, that agents from other countries – including Iraq and Iran – were operating in South Africa, and that murders were linked to counterfeit money.

Most startling were attempts to discredit Landman by alleging that he worked for Military Intelligence and that he had 'staged' the limpet-mine blast outside his house. Landman dismissed the claims, saying he would never endanger the lives of his family.

ANC intelligence agents also told the *Weekend Star* that they too were investigating the trade of red mercury in South Africa. 'There are a lot of deals now.' They were investigating links between the shadowy 'third force',[1] Mossad and extremist groups on the right wing. At least one undercover agent was being given protection because his life was threatened after his cover was blown. The agents said they knew red mercury weapons were used during the war in Angola.

By now police were convinced the killings were linked to red mercury, and were suggesting that powerful people – maybe governments – didn't want the trade to continue.

This coincided with a warning from Mike Louw, director of the National Intelligence Service, who told legislators in the agency's first public testimony that the country was awash with foreign agents trying to pick up nuclear secrets. He said the agents were trying to find South Africa's nuclear experts to either hire them or ensure that they did not go to work for countries with nuclear ambitions. A police source later confirmed that agents from a country in the Middle East had approached a number of South African nuclear scientists in an effort to recruit them.

Another source said US agents were in South Africa trying to work on the problem at source. 'They are trying to buy red mercury or steal it – anything to get it off the market.' He said two other people were killed

1 The 'third force' was a term used to describe a shadowy group of unknown killers responsible for a range of bloody covert operations, which included the stirring of violence in tension-filled black communities in Natal and the Johannesburg area. In the 1990s, it was blamed for numerous massacres which claimed the lives of scores of commuters aboard Johannesburg trains. Third-force activities were widely believed to be connected to the security forces of the previous South African government, but this was difficult to prove. The callous aim of these *agents provocateurs* was to portray black people as uncontrollable and blood-thirsty. The political message was simple: black people were not fit to govern. Similar acts of destabilization have continued since the election, although on a far more limited scale.

in Maputo in 1993 because they were trying to trade in the material. There was a hit list in existence and 'one or two' people were already being protected by the state.

Landman was also preparing for the worst in his investigation. He admitted he suspected his inquiry would eventually involve people in high places – people in the military or senior politicians. And he knew it might become 'sticky'. However, for the time being, he was prepared to go all the way.

By 9 July 1994, the *Weekend Star* investigation had started to focus on the central issue. The newspaper was quoting an Israeli businessman with strong political and security connections in Israel as saying that South Africa had become a 'supermarket' for deals in red mercury. He had been offered the substance in Cape Town in 1991, and he knew that at the time Israel was looking for the material as a vital component for the miniaturization of nuclear warheads. He passed the information to his partner in Israel, who used to work for Israeli military intelligence and later for the Israeli Atomic Energy Commission. He did not know whether the deal was struck. He said Israel did not need red mercury any longer, having acquired the means to manufacture it from former Soviet scientists who had immigrated to Israel.

And on page 1, under a headline 'Kidger link to "superbomb"', the newspaper raised the possibility that the chemical Alan Kidger was shipping, red mercury, could be used to make a small nuclear weapon – a device no heavier than 2 kg. The newspaper suggested that red mercury could represent a cutting-edge technology perfected years ago in the Soviet Union. In essence, the technology meant that Third World countries could make a nuclear device more cheaply and more easily with materials that were not controlled by international treaty.

Looking at the macabre nature of the killings and earlier suggestions that they were linked to the 'clean' bomb, the possibility that South Africa had been procuring red mercury for its own superbomb could not be dismissed. And Landman too had decided it was time to look more closely at this mysterious substance.

4 The Terminator

On 24 March 1993 State President F. W. de Klerk convened a special joint session of Parliament in Cape Town and announced in measured tones that his country had secretly built six atom bombs during the 1980s, and part of a seventh. As jaws dropped, he also had some good news to impart. He said they had all been scrapped in 1991, and South Africa was now a nuclear-free zone – the first country in the world to give up its arsenal voluntarily. He had taken the decision shortly after coming to office at the end of 1989 'in the national interest'. The global political situation had changed dramatically, and a nuclear deterrent had become not only superfluous but an obstacle to the development of South Africa's international relations.

All other work on the nuclear bomb programme had similarly ended, said De Klerk. It had been a very limited nuclear capability. 'No advanced nuclear explosives, such as thermonuclear explosives, were manufactured ...' From the outset the emphasis had been on deterrence, and there had been no assistance from other countries.

He said South Africa had never conducted a clandestine nuclear test. There was 'no certainty' that a 'flash' detected by a satellite over the South Atlantic in 1979, and widely suspected of being a joint test with Israel, was a nuclear explosion – and 'if it was, we were not involved'.

De Klerk continued: 'South Africa's hands are clean, and we are concealing nothing. Permission has now been granted by the government for full access to the facilities and the records of facilities, which in the past were used for the preparation of a nuclear deterrent capability.

'I sincerely trust that this unprecedented act, namely the voluntary revelation of all relevant information, will confirm the government's effort to ensure transparency. I also trust that South Africa's initiative will inspire other countries to take the same steps.'

De Klerk was scornful of suggestions that his country had not disclosed all its stockpiles of enriched uranium: 'Such allegations ... are beginning to take on the dimensions of a campaign. South Africa's present nuclear programme, which is directed towards commercialization, is in the process placed under suspicion and is harmed. Our country cannot afford this.

'Accordingly I wish to confirm unequivocally that South Africa is adhering strictly to the requirements of the Nuclear Non-Proliferation Treaty and that it will continue to do so.'

He said the decision to build a nuclear arsenal had been taken in 1974, when the 'Soviet expansionist threat was growing in southern Africa'. The threat had abated by 1989 with a ceasefire in Angola and other global political changes.

De Klerk had earlier instructed an 'Experts Committee' of senior officials of the AEC, Armscor and the SADF to evaluate the pros and cons of dismantling the nuclear devices and of South Africa signing the Nuclear Non-Proliferation Treaty (NPT) as a non-nuclear-weapons state. He ordered the experts to examine all aspects of denuclearization, including the dismantlement of the devices, safe storage of the enriched uranium and destruction of all the hardware and design and manufacturing information.

De Klerk also wanted a timetable setting out how quickly the country could join the NPT and sign a safeguards agreement with the International Atomic Energy Agency (IAEA).

He told Parliament that dismantling work had begun in early 1990, supervised by an 'independent auditor'. All enriched uranium in Armscor's possession had been recast and returned for storage at Pelindaba, the AEC's headquarters. Armscor's facilities had been decontaminated and were now used for non-nuclear commercial purposes.

At a press conference later, De Klerk said the NPT, which had been signed in July 1991, did not oblige South Africa to inform inspectors of its former status as a producer of atom bombs. Dr Waldo Stumpf, head of the AEC, said neither the power of the bombs nor their technical details would be disclosed, but it leaked out that they were roughly the size of the Hiroshima weapon, 10 to 18 kilotons.

It was said about a thousand people had worked on the programme which had cost R700 million to R800 million (more than $200 million). Expenditure had been hidden in the vote of state funds to Armscor and the AEC. Only a small number of Cabinet ministers had ever been fully informed.

A week before the De Klerk statement the Foreign Ministry had instructed South Africa's embassies around the world to schedule meetings with host governments on the morning of 24 March. They were not told why. The de Klerk statement was faxed to them only twenty-four hours beforehand.

There were congratulations from a number of world leaders. US President Clinton was said by his spokesman to have greeted the admission 'warmly', but he added that his country had longstanding concerns about South Africa's nuclear programme. The ANC said it welcomed the announcement, but that it would believe 'South Africa's hands were clean' only when there had been full disclosure of everything that had gone on.

It was indeed a momentous day, but was De Klerk's statement the truth? For twenty years or more South Africa had lied about its nuclear plans. Other than the ANC, few seemed to consider that South Africa's nuclear arsenal could have been bigger and better than the six and half crude devices disclosed. The press comment the next day was almost entirely positive and uncritical.

Would it have been fair to ask more searching questions? Yes, it would. As we shall show, plenty of information had been published which should have made people worry that they were now being duped.

As early as March 1960, Dr Ampie Roux, the head of the Atomic Energy Board, had said in an interview that South Africa was now capable of producing its own atom bombs, 'providing it was prepared to isolate the best brains in the country and give them all the funds they needed'. As will be seen, he got those funds and those brains.

Then there was the comment in 1968 of General H. J. Martin, the army chief of staff, who said his country was ready to make its own nuclear weapons and this was linked to the production of a missile then in development.

In his address to Parliament, De Klerk had said South Africa's atom bomb project was given the go-ahead only in 1974. But Dr Louw Alberts, Roux's vice-chairman, said in 1974 that South Africa had the technology and resources to produce a bomb, and boasted that the nuclear programme was 'more advanced than India's'. India had just detonated its own atom bomb.

And there was also the size of the AEC's plant at Pelindaba, where the enriched uranium for the devices was made. Were all those towering chimneys and production plants, spread over hundreds of hectares on the skyline east of Pretoria, producing only this measly arsenal? At the very least there were obvious inconsistencies to be ironed out. It was time to talk to the man who was given the job of supervising the destruction of the bombs. Acting alone, he had looked over the shoulders of the scientists who were dismantling the weapons at Advena, the top-secret nuclear weapons plant near Pretoria.

Professor Wynand Mouton leaned back in his chair with the ease and calm of a man with time on his hands and described the most chilling experience of his life. 'Oh, I was cold,' he laughed. 'You know, just to realize the enormous power ... It's not a big thing, you know – a metre or two long and about 70 cm in diameter. You realize, if things go wrong here today, I'm gone; but this city, Pretoria, is gone as well.'

Mouton, nicknamed 'The Terminator' by the South African press, was describing his feelings the day he saw, for the first time, one of South Africa's six and a half declared nuclear weapons. The nuclear physicist, former chairman of the South African Broadcasting Corporation (SABC), former president of the University of the Orange Free State and trusted adviser to the National Party government, had agreed to discuss in detail how he monitored the dismantling of the bombs.

Speaking from his home at Wilderness on the Cape coast, he said his involvement had started with a phone call in 1989 from a man who had been a student at Stellenbosch University during Mouton's period as lecturer in nuclear physics there. The caller, by this time boss of the bomb-makers at Advena, had requested an independent observer to monitor the dismantling programme, and the bomb-makers' choice – Mouton – had been supported by De Klerk.

Mouton said he did not know about South Africa's nuclear weapons programme until that point, despite being on the board of Armscor from 1972 until 1980 – a crucially important developmental period for the weapons programme – and despite being one of the country's most noted nuclear physicists. 'But if you have a uranium enrichment programme – and all the world knew this – then of course as a nuclear physicist you know that's the most important thing as far as the bomb is concerned,' he said. 'If you don't have that you can't make the bomb.

'My students would ask me why we hadn't built a nuclear bomb. I would ask them what we would do with such a bomb that we couldn't do with ordinary bombs. But then if you look back at the nuclear strategy, which I later became familiar with, the bomb was never to be used physically. It was supposed to act as a deterrent. We were alone at that stage. We had interference from the north, from big powers, even Russia. The bomb meant you could ask people to mediate or assist in some other way. That was the whole idea behind it.'

He said he was not concerned that he knew nothing of the bomb programme at that time: 'It never really worried me that I was not told about this. It was a war situation.' He added: 'I think there were nine people who knew everything.'

Did South Africa ever consider using the bomb? 'No, I didn't get that impression at all – not as far as I could gather from the documents and of course by talking to people.'

Mouton said it was decided he would report back to De Klerk on the dismantlement progress every two to three months. He recalled his first meetings with the President. 'Our conversation was more about the problems. We had to decide how we were going to do it. How people on the programme would feel. For a person to build a thing and then have to dismantle it is quite a traumatic thing.'

Mouton said he had known De Klerk while the politician was Minister for National Education and he himself a university principal. 'We saw each other – not frequently, but fairly regularly. Sometimes he came to the campus to open a conference. And when I retired from the SABC in 1985, he also asked me to become chairman of the South African Council on Education. I liked him very much, and I appreciated him. Probably he didn't have any problems with me. So I was terribly eager that I should do this work for him.'

What was the brief? 'I just had to be a monitor – they called me the "auditor". It was my job to see that the dismantling was done in an orderly, safe and responsible way. I had to control everything and report to him when there were problems.'

Mouton said he carried the responsibility alone, but worked closely with the scientists at Advena. 'I did it from here, from Wilderness, which is 1,200 km from Pretoria. You couldn't be there every day, so I got to know the people who were doing the job to see whether I could put my trust in them. I could.'

Although De Klerk had decided in November 1989 – only weeks after entering office – to terminate the programme, he did not issue written instructions until 26 February 1990. Mouton was appointed auditor the following month. The dismantling started in July and was completed by 6 September 1991. Mouton sat in on all the planning sessions and, when the first bomb was dismantled, he was standing next to it. 'It consisted of two parts, which were always stored separately. One was a spherical piece of uranium that had a hole in it, and the other piece consisted of a cylinder. All you do is shoot the cylinder as fast as possible into the sphere, and the bomb would go critical. The bomb was the Hiroshima type – a very simple structure'.

47

Mouton declined to discuss the weight of the device.

Could the dismantling have gone wrong? 'I think the chances of that were very small – especially the way we handled them.' But shouldn't there have been more auditors? 'No, it wasn't necessary – I had so much faith in the people working and the way they were doing it. I looked at their procedures, and I was never worried. It was such a splendid team of people working there.'

The President had felt it was unnecessary to have someone monitor the process, but the bomb-makers insisted that there be such a person in case doubts arose later.

Bomb documents were destroyed at the beginning of 1993, just before De Klerk's announcement. 'I think the general feeling was that we were destroying the bombs, and if we kept the plans people would say that although we had destroyed the bombs we could make them again quickly.' There was also a worry that someone could sell the designs. 'In any case, if we wanted to build a bomb again in future we would certainly do it differently – we would probably build something better.'

But why wasn't something more advanced built in the first place, considering South Africa's obvious technical capabilities? 'You start as simply as you can if you haven't got the experience. But I did notice that from the third one they made small changes. They were already learning, and I think it was just that it was an experimental phase.'

He said he could find no indication of Israeli or US assistance: 'This was a go-it-alone programme. If you look at the whole enrichment programme, it was the idea of Dr Grant[1] and some of his collaborators. It was their own thing. Of course they did study at certain places. But if you look at the bomb you know it's the simplest type. If there had been input from people who had made bombs before, I'm sure we would have built a more sophisticated one.'

Mouton was an observer when some of the enriched uranium was transferred the twelve or so km from Advena to the AEC's Pelindaba complex. 'We did this over four nights, for safety reasons, and I was there for two nights. I sat throughout the night and went along with the shipment. But when they were melting it, I looked at the procedures, then went off, and I would perhaps come a few weeks later. It depended on what they were doing. But, as I said, the important thing for me was to decide whether I could rely on these people or not.'

1 This is a reference to Dr Wally Grant, who was mentioned in Chapter 2, and whose work with the AEC is examined in Chapter 6.

Mouton said there were ten vaults at Advena. Six weapons were made, and there was enough material for a seventh. The enriched uranium had been made into small ingots and placed under the protection of the AEC.

We asked Mouton if he would do anything differently were he to do it again. He thought it might have been a good idea to keep some or all of the 12,000 documents, covering the design of the weapons-grade uranium plant and the bombs, for the IAEA, to remove any suspicions. The papers had been kept in a steel cage at the dismantlement centre. Said Mouton: 'I did have a bit of doubt whether it was really necessary to destroy them. The IAEA would have been happier if we had not.'

On whether he was happy that every nuclear weapon in South Africa was destroyed, he said: 'I have that feeling. You know, towards the end, I still said to them: "I've seen these ten safes. Have you got others?" They said: "Yes." I went along and they opened up. But there was nothing.'

But could there have been other bomb factories? 'No. It was such a huge effort for a small country like South Africa to make what it did.'

Mouton said that, within a few grams, all the enriched uranium had been accounted for. 'There weren't any losses of uranium that really made me wonder what was going on.'

We asked him whether it was possible that South Africa had separately made small, tactical nuclear weapons. 'I saw no sign of that. I had to look at the dismantling of the six devices but, talking to people, I didn't find any sign.'

But could there have been a secret programme? 'I suppose it is possible, but I would be very surprised if that was the case. For eighteen months I saw these people frequently, and there was never a hint of it. To make these bombs was exceptional for this country, and I would be very surprised if there also had been anything of this kind.'

Did he think it was possible that there could be other bomb projects that were beyond his brief? 'Yes, but I would be surprised, looking at the whole effort that went into this.'

Although it would have been more efficient for South Africa to have built implosion-type weapons, using less uranium, Mouton said he saw no evidence that it had.

But how did he really know how much enriched uranium was produced? 'Well, they gave me the figures. But then of course if they were lying – yes, oh gee whizz.'

Asked whether the weapons were handed over to the military,

Mouton said they were not. The bombs had been stored at Advena. But was it possible that the vaults were simply emptied of most devices before Mouton got there? 'Of course, if people wanted to do it they could have. You can never be 100 per cent sure about this, but I had no reason to suspect.' Was he happy he saw the whole programme? Yes. He was dealing with men to be trusted.

However, Mouton confirmed there were a number of right-wing-inclined people on the programme who were unhappy that the bombs were being dismantled. But if something had been taken, other people there would have known.[1]

Asked what his response would be if he later discovered that in fact there had been a separate bomb programme that had been kept secret from him while he was dismantling the six and a half devices, he said: 'I would be very alarmed about it – no, that would make me most unhappy.'

De Klerk told Parliament: 'It was Professor Mouton's task to satisfy himself that every gram of nuclear material had been accounted for and that all the hardware and design information was destroyed. This has been done.'

Having satisfied ourselves that Mouton was convinced there could be no more weapons, we drove down the coast to meet a man in the city of Port Elizabeth, home of the South African motor industry. We had an appointment with Nick Badenhorst, a former civil servant who has spent his lifetime studying the world's nuclear weapons programmes, including the one in South Africa. His view of Pretoria's effort contrasted sharply with Mouton's.

He was adamant De Klerk was wrong when he announced that only six and half bombs were made, all of which were destroyed. 'I don't believe we only produced that number. And I believe we produced more sophisticated and smaller devices.

'I do not know what De Klerk's reasons were for stating that ... I suppose if you are head of state you see things from a different perspective. One should always bear in mind that truth is relative.'

Badenhorst told us he believed South Africa still retained a formidable arsenal of nuclear weapons, consisting of two types of 155-mm cannon shells, 10-kiloton gravity bombs, so-called backpack bombs of 1 kiloton or less, nuclear-tipped cruise missiles, and Arniston and D-25 interconti-

1 The *Washington Post* reported on 12 May 1993 that two workers had to be dropped from the dismantlement programme and kept under continuous surveillance when they threatened to abscond with the bomb materials.

nental ballistic missiles (ICBMs). The stockpile also included thermonuclear weapons.

His claims were startling. Although the police and others had indicated that nuclear weapons still existed in South Africa, we were taken
aback by the breadth of knowledge and detail that an analyst such as
Badenhorst could extract from what had already been published.

Badenhorst, who had meticulously analysed every available detail of
nuclear matters and missile development over the past thirty years, is a
respected researcher whose counsel has previously been sought by US
nuclear academics. He had previously been unable to expound upon his
theories in public because of South Africa's draconian censorship legislation. 'It was an interest I never outgrew. I do not have anything classified
– all my sources are open. But in the apartheid years I could not have
risked saying anything. Now that there is a new openness, I can.'

But if South Africa had built nuclear missiles and thermonuclear
bombs, we asked, where would they have been used? He said the larger
devices were aimed at other capital cities: 'If the United Nations had
decided to invade us in the late 1980s because it had had enough of
South Africa's racial policies, we could have threatened those countries
that supplied UN troops.'

He believed the country's obsession with having the bomb stemmed
from the turn of the century and the Boer War with Britain: 'A lot of
people here got hurt, and it is out of that generation that our leaders of
the 1940s and 1950s came. They vowed to ensure that they would never
be hurt again by a foreign regime.'

He said the nuclear programme began in the 1950s, and argued that
South Africa's banishment from the Commonwealth in 1961, coupled
with the refusal by the US administration of John F. Kennedy to allow
arms exports, increased his country's determination to have an independent nuclear deterrent.

Badenhorst said that South African Prime Minister Hendrik Verwoerd
expressed this determination in 1965: 'He said it was South Africa's duty
not only to consider the peaceful applications of nuclear technology but
also the military applications.'

Badenhorst said that plans were advanced even further by 1967:
'From around that time it was rumoured that the Israelis were in South
Africa to help with the nuclear weapons programme, and also French
physicists.'

He believed South Africa obtained an atom bomb from another
nuclear power that same year: 'I found an obscure newspaper article

which stated that South Africa had acquired a weapon so revolutionary in design that its components were stored in different vaults. I do not know of any conventional weapon that is kept like that.'[1]

When did South Africa get its first home-made bomb? Badenhorst theorized that this could have happened as early as 1974. He believed that looking at developments in other countries helped to put South Africa's programme in perspective. He argued that South Africa must have developed implosion devices because they required much less uranium or plutonium than the gun type – the model declared by De Klerk. 'I do not accept that we only made crude gun-type devices. China built an implosion bomb using old buckets in which they melted down various chemicals to make the explosive lenses. We had high-speed computers and foreign physicists. The Chinese had hand-held calculators. I can't accept we would rather build a dinosaur.'

Did South Africa acquire neutron bombs? 'Yes,' said Badenhorst. 'I would even go so far as to say they did this in co-operation with Israel.' He added that this co-operation extended to missile development.

'I believe we have not only long-range missiles but ICBMs based on the Israeli Shavit. After completing one orbit of the earth, it has an accuracy of 1 km. For our purposes – blackmail, terror – this was good enough.

'If one takes account of court proceedings now at hand in the United States, South Africa was developing the Shavit with Israel since 1984. My conclusion is that from 1987 South Africa could have been in possession of one. Officially, we no longer possess delivery systems. But if one listens to the grapevine I believe we still have a nuclear weapons capability and missiles.'

We had become aware of Badenhorst's research after a specialist defence magazine, *African Armed Forces*, published a controversial piece he had written on the nuclear programme before South Africa's first democratic election. His story, couched as a hypothetical scenario, came shockingly close to what we had been told as fact. He said that nuclear weapons and delivery systems remained in South Africa – and would not be significantly reduced until the National Party government negotiated the governing system and constitution it wanted. The implication of what he was suggesting seemed to go some way towards corroborating

[1] A manager of the bomb programme later confirmed that South Africa had procured a nuclear weapon 'from a friendly country' in the late 1960s and, until 1981, it had been stored inside an underground vault in a disused mine in the Witbank area of the eastern Transvaal.

what was being claimed by the security police and others.

In a section of the article that was cut before publication in November 1993, Badenhorst said the Israeli Shavit missile, on which South Africa's Arniston missile was based, could probably send a small nuclear warhead about 10,000 km. 'In theory, this means that the whole of Africa, as well as cities such as Melbourne, Moscow, Berlin, Paris, London, Buenos Aires and Rio de Janeiro, could be targeted by the Arniston,' he said in the article. 'However, a more substantial warhead, and consequently a more powerful rocket, will be needed for what I suspect is the real reason for our "space" programme, and ultimately the building of the D-25 – the acquisition of a truly intercontinental ballistic missile.'

The D-25, he said, would reach targets beyond the range of the Arniston, and with a larger warhead. These would probably travel 16,000 km.

In the hypothetical scenario he sketched, Badenhorst effectively suggested that elements of the right wing could have become involved in nuclear blackmail. He said military 'rogues', in reality disciplined units acting on orders 'from the top', could hold the world to ransom with these missiles if their political demands were not met.

He suggested these 'rogues' might have threatened to fire one missile each at North America, Europe and Asia. He described a scenario in which there were frantic, UN-sponsored negotiations and political concessions from all sides, including the De Klerk government. This would eventually lead to the 'final dismantling' of the South African nuclear weapons delivery systems, he wrote. 'However, rest assured that notwithstanding thousands of IAEA inspections, some of these weapons and missiles will be preserved somewhere. Why? Because I cannot for one moment imagine that the present administration [De Klerk's] would want to leave the new South Africa completely defenceless against any future threat to its survival – be it communism, fundamentalism or any other 'isms.

'I do not believe they would want to repeat Prime Minister Neville Chamberlain's mistake of 30 September 1938, when he stated there would be "peace in our time". On 3 September 1939, Britain declared war on Germany.

'If, God forbid, the Government of National Unity should fall and one is faced with civil war and atrocities such as those committed in Rwanda, the people in South Africa who do not take part in this would retreat to safety and use the threat of these weapons to get the world community to intervene.' They would also be used if old-style communism started to re-emerge and threaten South Africa.

Badenhorst said that this scenario could later lead to nuclear black-mail – to ensure whites would get the best possible deal out of the political settlement. 'Yes, Israel has used this successfully in 1963, so that is probably where we took our cue.'

Yet again someone was telling us there was nuclear trouble brewing behind the scenes.

Badenhorst said the long-range missiles developed by South Africa were a strong indication it had sophisticated nuclear devices. 'You would not build such weapons to deliver a bomb made of TNT,' he said. He also pointed out that the United States had recently been very active in making sure South Africa had ended its missile programme run by Denel, the government-owned company that took over Armscor's manufacturing operations in 1992. (Denel has sixteen divisions, organized into five groups, and employs about 13,000 people.) In August 1995 a US demolition team destroyed giant steel hangers and two massive concrete slabs at a static rocket test site at Rooi Els in the southern Cape. Explosives experts were also expected to 'modify' a critical part of an assembly plant run by chemicals and explosives company Somchem at Somerset West, also in the Cape, to prevent further construction of long-range rockets.

The experts were to to ensure the company could no longer make solid-fuel rocket motors with a range of more than 300 km. This required reducing the depth of the pits into which rocket casings were lowered. Somchem would still be able to fuel short-range 'theatre missiles', but nothing bigger. Paul Holtzhausen, spokeman for Denel, said the Rooi Els site had been used to test booster rockets intended to launch a low-orbit satellite to monitor environmental changes. He said nothing about nuclear ICBMs.

But according to South African Trade and Industry Minister Trevor Manuel, the work marked the ending of South Africa's nuclear programme. 'With this, the country's nuclear programme will be fully terminated,' he said, appearing to contradict a statement by F. W. de Klerk that South Africa had never had any nuclear missiles. Manuel said the demolitions were part of South Africa's obligations under the NPT and the Missile Technology Control Regime (MTCR) – a club of nations committed to checking missile proliferation. The demolition was being carried out in terms of a deal struck in 1994 with the Clinton administration in which the US government agreed to support South Africa's membership of the MTCR. In return, South Africa had agreed to close its space launcher and missile programme.

The US demolition team was being paid $735,000 for the work from the non-proliferation and disarmament fund of the US State Department. The South African government had initially requested $5.9 million from the fund, according to news reports. US officials said Denel had suggested the fund simply write it a cheque and let the South African armaments manufacturer carry out the demolition work, which was the culmination of negotiations started between the Bush and De Klerk governments.

The struggle between the two countries over South Africa's missile capabilities was put down to commercial considerations, with the United States not wanting to lose satellite launching business to another country. However, Badenhorst believed it was further evidence that South Africa had developed the capability to drop a nuclear weapon on any city in the world.

It was by now clear we would have to investigate the background to South Africa's nuclear programme to establish whether it was possible there could still be nuclear weapons in existence.

And what of the murders and the alleged links to red mercury? The answer to the red mercury riddle most likely lay in Russia, where reports about the substance had been appearing since the mid-1980s.

5 Inside the Russian Matrioshka

As usual, there was mayhem at Kazan mainline station on the outer ring of the Moscow underground. People were rushing from the subway towards the trains that would carry them far away to the East – to Omsk and Tomsk in outer Siberia, and even to Vladivostok on the Pacific Ocean, some 6,000 km away.

But the way to the passenger compartments, and their precious empty seats, was obstructed by the hordes who had just arrived from the provinces. Many bore huge bundles of merchandise and garden produce to sell on the streets of the capital. The most desperate dragged their pets behind them – another commodity with which to earn a few precious roubles. It was chaotic, yet somehow people managed to keep moving.

A few minutes before its departure time, the diesel train at platform 10 rapidly filled up. It was heading for Ekaterinburg, 1,600 km away in the Ural mountains, and all the cheap seats were taken. Latecomers had to stand or squat, if they could find space in the corridors. The first-class compartments were, however, nearly empty. A ticket cost only £2 ($3.20) for the twenty-four-hour journey, but, apart from Western visitors, few travelling that hot dusty day in July 1992 could afford such extravagance.

The train had begun to crawl through the Moscow suburbs when George[1] sat down on the bunk bed opposite and issued a baffling request. 'My friend, before we get to Ekaterinburg, you must tell me everything you know about red mercury. The people you are to meet there will want to know everything.'

He was obviously anxious about the subject, and he was even more unhappy to be told that red mercury was regarded in Britain and the rest of the Western world as a hoax. 'But you must know something,' he said. 'Everyone in my city believes scientists in the West are making use of this substance just like we are. We know for certain the Americans are buying it.

[1] George is not his real name. He had come to Moscow from Ekaterinburg to meet co-author Peter Hounam, who had just flown in from London. Hounam was accompanied by John Large, a nuclear engineer who advises Greenpeace.

'I have been sent to Moscow to meet you because the Ekaterinburg City Council wants to open up its military factories to the West. We need to convert them to peaceful uses. We need to show journalists like you that we have a lot to offer.' He got more agitated. 'If you say you know nothing about red mercury, they will not respect you. They will blame me for inviting you.'

George, who was in his early thirties, eventually calmed down. He was thin, nervous and very earnest, and said he was a nuclear physicist by profession. Like many of his friends, he had found it was no longer easy to survive by working for state-run academic institutes at the equivalent of £10 ($16) a month.

As the journey continued, he began to relax. 'Look,' he went on, 'I know red mercury is said to be a hoax. The newspapers here say so too sometimes. But I promise you it is not. It is a very special chemical, made in our military factories, which has many uses.

'When it is first made, it is a powder which is dark red in colour. But we irradiate it in a nuclear reactor which turns it into a very heavy liquid, the colour of wine. It is very, very expensive, because it is very difficult to make.'

The train was trundling through featureless birch forests, and George talked late into the night. 'Free speech and ending censorship are important to us now. That is why I can talk to you. Go to any subway and you will even see people selling pornography, just like in London.'

He was worried about the economic crisis in Russia, but said the recent political upheavals were inevitable. 'Most people are still glad the communist regime has fallen,' he explained, 'but it has led to many bad things, like the growth of the Russian mafia who control the things like the red mercury black market.'

Then George lowered his voice: 'You know, my friend, that one of the uses of red mercury is for nuclear weapons. You can make them in a different sort of way – nothing like the ones you have in the West – and they can be used by underdeveloped countries. That is why our mafia are in the black market.'

Ekaterinburg is the capital of the region of Sverdlovsk, Russia's second-biggest industrial area, and George was proud of its history. It had been founded by Peter the Great because of the rich mineral deposits in the area, and by Russian standards had become relatively prosperous. In 1918 it was notoriously the scene of the slaughter of Tsar Nicholas II and his family, and more recently Boris Yeltsin had been born in its suburbs and risen to become its Communist Party boss.

In one of the most remembered crises of the Cold War, an American U2 spy plane, piloted by Gary Powers, was shot down there in May 1960. The US had sent him to photograph the military factories that had mushroomed in Ekaterinburg after the Second World War. In those days it was a 'closed' conurbation, barred to anyone without a permit; it was not opened to Westerners until early 1992.

The factories mass-produced shells, tanks, cruise missiles and even biological weapons using anthrax bacteria.[1] But business had been bad since the end of the Cold War. The emphasis was now on unbridled capitalism through the manufacture of Western goods. George was particularly proud of the former Cruise missile factory: 'Now it has a production line making Philips videocassette recorders.'

Ekaterinburg also seemed to be a centre of the Russian red mercury business, and George was anxious to introduce his friend Yevgeny Korolev, who knew a lot more than he did about it. Korolev was a city councillor and a local hero, having started a number of housing co-oper-atives that had created thousands of homes. Also, by training he was a nuclear physicist.

A bearded and gaunt figure, Korolev operated from an office in a mammoth apartment block he had helped to build. An old MiG fighter and a tank provided a sculpture in the square outside, and his office was strewn with papers and plans.

'You are asking about something that the authorities want to keep secret,' he said, 'but I don't mind telling you because it is time the world knew. This material does indeed have many uses, but you will want to know how it can be used in a nuclear weapon.' He turned up the volume of his television set and took out a loaded revolver. 'Don't be alarmed – this is just a precaution,' he said reassuringly, and laid the gun on his desk.

'Red mercury has two functions in an atom bomb device. It is an extremely powerful conventional explosive which can compress a ball of plutonium to above its critical mass and make it fission. It can also generate a powerful burst of neutrons which makes the fissioning more efficient.'

Korolev too said that in its normal form red mercury was a powder, but under special processing in a reactor it could be turned into a very heavy liquid. In this form it had a limited life of perhaps three months. It

1 In 1976, 200 people died when anthrax leaked out of a plant. At the time it was explained away as an epidemic caused by 'bad meat'.

was the fresh liquid red mercury that was used in nuclear weapons.

As well as fraudulent deals taking place on the black market, the genuine material was also being traded for huge sums and at huge risk by the Russian mafia, he said. People had been shot with long-range rifles, and there were stories of people being thrown alive from planes.

Korolev said the smuggling trade in the chemical was a major problem for the authorities, because the Russian mafia had penetrated the military industries and could control the supply. 'Red mercury can make very small nuclear weapons. Saddam Hussein could make an atomic grenade the size of a grapefruit that would blow a ship out of the sea.'

'It is a dangerous game,' he said. 'People all over the world want to buy it. Countries in the Middle East and the Far East are always in the market. Even Japan has bought some. Why do you think they want it? They want their own bomb.'

George then took us to Vitaly Mashkov, who was People's Deputy for the Sverdlovsk Region and a political ally of Yeltsin. At first Mashkov refused to make any comment about nuclear matters except to say that Russian scientists had a unique method of separating plutonium from irradiated uranium. Then, as he was leaving his office for another meeting, he linked this to red mercury: 'It is a great scientific advance – something that Russia can be proud of,' he said. But he added quietly: 'You must realize it is also a grave proliferation threat.'

The collapse of communism and the débâcle of the attempted coup against Mikhail Gorbachev a year earlier had evidently made people like Korolev and Mashkov less cautious about talking to journalists about nuclear secrets. It also became clear that highly placed people in Moscow wanted part of the story to come out about red mercury.

Two secret documents were leaked to a weekly newspaper which shed light on the deals that had been quietly going on for some time. They came from the Lubyanka building near the Kremlin, once the headquarters of the Komitet Gosudarstvennoy Bezopasnosti, or KGB, the Soviet security service, and now the home of its successor, the Foreign Intelligence Service (FIS). The FIS had been monitoring red mercury trading and had produced a detailed list of applications from sellers seeking official permission to export red mercury. It gave the names of Russian companies involved and the institutions acting as intermediaries, including the Academy of Science, the USSR Council of Ministers, and an association of Afghan war veterans.

The document indicated that many multimillion-dollar agreements to sell red mercury had been negotiated, of which some were probably hoaxes. One deal in particular – number 29 – stood out. It showed that a special presidential order had been signed by Boris Yeltsin granting permission to an Ekaterinburg company for the sale of large quantities of the chemical.

This linked up with the second document that had been leaked by the FIS. It was a copy of the order, dated 21 February 1992, which gave exclusive trading rights to Oleg Sadykov, head of a company called Promecology. The document allowed the firm to 'produce, buy, keep, transport and deliver' red mercury 20/20 and export it with an annual quota of 10 tons. The value of this at the quoted black-market rate was in excess of $3,500 million!

At Promecology's penthouse suite of offices overlooking the Moscow river and the White House, home of the Russian Parliament, Sadykov was not happy to be interviewed. Pacing agitatedly up and down his corridor, he refused at first to say anything. Eventually, he was persuaded that the leak of the FIS document needed a response, and he then spoke almost non-stop for two hours.

Sadykov said his company was being allowed by Yeltsin to make a lot of money from red mercury sales to subsidize a massive project to reclaim contaminated Russian rocket sites covering millions of hectares at Bykonur, Kapustin Yar and Plesetsk. Waving his hands and thumping his desk with enthusiasm, he claimed red mercury could create new technologies, faster semiconductors and cheaper methods of energy generation.

On nuclear weapons, he said the material allowed the construction of very small nuclear weapons, perhaps no bigger than a pen top. 'We are only allowed to deal directly with governments where the final customer's identity is known and approved of, and where no re-export is permitted,' he said. How much did his red mercury sell for abroad compared with the black-market price? 'Ours costs $500,000 a kilogram. Stolen material is cheaper – but then stolen goods are always cheaper.'

By now he was getting into his stride, disclosing that red mercury, in the form that was leaking on to the black market, perished after several months and became useless – unless buyers had the facility to refresh it. When it was delivered from the production plant, it was in the form of a dark-red honey-like liquid, but as it deteriorated it turned into a powdery sludge.[1]

1 Sadykov was later interviewed for a *Dispatches* programme aired by Channel 4 Television in Britain and produced two jars which he said contained the basic material from which red mercury was synthesized. One bottle, which was supposedly fresh,

Sadykov said the black-market sales of red mercury in the West posed a big threat to world security which Russia appeared powerless to stop. 'It is essential for the President to solve this problem right now. The fascists and communists are trying to use it to disturb the political situation. We want to stop the mafia and do some kind of deal with the West.'

Sadykov also said that the old Soviet authorities had been secretly selling red mercury to US businessmen for many years, and that the US government had full knowledge of its properties. He confided he was in the process of agreeing a contract with a Los Angeles company, API International.[1] A letter of intent had been signed to sell them no less than 50 tons of red mercury, worth a staggering $50 billion.

Sadykov said the Russian Ministry of Atomic Energy was fully aware of the potential applications of red mercury, and they should be questioned about it. The trail therefore led on to Yevgeny Mikerin, head of its science and technology department.

A few weeks earlier Mikerin had told the *Guardian* newspaper in London that the material was an exotic radioactive substance used in microelectronics, and not a hoax. Asked about this remark at his office in the Ministry, Mikerin said he stood by it, but he believed suggestions it was used in nuclear weapons were false. 'It could be true, but my Ministry has no knowledge of this.'

He grew more uneasy when confronted with the leaked FIS list of transactions. 'I can see this list contains the name of our Minister, Viktor Mikhailov, and our President. This is of concern to us, and we would like a copy so we can investigate.'

Mikerin promised to forward the findings, but no response was ever forthcoming. However, later, in an off-guard moment, Mikhailov told a conference that Russia was able to make a new miniature type of weapon that could be detonated in its hundreds on the enemy, wiping them out without harming Russia's own troops. Later, in an interview in *Pravda*, he seemed to hint that these weapons were 'mini-neutron bombs' that could kill people without damaging buildings.

appeared to contain a dark treacle-like substance. The other, which Sadykov said needed refreshing, was partly liquid and partly granular.

1 The Los Angeles company was headed by Jesus Godinez, a real-estate and car-part salesman. Confronted in LA, he said his company was acting as a broker for multinational companies in the West, including major oil companies. At one stage he had made several trips to Angola in search of supplies. At the time of going to press, he said he had not yet succeeded in importing any red mercury into the United States.

Around the same period General Yevgeny Negin, an academician and leading nuclear weapons expert, raised similar speculation when he said his country had developed a nuclear weapon 'in which a doubling of yield is achieved with a hundred-fold reduction in weight compared with existing devices'. This description of a new type of mini-nuke echoed the remarks of Yevgeny Korolev.

According to Dr Frank Barnaby, a British nuclear physicist who closely follows developments in nuclear weapons, Negin's remarks, if correctly reported, must mean that Russia is using a new technology unreported in Western scientific literature. He said such a tiny type of nuclear warhead would be impossible to construct using fissile materials such as plutonium-239 and uranium-235, the basic components of Western nuclear devices.

Yeltsin's apparent backing of Sadykov's entrepreneurial activities with red mercury soon sparked a burning row. The two men were attacked in the Russian Federation Parliament by former Vice-President Alexander Rutskoi, a bitter critic of Yeltsin's cavalier economic policies. In a long speech televised across Russia, he accused Yeltsin of squandering Russia's strategic assets. Bashing the podium with indignation, he continued: 'Some brilliant minds have come up with a new element in the Mendeleyev [periodic] table. They are sending abroad this substance that does not exist in nature.'

Rutskoi's remarks had to be taken seriously. He was not only a prominent Russian politician, he was also a veteran army general, renowned for his heroism in Afghanistan. Yeltsin was also about to go to the country with a referendum on a new constitution and faced a growing band of hostile People's Deputies. He had no alternative but to take some action. A police investigation led by a public prosecutor was ordered, and Sadykov's licence was rescinded. The boss of Promecology went to ground, and rumours began to circulate that he was dead. Orders were also sent out from the Kremlin to control the red mercury trade.

Then Rutskoi himself seemed to fall in line. In a remarkable volte-face he publicly recanted, saying he no longer believed that red mercury existed. He had spoken to scientists in Russia and had come to the conclusion that 'this was the hoax of the century'. Later the public prosecutor dropped his inquiry, telling the Itar-Tass news agency: 'It has been established that none of the enterprises or research institutes has ever synthesized or made a product with the qualities and characteristics of red mercury.'

Rutskoi's reversal of opinion may have been a genuine realization that he had made a major blunder, but there was an alternative explanation. Several sources told us that the United States had put heavy pressure on Yeltsin to calm the controversy and extinguish public comment. It was, however, evident that public statements in Russia differed from what people were saying privately. Several months elapsed before research for a *Dispatches* programme, 'The Pocket Neutron', for Channel 4 Television in Britain shoved the issue back into the spotlight.

The director of the programme, Gwynne Roberts, went to Moscow and, after patient research, obtained a series of confidential documents. They had been gathered by an aide to Yeltsin's political office who had been given instructions to find out about red mercury.

One document had been written by Sadykov, apparently for Yeltsin's information, and vividly expanded on what Promecology's boss had disclosed to Hounam in the summer of 1992. It accused some Russian businessmen, acting for red mercury producers, of blatant dishonesty:

To achieve their aims, they try different methods of fraud – they even sometimes use false specimens and certificates ... The illegal deliveries of red mercury abroad were carried out by top Communist Party officials and Russian ministries involved in the production. In exchange, these organizations would have a separate state budget. Some of the money was used to back communist movements abroad and support further scientific research.

He estimated the illegal export of red mercury could amount to almost $100,000 million. He said an organization called Mercury, with its headquarters in Switzerland, was dealing with the Russian side. The report went on: 'A so-called specialized group of KGB collaborators and specialists from the Ministry of Defence took part in this affair. Recently, some operations involving the export of party funds were carried out under the label of red mercury transactions.'

He said that even more recently there had been an effort to legalize the purchase from Russia by Western buyers: 'Those involved in all these deals had to mask them and, on their initiative, a campaign was initiated in the mass media to persuade the Russian authorities that red mercury did not exist.'

Sadykov said that, since he had been granted the presidential order, other groups had been locked in a struggle 'to protect their turf' using senior Russian politicians. He warned that his company could not cope alone against the illegal exports of red mercury and the corruption that went with it, and called for the support of the Defence Ministry and Customs.

Also among the documents obtained by Gwynne Roberts was a top-secret report for Yevgeny Primakov, Yeltsin's new intelligence boss, prepared by his First Chief Directorate, Technical Branch, on 24 March 1992. It is worth reporting at length.

'All the companies that tried to buy this product were small consultative companies engaged in broking activities,' it said. 'These companies did not disclose their interest in this product, its applications and the ultimate consumers, and often they were not named on official registers.'

It listed the main applications of red mercury as: 'The production of fuses of high accuracy for conventional bombs; the production of fuses for nuclear bombs; the starting-up of nuclear reactors; the production of coatings for military equipment to avoid radar detection and the production of warheads for self-guided, high-precision missiles.'

It continued: 'According to information which is not totally reliable and which requires additional checking, this substance can be used in some modern technologies that are not known of in our country: the production of high-speed electronic components; paper for banknotes; refining gold from ore and some types of industrial waste.'

It said Western companies Rockwell, General Dynamics, Westinghouse, Messerschmidt Boelkow Blohm, Siemens and British Aerospace were engaged in activities connected to red mercury.

The report said the chemical was a mercury salt of antimony with the formula $Hg_2Sb_2O_7$. This was first produced in the USSR in 1968 at Dubna, a major nuclear research centre where the reactor was suited to implanting the material with strontium, caesium and other isotopes.

It continued: 'Red mercury was produced at plants run by the former Ministry for Atomic Energy in such towns as Sverdlovsk-33, Chelyabinsk-40 and Sverdlovsk-66,[1] and the laboratories of the Academy of Science at Novosibirsk, but in very small quantities ... As a result of this process, they obtained a substance with a density of up to 23 grams per cubic centimetre.[2] The product can be kept for no longer

1 It is estimated that more than 700,000 people in Russia live in closed military cities. Many such complexes were given the name of the region in which they were built and a number. They still do not appear on Russian maps.

2 This density baffles many Western scientists as it is higher than any other known substance, including pure metals. Mercury as used in thermometers has a density of 13.6 g/cm3 . $Hg_2Sb_2O_7$ is a powder in its natural state and has a density of 9.6 g/cm3 ; pure plutonium, one of the heaviest materials known, has a density of just under 20 g/cm3 .

than four to twelve months, depending on the isotope used.'

The Russian intelligence service said that, according to specialists, there is only one reactor at the European Centre for Nuclear Exploration in Switzerland (CERN) that can be used for implanting red mercury with isotopes, but they believed some modifications and additional experimentation would be needed. 'This factor, as well as the availability in the USSR of large quantities of red mercury stockpiles, explains the special importance of this country in its production.'

The report quoted a price of $340 dollars a gram for what was described as 20/20 red mercury, and $380 for 20/23 – more than twenty times the price of gold. The substance was said to be carried in standard lead-coated containers, each weighing 30 kg and carrying a 5-gram specimen container.

'Thanks to the high density of this product, such containers are not large. The presence of the specimen is important to avoid forgeries.'

The report said shipping routes from the Russian Federation were via intermediary companies in Hungary, Bulgaria, Poland, Germany, Switzerland, Austria and Finland. The final consumers were large companies in the United States and France that are connected to the nuclear or space industries. 'And the consumers of this product are Israel, Iran, South Africa and Arab countries, such as Iraq and Libya, that are striving to have nuclear weapons.'

It said one of the Hungarian companies, called Ferrometa KFT, was headed by an ex-Dubna employee called Laslo Sege. It claimed he was centrally involved in delivering red mercury to US companies that had given written guarantees that they would use it only for civilian purposes within their country. Hundreds of kilograms were being exported there from Europe. 'Such firms as RP Trading Co. (Canada) and Euro-Professional (US) tried to find the companies supplying red mercury. It is believed South Africa is behind those firms.'

Before it was decided that special licences had to be obtained in Russia for the export of red mercury, 'there were plans to export it illegally through the embassies of Iran and Libya in Moscow ... We do not know for certain what happened after that.'

The report concluded: 'The illegal export of red mercury has probably been carried out since the mid-1970s. At the same time, both the price and the demand for red mercury have greatly increased.'

The trips to Russia showed one thing at least: it was difficult to dismiss the idea that red mercury was simply an invention of fraudsters and rouble-launderers, as had been alleged in the West. The Russian reports also stated that South Africa was actively and secretly buying the material from Russia, further raising the question of whether red mercury was linked to the development of advanced nuclear technologies in the Republic.

6 Nothing More to Hide?

Evidence from Russia of red mercury being bought by South Africa for nuclear use and Nick Badenhorst's painstaking research into advances in weapon and missile developments gave a different perspective of the Republic's nuclear programme from that of President F. W. de Klerk in his 1993 speech. There must have been many other people, linked to the programme, who knew that South Africa was much more advanced than Parliament had been told.

Of course the authorities knew they were all gagged by the Official Secrets Act and the Atomic Energy Act, and would never talk, but in South Africa nothing is ever conclusive. In 1994 sixteen scientists, engineers and administrators from the nuclear programme blew the whistle in a most extraordinary way.

South Africa's *Sunday Times* newspaper splashed a story revealing that this disgruntled group were threatening to expose closely guarded secrets unless they were paid R4.5 million ($1.2 million) in redundancy benefits – equivalent to salary for two years, plus benefits. A spokesman admitted to reporter Peter De Ionno that the threat amounted to blackmail. He said his colleagues were prepared to construct bombs for anyone if their money was not guaranteed.

'We want a settlement,' he said, 'but negotiation has failed and we don't want to have to take this to the industrial court ... I am not ashamed of what we did, but I cannot get a job. We are treated like outcasts. We are South Africa's nuclear casualties.' He warned that the disclosures would prove embarrassing for the National Party, Armscor, and its offshoot Denel, which controlled Advena, where South Africa's nuclear weapons had been produced.

Contradicting De Klerk's assertion that no foreign help had been received, he said his group had secret details of South Africa's past cooperation with Israel on missile technology and details of a process Israel had supplied which transformed a satellite launcher into a nuclear ballistic missile.

He said South Africa's space programme, scrapped on US insistence in

1993, was originally intended to use a clone of the Israeli Jericho-II two-stage missile to deliver nuclear devices. More than 200 South Africans had covertly worked in Israel on the missile programme between 1989 and 1992. A three-stage missile known as RSA-3 had been built, he said, and had been fired in static tests. And two all-terrain mobile launchers had been built and tested at a Denel proving-ground in 1988 and 1989.

Also, in a R200 million ($55 million) deal, South Africa had bought an explosives system that could stop a missile at a predetermined point in mid-flight, and strike a target within a kilometre. The rebels' spokesman appeared to be referring to a Fractional Orbital Bombardment System, or FOBS, by which an intercontinental ballistic missile is fired into a low earth orbit and then halted by reverse-thrust motors to return to earth above its predetermined target. If South Africa had this technology, it also implied it had sophisticated nuclear warheads for an ICBM.

The spokesman told the *Sunday Times* that after South Africa's 'dirty' bombs had been completed, more powerful ones were developed in secret on behalf of the SADF. This programme was stopped in 1989, but he said it had included 'thermonuclear hydrogen bombs'. 'What is the deterrent value of a 20-kiloton bomb when your enemy is threatening you with a 100-kiloton bomb?' he asked. He said his colleagues also had first-hand information that would identify sources for specialized equipment for nuclear bombs in Britain, France and Germany.

The *Sunday Times* story seemed incredible but there is little doubt it was genuine. A spokesman for Denel confirmed that sixteen staff members had been made redundant and talks with them had broken down because of their 'unfounded and unreasonable claims and expectations'. He said media intimidation had left Denel disillusioned at the conduct of people 'with high technology standing for whom Denel has only the highest regard and sympathy'.

This sympathy did not last long once the *Sunday Times* hit the streets on 27 March 1994. Paul Holtzhausen, Denel's group communications boss, said the threats could jeopardize South Africa's relations with other signatories of the Nuclear Non-Proliferation Treaty (NPT). Armscor said any disgruntled nuclear and rocket scientist who disclosed information about South Africa's nuclear weapons programme would be liable to charges under legislation preventing proliferation of weapons of mass destruction. The ANC said it was worried about the information falling into the wrong hands.

By 29 March the matter had been rushed to the Supreme Court in Pretoria, where Gideon Smith, an Armscor senior manager, said in an affidavit that the information already published had harmed his country's chances of becoming a member of the Missile Technology Control Regime. He said the United States was worried, and that if further information was disclosed South Africa's chances of joining would be slim. He applied for an 'urgent interdict' preventing the sixteen, whose names and addresses were listed, from 'disclosing any information in connection with the obtaining, supply, marketing, import, export, development, manufacturing, upkeep or repair of, or research in connection with munitions on behalf of Armscor or any of its subsidiaries'. Just in case something was missed out, it also requested that the rebels be forbidden from disclosing any classified information to any unauthorized person, including the media.

As seemed inevitable, the order was granted by Mr Justice Spoelstra and the sixteen rebels were silenced.[1] However, the information already released cast doubt on South Africa's proclaimed transparency. It now seemed hydrogen bombs had been developed, and also long-range nuclear-tipped missiles.

And yet De Klerk and Professor Wynand Mouton had said that each device had weighed nearly a ton. The first two were apparently usable only for testing or 'demonstration' purposes in an underground shaft, as a warning to an enemy. The remaining four that were completed late in the 1980s were fit only for dropping over a target from a plane, and virtually no more advanced than the one the United States had dropped on Hiroshima in 1945. None of this gelled with the rebels' story. According to them, South Africa was up in the big league in terms of developing nuclear weapons and delivery systems.

The origins of South Africa's nuclear programme go back fifty years, to 1944, when Britain was deeply involved in the Manhattan Project to produce the atom bomb. The bombs being prepared for the US raids on Hiroshima and Nagasaki were nearing completion, and there was a desperate need for uranium. Sir John Anderson, the British Chancellor of the Exchequer, wrote a coded telegram to South Africa's Prime Minister Field Marshal Jan Smuts requesting him urgently to check on sources of radium and pitchblende ore.

1 By September 1995 the Denel sixteen's legal case was still grinding on. The court order preventing them from discussing their grievances with the media was still in place and the group was under surveillance.

To those in the know, any minerals containing these materials would also be rich in uranium. Smuts ordered a search, and engineers with British-supplied Geiger counters were sent roaming the bush. Substantial deposits were found on the gold reefs west of Johannesburg and in South West Africa (now Namibia, which is one of the world's largest suppliers). South Africa thereby became a major supplier of the raw materials for the West's nuclear programmes.

The Atomic Energy Board (AEB), which became the Atomic Energy Corporation (AEC) in 1982, was formed in 1948 by Act of Parliament and held its first meeting in March 1949, taking control over all nuclear matters from mining to the production of atomic energy – both seen as highly profitable enterprises.

The fact that South Africa produced not even a watt of nuclear electricity for public use for another thirty-five years is the first clue that the country's vast investment in nuclear research and development had another central purpose.

Through the mid-1950s, the country was investing heavily in training. Nuclear physics departments were opened at the universities of Witwatersrand, Cape Town and Stellenbosch, and the Council for Scientific and Industrial Research, a state-run body, began work on particle accelerator research. It has been reported that by this period research work on a nuclear weapon design had already begun. By 1954 the government had started providing bursaries for physicists to study overseas and a delegation had been dispatched to Europe to study the industrial uses of atomic energy. It paved the way for the dispatch of large numbers of students to France, Germany, Britain, Sweden and the United States.

By 1957 the Atomic Energy Board's remit was extended, worrying some senior scientists. Dr Ampie Roux, the AEB's research director, began to formulate a new set of objectives. On paper they seemed innocuous enough. Item 2 in his list was 'the study of further steps in uranium processing', item 3 was 'the study of the properties of uranium in relation to its use as a nuclear fuel' and item 4 was 'the study of economic heavy-water production'. But taken together they could be seen as sanctioning the first steps to the production of weapons-grade plutonium or uranium.

In the summer of 1958, the members of the AEB split. The Board's expurgated official history, *Chain Reaction*,[1] states: 'The division of the

1 *Chain Reaction* by A. R. Newby-Fraser (Atomic Energy Board, 1979).

Board into two camps derived in essence from differing legal interpretations of a small phrase contained in the Atomic Energy Act.' The phrase is not identified,[1] but it was clearly of considerable importance: 'Feelings were running high, so strongly in fact that a very substantial delay was incurred before the Cabinet gave the go-ahead for the programme.'

The Board's secret row raged for more than a year before the objections of the dissenters were overcome, the 'logic of the arguments of the majority' were accepted by the Cabinet, and 'The green light flashed for the Board.'

It seems likely this was the point of take-off for the bomb programme, code-named Operation Kerktoring (Operation Church Tower).

Given the go-ahead, Roux lost no time in beginning to realize what was clearly an expensive dream. The AEB had been occupying offices in part of the fourth floor of the Merino Building, a block in central Pretoria; apart from Roux there were just two engineers and a small support staff. But now that was all to change.

Surveyors had already been looking for a vast site that could accommodate acres of buildings and a daily flow of 5,000 cubic metres of water for the plant and equipment. It was found 35 km from Pretoria in the Magaliesberg mountains, where the Crocodile river runs through a valley, providing plentiful amounts of water. Farms were quietly bought up before their owners realized the purpose to which their land was about to be put.

The official history records: 'From then on the tempo of construction was maintained at high pitch and, one after another, various buildings sprouted from what previously had been a low hill covered with sparse waving grass, rocky outcrops and clumps of indigenous trees; thornbush, kareeboom, and bushes bearing the national flower, the protea.'

Naming the site proved easy. Down the hill was a camping spot with a café called 'Pelindaba', meaning, in the local tribal tongue, 'the discussion is finished'. That name was adopted for the new campus.

Roux's prestigious Pelindaba campus was soon growing fast, with separate buildings for chemistry, metallurgy, engineering and several other disciplines. He could reflect that one of his early objectives had been achieved: a centre for nuclear research that would proclaim to the rest of the world that South Africa was now in the big time.

On the other hand, his other major objective would have to remain

[1] A small omission was any hint of a nuclear explosives programme in more than 200 pages.

secret. His organization was already taking its first faltering steps towards mastering the enrichment of uranium. This was the difficult process of extracting from uranium ore – composed mainly of atoms of U-238 – the small quantity of U-235 that it also contains. It was the U-235 that South Africa needed, either to build a power reactor or to produce a bomb. This programme was called Project XYZ.

Recalling this period, *Chain Reaction* says defensively: 'No one was under any illusion as to the politically sensitive nature of uranium enrichment, and the malicious interpretations which even at this early stage would have been placed on any suggestion of research into enrichment processes. Accordingly, the project was classified.' This explanation is not so credible if, as it maintained, the AEB was interested only in peaceful applications of nuclear fission. In the same period, the West Germans were working on enrichment techniques and were open about how they were progressing.

The AEB was so determined to keep the work secret that it was not even located at Pelindaba. Scientists and engineers were moved into a former motor accessory store in Du Toit Street in central Pretoria, which was made to look like a commercial engineering workshop. Later the project outgrew this shabby building, and Shamrock Building in Skinner Street was taken over.

By 1964, considerable advances had been made, and it was time to ask the government for yet more money to build a prototype enrichment plant. Prime Minister Dr Hendrik Verwoerd was invited to Pelindaba for a briefing and, says the official history, he immediately asked whether some of the formalities could be bypassed. Said the history: 'The impact of this whole-hearted support by the Government was so great that by the end of December 1964, instead of then calling for tenders, the Board already had the building completed – physical manifestation of the drive and urgency which has characterized the enrichment project.'

By now, with Verwoerd's personal backing, all the omens were good for the AEB's new National Nuclear Research Centre. A twenty-megawatt research reactor, christened Safari-1, went critical in March 1965. It was supplied by Allis Chalmers of the United States, who also undertook to supply the enriched nuclear fuel it needed,[1] and it was safeguarded by the IAEA.

Britain was equally compliant on the nuclear front. Many South

[1] In 1975, court action initiated by the black caucus in Congress forced the suspension of deliveries of fuel.

African nuclear scientists travelled to British universities for training, and there was close collaboration with Harwell, the Atomic Energy Research Establishment in southern England. Although the Safari-1 reactor was fuelled by the United States, the fuel rods themselves were produced largely at the AERE. Of 86.3 kg of weapons-grade uranium supplied between February 1965 and April 1975, 64.3 kg was supplied from Harwell – enough for a few nuclear weapons. An audit of these supplies appears to account for most of the material, but experts admit some plutonium or highly enriched uranium could have been diverted and replaced later with illicit supplies, perhaps from the People's Republic of China.

There have been repeated complaints that fuel in Safari-1 could have been periodically reprocessed to extract weapons-grade plutonium. Though this suggestion is always strongly denied by Pelindaba, it is nevertheless surprising that the United States was willing to install a reactor with a potential military application. Safari-1 came on stream just two years after a voluntary UN arms embargo was agreed by the Security Council.

When the reactor had been inaugurated by Prime Minister Verwoerd, he seemed to recognize this point. He told workers: 'It is the duty of South Africa not only to consider the military uses [of uranium] but also to do all in its power to direct its uses for peaceful purposes.' Was this an admission, at least in part, of a secret military programme?

Dr A. Visser, a board member of the AEB, hoped so. He publicly advocated production of a bomb for prestige purposes and to use against 'the loud-mouthed Afro-Asiatic states'. He added: 'Money is no problem. The capital for such a bomb is available.' Dr Wally Grant, speaking on the AEB's behalf, said: 'On several occasions the director-general has indicated that South African scientists, in common with those from most developed countries, do have the ability to develop nuclear weapons ...' But he added, only half-reassuringly, that there was no military research being done in this area. As will be seen, South Africa was by the late 1960s developing the idea of peaceful nuclear explosions for use in mining – something that was in reality untenable, but which provided an ideal cover for its secret military programme.

Safari-1 is still functioning as a research tool, and we were given a tour by scientists who were obviously proud of its contribution to research.

The developments in South Africa have to be seen in the context of what was happening elsewhere. In the 1950s the United States was forging ahead with its development of both atomic and thermonuclear weapons (the hydrogen bomb). Across the northern hemisphere the Cold War was raging, and Britain, then South Africa's mother country, was developing its own independent nuclear deterrent.

The atom bomb weapons that emerged from that programme were carried by long-range Handley Page Victor, Hawker Siddeley Vulcan and Vickers Valiant bombers, which could range over the whole world by using runways in friendly countries or by inflight refuelling. In war, one key stopping-off point would be South Africa.

It emerged from our research that in this period Britain felt so confident of South Africa's loyalty that it even based nuclear weapons on its soil. A senior South African military source said 'Kaalpan', an army base near Warrenton, north of Kimberley and at the centre of the national rail network, was a strategic nuclear store for the Commonwealth in those days.

However, from the late 1950s South Africa was becoming increasingly isolated in the world and there was mounting internal civil disorder because of its apartheid policies. The issue was brought into sharp focus in February 1960, when the British Prime Minister Harold Macmillan paid an official visit to the country and gave a now famous address to Parliament in Cape Town. 'The wind of change is blowing through this continent,' he told his audience, 'and, whether we like it or not, this growth of national consciousness is a political fact.' Verwoerd furiously replied: 'There has to be justice not only for the black man in Africa but also for the white man.' He won loud applause.

But, as if to reinforce Macmillan's point, the racial strife worsened six weeks later. Tragically, 56 died and 162 were injured in the Sharpeville massacre, when South African police opened fire on a crowd of 15,000 who were protesting at the pass laws, which controlled the movement of blacks.

South Africa was now untenable as a British nuclear storehouse. In March 1961 Verwoerd told a meeting of Commonwealth Prime Ministers in London that he would leave the Commonwealth when his country became independent the following month. Said Verwoerd bitterly: 'It is clear after the lead given by a group of Afro-Asian nations that we will be no longer welcome.' He also wanted to spare Britain any embarrassment.

In 1962 Nelson Mandela, who had been on the run accused of leading strikes against apartheid, was jailed for five years for incitement. Then in 1963 the Organization of African Unity (OAU) was formed, making the elimination of apartheid one of its main aims. It began to have increasing influence over UN policy and the call for sanctions against South Africa.

In this period, the Reverend Martin Luther King was leading his own civil rights movement in the United States. In 1963 he made his famous 'I have a dream' speech. Inspiring others fighting for equality all over the world, he said the struggle would go on until 'justice flows like water and righteousness like a stream'. President John F. Kennedy backed him all the way.

In 1964 Ian Smith became premier of Rhodesia and threatened to declare independence unilaterally if Britain insisted on blacks being given the vote. A week later Mandela appeared in a Pretoria court accused of conspiracy to overthrow the government by force. He pleaded guilty, saying from the dock: 'I do not deny that I planned sabotage. We had either to accept inferiority or fight against it by violence.' He was sentenced for treason, and spent twenty-seven years in jail.

This, then, was the background to South Africa's new-found pariah status and Verwoerd's determination to go it alone. He would not see his National Party's policies watered down – after all, he had been the prime mover of apartheid.

As he sat in his vast office on the first floor of the Union Building in Pretoria, it must have been some comfort to know that the nuclear programme could provide him with a deadly trump card.

By the end of 1967, researchers hidden away in the Skinner Street laboratories believed they had perfected a technique of uranium enrichment known as the 'vortex-tube' method. South Africa later claimed this was a considerable scientific achievement, but evidence in fact points to its being remarkably similar to a West German development known as the Becker nozzle system, after its inventor, Professor Erwin Becker, of the Institute for Nuclear Processing Techniques in Karlsruhe.

Whatever the truth, South Africa's technical progress was rapid. The system was proven on a small scale at the 'X-Plant', developed by the Skinner Street team, and plans were laid for a much bigger facility. A point of no return was reached in 1968, as the official history described in dramatic terms.

It said tension was high when an independent committee reporting to the Cabinet and chaired by industrialist, Dr H. J. van Eck, conducted a three-day inquiry at Pelindaba. Its top-secret task was to assess whether the prototype's technology could be scaled up for a much bigger plant. On Friday 19 April, on the conclusion of the hearings, Van Eck dictated the committee's unanimous recommendations: 'As each page was completed, stenographers dashed for their machines and transcribed their shorthand notes into the final written forms.'

It was the committee's opinion that a pilot plant should be erected before embarking on the construction of a full-scale installation. Once again there was clearly no time to be lost, and the project charged on. The AEB split and formed the Uranium Enrichment Corporation of South Africa (UCOR) with Ampie Roux as chairman. An equally important driving-force was Dr Wally Grant, designer of the vortex-tube system, who had now become director-general of the Board. Together they set forth to build a new facility – to be known as the 'Y-Plant'.

Before Van Eck's committee had even sat, a site had been selected within the perimeter of Pelindaba but as far removed as possible from the Safari-1 reactor complex. There were geological problems there, but the area met the main requirement. It would be possible to erect two barbed-wire barrier fences with gun posts and a road in between for armed patrol vehicles. As the AEB later admitted, the requirement was 'seclusion from inquisitive passers-by'. There would be no welcome for KGB or CIA visitors or any curious Safari-1 scientists across the hill.

In naming the site, the AEB's love of the local tribal language again came to the rescue. The word 'Valindaba' was chosen, meaning 'the council is closed'. The preferred translation was 'no comment'.

However much it might have wanted to keep Valindaba secret, the AEB recognized there would have to be limited disclosure. The plant would require a number of tall chimneys to carry exhaust gases high into the sky. The tops of these would emerge above the mountain ridge, rendering them easily visible from the public road to Pretoria. The completed colossus would soon occupy an area of more than three football pitches, with service buildings taking up a similar area. No spy plane or satellite could fail to mistake what was going on in the valley of 'no comment'.

The AEB's historian tells in dramatic tones how Prime Minister John Vorster broke the news to the Cape Town Parliament on 20 July 1970: 'An air of anticipation pervaded the Chamber where the Members of Parliament were assembled, the feeling of expectancy almost palpable, for word had passed that the Prime Minister was about to make an announcement of particular import ... This was to be the first public release of one of the best-kept secrets in the country – a project that was a truly remarkable scientific achievement ...'

Vorster publicly praised Drs Grant and Roux for their inspired leadership of the research programme. He said it would have been foolish not to exploit South Africa's uranium ore resources. Then he announced an ambitious civil programme: 'South Africa finds itself on the eve of a large nuclear power programme of its own, of the order of 20,000 megawatts electrical, by the end of the century. If such a programme can be based on enriched uranium, it will result in a very marked capital saving. However, such a course can only be followed if the supply of enriched uranium can be guaranteed, which, in the difficult world in which we live, implies our own production.'

The Y-Plant construction programme was now public, but deliberate confusion was spread about its purpose. It was simply referred to as the 'pilot facility', implying it was another prototype.[1] The official purpose, said the AEB, was to 'confirm predictions, derive operating data and pinpoint problems'.

In reality the Y-Plant's performance remained classified – covered by the 'strict stipulations' of the Atomic Energy Act on secrecy, by which people could face sentences of up to twenty years for talking – and it was only after De Klerk's 1993 announcement that it became clear that it was manufacturing fissile material for the A-bomb.

Vorster's commitment to a massive peaceful nuclear programme was at odds with professional opinion. Only three years earlier the AEB had announced it had scrapped its plutonium reactor programme, because there was no foreseen need for large nuclear electricity generators. South Africa had a planned vast investment in coal-fired power stations, and the country's reserves of coal would last well over 300 years.

But Vorster was not just announcing one reactor, or even two. To generate 20,000 megawatts of electricity, which at the time was more than the country's entire power requirement, would have meant building at least three huge reactor complexes every decade for the next thirty years.

As history has shown, South Africa built only two reactors, which started producing electricity in 1984, with a total generating capacity of 1,800 megawatts. Both are situated at Koeberg, 30 km from Cape Town, and they alone cost the country R3,000 million ($820 million).

As became public knowledge after De Klerk's 1993 announcement,

1 In 1978 the AEB announced the Y-Plant had been so successful that further expansion of South Africa's enrichment capacity was now planned. This led to the opening of the Z-Plant in the 1980s, ten times bigger still. Its official purpose was to make 3 per cent low-enriched uranium fuel (LEU) for two civil nuclear reactors in the Cape. It produced 300 tons a year, of which the Koeberg reactor took 200 tons and some of the rest was sold. It was closed in early 1995 because it was not economic in competition with cheap supplies of uranium fuel from Russia. It has, however, been suggested that fuel from the Z-Plant may have been fed into the Y-Plant, making its output of weapons-grade uranium even bigger. There have been similar stories about LEU obtained illicitly from China.

the Y-Plant was a full-scale manufacturing facility which was never meant to serve the civil programme. Enriched uranium for Koeberg and Safari-1 was largely imported from France and the United States until the mid-1980s, when the Z-Plant, the low-level enrichment facility, came on stream at Valindaba.

It seems clear, therefore, that South Africa's plans to build nuclear weapons were well in train by the inception of the Y-Plant in the early 1960s, and do not date from 1974 as De Klerk maintained in his 1993 announcement.

The row at the AEB in 1958 indicates that some leading nuclear scientists were strongly opposed then to a military programme, and a number of senior board members quit the AEB because of their concerns. Nevertheless, South Africa remained an honoured member of the nuclear community and continued to play an active role in collaborating with other members of the IAEA, formed in 1957.

One of its governors for ten years, from 1959, was Donald Sole, later the South African ambassador to Bonn and Washington, and a key player in the procurement programme for material which could be used in nuclear weapons technology. South Africa retained its permanent position on the IAEA's board of governors until 1977, and ceased attending general sessions only in 1979.

It seems that, whatever the suspicions about the activity at Valindaba, countries were prepared to accept South Africa's assurance of innocence. This even prevailed when, in July 1968, Russia, Britain and the United States signed the Nuclear Non-Proliferation Treaty controlling nuclear weapons and, to the dismay of other countries, South Africa refused.

In trying to explain the decision, the AEB described the treaty as 'a laudable move which all sane countries support in principle'. But it added: 'Regrettably it embodies the possibility of the infringement of sovereignty and the retardation and inhibition of essential nuclear development ... As a responsible country [South Africa] has made it plain that it will not do anything which encourages the proliferation of nuclear weapons.'

With the enrichment development programme then moving quickly, there can be little doubt why South Africa refused to sign the NPT.

The Y-Plant was commissioned in 1974 and began to operate in 1975. It worked continuously until 1990, when it was shut down. There were three separate buildings joined together by pipework. Building 1 was where uranium was enriched from its natural level of 0.7 per cent U-235 to 3 per cent. Building 2 took the enrichment to 14 per cent, and Building 3 took it to its final level – over 90 per cent. Only Building 1 still contains enrichment plant: the others have been emptied, and one is now used for laser enrichment, regarded as a much more efficient process.

Building 1 is bigger than a cathedral and packed with thousands of metres of stainless-steel pipes, compressor units and electric motors. Markings indicate that all the equipment was produced in South Africa, which, if accurate, shows that South Africa made an astonishing technological leap.[1]

How much weapons-grade uranium did it produce during the fifteen years it operated? The figures computed by the IAEA in 1991 suggested 400 kg, enough for six and a half crude devices. But does the evidence support this relatively small amount?

According to the AEC, the Y-Plant never worked at its full design output of 20,000 separative working units a year, equivalent to 120 kg of bomb-grade uranium. The AEC says 'chemical reactions and inefficient mechanical processes' greatly reduced its performance.

The AEC also asserts that the plant began producing in late 1977. It argues it worked at half capacity from then until 1990, or for little more than twelve years. Even at half its design output, however, the plant would have produced more than 700 kg in this period – enough for fourteen crude atom bombs. But, says the AEC, some of the output was diverted to Koeberg and Safari-1 and the real output figure was around 400 kg.

Given the AEC's licence to lie about these matters in the past, there is little cause to accept this story, and it is clear that the intelligence community in the United States did not. In March 1993, shortly before the De Klerk bomb announcement, a *Washington Post* staff writer, Jeffrey Smith, reported fears that the IAEA was 'treading too softly' with South Africa. It said the intelligence community was worried that some highly enriched uranium and other components of nuclear warheads had been hidden. Smith added: 'US suspicions are based partly on what officials say is highly sensitive intelligence collected on the South African programme from human sources and photo-reconnaissance satellites.'

---

1 It is now known that many items were imported from West Germany, as will be discussed later, but there was no evidence of this when we were shown around in 1994. A source told us that it was normal practice during the era of sanctions for military manufacturers to have a special section for removing labels and identification numbers on imported equipment and, if necessary, replacing them with false ones.

Before the Republic signed the NPT, the US intelligence community had secretly credited the government with developing a nuclear arsenal of perhaps six to ten warheads during the 1970s and early 1980s. Smith also heard from US officials that South Africa had developed nuclear weapons that could be fired from field artillery – a story we were to hear in South Africa too.

Two months later Smith returned to the subject, reporting that proliferation experts were intending to analyse the ink and paper used in the operating records of the Y-Plant, 'to resolve lingering US worries'. The tests were meant to assess the age of the records. US intelligence agencies had earlier obtained information that 'a lot of stuff [in the operating records] was altered or filled in', the *Post* said, during a period of several months when the AEC had claimed the records had been mislaid.

Smith said some US intelligence officials suspected that the AEC, or perhaps some renegade officials there, had fabricated documents after the bomb programmme had been halted. The object would have been to understate the production of bomb-grade uranium. It had been calculated the 400 kg in store were about a third that intelligence experts estimated had been produced if the Y-Plant operated at full capacity. 'It's the minimum possible, reflecting what might have happened if everything went wrong,' one official told him. In November 1993 a US intelligence estimate said it was still not possible to assess whether the Republic had declared everything, further undermining the IAEA's contrary view.

Leonard S. Spector, a leading nuclear proliferation expert with the Carnegie Endowment for International Peace, called on the IAEA to press South Africa not only to surrender any missing fissile material but also to turn over other nuclear warhead components. 'If they don't find and destroy these components, the arsenal could be reconstituted,' he said.

Contrary to the AEC line that the Y-Plant functioned from late 1977 until 1990, or just over twelve years, at half output, there is evidence that it was much more productive. The complex was officially opened in April 1975 by the Prime Minister, John Vorster.[1] He expressed his delight at the successful operation of the plant and how the enrichment process had 'been proved in practice'.

1 Vorster was asked by the magazine *Newsweek* in May 1976 whether South Africa's defences included a nuclear capability. He replied: 'We are only interested in the peaceful applications of nuclear power. But we can enrich uranium, and we have the capability. And we did not sign the nuclear non-proliferation treaty.'

By this point, the plant was 'very successful' according to a government official at the time. A production manager who showed us around the Y-Plant in 1994 told the same story. He had been there from the beginning, he said, and after some minor teething troubles in 1975 the plant was producing at full output by 1976. He was proud of how it hardly ever malfunctioned, despite its enormous size, spread as it was across three buildings: 'All the years it was functioning, until it closed down in 1990, it worked like a dream.'

Taking this evidence, it is likely the plant operated close to its maximum capacity of 120 kg a year for fourteen years – two years longer than the AEC now claims. The total production of highly enriched uranium would have amounted to more than 1,500 kg, enough for twenty-eight crude bombs or double this figure if a more advanced design had been adopted.

It has also been suggested that even larger quantities of weapons-grade uranium could have been produced if low-enriched uranium was used as feedstock instead of uranium ore, or if South Africa had secretly imported highly enriched uranium. In November 1967 the magazine *Newsweek* reported that France was clandestinely helping the Republic's nuclear programme. It said France had offered to supply highly enriched uranium for the Safari-1 reactor if negotiations with the United States failed, and added: 'The French have hinted that enough fissionable material might be supplied for military purposes as well.' Two British newspapers, the *Daily Telegraph* and the *Financial Times*, followed this up in July 1970, with stories that France was now supplying enriched uranium to the Republic.

In 1978 it was reported that the Anti-Apartheid Movement in Bonn had uncovered evidence that a separate 'commercial' uranium enrichment facility was being built with German assistance at a chemical plant called Sasol 2 near the towns of Evander and Trichardt, 140 km east of Johannesburg. The project was said to be going ahead under unprecedented secrecy, with deliveries under two code-names, 'black' and 'white'.[1]

This enrichment plant, according to the AAM researchers, was being built at breakneck speed to be ready by 1981/2. They said many German companies were working flat out to produce vital compressors and other equipment. And financing was allegedly provided by a consortium led by the French bank Credit Lyonnais under the cover of the Koeberg project.

1 From *The Nuclear Axis* by Zdenek Cervenka and Barbara Rogers (Julian Friedmann Books, London, 1978).

Sasol 2 is an extensive chemical complex with its own airstrip and impenetrable security. We heard other stories that there was an underground facility in the area, known as the 'black reactor'. We were also told by a highly placed official within South Africa's National Intelligence Service that a KGB agent had been spotted in the area of Evander and Trichardt in this period, but the NIS had never managed to establish on what he was spying.

In November 1981 the *Washington Post* quoted US intelligence sources as saying that South Africa was importing unsafeguarded low-enriched uranium from China via an intermediary in Switzerland. The fuel was said to be for South Africa's Koeberg civil nuclear reactors, which came on-stream in 1984. But France, which built the reactors, also provided its LEU. The AEC will not admit to any clandestine imports of nuclear material, leaving unresolved just how much might have been amassed for nuclear weapons.

The evidence indicated that South Africa had the capacity to make far more than the six and half bombs declared by De Klerk. As we were to discover later, these were only the military's 'museum pieces'. In the 1980s they were superseded by much more advanced weapons for which there were plentiful supplies of HEU.

When was South Africa first in a position to make a bomb from weapons-grade uranium? The official story is that its six and a half weapons were completed between 1979 and 1989. The first, apparently code-named 'Melba', could only have been detonated for test purposes in an underground shaft. The second, in April 1982, was better engineered but was also a test device. Officially, there was no deliverable bomb until 1987, when the third device came off the production line.

If the Y-Plant production manager was correct, however, enough Y-Plant material could have been ready to fashion a weapon as early as 1976. As will be seen later, South Africa was apparently stopped from testing one the following year, and, if South Africa was secretly importing high enriched uranium, the first device could have been made even earlier.

Nick Badenhorst recalled a newspaper story from the late 1960s that said the country had acquired a revolutionary weapon 'whose components were stored in separate vaults'. This seemed to imply it was an A-bomb.

A source working for the nuclear weapons programme in 1981 told of an intriguing incident that seemed to fit with this report. 'One night we realized there was something fishy happening involving army trucks,' he said. 'They went to a mine in the Witbank area to collect a bomb. There was talk that the Israelis, the Russians or some other foreign power had brought one into the country many years earlier. When they got to the mine, they had to cut open a door to get the weapon out because they had lost the keys. It was brought back to us in a wooden box, larger than a coffin, and placed in one of the vaults.'

The source also said that in the 1980s South Africa was making not A-bombs but thermonuclear weapons, including the neutron bomb. Later, when we got to know him better, he described his reaction when he saw De Klerk's announcement in 1993 about the nuclear programme: 'I was watching the news on television. I sat there in amazement. The statement was bullshit. The generals were running him.'

Nevertheless, South Africa's story has been believed, and the Republic is once again a member of the international nuclear community. Under the rules of the NPT, a country is under no obligation to admit it has ever had nuclear weapons: it merely has to confirm that, from the time of becoming a signatory, it is not a nuclear weapons state.

The Republic became a treaty member on 10 July 1991, and signed a Comprehensive Safeguards Agreement with the International Atomic Energy Agency two months later, on 16 September. On 30 October, as required by the agreement, it submitted an inventory of nuclear materials.

The prime object of the agreement with the IAEA was to allow its inspectors to check on the amount of enriched uranium South Africa had produced in the past. If this coincided with the quantity used in the six and a half devices, then it was reasonably certain that no bombs were missing.

The IAEA weighed the uranium ingots being kept in an underground vault at the AEC. There was around 400 kg. It checked the production records of the uranium enrichment plant, including handwritten records. They seemed to tally (although many pieces of paperwork had been doc-tored to disguise the identity of customers and suppliers). The six devices and the partially completed device were each said to contain about 55 kg – a total of about 385 kg. The mathematics seemed roughly correct.

In accordance with its charter, the IAEA carried out these checks in secret and it took two years. It was clear to its inspectors that the 400 kg had been used in nuclear weapons, but nothing could be disclosed until De Klerk finally went public in March 1993.

Six months later, the IAEA issued a report saying: 'It is reasonable to conclude that the amounts of highly enriched uranium which could have been produced by the pilot enrichment plant are consistent with the amounts produced in the initial report.'

The world was therefore assured that South Africa was now a nuclear-free zone and had no more nuclear weapons. But was the IAEA right to be so certain? Between De Klerk's decision to end the programme in 1989 and signing the NPT in July 1991, there had been plenty of time to fiddle the books. Furthermore, the IAEA's record was hardly glittering. It failed to spot that Israel had a massive nuclear programme, or the programmes of Iraq, Iran, Argentina, Brazil and North Korea.

7 'Get Out, or You'll Die!'

The passionate televised plea by Armscor executive André Buys in January 1995 that people should stop in their tracks if they were involved in the dangerous red mercury game echoed the feeling of the police team investigating the killings. They had reached the conclusion that South Africa had become an international trading-post for the material, and every deal struck amounted to a life-or-death gamble.

Lieutenant-Colonel Charles Landman was also concerned about our safety as we delved more and more into this underworld. 'These are dangerous and sometimes desperate people. You must be very careful,' he warned – showing remarkable foresight, as it was to prove.

There was a steady influx of tips, some anonymous, from people reporting that the black market in red mercury was flourishing. Many came from the Johannesburg area, where the majority of commodity dealers are based. Paperwork in circulation showed the going rate for a kilogram was between $300,000 and $400,000. A commission of a few per cent on a 20-kg container could set up a deal-maker for life. And this is what drove people on, even though an overwhelming number of deals were either never completed or straight frauds.

Occasionally, substandard red mercury was touted around, labelled 'commercial grade'. Then there were the counterfeit merchants, who doctored ordinary liquid mercury with a red powder in an attempt to hoodwink the ignorant. It was the same experience as in Russia. Attempts at getting a few grams of the real thing inevitably failed. Perhaps, as the nuclear establishment was saying, the material didn't exist. But there was another explanation: people with a genuine source of supply wanted guarantees that a substantial quantity would be bought before releasing even a small amount for testing. And we didn't have a handy $7.5 million for a bottle of it.

One thing was sure: middlemen elsewhere in the world were convinced South Africa must have warehouses full of the stuff. This was clear when we tapped in to the 'daisy chain' – an international network of commodity dealers, usually based in Europe, who mostly communicate by fax. One woman in Johannesburg told us she would be a billion-aire if she could have filled just a few of the purchase orders she got. She had requests from all over the world.

From the South African end, numerous containers in various shapes and sizes were being proffered, and in some cases it was possible to photograph them. Many were heavy olive-green canisters with what appeared to be Russian markings stencilled on the side. Sources said they had been smuggled in from Mozambique and Angola, significantly countries that had once played host to large contingents of Soviet military forces. We were told the Russians tested new weaponry there, including some that used red mercury.

Amazingly, a number of dealers were prepared to talk of their experiences if their identities were not disclosed. They had lived through plenty of failures, but they had one thing in common: they believed red mercury did exist and was being used for military weaponry. The idea that the substance could be a hoax was laughed at. They pointed out that the trade had being going on since the early 1980s at least, and no hoax had that sort of shelf-life.

They often claimed that they were trading legally as long as the red mercury they were peddling had not been made radioactive. It was impossible to verify if any of the successful deals they boasted about were genuine, because even if paperwork was produced it had been copied and could have been forged. But their tales were colourful, and if only a fraction of them were true the picture of the black market in South Africa was scary.

One Johannesburg trader, who seemed particularly knowledgeable, identified one of the photographed canisters as part of the battery package for a Russian-made SAM-17 missile and another, older, container as a similar device for an earlier SAM. He said: 'They are reputed to contain a crude form of red mercury. The canisters come from Angola and Mozambique, but the stuff inside is rubbish. It would need refining extensively to be of any real use. The old stuff can be recharged, but it costs lots of money. It's cheaper to buy it new.

'The old containers used to be sought after, but not any more. The good stuff coming here now is coming via Germany, where the Stasi [former East German secret police] structures still exist and people want to make money. There are now many more tests than there were, and further refinements to the product.'

He said red mercury was used as a 'detonator and an explosive' but he did not know how. Fifty grams of crude red mercury 20/20 from the old canisters was less effective, he said, than 0.75 of a gram of the new material. The clue to the value of the red mercury appeared to be in its designation – RM20/20, RM50/50, RM90/90 and RM100/100 – and arms dealers believed the 50/50 and 100/100 to be particularly 'good stuff'.

Among the numerous examples of allegedly good stuff was a torpedo-shaped 500-gram canister that could fit in the palm of a hand. On the side was a label saying it contained red mercury PR50/50 made in the United States, and the canister was completely smooth, with no obvious entry point. It was in the hands of two men in the Johannesburg satellite town of Germiston, who said they were acting on behalf of its owner, who was based in Windhoek, Namibia. 'We are sure it is genuine,' one said. 'The owner has shelled out R50,000 [$13,700] for it.' He showed that when it was put near a watch the pointers stopped. It also affected television reception, although it gave no reading at all on a Geiger counter. He was disappointed at our lack of interest.

The final outcome was typical of so many deals, as we heard from the broker a few days later. 'We decided to break into the thing and see what there was inside,' he said. 'The owner agreed and was on the end of a phone from Windhoek as we did it. We got a hacksaw and cut off one end. Out poured a whole lot of ordinary mercury metal, and then a little magnet fell out. The owner was not a happy man. He started to weep, he was so shattered. All his money had gone up in smoke.'

A former member of the SADF's élite Thirty-Two Battalion claimed he had been given a dramatic demonstration of red mercury's explosive properties by sellers in Namibia. 'I got into it by chance,' he said. 'I was buying and selling commodities and was shown a hoard of red mercury in the desert near Aus. I was offered a kilo for R600,000 ($164,000) but wasn't interested. There was a large, heavy ball with P20/20 that had Russian writing on its side.

'I had told them I was a buyer and wanted a demo because two Italians wanted 100 grams. They then offered to do one. They mixed small amounts from two substances. It was like a bomb. It destroyed completely a Mitsubishi truck. They used only a small sphere, about 5 cm across.'

The former soldier added: 'When brought near, it killed our digital watches, and when we held it close to a television, it reduced the signal to a dot on the screen. It was like a red powder, a red dye. They said it wasn't active, but was highly carcinogenic. They had a number of plastic containers.

'Back in South Africa I was told not to get too deeply involved because dealing in red mercury amounted to being threatened with death.'

He said he was also offered red mercury in Tanzania, Kenya and Zimbabwe. His sources had said it was used to make bombs and nuclear warheads.

A dealer in the Transvaal region north of Johannesburg said he could obtain RM20/20 in quantities of up to 80 kg. He would not say where it came from, but some was available in the Johannesburg area. He offered half a kilogram for testing purposes for a mere R500,000, but he wanted trust accounts opened in London and Johannesburg to show our bona fides before any deal could be finalized. His price, he said, was based on the 1993 base rate in Russia of $338 a gram, plus his mark-up.

Another dealer was worried about staying in the business: 'I'm scared and don't want to end up like that chap in the boot of his car.' He claimed he had been trading in red mercury for years and had spent four months in Switzerland, mainly in Geneva, in the 'daisy chain'. He described this as a loose-knit group of commodity dealers prepared to buy and sell anything for a quick buck. This network was used to source materials such as RM20/20, plutonium and another rare, expensive and mysterious substance, osmium-187. He had handled all three, he said, on behalf of local clients, as well as RM50/50, which he described as more potent than RM20/20.

The broker said he also knew of a deal in 1992 in which Belgian buyers had sold a consignment of red mercury to a Middle Eastern country, probably Iran. He said Russian, Cuban and Iranian military personnel had been in the market.

He showed a file of deals in which he was allegedly involved. It contained a Russian scientific analysis of RM20/20 dated August 1993, and correspondence in Russian. An extraordinary claim that right-wing extremists were buyers was unsupported by any documentary evidence and seemed incredible. However, we later met another Johannesburg dealer, allegedly with Russian connections and an ex-KGB assistant, who said this was true.

An intelligence source told of a wealthy man of Russian extraction who had been deeply involved in the red mercury trade in South Africa. His links with dealers in the Soviet Union went back to the 1970s, and he travelled to see them at short notice under great secrecy. In 1993 he had allegedly helped to arrange the immigration to South Africa of a number of skilled women scientists and engineers with military intelligence connections. One had later fallen in love with a broker in South Africa and had become involved in the trade herself. He suggested some of the other women would have the knowledge to trade successfully in red mercury.

Another source, a pilot who has operated in Africa for years, said red mercury had become a joke on the continent. He had received many offers from customs officials, and knew of what appeared to be large caches, particularly in Mozambique, where a Renamo[1] soldier was offering twenty litres of the material for R300,000 ($82,000).

A Johannesburg businessman came forward claiming he had access to a consignment of outdated red mercury that had been shipped into South Africa through Lanseria Airport, north-west of Johannesburg. He was warned, he said, not to open containers except in a properly equipped laboratory.

Lanseria, a small regional airport, was mentioned by other sources, who said there were virtually no customs checks. It was used by buyers from the Middle East, we were told, and in early 1994 an aircraft went missing *en route* to Europe. 'It either went down or was hijacked,' said the source. Apparently it had been carrying 100 kg of high-grade red mercury.

Another source told of a dealer in Pretoria who was said to control a large stock of red mercury from ex-Russian sources. He said there had been two other unpublicized deaths linked to red mercury trafficking in Maputo, the ocean capital of Mozambique. The source said Alan Kidger had been involved in a deal to sell twenty flasks, and one had already been passed on to his Arab buyers before his murder.

One informant was none too happy to talk about his involvement in an attempted red mercury deal worth R29 million ($8 million). He was identified in leaked documents, and he therefore had no choice. This was no opportunist wheeler-dealer of the type we had met by the score in Johannesburg but a top lawyer in Stellenbosch, a university town in the wine-growing area near Cape Town. For Johann Marais to be involved with a material that was apparently bogus and valueless was a surprise; we expected him to say it was all a hoax. His story was, however, much more interesting. He admitted the deal 'might' have been for the South African military, and it had had the official sanction of four government ministries and a giant banking group.

At his busy offices in Stellenbosch's town centre, Marais first fiddled with his pencil and consulted his local law society on the phone. He wanted some advice on client confidentiality, but this seemed to be no problem and he began answering questions. He said he drew up a contract and

[1] The Portuguese acronym for the Mozambique National Resistance (MNR), which was a creation of the Rhodesian security forces and later taken over by South African Military Intelligence. Its aims were to destabilize the Marxist-backed government of Mozambique.

agreed to act as stakeholder for the buyers and sellers. 'I asked what it was used for, and I was told it was used as an explosive for bombs – nuclear bombs. I was also told it could be used as a rocket propellant,' he said.

Paperwork showed that Marais's client was Tertius Theart,[1] a small-time property and commodity dealer in Cape Town, who had 'involved himself in other deals'. Marais said indignantly: 'I wasn't dealing in it myself: I was just facilitating funds.'

He maintained he had never represented Armscor or the military in the deal: he was simply going to hold money in a trust account for the brokers involved. 'It might have been mentioned that the military would have been the purchaser, the military or Armscor was possibly the buyer, but I don't know who was involved: I was just the legal representative.'

He said this was his only red mercury deal. 'My first involvement was in January 1994. I was consulted by this one person for one transaction. He consulted me on a number of occasions. This person was a client of mine for a number of years – a commodities broker. I was just the man in the middle.'

In any deal of this nature, he said, people pay the purchase price into a trust account and when transfer takes place the lawyer gets notice to release the money to the seller. 'In this case the deal didn't go through because the deal collapsed.'

He said the red mercury, coded PR50, was coming in two 20-kg canisters, and with each one there was a sample of what was inside. 'I don't know whether the RM was radioactive,' Marais said. His involvement started when he received a letter from another attorney saying that he had people who might want to buy. 'I replied saying this was interesting and asked him to explain how it was done. I got back the wording of the guarantee that had to be used, and my document was drawn up.

'I was told that the merchandise was in southern Africa and had been taken to Pelindaba [headquarters of the Atomic Energy Corporation] for testing. For some reason the deal never went through.'

Marais said he had made inquiries to find out whether it was legal to deal in red mercury. He had approached the Departments of Mineral and Energy Affairs, Trade and Industry, and Finance, as well as the Reserve Bank, the state central bank. 'All of them told me that it was legal to trade in it and no special permits were required. And they knew exactly what was involved.

'My bankers, Absa [the biggest banking group in South Africa], also

1 The documents also showed Theart was linked to Dirk Stoffberg, an arms dealer who was shot with his wife in 1994. Stoffberg's death and his red mercury dealings are recounted later.

made inquiries to see if it was legal. My bank has a special investigation team in Johannesburg, and I asked them because it would involve them too. Their answer was also "Yes, you can do it."'

However, a spokesman for the Absa banking group claims it was not Marais who alerted them. He said Marais had asked the manager of his local bank in Stellenbosch to tell him when the R29 million cheque had been deposited into his trust account. 'He told the branch manager that it would be a Reserve Bank cheque, in connection with a transaction for red mercury, which was supposed to be coming from Switzerland.' The spokesman said the manager then alerted Absa's head office in Johannesburg that such a large sum was expected, and this triggered their probe.

Bank investigators had spoken to people at the Reserve Bank, which is state-owned, and other government ministries, and no one knew about a cheque being issued. 'They denied that such a deal was taking place,' said the bank spokesman. 'They added that if such a thing were being bought by government it would have been done at a much higher level.'

He said most of the ministries approached by Absa investigators appeared to know about red mercury, although an official in the Department of Mineral and Energy Affairs had dismissed it as 'a lot of rubbish'. 'All the managers involved were warned to hold clearance of the cheque for fifteen days if it arrived,' said the spokesman. The deal then never went through. He added that so-called red mercury deals were becoming a more common white-collar crime.

There were yet other clandestine meetings with people seeking technical advice about red mercury, most of them budding black-marketeers who were out of their depth. They believed they had a source of the chemical, or some other nuclear material,[1] but needed a buyer – or

1 During our investigation we came across a number of nuclear materials being traded almost openly in and around Johannesburg. We found containers purportedly containing cobalt-60, krypton-85, caesium-137 and uranium hexafluoride-6, among others. We confirmed that one container held uranium-308, one of the more common commodities available. However, the authorities said the material was not a serious problem because quantities were small and most, if not all, the substances had been stolen by petty-crime syndicates from mines, which needed a range of radioactive substances for specialized applications deep underground. But a black market in nuclear materials had apparently taken hold, based largely on such thefts of small quantities. However, we were told, if buyers were prepared to follow these black-market chains long enough, they would lead to other, more dangerous, materials – including enriched uranium and plutonium. One explanation was that, with its good communications infrastructure and hotels, South Africa was a logical trading-post for any deal concluded in the southern-African region. There have been numerous reports of nuclear materials being available in Mozambique, Angola, Zaïre, Namibia and Congo.

they had a buyer and were looking for supplies. They were so bent on making a fast buck they forgot that they were yapping to people whose job was to write everything down and publish it for a mass audience.

One call came through in August 1994 that turned out to be deadly serious. It was from the boss of a thriving security company, working for major Johannesburg enterprises. He wanted to know how to get a sample of red mercury tested, and how much it might be worth. Had he got any? 'I hope so,' he said. 'We have access to this very heavy container, and it looks military. Somehow we think it is genuine, because the people who are offering it wouldn't dare cheat us.'

Piet,[1] who was ex-military, opened up a bit more later that day at a meeting in the coffee-bar at Killarney Shopping Centre in Johannesburg: 'My client is a wealthy professional man here who would not normally soil his hands with these things. The problem is he has had a bit of bad luck. On behalf of some Israeli friends, he was doing a currency deal with a man in Kempton Park [outside Johannesburg] and the money has vanished – probably spent.'

Piet lowered his voice: 'Of course my firm has been handling that aspect on behalf of my client. We could get very nasty with this fellow, and he is naturally very frightened. Somehow he has got the impression we are linked to Mossad, and he saw the stories about Mossad and these killings. As a result of that, he has offered us a compromise – he has something that could be worth R30 million ($8 million).

'He has this container which is supposed to hold 20 kg of red mercury. It came originally from Angola, from people there who had close links to the Russian military advisers who were there during the civil war. If this is genuine then we have a legitimate buyer who has the cash available. The problem is the testing. Can you arrange it for us? You can publish the results, but keep our names out of it.'

The answer in principle was yes, we could indeed help. The AEC was happy to conduct an analysis and hand the container back afterwards with no questions asked. It was a surprise to discover that this illustrious organization, which secretly helped make the South African atomic bomb and which maintained that red mercury was bogus, was prepared to provide a service to test it. How could it know what tests to carry out

1 Not his real name.

if, as it said, the material did not exist?[1]

It was an intriguing puzzle which would be fascinating to solve, but co-operating with Piet raised an ethical dilemma. Should journalists be getting directly involved in this murky business, and possibly facilitating a deal that might enable someone to make a nuclear weapon? The potential physical danger was another aspect. And what if the material turned out to be highly radioactive? The AEC would be bound to impound it and tell the police.

And did Piet, who clearly knew a thing or two about life – and probably death as well – have any idea what red mercury was used in? 'I'm told it can be used in nuclear weapons,' he said calmly. 'My clients are aware of that too, but they know the buyers and are happy to sell to them. We want to go ahead as soon as it can be fixed.'

The moral debate raged for about fifteen minutes before curiosity, and an added twist to the plan, overcame any doubts. With Piet's agreement, it was decided to ask Landman, the detective probing the killings, to secretly monitor the testing of the goods. The drama therefore moved a few days later to the luxurious Sandton Sun hotel in Johannesburg's northern suburbs for the hand-over of the container for testing.

Three adjacent rooms had been booked at the expense of Ferdi,[2] the seller who had allegedly defaulted on the currency deal. Piet was in the middle room waiting for Ferdi and the container to arrive. The reporters were in another with the police and their listening equipment. A police forensic scientist, armed with a Geiger counter, was standing by in the third.

Ferdi arrived looking nervous, but he was taking no chances. With him was an American, who was introduced as the ultimate owner of the goods, followed by two armed guards. One, a burly Afrikaner, had an automatic rifle. The other was bowed down by a cylindrical object that looked like a large car starter motor. This was the precious red mercury.

As the tape-recorders whirred in the next room, Piet explained that there was one elementary test he wanted done on the spot. He opened the interconnecting door to allow the forensic scientist to scan his Geiger counter over the object. Apart from the normal background reading, there was nothing to register, but both Ferdi and the American seemed

[1] Other sources claimed that South Africa's Council for Scientific and Industrial Research had at one time provided a service testing red mercury, before the work was transferred to the AEC. They said the AEC was visited regularly by a number of dealers and that it was buying red mercury to keep it off the black market. Of course, the AEC denies this.

[2] Not his real name.

unfazed. 'Look, this material is slightly radioactive,' said Ferdi, 'but the container stops it leaking out. Feel the weight. You can see it contains something heavy. It has to be tested with proper equipment.'

He then explained he was not prepared to part with the container unless there was some way of guaranteeing its safe return. Piet had an idea: 'There is no problem. My colleagues can take the thing to the AEC, and I'll stay here with you and your gunmen as a temporary hostage.' Ferdi began to turn the idea over in his mind and then rejected it. 'Piet, you're not worth as much as the red mercury. We'll have to think of something else.'

Early the next morning, a way around this obstacle had been agreed. Representatives of the buyers and sellers would take the 'starter motor' to the AEC, hand it in, and wait for it to be returned by the laboratory after the test had been conducted.

The next stage became a fiasco, as a police video of the event graphically showed. The container was seen being manhandled on to a laboratory bench by a white-coated scientist. He unscrewed a cap on the top, close to its outer edge, and withdrew a long pencil-shaped tube. Talking to the camera, the scientist noted that the end of the tube was broken. He said a small laboratory sample had spilled, and the device was a typical container for radioactive materials which was now completely empty.[1]

Ferdi and Piet got to hear of this when the container was returned a few minutes later, but once again Ferdi was not surprised: 'The bastards are lying. Of course there is something else in there. Look how heavy it is. We know where it came from and we know it contains red mercury. They haven't opened up the main part of the container.'

It was a deal that would not die. From Ferdi's viewpoint, it would save his skin and set him up in riches for the rest of his life. He no longer seemed to mind that Peter Hounam, whom he now knew to be a journalist, was sitting in on it all. Piet also seemed more than keen for the transaction to succeed. But how was the material to be tested? The Gazebo coffee-lounge at the Sandton Sun hotel became a red mercury conference centre for the next two weeks as meeting after meeting was convened there.

Ferdi first came up with a plan to hire a nuclear physicist, who had recently retired from the AEC and who was a family friend, to test it in his private laboratory. 'He knows all about red mercury. He has the

---

[1] The police video showed that the scientist made no attempt to unscrew a central bush on the container or to open a lead seal, both of which seemed to give access to the interior.

94

equipment. He is very nervous, but I think he will do it,' opined Ferdi. Then the scientist's nerves apparently failed.

One meeting took place at Ferdi's house, to allow a further inspection of the goods. The place was guarded by a dozen armed men, several with automatic rifles. A detachment was watching the gate with binoculars from a small caravan they had imported. Hounam put the container on a set of bathroom scales and found it weighed 25 kg. Measuring its dimensions, calculating its volume and then its density, it turned out to be as heavy as solid lead, although it appeared to have an interior chamber.[1]

Ferdi then brought an Angolan into the room who said he had been trained in red mercury technology in Russia and Lithuania. He drew vague diagrams of how it could be tested, and maintained that a crude atomic bomb could be made if the contents were mixed with terbium and potassium. 'The red mercury is like red mud,' he said. 'I promise it is in there.' He said generals in Angola were involved with the deal, along with, improbably, a relative of the Angolan Prime Minister, José Eduardo dos Santos. Apparently, Russia had been supplying red mercury to the Angolan army, and it was leaking on to the black market.

The meeting was interesting, but it took the deal no further. Ferdi plucked up courage to make an approach to the AEC again. It was another setback. 'I rang and spoke to a Dr Bouwer. He agreed to see me. At first he was very friendly when I arrived at Pelindaba. He said he had just to make a call and then he would take me to see some red mercury in his laboratory there. But whoever he called on the phone asked for my name, and the whole thing went cold. I was shown the door. It was a complete change of attitude.'

Finally, after a fortnight, a possible solution was agreed. Everyone was to fly by private plane to Windhoek, capital of Namibia, where a secret laboratory could do the tests. By this stage Ferdi was so anxious to see the deal through that he offered to pay all the costs, and was also prepared for journalists to go along. The arrival of Dr Frank Barnaby from Britain to oversee the test was an added attraction to Piet, who was still anticipating that Ferdi would pull another fraud. And Gwynne Roberts, the Channel 4 director for whom both Hounam and Barnaby were working at the time, also went along.

A twin-engined Cessna was soon waiting at Rand Airport, Johannes-

[1] The outer casing was part steel and aluminium, with some lead inside that. Lead has a density of 11.3 g/cm3.

burg, and so was the canister, hidden in a cardboard box. Unhindered by any policeman or customs officer in the terminal, it was secretly smuggled into a compartment in the nose of the plane. In Windhoek the parties separated – the buyers and journalists to the Safari Sun Hotel, and the sellers to the Hotel Furstenhof. The tests were to take place the next day, at a secret location.

Four frustrating days later there was still no sign of action. By this stage, two other containers were on offer, which allegedly had fresher material, but the sellers were apparently not prepared to do the test until Piet and his client produced guarantees from a Swiss bank. Rows went on until late into the evening, and then Hounam gave them an ultimatum. He and his friends would wait one more day before pulling out. There were more discussions which at last reached a conclusion: the test would take place after breakfast in the morning.

There had been plenty of time to wonder who was in the market for the battered containers, assuming there was something in them worth buying. Piet's client appeared bona fide: he was a respected figure in Johannesburg's affluent northern suburbs. But, as the squabbling and waiting went on, it became clear from overheard snippets that others might also be bidding. Shady characters frequented the Safari Sun, and periodically spoke to Ferdi.

Hounam returned to his hotel room at 11.30 that night and thirty minutes later the phone rang. A voice said slowly: 'Mr Hounam. You must get on the plane to Johannesburg as soon as you can. If you stay you are in great danger.' The caller had a Middle Eastern accent. Could Hounam be on some Arab hit list? He hardly had time to collect his thoughts before the phone rang again. It was the same man.

'Mr Hounam. We have booked you on the 1.30 p.m. flight from Windhoek to Johannesburg tomorrow. Will you be on it?' Again the caller put the phone straight down.

Barnaby and Roberts joined Hounam in his room to decide on strategy. It was agreed that the advice must be heeded, and in any case the chances of the tests taking place were by no means certain. But getting on the flight that had been so kindly booked by the menacing caller was not wise. If this was a serious threat it could be a trap.

Fortunately, a private plane was available at first light, and it was decided to stay together until it was time to go. Then there was a knock on the door. There stood a burly Afrikaner who was clearly in a highly agitated state. He was a friend of one of the red mercury dealers, we recognized, but why had he suddenly turned up? Speaking through the partly open door, he said: 'I mean you no harm, Mr Hounam, but this is a matter of life and death.' He announced he was linked to South African Military Intelligence and begged to speak privately. Pulling out a large automatic from his belt, he handed it into the room butt first, and then came in.

'Don't be too alarmed,' he said, shaking with anxiety, 'but I have just heard that a contract was taken out on your life. It happened an hour and a half ago. You must take what I say seriously. They mean to do it. My information is that the terrorist group Hezbollah[1] have you on a hit list. They think you are MI6. There is no danger in South Africa, only here.'

Our visitor said it was his duty to stay with us all night and take us to the airport at dawn, provided we trusted him. A snap decision had to be taken. Was this huge, friendly but highly on-edge character there to protect us or to shoot us? We need not have worried. Right through the night he patrolled outside the room or kept watch from the window with gun in hand. In the early hours he started to chat. He said he knew all about the red mercury. There were a lot of frauds, but Windhoek was a centre for real deals and there was a nearby laboratory[2] that tested the chemical.

Half an hour before the plane was due to take off, a car arrived in the half-light outside and flashed its lights. It took us to the terminal – and safety.

Who had been behind the calls? Was it someone who wanted us out of Namibia[3] who was simply making an idle threat? Or, as our midnight caller said, was it all too real, and had we had a brush with the shady people who were behind the mysterious killings in South Africa?

[1] We were later told by other sources in South Africa that Hezbollah, the pro-Iranian terrorist group, were in the market for red mercury from a base in Cape Town.

[2] Documents accompanying one of the canisters indicated it had been tested for red mercury at a laboratory in a mine 40 km from Windhoek. It was run by Tsumeb Corporation, but mine managers at the gatehouse (we were not allowed any further) denied there were any testing facilities capable of providing verification. They also said they knew nothing about red mercury.

[3] Shortly after this trip to Namibia, Koos Theyse, the local deputy police commissioner, gave a public warning about the dangers of looking for red mercury in military weaponry. He said tribespeople in northern Namibia had heard of the value of the substance and been told it was to be found in Russian land-mines, mortars and missiles left over from the Angolan war. Theyse said 'scores' of people had been killed or injured trying to open them, having paid as little as R80 ($22) for them. We also learned that a terrible rumour had circulated in southern Angola that albino tribespeople had red mercury inside their skulls. A number had been decapitated and, as a result, special protection had to be arranged for others who naturally feared for their safety.

Piet and Ferdi never did a deal after this. But we later confronted Piet's client and asked him on whose behalf he was trying to buy red mercury. After the Namibian débâcle, we felt we deserved an answer. 'My people are based in Israel,' he said. 'There's no problem in getting it in to Israel. There is no customs problem whatsoever, and we can have it tested there. If the product is good, fine – they will buy it on the spot. You get there in the morning and it can be done that day by the top people.

'Ultimately, the people we were dealing with were acting for the Israeli government. The Israelis know the full value of this material.'

8 Death in Paradise

We knew people were dying because of red mercury; that the substance originated in Russia; that it had an application in nuclear weapons; that it had attracted the interest of a lot of strange people; and that the issue was upsetting authorities in South Africa and elsewhere. We also realized that, outside of Russia, South Africa had become the focus of the story. But why South Africa? A hint of what was to come started to emerge after yet more killing, this time of a notorious arms dealer and his wife who were found dead at their luxury Schoemansville home overlooking Hartbeespoort Dam, which nestles in the hills of the Magaliesberg range about 70 km north-west of Johannesburg.

Dirk Stoffberg, alias Derek Strauss or François Borg, had survived, even flourished, in the murky world of arms deals and espionage for more than two decades. He had remarried in July 1993 after meeting a German woman called Suzanne Tanzer in Europe. They had settled in an idyllic house overlooking the dam, which reminded them so much of Switzerland. In a television interview with the South African Broadcasting Corporation (SABC) a year before his death, he had said he was quitting the arms world.

Talking about his exploits on camera to film-maker Jacques Pauw, he said: 'To me it's something out of the ordinary. It's something not every person wants to do. It is exciting. You pit your wits against the rest of the world. You play international chess – see who comes first and who succeeds. My whole life, I've been after the unusual.' However, what he didn't say was that he had started dealing in something far more dangerous – red mercury.

Pauw, who went further than any other South African journalist to expose Stoffberg, described him in his hour-long documentary as a 'flamboyant playboy' with a life of Italian sports cars, French champagne and racehorses. He said the seven-times-married arms dealer was a lavish entertainer and 'irresistible to women'.

His activities at one point saw him living in a plush suite of the Hôtel National in Lucerne, Switzerland, a haven of luxury shared with the rich and famous. From here he co-ordinated his espionage activities and cemented his arms deals.

This larger-than-life character was proud of his achievements and a man prepared to sell anything to anyone – so long as the money was good. He had started his career selling conventional weapons – tanks, helicopters, small arms and, later, missiles. Soon he was dealing with some of the world's most notorious nations – Iran, Iraq and Libya. To them he sold mustard gas and other horrible chemicals, and even tried to sell enriched uranium.

He had spoken openly to Pauw about his exploits, backing up his claims with documents. Security sources would later speculate that his 'going public' might have been a factor contributing to his death. Even if he had not disclosed sensitive information that might hurt others, by talking openly about his life he could have been a threat to those who would rather remain in the shadows.

He had discussed his secret trade with Israel and disclosed too that he had been dealing in red mercury, but he refused to talk about either subject on camera for Pauw. However, Stoffberg revealed he had worked for the National Intelligence Service for about fifteen years, before being forced out. He had then moved into the arms trade. During the 1980s, he made huge sums of money and frequented only the best hotels in Europe while there on business. He was working through a network of front companies, among them the Atlantic Bankers Corporation in the British Channel Islands. Then, said people close to him, as the market became flooded with weapons, he increasingly turned to selling chemicals.

Stoffberg broke into the international arms trade in the mid-1970s when he started manufacturing a Rhodesian-designed machine pistol which he sold to Iran and other countries. In 1979 he pulled off his first big international arms deal, an illegal transaction in which he sold fifty US-built tanks and 7,500 rounds of ammunition to Taiwan. The deal was worth $36 million. He brought his fat commission back to South Africa in suitcases, which he kept stashed away in a cellar under his house. He and his wife at the time, Linda Stoffberg, then lived off this mountain of cash after 'washing' the dollars with the help of friends in the banking system.

In August 1980 he said he met William Casey, campaign manager for Ronald Reagan and later director of the Central Intelligence Agency (CIA), at a restaurant in London. Stoffberg said Casey had approved a plan for him to act as middleman in a deal to supply 155-mm guns to Iran in return for the release of the fifty-two American hostages there.

Nigerian officials were later bribed to provide the end-user certificates. Ten years after his meeting, Stoffberg would testify before a Congressional hearing into allegations that Reagan's campaign team had secretly plotted with representatives of Iran to delay the release of the hostages until after the 1980 presidential election, thereby cheating President Jimmy Carter of a diplomatic coup. It had become known as the 'October Surprise' affair. The US investigation never found any convincing evidence to support this theory, and also found 'inconsistencies' in Stoffberg's evidence. He was found guilty of breaking US sanctions on Iran. However, the authorities said he had provided 'substantial assistance' and he was subsequently sentenced to only eight months in jail. That effectively meant he was released immediately. By this time – in January 1992 – he had spent R400,000 ($109,000) on lawyers.

In 1984 Stoffberg was in London again, this time, he claimed, to meet Vietnam War hero Colonel Oliver North, who was also named in the 'Irangate' arms-for-hostages scandal. Stoffberg said on this occasion he was asked by North to arrange a supply of weapons to Iran in a contract worth $320 million. South Africa was to be used as a conduit for the weapons, with the first transaction to be routed via Mauritius. North has never admitted to any meetings with Stoffberg.

In 1986 Stoffberg was charged by Armscor for trading in R16 million ($4.36 million) of weaponry without a permit. He appeared in court, but there were no witnesses available and the case was thrown out. Stoffberg considered it was a warning from the giant South African armaments corporation not to step out of line.[1]

By 1987 Stoffberg had turned to politics. The liberal Progressive Federal Party (PFP) announced that it was considering him as a candidate in the 1987 election. He was to stand for the PFP in the Modderfontein constituency, a National Party stronghold secured by Defence Minister General Magnus Malan. He came close to getting the nomination, but some members of the PFP became uncomfortable when details of his background started to emerge. The PFP had not been fully aware of his right-wing tendencies.

By the end of that year he had settled in Europe and had become a

1 For a period in the mid-1980s Stoffberg lived in a small hotel near Frankfurt. Peter Hounam, who was working for the London *Evening Standard* at the time, visited him there to question him about a missile deal involving Iran. Talking incessantly into the night, Stoffberg admitted he was dealing in arms, and was supplying goods to South Africa in defiance of sanctions. He got blind drunk, and at one stage pulled out a gun. Later still he started talking about the loneliness of his existence and burst into tears.

full-time member of the four-man Adler Group, an intelligence, black-mail and assassination squad. He set up home in the Hôtel National in Switzerland and started to co-ordinate the group's activities.

Dirk Stoffberg had admitted his involvement with Adler and had made it clear before his death that he had a hand in the murder of the ANC chief representative to Paris, Dulcie September, whose bullet-riddled body was found outside her office in March 1988. ANC representatives across Europe were gripped by anger, grief and confusion. South African agents were immediately accused of committing the murder, but the government denied complicity.

French police detained five suspects, and then released them. French intelligence agents told the press that one of them was Stoffberg, and that he headed a South African assassination unit in Europe. They suspected his involvement in the killing of September.

Before his death, he had openly spoken of the murder to Pauw, but when confronted on camera he simply responded: 'No comment.' Further inquires revealed that detectives at Britain's Scotland Yard had questioned Stoffberg at Heathrow Airport in London. With him was a man called Mitchell. Detectives found a number of names of ANC representatives in their possession. Stoffberg said Mitchell had given him the list. When detectives asked what it was, he replied it was simply a list of addresses of friends 'for Christmas cards'. When he was asked whether it was an ANC death list, he told Pauw: 'No comment.'

Earlier, in an interview with a newspaper, his response was different. 'These were fifty targets, put it that way.' Then he laughed.

Mitchell was acting as a courier. He had worked out of an office next to the Malawian embassy in Geneva, Switzerland. Said Stoffberg: 'There was certain military equipment required – I didn't use direct contact with Armscor.' Mitchell was an agent for Military Intelligence and the messenger. Asked why Mitchell had to bring the ANC death list to Stoffberg, he said: 'No comment.'

In June 1988 the London magazine *Private Eye* reported that a British businessman called David Mitchell was approached by South African Military Intelligence to move money around and set up front companies. The article said Mitchell shared an office in Geneva with the Malawian consul. The South African Defence Force denied that Mitchell worked for them.

After the Dulcie September killing, Stoffberg telephoned his estranged wife in South Africa, Linda Stoffberg, and said he was in a lot of trouble and she would not hear from him for a while. 'He was very nervous,' said Linda. But she said he was clearly proud of his achievement, sending back to South Africa many newspaper clippings of the September killing.

Also, he had told German journalist Jürgen Roth that he was involved in the assassination: 'He admitted he was part of a network that organized the killing of September.' However, Stoffberg was not in Paris at the time. After the murder, it was reported in South Africa that a professional, highly trained unit of assassins was targeting ANC representatives in Europe. Newspapers called it the Z Squad. Asked whether he was part of it, Stoffberg again replied: 'No comment.'

Scotland Yard told Roth that Stoffberg was behind a network of people who had organized the assassination of September. Said Linda Stoffberg: 'He admitted he was heading the squad that had been reported in the South African press. He said he was part of a very powerful organization.'

The French press said South Africans planned the killing, but that a professional hit man, probably a former Foreign Legionnaire, had pulled the trigger.

Stoffberg, a highly trained former South African agent, apparently had been associated with Adler since 1982. It was a classic operation for the South African security services, and it fitted with the *modus operandi* of the world's intelligence agencies, which routinely hire freelancers to do their dirty work so that they can disown them if necessary. Throughout the 1980s murder, bombings and harassment would stalk ANC representatives across the world. On top of the September murder, Stoffberg admitted that he and Adler had been involved in the killing of a man in a Hong Kong hotel in November 1983.

Analysts would conclude later that the Adler Group was indeed a unit of freelance killers in touch with various intelligence services around the world, including those of South Africa. Stoffberg had already claimed that, among other duties, Adler was an assassination squad for the CIA, and that he had done undercover work in Europe for the CIA, along with South African agencies.

It was during his full-time involvement with Adler in the late 1980s that Stoffberg had met Suzanne Tanzer, who said she had been attracted by the James Bond world in which he lived.

Her friend, commodity broker Margaret Turner, said the couple had met after Suzanne had been introduced to a Captain Hennie de Bruyn, on a train to Frankfurt, where she proposed to live. 'She told him she had been cheated out of 75,000 Deutschmarks ($53,000) in a deal with an Iranian who was to buy diamonds from her.' A week later, Stoffberg contacted her. 'Obviously de Bruyn was South African intelligence and had told Stoffberg about her contacts with Iran. She fell head over heels with him.'

By 1990, at the end of the Iran–Iraq war, Stoffberg became involved in the smuggling of war chemicals. He said he was doing a deal that involved Libya on behalf of the CIA, which was trying to establish the trading routes for such materials across Europe. He was communicating with a front company in Tunis which was being used by Libyan intelligence, he said.

Stoffberg supplied weapons of mass destruction to some of the world's most notorious dictators, but he said he was just 'a soldier, fighting behind the battle lines'.

He also was said to have had dealings with the South Africa's Atomic Energy Corporation, whose huge Pelindaba nuclear research complex could be seen across the dam from the Stoffbergs' patio.

Stoffberg was finally arrested and jailed on the Swiss–German border on 24 April 1991, under arms control laws, for attempting to sell 1,000 9-mm handguns to a US Customs official posing as a Chilean broker. His nuclear and chemical deals were stopped. In November he was extradited to the United States, where he would later testify in the Irangate arms-for-hostages scandal.

The stress of his life finally started to catch up with him. A security source who knew him said his contacts had started to dry up, particularly after the television interview. 'He had become the world's worst spy,' said the source. 'No one wanted to deal with him any more.'

At the time of his death, Stoffberg was believed to be short of money. The bottom had fallen out of the weapons market, his German wife's money had dried up, and, like Don Lange, Kobus du Preez and Wynand van Wyk before him, he feared that he was about to be eliminated. He had said earlier: 'You do receive threats and you don't take them lightly. You try to be careful.'

Turner said the couple had returned to South Africa in 1992 and started dealing in what Suzanne Stoffberg described as chemicals. Suzanne had abandoned two teenage sons and a husband in Germany to marry Dirk, and was still mesmerized by him. She told Pauw: 'From both sides, we love each other very, very much, and I think our love is so strong it will be for ever.'

But it did not seem like that to the owner of a local restaurant. He said it was embarrassing to see the Stoffbergs. 'Dirk would never let her out of his sight. He got annoyed if she looked at another man. If she went to the toilet he would stand outside the door, and they would frequently have terrible rows. They were a very unhappy couple.'

Dirk Stoffberg (fifty-eight) and Suzanne (forty-three) died on 20 July 1994. They were found lying in pools of blood on their balcony, whose beautiful vista of paradise – the deep-blue dam, the multicoloured yachts and the wild, rugged Magaliesberg mountains – was an incongruous backdrop to the horror of the killings. Neighbours heard shots and telephoned police. It appeared he had shot her, then himself. Two weapons were found. Bullets also peppered the inside walls of the house, indicating that whatever happened did not happen quickly.

But some friends of the family refused to believe Dirk Stoffberg had killed Suzanne or himself. A business associate, who said he had spoken to Stoffberg only an hour before his death, told us: 'He was very excited about a deal he was putting together which involved selling teak from the Sudan. He stood to make about $5 million. He had been working on the project for months and had already spoken to potential buyers in South America and Britain.'

Love letters the Stoffbergs wrote to each other only three years earlier told of a passionate affair. Could this all have gone so horribly wrong so soon?

The night the couple died, Suzanne was on the telephone talking to one of her sons in Germany when she screamed. And then her son said there was silence. Not long afterwards Stoffberg, or someone impersonating him, phoned his sister, Vicki Oxley, in Pretoria and told her he had shot Suzanne and was about to kill himself. In a statement to police, his sister said she had received a telephone call from Suzanne on the day of the killings: 'She said she and my brother owed her former husband R180,000 [$49,000], which should have been repaid in April. Her former husband had phoned her and asked when he was likely to get the money.'

Suzanne told Vicki that she had explained to her ex-husband that they did not have the money, but would repay him in December. He had asked for a security bond on the house, which he promised to return when the loan had been repaid. Dirk had opposed the idea, and his wife was phoning to find out what his sister thought about it. Suzanne then said her husband wanted to speak, and he took the receiver.

He said he had told his wife she could have a divorce if she wanted one and that she and her ex-husband and their children could have the house and the possessions. He would leave. 'Dirk said: "All I want are my books and a few personal possessions." He went on to say: "I cannot take it any more," and spoke of Suzanne's heavy drinking and her behaviour under the influence of liquor – throwing things about the house and breaking them,' said Vicki. 'He said that her family hated him.'

Vicki said she had been aware for months that the marriage had not been a happy one. 'At 8.30 that same evening, my brother phoned me and, in a calm voice, said: "Please come and fetch the dogs. I have killed Suzanne and am now going to kill myself." He put down the phone. At once I tried to phone the house, but there was no reply.'

Dirk Stoffberg had apparently murdered his wife, then turned a gun on himself. Both had been shot through the head. An open and shut case. Or was it? Soon afterwards, police said they believed the couple might have been murdered and were investigating a link between their deaths and red mercury. Stoffberg had been working on a red mercury transaction just before he died. A small, cylindrical canister purportedly containing the substance had been photographed on the sofa in his house. The picture had been found after the killings, but no one knew what had happened to the canister.

A blue file containing sensitive documents belonging to Stoffberg was smeared with blood on the inside back cover when it was found by a family friend. It contained documents on red mercury, and on the cover it mentioned the name of a Malcolm Roelofsz and the year 1994. It revealed that Stoffberg had been involved with red mercury in December 1993, when 60 kg were being offered by Roelofsz for $250 a gram. Roelofsz also said he had highly enriched uranium for sale.

Stoffberg had sent two faxes to one Zuhdi Alkatib in Jordan, offering him the red mercury and enriched uranium. A note in Stoffberg's handwriting, dated February 1994, said Alkatib was in South Africa and would contact him.

Blood was spattered all over the house. One trail of blood spots led down a corridor towards a large office where Stoffberg kept his safe. Had someone been chased through the house? A gardener told police he heard someone running down the outside staircase immediately after shots had been fired. And there were stories, discounted by police, that investigators had a secret witness who had seen a short, olive-skinned man, described as 'rather squat', running down the stairs and out of the house with files under his arm two minutes after the shooting.

Meanwhile, we were told by a man close to Military Intelligence that for some time Stoffberg had been under surveillance by a police unit called C10, which was working closely with the Directorate of Covert

Collection, part of MI.[1] They had been photographing Stoffberg's visitors and operating telephone intercepts. 'Dirk may also have been under surveillance from other security divisions,' said the source. Police could not confirm that he had been under surveillance at all.

Also, police were outraged to have discovered that some of Stoffberg's business papers were removed from the death scene by a man from MI and a woman from NIS. Detectives were trying to retrieve the missing files and investigating why Stoffberg's business affairs were of so much interest to the intruders. Mysteriously, a safe had also gone missing from Stoffberg's study. Had they been looking for the red mercury file, which was taken before they arrived?

On top of his dealings in red mercury, documents showed that Dirk Stoffberg was working on other large projects. He was trying to sell diamonds from Russia and the Central African Republic.

A number of people connected to the Stoffbergs said they received death threats after the killings. They included sixth wife Linda Stoffberg, daughter Cheryl Stoffberg and Margaret Turner, who said she was a close friend of Suzanne Stoffberg and was acting as executor of her estate. Turner had been offered money by three people who believed she had some of the Stoffberg files.

On top of the threats, Linda Stoffberg was virtually abducted by a man who was apparently connected to the security service. She told Pauw that he took her to a bush camp surrounded by an electrified fence. There, he and two others asked her questions about Stoffberg.

'I was telephoned and asked to go to Dirk's house, where I would be picked up. And I was taken round and round the dam, eventually to a farm where I was questioned by three men. Their names were not revealed to me. They wanted to know if I had any of the recent documentation. They questioned me on documents about certain substances. They were also interested in certain diamond documents, and a couple of others too.'

[1] C10 was based at Vlakplaas, which was widely reputed to be the home of the SA Police's death-squad units. According to court testimony, C10 was 'known throughout the country as the specialists, professionals in difficult matters'. Three police generals – former CIS chief Lieutenant-General Krappies Engelbrecht, former deputy commissioner of the SAP Lieutenant-General Basie Smit and former divisional head of the Crime Combating and Intelligence Service Lieutenant-General Johan le Roux – were implicated by Mr Justice Richard Goldstone as 'depraved' officers involved in 'a horrible network of criminal activity', some of it associated with C10. Engelbrecht is also accused of warning the head of the SADF, General Kat Liebenberg, the night before Judge Goldstone's investigations team raided the top-secret Directorate in November 1992. The raid led to the purge of twenty-three senior SADF officers by de Klerk, a move that embittered many in the military.

But was red mercury ever mentioned? Pauw asked. 'Yes, it was,' she said. 'They wanted to know if I had seen any documents referring to red mercury or the actual connection between Suzanne and somebody in Jordan. And that was it.'

Stoffberg's daughter Cheryl was probably the closest and dearest person to Dirk. Although she lived 1,500 km away in the Cape, he shared his innermost secrets with her. She said repeatedly she believed her father was murdered, and that days before his death he told her he was worried for his safety.

She told the SABC: 'He said there were certain people who were after him. He believed his life was in danger, and he asked me to destroy documents should anything happen to him. He said the documents were dangerous, and I destroyed them.' From the beginning of 1994, he had sent her documents relating to red mercury. She refused to explain the contents. On red mercury, she said: 'He said it was dangerous, and he wanted out.'

Asked why she thought her father feared for his life, she said: 'I believe it was related to red mercury ... I have no doubt about it.' She refused to say who wanted to kill him. After his death she was approached by a man: 'He threatened me. He said if I pursued this I was dead meat.'

Linda Stoffberg, who kept in close contact with her ex-husband, told a similar story. She had been allowed to remove her ex-husband's personal items after the killings, and also got rid of documents. 'I destroyed anything that vaguely resembled red mercury. I just thought it was too dangerous.' She knew the risks, having lived through years of sensitive weapons deals during her marriage. Asked if she knew what red mercury was, she said: 'No. I don't want to know either.' She believed a deal had 'gone wrong', and was convinced that Dirk and Suzanne had been murdered because of red mercury.

Dirk Stoffberg, who in his younger days had been a bank clerk, had been running an import–export company from premises in Midrand, north of Johannesburg, before he died. He clearly knew he was treading a tightrope with his red mercury dealings. He had secret business links with Don Lange, the Durban arms dealer who had been murdered. Documents showed they had worked on at least one red mercury deal together, and police were beginning to fear there was an orchestrated attempt to eliminate people trading in nuclear materials with the Middle East.

Ten days before Dirk Stoffberg died, he told his closest friend, a colonel in MI, that he was worried about his safety. The colonel, tracked down by the Jacques Pauw, agreed to speak on condition he was not identified. He said Stoffberg had told him that he knew someone in Pretoria who had contact with another person who was in possession of red mercury – or 'red dust', as Stoffberg called it.

Stoffberg also had enemies partly because of his personality. As well as being temperamental, violent and intolerant, he was often a rampaging drunk who constantly abused his wives.

Suzanne Stoffberg also drank heavily, and was behaving oddly shortly before her death. Her friend Margaret Turner told us she had never liked Dirk and was trying to persuade Suzanne to leave him. 'He used to hit her.' Suzanne had also reportedly taken to stripping off her clothes and running naked around the neighbourhood.

But even more odd was her husband's strange passion – he idolized the Third Reich. Linda Stoffberg recalled he had a prize collection of Hitler memorabilia and would strut up and down his patio wearing Nazi uniforms. She showed us one of them.

'This was his prized possession. It was on a dummy, but the poor old dummy fell apart and I threw that away. It had all its badges and things which have fallen off over the years of moving around.' Hitler was his idol. 'He was a neo-Nazi and believed in Hitler's policies. He believed the world would have been a better place had Hitler survived. He had two or three Hitler uniforms, which I still have, and every book, every piece of documentation that ever came out about Hitler. In fact at one stage he tried to start his own little neo-Nazi party going here. But it didn't work too well.' Ironically, Stoffberg was also a peace monitor for South Africa's first all-race election in 1994.

A police intelligence source said Stoffberg had dealings with right-wing groups in South Africa and had attended a number of meetings. He speculated that he could have been buying nuclear materials, including red mercury, for paramilitary groups on the right wing.

He also said that he believed Stoffberg was selling 'sensitive materials' to countries in the Middle East to generate money. 'I personally believe he was in financial trouble and was prepared to talk. I think he was prepared to go out and tell the whole truth. I believe it was somebody in this country from a right-wing group who killed him.'

A hoard of documents found in Dirk Stoffberg's house after his death paints a vivid picture of clandestine dealings in nuclear chemicals. Red mercury, weapons-grade uranium and heavy water were among the notorious materials he was peddling – probably at his peril.

Documents show that Stoffberg was in league with a Durban arms dealer, Malcolm Roelofsz. Some relate how, early in 1994, the two men were trying to sell 60 kg of red mercury for R48 million ($13 million). Another document lists a variety of substances which add up to a recipe for mustard gas.

Roelofsz's son later threatened television producer Pauw after the arms dealer had featured in a documentary on red mercury. 'You're finished,' he told Pauw. 'You have no future left.' Said Pauw: 'I think this is an indication we have struck a raw nerve.' Pauw had filmed what he was told was red mercury dust, and said documents he had obtained suggested that Stoffberg and Roelofsz were happy to sell both red mercury and mustard gas.

Intelligence agencies, understandably, did not want such a haul of sensitive documents to fall into the hands of journalists. Stoffberg's most closely guarded secrets were kept in cupboards, filing cabinets and boxes in his office. Piles of them disappeared. Agents of MI, NIS and the CIS raced to the scene on hearing about the deaths. Many of the documents had already been taken. And they took some of those remaining.

Said Linda Stoffberg: 'A lot of people were looking for documents, and a lot of people appeared from nowhere. Nobody – especially the family – knew who they were. Some of them claimed to be friends of Dirk and Suzanne.'

We saw a number of documents, including some that detailed Stoffberg's business dealings with Roelofsz, dating back to the early 1980s. The two of them were trying to trade not only in commodities such as oil, emeralds and timber, but in weapons and dangerous nuclear substances.

One such substance was uranium trioxide, or U_2O_3. Inquiries about this product left us mystified. There seemed to be very little known about it among nuclear scientists we approached, and no descriptions in standard textbooks. Its cost is more than 100 times higher than that of plutonium (about $1.2 million a kilogram). However, one black-market trader said it had been produced by 'two or three' countries, including Russia and South Africa. Its price was $100,000 a gram, but desperate countries had been known to buy it for many millions of dollars a gram. The trader said this 'white, crystalline powder' was used to 'breed' highly enriched uranium in a nuclear reactor or other suitable vessel. Only tiny quantities – a few milligrams – were needed to initiate what was effectively a cheap enrichment process, he said. With red mercury, it too could be used to build a bomb. We could not verify any of this.

However, we saw a number of documents from companies purportedly selling the material at prices of up to $140 million a kilogram. And it was also a deal potentially worth $60 million and involving uranium trioxide that caused a major row between Stoffberg and Roelofsz, according to documents found at the death scene.

In 1990 Roelofsz and a man called Rashid, sometimes referred to as 'The Priest', faxed a message to Stoffberg, under the subject heading 'Books':

> My very good friend and brother Raheel has made contact with me. He was unable to meet with you due to the very tense situation in the Middle East ... He is moving goods; to an African state as he discussed ... So as to make 100 per cent sure buyer gets what he wants I am now releasing formula to you so there is no mistake as he is investing a further $35,000 to move goods to pick-up point.

R. Sheriff Consultants, with offices in Durban and London, were in correspondence regarding the same material, referring to it also as 'Books'. The writer, R. Sheriff, said he hoped the fax did not fall into the wrong hands. This is how he described the goods in correspondence:

> Item: Uranium trio oxide;
> Contents: 95 per cent pure uranium, MX-D 1979 radio active, 3 per cent uranium oxide;
> Capacity: 278;
> Packing: Triple glass scale;
> Markings: Open in lab. Very sensitive. Handle with care.

The message then said that the material had been sealed in 1979 and the quantity was between 300 and 600 grams.

In another fax about the same transaction, Roelofsz wrote that the price of the trioxide was $120,000 a gram, but the buyers were looking for it at $20,000 less.

He said it would be transported to a place of the buyer's choice for inspection 'via the embassy', and that the material would have 'no legal documentation, as per buyer's request'.

It was clear from a fax from Stoffberg that the buyer for this substance was a government, not an agent, and therefore had to be handled 'with great delicacy'.

We examined further documents, letters and faxes relating to business between Roelofsz and Stoffberg dating back to the early 1980s.

Roelofsz's faxes to Stoffberg often started off cordially: 'Hello Old

Friend. I trust that you are well.' Their relationship by fax between Roelofsz's offices at Umhlanga, near Durban, and Stoffberg, either in Johannesburg or somewhere in Europe, made fascinating reading. Most of the faxes and other communications between the two were friendly and often cryptic, dripping in mystery. They almost always discussed the trade of one commodity or other, along with the letter of credit and other banking arrangements. But on at least one occasion they fell out over a deal. In 1990 they had a furious row by fax, each one accusing the other of being crooked.

Stoffberg faxed Roelofsz from Switzerland in November, referring to someone called Raheel. In capital letters, the fax read: 'This must all be some sort of sick joke! For so many weeks now I await your firm arrival – then at the last moment always you find another excuse (sorry I cannot accept this nonsense repeatedly, what kind of fool do you take me for?).'

A few weeks later, Roelofsz's handwritten fax to Stoffberg read:

I am absolutely shocked by your silence ... If you cannot do the business, please say so ... a pretense to get money makes you nothing but the lowest common thief. You have a lot to answer for, especially the $10,000 for travelling, the $35,000 to move the goods and the $1.8 million Raheel has sent on November 15 to secure them ... Just pay back the $10,000 and pay the balance ... You cannot disappear, your photo was taken in Zurich and your every movement monitored. We know where you are and that you have received all my faxes.

Stoffberg responded furiously: 'I am not impressed by your sanctimonious attitude. At the first meeting you could not stop talking about yourself and how wonderful you were.' Stoffberg finally accused Roelofsz of going 'berserk': 'If I had a twisted mind, I could retaliate against you all in a similar manner. You have, by a childish stupid act and absolute indiscretion, destroyed all I had established here. You will hear from one of my people.'

When we visited Roelefsz at his small metal fabrication works near Durban, he at first denied being an arms dealer or trading in red mercury. But under pressure he admitted he had tried to sell a variety of materials that could be used to make nuclear weapons.

Did you have no qualms about what you were selling, we asked? He replied that he did not. Eventually, after a heated, ongoing exchange, a visibly shaken Roelofsz said he had made very little money out of his dealings and he was now living in a rented house. He said he had been dealing with a trader known as 'The Priest', from Pakistan, who he now believed was dead. He also believed that Stoffberg had been selling highly enriched uranium to Jordan. Roelofsz claimed Stoffberg was penniless when he died, and believed he was fed up enough to kill Suzanne and then shoot himself.

Stoffberg's association with nuclear issues started many years ago. Months before he died, he admitted he had carried 'nuclear bits and pieces' to Israel in the 1980s, using his Swazi-registered aircraft. Most of the cargos he shipped with this plane were South African armaments, destined for a variety of destinations across the world, sources told Peta Thornycroft, a reporter for the Durban-based *Sunday Tribune*. A select few consignments had been shipped to Israel, they said. His company, which operated on forged documents, was called Air Swaziland, and had offices at Lanseria Airport, north of Johannesburg, Thornycroft's story said. The company was closed after an Interpol investigation in 1981, and the plane was seized by a French company that had arranged a lease for Stoffberg and his associates.

He would never tell anyone – including ex-wife Linda or his grown-up daughter Cheryl, his closest confidantes at the time – what he was transporting from South Africa to Israel, except that the cargo was connected to the nuclear industry.

It was clear from the Stoffberg paper trail that Suzanne Stoffberg was also a dealer in unusual commodities. The documents showed she had a long-standing business relationship with a trader in Jordan and, strangely, had compiled what looked like an intelligence report on her Hitler-loving husband.

The former Suzanne Tanzer claimed to have met Stoffberg in her native Germany, fallen in love with him, and left her husband and two children. Whether she was in reality an intelligence agent in Germany (and, if so, for whom), an arms dealer in her own right or just a woman who fancied a change is not clear. She was certainly not just a simple loving wife who lost her heart, her looks and her family to a rampaging drunk who constantly abused her.

There was speculation among security agencies that Suzanne was working for East German intelligence and had a false passport. A CIS security police officer, who was one of the first to arrive at the crime scene, said that among the documents he found a long typed statement signed by Suzanne which listed all her dealings with Stoffberg since they had met and married. It told how they met and how they were arrested at the German border with papers on how to build a nuclear weapon bomb and a 'recipe' for red mercury. She had managed to tear the papers and flush them down the toilet. The police officer said it was a curious thing – almost as if she was writing an intelligence report on all her dealings with Dirk and his friends for some agency or other.

Said the police officer: 'What bothers us is the way she was shot, on top of the head, and that there was blood smeared high up on the walls of the garage. She apparently was made to go on her knees before she was shot, and she had more than one wound. Also, there were a lot of bullet marks in the house.'

Turner told us: 'When I heard of the shooting, I went straight to the house. The bodies had been taken away and I started to clear up. The police had removed some of the documents, but there was a file of papers that was smeared with blood on the inside. I found another file in an old school desk which contained their latest red mercury dealings.

'Apparently Suzanne's son had been on the phone to her. She was cheerful, then he heard a scream – no row. Then there was silence; then three shots.'

Turner, looking at clues she had picked up at the crime scene, speculated on what might have happened. 'The puzzling thing is that she must have screamed, put down the phone, run outside to the car and been shot there under the chin. The bullet went out of her forehead and didn't kill her. The car was covered with a spurt of blood and a trail went right up the stairs. She must have tried to run back upstairs and been shot twice more, through the temple and through the back of the head.

'He was shot in the head. In Suzanne's office there was blood-covered toilet paper in the waste-paper basket. Someone must have gone to the bathroom, taken the toilet paper, wiped themselves, and then left it in the office. The file had been smeared with blood on the inside. This all seems to be inconsistent with the idea that Dirk did the killing. There was no row. He was an expert shot. Why would he look in a file before killing himself – and why clean himself up?'

Said the CIS police officer: 'The bodies had already been taken away, and people were clearing up. I saw a lot of documents on a large table, as if he had been pulling out papers to refresh his memory of past deals. Also, there were two boxes full of papers. We only looked through the files on the table. One document related to red mercury – I don't remember which country it was from, but there was an Indian guy called Singh and someone called Basil apparently involved in a lot of the transactions. Singh was apparently involved in luxury cars, such as Mercedes and

BMWs, for Botswana. There was stuff on emeralds and diamonds. Some of the papers dealt with the Middle East. A lot of the documents referred to deals for Armscor.'

He said he had reported his findings to his colonel in Pretoria.

'Other documents were from Kuwait or Saudi Arabia, and still others concerned shipments of teak in Uganda, which were destined for Brazil,' said the police officer. 'Someone I knew in the NIS telephoned and said he wanted to see me. A woman called Sue also had telephoned, and she wanted to see me too. I arranged a meeting which was attended by my colonel, who later told me the woman was actually from MI.' Linda Stoffberg said the MI and NIS agents were looking for a particular file. They found and removed it.

Police investigating officer Lieutenant-Colonel Charles Landman said: 'The scene very much looks like an incident where the husband shot the wife and then shot himself. But there are certain peculiar things that we are busy investigating. If they were murdered, it was a very professional job to make it look like a murder/suicide.'

Asked who stole documents, Landman said: 'We have the names of certain individuals and we also know that certain government departments are involved in removing certain of the documents. We are looking into that.' He was investigating charges that agents of MI and the NIS removed papers.

Strangely, the police who originally investigated the deaths did not call for blood samples to be taken. Both bodies were cremated.

An indication of Stoffberg's violence came through when he explained to the SABC that while in Europe he carried a German combat knife, which he once used to cut the face of an accountant who tried to pass him a bad cheque. 'It was a warning,' he said.

Violence was also a theme of business deals. Dirk forced Suzanne and his business associates, including retired military general Willem Lombard, to sign a document that bound them to secrecy on penalty of losing a limb, tongue or eye.

But at the end of this tale of love, tragedy, espionage and arms deals, it is clear that of all the secrets, the Stoffbergs' trade in red mercury was their most sensitive. And it was their involvement in the trading of this material that would ultimately lead to breakthroughs in our investigation.

Of all the killings, Dirk Stoffberg's was the one that placed red mercury closest to the door of the security services. He was in the business of trading sensitive materials, some of them nuclear; he had an international network of contacts; and he had an open door through to South African intelligence agencies.

And, from the paranoia he displayed over red mercury, and the panic of the intelligence services, it was clear that he was trading in a dangerous, secret substance that official bodies in South Africa clearly knew existed. Even documents relating to this trade were marked by the Stoffbergs 'FYOM' – For Your and My Eyes Only. Secrecy was no joke. Before their deaths, they too would have realized that people trading in the material were being murdered.

The Stoffberg killings demonstrated vividly that the trade in red mercury in South Africa was not just the domain of chancers, crooks and other wheeler-dealers. Dirk Stoffberg was a man who had considerable international experience in buying and selling all kinds of armaments, along with nuclear and chemical materials. It was unlikely that he had been deceived by con men selling 'red paint'. Far from it. In the weeks to come, his death would throw up alarming testimony to show why South Africa had become inextricably part of the world red mercury trade.

9 Red Mercury is a Hoax – Official

Bizarre stories of red mercury began to circulate in Western newspapers during the 1980s but received scant attention. Nobody appeared to know what it was used for or even if it existed. There were wacky tales of samples being seized in Italy, Germany, Switzerland, Poland and Bulgaria, accompanied by other rarities such as osmium-187 and scandium. Apparently the buyers were from the Middle East, with Libya and Iraq active in the market. Smugglers were said to be charging more than £250,000 ($375,000) a kilogram, and the price alone made the stories seem improbable.

The reaction of Western governments to this trickle of stories was uniform. They condemned the deals as hoaxes, perpetrated by organized crime groups such as the Russian mafia, and pictured the buyers as gullible buffoons. The British Ministry of Defence said snootily: 'There is no evidence that red mercury exists' – a line that is still used when questions are asked in the British Parliament.

The US Department of Energy in Washington said any samples it had obtained were useless – like coloured water. 'Careful consideration of the claims made for red mercury makes it apparent it does not exist.' It said it was interested in the stuff because it was often linked to sales offers for alleged nuclear weapons materials.

In its newsletter, *Critical Technologies*, the Office of Non-Proliferation Support at the DoE said red mercury had become one of science's unicorns. 'Take a bogus material, give it an enigmatic name, exaggerate its physical properties and intended uses, mix in some intrigue and voila! – one half-baked scam, but one with some income potential … In scam after scam over many years, nobody has produced anything extraordinary and surely nothing justifying a half-million-dollar price tag.'

Nevertheless, the DoE's Office of Threat Assessment along the corridor was publicizing a special phone number for people with information about red mercury. And its deputy director, Thomas Blankenship, was under orders to file away everything he could find. He said: 'I don't discount that a version of red mercury has some military use, but I don't believe it is important and I am not sure what it is.'

Why did the stories persist, and why were people prepared to be fooled after being warned about frauds and samples of coloured water? One explanation from Blankenship, echoing the comments of police forces in Germany and Italy, was that some deals were sophisticated money-laundering scams.

A Russian company would offer to sell some red mercury to a Western firm it was in league with, and agree to pay a forfeit if it didn't deliver the goods. The intention was for the deal to fail, so that the Russian company was forced by law to pay the forfeit. It knew the Russian authorities would allow it to exchange roubles for Western currency at a good exchange rate to meet the debt. The two parties to the deal would then split their ill-gotten profits.

Research showed that such scams were indeed being used to launder roubles, but it begged one important question. If the Russian authorities were falling for this trick, they must have been satisfied that a genuine red mercury deal was originally intended – and *ipso facto* that there was such a thing as red mercury.

The chorus of denials in the West did not stem the stories of mega-dollar deals emanating from the former Soviet Union, which continued into the 1990s. The Bulgarian authorities revealed that a quantity of red mercury had been seized, hidden in a missile warhead. It was being sold to a foreign government, and several Russians had been arrested.

When questioned, the Bulgarian Interior Ministry seemed to know quite a lot about red mercury – enough to warn that it must be handled carefully. Said its spokesman: 'Competent services have recently received signals that there is illegal trade of raw materials and substances that present a danger to the life and health of people and to the environment. For example, several times there have been quantities of so-called red mercury found on the black market. After consulting specialists, it became clear that this is an industrial compound of several elements with strong radioactive and toxic impact. In contact with skin or respiratory organs, there can be irreversible consequences to the human body, including death.'

The *Los Angeles Times* reported that Yanko Yanev, head of Bulgaria's Atomic Energy Committee and a nuclear chemist by profession, had obtained a seized container of red mercury. His scientists found it was not radioactive, but its red colour perplexed them and it was clearly of Soviet military origin. 'They think it is an amalgam of mercury and tellurium,' said Yanev, pointing out that mercury and tellurium isotopes are present during a nuclear explosion. He believed the mystery container could be a leftover from a Soviet missile system. 'I really regard this as a problem,' Yanev told the newspaper. 'It's such a disorganized situation now [in the former Soviet Union]. I don't know what red mercury is. It could be for a missile, it could be for anything. They are now selling everything on the black markets, maybe only to get food.'

The problem seemed to be mounting in Eastern Europe. The head of the Hungarian police's organized-crime division was alarmed that hundreds of local businessmen were trying to sell red mercury. Professor Giorgy Marx, head of nuclear physics at Budapest University, was brought in to advise. He told newspapers that red mercury 20/20 'could cause the kind of chemical explosion to create nuclear fission in plutonium warheads'. Hungary's main newspaper, *Nepszabadsag*, put it similarly: 'It might be a detonating substance for plutonium bombs.' It added that several recent murders in Vienna might be linked to the traffic.

Another newspaper story said that police in the Ukrainian city of Poltava had arrested thieves carrying 180 kg of red mercury that had been stolen from a plant at Tambov in Russia. The material was not treated as a fake, because the report went on to say the red mercury had been returned to its owners.

One amazing event from August 1991 stood out from all the others. Thirty-five Czech red-beret paratroops and fifteen military police were landed by plane at one of the country's main military airbases, at Mosnov near Ostrava. The personnel on the base were held at gunpoint while commandos shot their way into one of the storage buildings. They had been told that a consignment of red mercury was hidden there, and were under orders to find it. Hooded troops tore the place apart, injuring some of the base personnel in the process.

The embarrassed commanding officer of the invasion force found nothing, and the action sparked a local scandal. A secret parliamentary inquiry was held, during which one of the investigators committed suicide. Why was the Czech army shooting up its own base seeking an apparently mythical substance? The answer never came out. Martin Sendrych, the Czech Interior Ministry's spokesman, said his police force had confiscated red mercury after several smuggling arrests, but now viewed the material as 'of no strategic military value'.

In March 1992, the Norwegian newspaper *Bergens Tidende* reported that a local company had been offered 6 to 8 metric tons of heavy water and 22 pounds of red mercury; both, it said, were used in the weapons industry. The reports of seizures kept coming, and at last a British newspaper, the *Independent*, began to take an interest. In April 1992 it tracked down Marco Affatigato, a former Italian neo-fascist, who was apparently trading in red mercury from an office in Valence, southern France. He had once served a twelve-year sentence for membership of Ordine Nuovo, an extremist right-wing group that was banned in the 1970s and had been investigated for a series of attacks on trains. He told the newspaper that for two years he had had an exclusive franchise to sell red mercury, and he was getting supplies from the Ukraine.

Affatigato said the KGB and ex-military officers in Russia were stealing it from the production plants and smuggling it across the border. It came in containers weighing 1, 5 and 30 kg and was given various names such as 'Vin Rouge' and 'Beaujolais' because of its colour. The most common type was 'red mercury 20/20', but there was an expensive and rare version called 'red mercury 20/23' which came 'with a stick of uranium down the middle'.

He told the newspaper there was also a scam in operation, because the material deteriorates with time. 'After three months [red mercury] is no longer usable for the purposes for which it was created. If you calculate the time between leaving the factory and going into store and then being delivered at Vienna, Zurich or Geneva … that takes six to seven months. By that time it is no longer any use.'

The Italian said a buyer on the black market sometimes doesn't know this and therefore 'gets screwed … He's going to buy the product at above the official market rates, for about $500,000 a kilogram. Multiply that by 30 and you get a tidy sum.'

Affatigato boasted that his biggest customer was a member of the House of Saud, the family that rules Saudi Arabia, whom he had met in Paris. The end-user certificate showed his supplies of red mercury were for the jewellery trade.

The *Independent* was not convinced by Affatigato's claims, or those of others its reporters had grilled, but it grew alarmed at the lack of official action: 'Whatever the truth, it is surprising to say the least that the police and intelligence departments of half a dozen countries have shown so little interest in pinning down the source of the traffic or in securing any convictions in what, if it is a fraud, could rank as the sting of the century.'

We later learned from several sources that Saudi Arabia was one of the biggest buyers of red mercury, and had up to three jet aircraft on standby to fly to any city where it was available. There was a Lear Jet equipped with basic equipment to verify the authenticity of the material being bought. There was also a Boeing 727 with a large conference suite at the front and a lead-lined laboratory at the rear. A trader who said he had been inside this plane was impressed with the equipment: it included fax machines, sophisticated communications systems, glove boxes for handling radioactive materials, hot cells and analysis instruments. He had heard that a Boeing 747 had recently been added to the fleet.

Most journalists poking into the matter were soon baffled by all the inconsistencies, and they got no help if they turned to the UN's International Atomic Energy Agency in Vienna, where officials were sitting firmly on the fence (and still are). A spokesman admitted it had received inquiries from a number of countries, including from the Ukrainian government, asking if there were restrictions on the cross-border trafficking of red mercury. The IAEA could not give a definitive answer because, it was said, the chemical was not on its 'trigger list' of dangerous substances specified in the Nuclear Non-Proliferation Treaty. This list deals only with fissionable materials such as plutonium and uranium, and any case of illegal trafficking of these has to be reported within twenty-four hours.

Hans Blix, the director-general, ventured that red mercury was a hoax, but refused to be categorical: 'There are a lot of crooks around who want to make money.'

The IAEA said it had no plans to investigate the confiscations taking place. This remained IAEA policy even after a UN nuclear inspection team found evidence that Iraq was taking an interest in the material. On a visit to Baghdad, in the wake of the Iraq–Kuwait war, the team discovered a cabinet full of papers about red mercury, some from Western arms dealers who were offering the stuff. The UN's nuclear specialists had been sent to oversee the destruction of Saddam Hussein's atomic weapons programme, but the team put all the red mercury files back, believing they were of no significance.

A team member later said he knew nothing about red mercury and was therefore not in the least bit curious about the find. He had not seen reports, then emanating from northern Italy, that Iraq, Libya and other countries were buying the material in the belief it represented a new nuclear weapons technology.

Romano Dolce, a public prosecutor in the Italian mountain resort of Como, near the Swiss border, was running a major investigation into the smuggling of nuclear materials, and had picked up evidence of Russian-made red mercury passing through his patch. It was, he announced, bound for the Middle East and, we learned, South Africa.

He agreed to a meeting at his office in the city centre, close to the mountain-fringed lake which has made Como a major tourist centre. Fiddling with a combination lock, he opened up a metal cupboard full of papers which had been gathered by his local force of customs police – the Guardia di Finanza. 'You can see we have been dealing with this problem for some time,' Dolce said, pointing to a list of thirty cases of nuclear smuggling that appeared to involve red mercury. 'This material is passing through here because it is conveniently close to Switzerland, where most of the financial aspects of the deals are completed. The banks there are well aware of how these materials must be bought and sold, and provide special facilities. There are also special laboratories that can verify the chemical sample is genuine. We pick the trail up when people drive to Italy, heading south.'

Dolce disclosed that much of his evidence had come from paperwork seized during arrests, and from telephone taps, which he was able to authorize easily. 'We have listened in to many conversations, and we believe this material is genuine. We have seized samples, but nothing that we think is the real substance. The trouble is I can get no straight answers – either from the IAEA in Vienna or from our own security police. When we make arrests they all descend on me – even the CIA – but then they leave without telling me anything.'

He said he was conducting Italy's first judicial investigation into the red mercury traffic. It had begun when two informants had come to his office and said the smuggling through Como was the tip of an enormous international scandal. Since then he had found documents in Russian, Czech, German, French and English, as well as Italian. 'If all these deals are frauds, why are so many people, including governments, prepared to be cheated?'

In one arrest, in the northern city of Milan, his police had picked up three Hungarians and an Austrian. They had with them two small containers, each weighing a kilogram, of what was allegedly red mercury. This was tested by the director of Italy's Atomic Energy Agency and found to be a 'powdery mixture of mercury and antimony'. Dolce said he was certain from his research that Iran, Iraq, Libya, Israel and South Africa were major buyers, but he added: 'Even Western countries are interested. It is worrying. There has to be some sort of international investigation of all these matters.'

In fact in May 1994 it was Dolce who came under investigation. Sensationally, he was arrested by police probing, it was stated, 'the illegal trafficking of weapons and atomic bomb components'. More than 200 police took part in a swoop on the public prosecutor's offices, his home and the premises of five others who were arrested at the same time. He was suspected of having links with organized crime groups which smuggled weapons, explosives and radioactive materials from the former Soviet bloc.

Lieutenant-Colonel Carmine Adinolfi, head of the squad, said further arrests could follow as part of the year-long probe. He would not say if any weapons or nuclear material had been seized. Dolce was clearly regarded as the gang leader, as the others snatched were suspected petty criminals in the Como area. He spent some time in jail before being put under house arrest in his home town of Rimini. All his files from the red mercury probe were removed, and the investigation was effectively ceased.

Dolce was eventually released from house arrest on the orders of a judge and he returned to Como. In early 1995 he resigned as a magistrate, but as this book went to press in September 1995 the prosecutors in Brescia had still not finally decided whether he would face charges. It was now being alleged that he had faked a number of police enquiries in conjunction with a secret service informer. Dolce maintained he had been targeted to thwart his investigation into nuclear smuggling.

While Dolce was banged up in jail, the rest of Europe suddenly awoke to the warnings he and a few others had been voicing that the world was in imminent danger from nuclear smuggling, and from terrorists or demagogues fashioning a crude type of nuclear weapons device. The number of seizures of radioactive samples was growing. One foolish trafficker had managed to burn a cavity in his belly by hiding a phial of caesium-137 under his shirt. In Germany, two seizures of plutonium-239, the fissionable component of an implosion-type atom bomb, ignited concern, and the heavyweight press flew in from the United States. One batch was of exceptional purity and was identified as coming from Russia

The *Washington Post* complained in August 1994 that international agreements to control smuggling were needed urgently, and yet plans to implement them were in disarray. The *Post* went on: 'A two-year US effort to help Russia keep its nuclear materials from falling into terrorist hands has largely failed to get off the ground because of US friction with top nuclear experts, low funding and inattention at the top levels of the Clinton administration.'

Time magazine sent out reporters to Russia to file in depth on the situation. 'As factory subsidies erode and payrolls shrink, thousands of Russia's most talented researchers and millions of factory workers are struggling just to survive. They have thrown open their doors on a back-country yard sale, offering all-comers bargains in everything from highly sophisticated conventional weapons to rare and strategic metals.' The US Secretary of Defense told *Time*: 'This is a very worrisome problem,' but added hopefully, 'The only good news I have is that it does not seem to be happening with nuclear weapons.'

Time spotlighted, as we had, that Ekaterinburg was the centre of the trade. It said the former military city had become 'a shopping center for the hottest market in restricted products, the rare and strategic metals trade'. It found there were staggering profits to be made, and explained how this was done:

> More sophisticated buyers cultivate contacts with a small community of international brokers, mostly Germans and Americans, who work out of Switzerland. These brokers have sanitized their operations so thoroughly that they never actually meet the seller ... couriers deliver the seller's metals and the buyer's cash to one of the Swiss banks specializing in the metals trade. There, the metals are tested by an independent laboratory for atomic count and purity.

However, *Time* had also found that some middlemen were dispensing with any pretence at legitimacy and were travelling around with bodyguards, scientific experts and suitcases of cash. 'The sellers are most likely to be Mafia-connected hustlers or former KGB agents, some of whom have even set up joint ventures with former CIA agents to smuggle strategic materials. The trade is so brisk that Estonia has emerged as one of the world's leading exporters of rare metals even though it produces none.'

It was precisely what George, our contact in Ekaterinburg, and Dolce, in Como, had been saying. Russia was leaking deadly substances, and no one seemed to be offering a finger for the dyke.

Russia had become notorious as a Shangri-La for the quartermasters of terrorism around the world, but what of red mercury? The Western media yawned, scratched their heads, and went back to sleep. It was either too complex an issue or too big a burden on travel expenses to resolve. Alternatively, like good lobby fodder, they accepted the official line that investigating it would be like chasing after rainbows.

Five thousand miles away in South Africa, however, the topic was fizzing. The police investigation by Landman was headline news, and a lively debate about red mercury was occupying many column inches. The Johannesburg *Weekend Star* was pursuing a full-scale investigation, others were intermittently following up leads, and a few were being downright contemptuous of the whole issue.

The writer of a satirical column, 'A Letter to Soweto', in the *Weekly Mail & Guardian*, speculated that red mercury might be produced as a by-product of tomato ketchup. He also conjured up a sales spiel for miniature atomic devices: 'Next time a big bully kicks sand in your face on the beach, hit him with a nuclear bomb hidden in an ice-cream cone.'

In a piece entitled 'Nuclear Weapons – Little Green Men?', the *Financial Mail* suggested the red mercury stories were designed to smear Israel, after allegations that its security service was behind the killing of Alan Kidger. Ken Owen, editor of the *Weekend Star*'s rival, the *Sunday Times*, complained of 'wild tales of red mercury, a substance that no reputable scientist believes exists … it is fun journalism, and nobody takes it seriously, but it does displace the day-to-day reporting of the South African revolution.'

Owen is one of South Africa's best journalists, but he seemed to be forgetting that weapons scientists the world over, many of whom were possibly researching secret red mercury applications, could never admit the substance's existence. He also seemed to accept without question the line of his country's Atomic Energy Corporation, which was parroting the official story coming from Europe and the United States. At its vast nuclear plant in the Magaliesberg mountains, west of Pretoria, where for years it kept up a pretence that South Africa had no atomic weapons, spokeswoman Lola Patrick said there had been dozens of reports that the chemical was on sale in the Republic: 'We have been contacted at least once a month in the four and half years I have been here. All the reports have proved to be hoaxes.'

She added: 'All sorts of weird and wonderful properties were claimed by those touting substances called red mercury, which they were offering for prices of up to half a million dollars a kilogram. Usually claims are made that it has got some wonderful intrinsic value in the nuclear arms industry or in the production of medicine.'

On one occasion the red mercury on offer turned out to be a red powder. In another instance a bottle was painted on the inside with red nail-polish. Patrick was clearly not a believer: 'As far as the AEC is concerned, red mercury does not exist.'

Similar advice was being given in a confidential report to the police's

Bomb Data Centre in Pretoria. It came in a report written by Dr S. J. van der Walt, a scientist at Mechem, the Pretoria-based chemical and explosives manufacturer. He said a paper on red mercury by Dr Frank Barnaby of Britain for the magazine *International Defense Review* was the best technical discussion he had seen on the subject. However, he did not believe a thesis advanced by Barnaby that red mercury could produce sufficient heat, when detonated, to cause fusion in a neutron bomb. Van der Walt concluded: 'Red mercury seems to be a figment of the imagination. None has been investigated by independent scientists, to my knowledge, and found to conform to the claims made for it ... If it is used in nuclear weapons at all, it may be only a carrier for radioactive isotopes ... Without enriched uranium or plutonium, red mercury remains only a toxic hazard.'

Barnaby, the British expert cited by Mechem, had in fact become one of the West's leading experts on red mercury. For two years, he had been a consultant to a number of TV programmes on the subject screened by the British television series *Dispatches*. And, as a nuclear physicist who once worked on his country's nuclear weapons programme and later became director of the Stockholm International Peace Research Institute, he was highly qualified to solve the mystery.

When first embarking on the quest for this substance in 1992, he decided his first task was to find out what was known in the West. Specifications faxed from Russia showed that red mercury was a compound of mercury, antimony and oxygen with the chemical formula $Hg_2Sb_2O_7$. Delving though databases at his local college, King Alfred's at Winchester, Hampshire, he traced only one reference: an abstract of an article written in 1968. The British Library's Science Reference Department in Holborn, London, provided a copy of the original dusty report, which showed that Dr Arthur Sleight of the American chemical giant E. I. DuPont de Nemours, in Wilmington, Delaware, had synthesized the material as a red-brown powder.[1] Sleight predicted no special properties for his creation of so long ago, but Barnaby was delighted to discover the reference: it could no longer be said that the basic chemical,

[1] Sleight's article appeared in the journal *Inorganic Chemistry* in September 1968. He is now professor of chemistry at Oregon State University and breeds llamas at his nearby ranch in his spare time. Interviewed there, he said he did no further research into the chemical and was not aware that DuPont had. However, he did not dismiss the possibility that the Russians, with their expertise in materials science, had managed to form it into a liquid with special properties.

defined in the Russian specifications, was a complete sham.

Barnaby is a veteran traveller who speaks at scientific conferences all over the world. He travels light – a couple of drip-dry shirts, a pullover and a spare pair of trousers are his preferred kit. When it became clear that answers to the technical mystery lay in Moscow and beyond, out came his battered duffle bag and off he went with the television research team.

It took several trips, dozens of meetings in back rooms and lonely waits on snow-blanketed street corners for snippets of news before he was satisfied he had some of the answers. One of the sources was a nuclear chemist who had worked on testing red mercury samples; another knew of its application in nuclear weapons. At first the Russian specifications for the material were inexplicable, but, as these experts and others opened up, Barnaby began to form a clearer image.

He learned the material had been produced as long ago as the mid-1960s at a nuclear research centre at Dubna, near Moscow. All through the days of the Cold War it had been kept a closely guarded secret, gradually being refined and adapted to new applications. Eventually it had become part of a new range of nuclear weapons for the Soviet bomb programme. Barnaby realized that if the potential of the weapons was as people were saying, the Soviets probably had an edge over the West in the days before the collapse of communism.

His first problem in understanding the technical complexities had been the strange composition of the Russian version of the material. Sleight had produced antimony mercury oxide as a powder, but all the evidence from Russia showed it could be turned into a gel that flowed like honey. Barnaby learned that in Russia a very pure form of the powder was dissolved in ordinary mercury metal, the type used in thermometers. It was then put in containers which were placed in the heart of a nuclear reactor for about twenty days. Under intense neutron bombardment, and perhaps with the addition of catalysts, the material was transformed and became a very thick and heavy cherry-red liquid.[1]

One five-megawatt nuclear reactor, Barnaby was told, could take six containers each with 40 grams of the mixture. The production of large

[1] Apparently the procedure was quite complicated and entailed mixing the powder with ordinary mercury in roughly equal molar weights, then adding other chemicals whose recipe was a closely guarded secret. After irradiation, the mixture was heated to evaporate off the remaining mercury metal, leaving behind the gel. According to the precise ratio of molar weights, various types of red mercury were fabricated, each with a different application. RM20/20 represented the fact that the molar weights of the mercury and antimony were identical.

quantities was therefore very difficult, with the entire Russian output amounting to about 60 kg a year. He was told the material was made at the closed Russian military cities of Krasnoyarsk-26 in Zhelenogorsk, Penza-19 in Zarechnly and possibly in Kazakhstan, with the red mercury powder coming from a plant in Ekaterinburg. Different types of red mercury were produced and given different code-names, such as RM20/20, RM16/24 and RM18/22. RM20/20, the type listed in so many of the Russian specifications, was allegedly used in nuclear devices.

Once the gel RM20/20 had been produced, there was a further crucial step before it could be used in an atom bomb. Radioactive chemicals known as transuranic actinides (an example would be californium-252) had to be added in minute quantities, but, once added, the gel would begin to deteriorate after about thirty days and would become substandard.

How was this used in nuclear bombs? Barnaby believed that two types of bomb were possible with red mercury. In a normal atom bomb, a ball of plutonium, encased in layers of beryllium and uranium, is surrounded by high explosive. When this is detonated, the violent inward shockwave causes the plutonium core to shrink in volume and become denser. This makes it exceed its critical mass, initiating the process known as nuclear fission. At this split second, a neutron gun fires neutrons into the plutonium. This multiplies the number of chain reactions, and causes the familiar mushroom-cloud explosion which can be measured in thousands of tons of TNT.

Barnaby found that a modified form of this type of atom bomb could be made with red mercury. Capsules of RM20/20 would be embedded in the high explosive that surrounds the plutonium. When the high explosive was detonated, and before nuclear fission took place, the red mercury would form a uniform layer between the explosive and the plutonium core. He believed it would then have several functions. It would reflect neutrons back into the core, replacing the beryllium layer for this purpose. Also, its high density would prevent the outward expansion of the plutonium when it fissioned, stopping it from disintegrating too quickly. This replaced the function of the uranium layer. And the presence in the red mercury of an actinide like californium-252, which is a powerful neutron emitter, would supplement the effect of the neutron gun. Such a weapon would produce far more deadly neutrons than the other type of device. Barnaby describes it as an unusual combination of an atom bomb and neutron bomb.

The other type of red mercury weapon that Barnaby heard about in Russia would take this a deadly step further. A small quantity of red mercury would be enclosed in a layer of spherically shaped explosive charges. When these were detonated, they would implode and put the chemical under enormous compressive force. In turn, this would make it release very high levels of energy that were bound up in red mercury's crystal structure. This energy could cause a few grams of deuterium[1] and tritium, both rare isotopes of hydrogen, to undergo a phenomenon known as fusion. This would produce the gas helium and a massive emission of neutrons and energy.

Barnaby reckoned that a bomb fabricated on these principles could weigh 4 kg or less. Given the high density of red mercury, the entire device might be no bigger than a grapefruit but have a yield of several kilotons. He realized that if all this was true, the world was at the dawn of a new type of nuclear weapon – one that could give any two-bit dictator muscle.

Its technical name was innocuous enough – the 'pure-fusion device' – but its properties were terrifying. Detonated in the air above a town or a battleground of tanks and artillery, it would produce a massive flux of high-energy neutrons that would penetrate all metal and concrete. Within range of the detonation, all life would be exterminated, leaving most of the buildings and vehicles intact.[2] The neutrons would make the area radioactive, but the radioactivity would decay within an hour or so, rendering the ground safe to occupy.

This contrasts with the types of neutron weapon deployed in the West, which leave residual radioactivity. This is because they require a nuclear fission device – in other words an atom bomb – to generate the very high temperatures for fusion.

As Yevgeny Korolev had told us way back in Ekaterinburg: 'Red mercury can make very small nuclear weapons. Saddam Hussein could make an atomic grenade the size of a grapefruit that would blow a ship out of the sea.'

Barnaby's technical findings were eventually published in *International Defense Review* in June 1994 under the heading 'Red Mercury – Is there a pure-fusion bomb for sale?' He was expecting either ridicule or fury from the nuclear establishment around the world, but there was mostly silence – and suspiciously little curiosity. On the other hand, if our own findings were right – that there was a conspiracy afoot between

1 Deuterium is a component of heavy water. Most neutron-gun designs also use small quantities of tritium and deuterium. As will be seen later, South Africa was secretly acquiring both these materials, although they were allegedly not used in the six and a half atom bombs admitted to by De Klerk in 1993.

2 The neutrons ionize the cells of the body, destroying them. They have a particularly serious effect on the central nervous system, quickly incapacitating victims.

Russia and the major Western powers to muffle all speculation – such a reaction was to be expected.

Barnaby put it this way: 'It is not clear why the authorities are so dismissive of red mercury as an ingredient in nuclear weapons. Perhaps they do not want to admit that the Russians have stolen a march on the West by developing a revolutionary new type of weapon, or they may not want to embarrass President Boris Yeltsin by acknowledging that he allows such a strategic material to be smuggled out of Russia. It is also possible that red mercury is already taken seriously by many governments and that public pronouncements of the substance as a hoax serve merely to divert attention. But, given the serious consequences of a flourishing trade in red mercury, the West should face the facts about it and grapple with the issues raised by them.'

There was one other expert who was even more alarmed than Barnaby. Dr Sam Cohen is now retired, but his mind is as sharp today as it was in the fifties when he worked as a nuclear weapons analyst on the Manhattan Project, the Allied nuclear weapons programme. Later he was credited with inventing the concept of more effective, and 'cleaner', neutron bomb devices. In 1993–4 he began delving into reports of new types of neutron bombs in Russia, and he reached the same conclusion as Barnaby – that there was indeed a new technology, unpublicized in the West.

Cohen even discovered that secret research was being conducted into a new class of high-energy chemicals in his own country – at the Department of Energy's Sandia National Laboratories in New Mexico. He had heard that this research included red mercury, and the new science was dubbed 'ballotechnics'.

By putting certain special chemicals under intense pressure from conventional explosives, the material could release huge amounts of energy at super-high temperatures. Cohen quoted an assessment from a classified presentation by a scientist at Sandia who said: 'Under certain conditions, chemical energy density transformations obtained can be greater than with high explosives and the power exceeds that of high explosives.'[1]

1 In October 1994 the Los Alamos National Laboratory, the premier US nuclear weapons design centre, announced it was conducting controlled fusion energy experiments in conjunction with scientists from Arzamas-16, its Russian counterpart. The statement said the project had brought together, for peaceful purposes, the scientists who designed the Russian and US weapons of mass destruction. 'These experiments are part of an unprecedented scientific collaboration ... encouraged at the highest levels of both governments.' It added that the detonation of high explosives had been used to produce nearly 40-million-degree temperatures in a tiny part of a gas and had produced fusion reactions.

Commented Cohen: 'This is exactly the principle of a small fusion bomb ignited by a substance like red mercury.'

In September 1994 he published his blunt conclusions about the consequences of this technology in a long article in the New York-based magazine *Spin*. 'I'm talking about a world where any nation, no matter how small – any cell of terrorists for that matter – could get its hands on a cheap micro neutron bomb the size of a baseball. Just one of these pint-size killers, equivalent to 10 tons of TNT, and capable of dispersing deadly neutrons more than one third of a mile, could easily and efficiently annihilate many thousands in a downtown district or in crucial government buildings – detonation that would make the World Trade Center bombing [in New York] seem like the explosion of a single firecracker.'

In April 1995 *New Scientist*, the respected weekly magazine published in London, weighed in with a leading article:

> A week after the bomb attack in Oklahoma City and a month after the nerve gas attack in Tokyo, it is impossible not to feel a deep chill at reports that 'red mercury', the ultimate terrorists' weapon, might really exist.
>
> Red mercury was supposedly developed in the Soviet Union, and stocks have periodically been offered for sale in the West by figures from Russia's underworld. It has been described as an explosive so powerful that it could trigger fusion in a small volume of tritium and deuterium, thus making it possible to build a neutron bomb the size of a baseball.
>
> Enough doubts remain to make two things worth doing. First, every rumour about red mercury should be investigated, if only because the trail may lead to an arms dealer with ex-Soviet connections. These are people who might have access to illegal plutonium, which it is just as vital to intercept. And secondly, the International Atomic Energy Agency should consider strict controls on sales of tritium.

Down in South Africa, press comment on red mercury was beginning to rattle South Africa's nuclear establishment, particularly when the views of Barnaby and Cohen were quoted. Establishment nerves were further jolted in January 1995 by a documentary broadcast by the SABC called 'The Colour of Death' made by investigative reporter Jacques Pauw for the peak-time current affairs programme *Agenda*. It brought out more evidence about the black market and the killings, and aired suspicions that Armscor was involved in red mercury deals.

After the documentary was aired, there was a live televised debate on the subject in which Armscor was represented by André Buys, senior manager of planning and a former head of South Africa's nuclear weapons programme during the 1980s. Said Buys on air: 'Armscor received numerous offers of red mercury, from anonymous calls and from people whom we didn't know. They just come up to us and introduce themselves ... but right from the start we were always under the impression that red mercury doesn't exist.

'Somehow these people were under the impression that we should be very interested in it. It was said in Russia that South Africa would be one of the prime clients for red mercury, and they were very frustrated if we sent them off.'

He was adamant that Dirk Stoffberg and Don Lange, who had recently died amidst allegations of red mercury peddling, had never worked for Armscor. 'Mr Stoffberg was an arms smuggler. He is not the type of person that we have had any dealings with. In Armscor we try our utmost best not to make use of the services of agents, because it is very difficult to distinguish between an honest one and an arms smuggler. Mr Stoffberg tried to portray himself as an agent of Armscor, which he was not. Neither was Mr Lange. He masqueraded as an Armscor agent, but we never did any business with him, and that was it.'

These remarks caused some amusement within South Africa's arms industry, where it was commonly said that Armscor relied heavily on agents – some of them highly suspect – during the days of sanctions. Furthermore, a few weeks before Buys appeared on this programme, Armscor had officially admitted Lange had done work for them.

Buys was particularly keen to nail the lie that red mercury was a valuable nuclear weapons material: 'The red mercury story is a hoax that has got out of hand ... I have no doubt that there could well be a connection between murders in South Africa and red mercury, because we know these people are arms smugglers. We know that this commodity, which is a phantom substance, has achieved a value of ridiculous proportions – it is more than ten times the price of gold. And there is this feeling among the smugglers that there are certain countries that are desperate to have it – including South Africa.

'I can imagine these smugglers could purchase some of this material in the hope they can make a big profit, and when they are frustrated, when we don't want to buy it, they try to get their money back ... that's when it gets extremely dangerous. I'd like to warn everybody: if you are involved in red mercury, you must stop.'

However, a few days later the debate was joined by Roelof 'Pik' Botha, the South African Minister for Mineral and Energy Affairs and a Foreign Minister in the former Nationalist government of F. W. de Klerk. In a speech to a nuclear conference at a hotel in Midrand, near Pretoria, he trumpeted the achievements of Koeberg nuclear power station but added: 'If we are to ban nuclear power because of radioactivity, perhaps we could turn to red mercury. At present there is a lively debate in South Africa on this subject. Perhaps you can assist us in ascertaining whether red mercury is a hoax or a hope – to convert into fuel for electric power stations.'

Botha's press aides explained that this was intended 'as a joke'. In the light of our Russian experience, the question was whether Botha intended it to be construed that way.

10 Tickling the Dragon's Tail

A go-between had arranged a number of meetings around Pretoria with a man who had directly worked in South Africa's nuclear weapons workshops during the 1980s, but each time he failed to show up. It was explained that he was very nervous, that he was worried he would be accused of treachery. He imagined he was being watched, and on one occasion had arrived at the door of an agreed rendezvous spot only to go back home.

Dion,[1] the man who had told us the story of the bomb removed from a mine at Witbank (Chapter 6), was no different from dozens of others whom we had finally managed to interview, except that he could provide first-hand knowledge of the sanctum where Armscor's nuclear weapons were secretly stored. It was agreed we would have one last go, and arranged to wait at a thatched bar 80 km from Johannesburg. It turned out to be a reassuringly safe distance, and this time he made it through the front door.

He had worked as an Armscor manager at the organization's Kentron Circle nuclear weapons assembly plant (later renamed Advena) and, unlike many, he had once had access to a number of other sensitive sites. The first question we wanted to resolve was how much weapons-grade uranium had been made at the Y-Plant in the fourteen years it had functioned. Officially this was about 400 kg, enough for seven A-bombs. But as we outlined in Chapter 6, it could well have been more.

Lubricated by a couple of cans of Castle beer, and a brandy and Coke, Dion lost some of his reticence and began to explain. 'There were regular deliveries of the uranium from Valindaba,' he said. 'They produced tons – far more than what they say. It was driven across in the boots of cars. It was stored inside an aluminium case with a lock. We called them "cookies". They were moved in 3- or 4-kg lots.'

He added: 'The bombs were the size of a soccer ball. One part of the bomb would be kept in one vault, and the remainder in another, and you

[1] Not his real name.

could not get access to both at the same time.' This fitted with video footage of the vaults issued by Armscor. There were ten in all, each easily large enough to walk in.

Coded locking devices were used to prevent unauthorized access, and two personnel had always to work together when moving parts of the devices, each checking the other's actions. There were two access codes for each vault, with a number of mechanical and electronic locks. A third code was needed to assemble a device, and to arm one required a key, along with a fourth code from the President. The arming process required seven people.

In the life of the nuclear programme, the vaults were allegedly used for only the six and a half devices that have been officially admitted. But Dion told a different story.

He said each vault was large enough to take several warheads. They were standing on racks like a baker's trolley. 'Sometimes I saw six of these half soccer balls in one vault. The other part of the bomb would be in one of the others, but all the vaults were used. In fact later on they added some portable walk-in safes for additional storage. The volume was too much to store in the initial ten vaults, so others had to be brought in.' Professor Wynand Mouton had told us earlier that there were other safes at Advena, but they had been empty when he inspected them.

We asked Dion whether the bombs being stored were crude atom bombs. 'Of course not: they were the latest design – thermonuclear and neutron bombs.' He said the highly enriched uranium for each device weighed 25 kg, not more than 50 kg as Mouton had indicated.

This was confirmation that De Klerk's account was false. Dion had brought correspondence showing when he was employed by Armscor and when he went to work for Kentron Circle, the subsidiary that took over nuclear weapons design and production in 1979/80. He had seen the 'cookies' and also the daily records. He added: 'The paperwork was shredded as soon as it was finished with. It showed the plan was to make twenty-five, but I think there were only twenty-four completed – that was how much enriched uranium was brought in.' He said in his period at Advena about seventeen bombs were built – all advanced designs.

Dion said a 'high-powered colonel' from the quartermaster-general's office ran the building. With the help of Military Intelligence agents, employees were kept misinformed about what was going on. There was a deliberate policy of circulating disinformation to keep everyone confused: 'There were two or three guys from army intelligence with us.

Their job was to mislead people. They would go to one section of guys and give them a certain story, and give another section a different story. It created lots of uncertainty.'

He believed that one of those 'stories' was that all South Africa's nuclear weapons had been destroyed. 'They tried to make me believe that it had been done, but I think it was a cover story,' said the former Armscor manager. 'You don't just melt these things down: there were millions involved.

'They came to see me after I left Advena, and before De Klerk made his announcement. They said: "Don't worry about what you see in the papers about us dismantling the stuff." They wanted to let me know they were still busy, and that what was said in the papers was all I was supposed to know.'

Dion's testimony indicated that the crude six and a half weapons, known as gun devices, did indeed exist as De Klerk had said. However, it seemed they dated from an earlier period in South Africa's nuclear pro-gramme – probably the late 1970s – and had been superseded by much more advanced technology. Dion also recalled that nuclear material from earlier bombs had sometimes been 'borrowed' to make more advanced models.

This was powerful testimony that South Africa's nuclear programme was much larger than admitted, but it flew in the face of international opinion. The Institute for Science and International Security (ISIS), a think-tank in Washington, conducted a special study of South Africa's programme. David Albright, its director, was allowed to interview AEC and Armscor officials and to visit some of the nuclear sites. His report, published in May 1994, restates South Africa's official line on the nuclear weapons programme and appears to confirm the De Klerk decla-ration.

Albright was told the AEB had completed its first device, christened 'Melba', in September 1979, but it had been fit only for underground detonation on a rig. Then Kentron Circle/Advena took over and in April 1982 finished a second, another 'pre-qualification' model, which was also unsuitable for deployment. The ISIS report explains: 'Armscor engi-neers emphasized reliability, safety and security ... design refinement and requalification of the hardware took several years ... The first qualified gun-type device was not completed until August 1987. This could be delivered by a modified Buccaneer bomber. By the time the programme was cancelled, three more deliverable weapons had been completed.'

Albright was full of praise for De Klerk's actions in dismantling them: 'South Africa's renunciation of nuclear weapons is a major success for international efforts to stop the proliferation of nuclear weapons.'

However, others studying the published evidence were more worried about the inconsistencies in South Africa's story. The Oxford Research Group, a British think-tank of nuclear scientists, queried the disclosures by de Klerk and the AEC. In a paper prepared in February 1995 for delegates to the Nuclear Non-Proliferation Treaty review conference in New York, it asked why South Africa's programme was apparently so primitive, and way below its capabilities.

The ORG commented: 'A country able to design and construct sophisticated uranium enrichment facilities and develop a laser isotope separation system inevitably has a cadre of scientists and engineers able to design and fabricate sophisticated nuclear weapons.' It said such scientists would be capable of designing implosion weapons rather than the gun-type, which allegedly used more than 50 kg of highly enriched uranium. 'An implosion weapon could use 20 kilograms.' The ORG said:

> South Africans would have been able to construct about 20 nuclear weapons rather than six; weapons that could have been used on delivery systems more sophisticated than combat aircraft, such as surface to surface missiles.
>
> With South Africa's space-launch capabilities and ambitions it is hard to believe that its strategists had not developed nuclear warheads more sophisticated than their primitive gun-type design ...

The paper said it was raising these suspicions because, under the De Klerk government, all documents relating to the nuclear weapons programme had been shredded and important facilities involved in the programme were totally destroyed. It then posed a string of blunt questions: 'If there was nothing to hide, why was all the evidence deliberately eliminated? Exactly how much highly enriched uranium was produced in Valindaba and at what enrichments? Were more nuclear weapons produced than those admitted to? If so, what happened to them? Had some group hidden nuclear weapons away? Had South African nuclear weapons designers developed implosion-type weapons? If not, why not? If Israel, India and Pakistan can produce up-to-date nuclear weapons, it is, to say the least, hard to believe that South Africa could not have done so as well.'

One of the authors of the paper was Dr Frank Barnaby, the expert on nuclear proliferation who has also studied the red mercury mystery. Six months after the ORG paper was circulated, he said there had been no response. 'It is a pity the new South African government does not see the merits of what we have said. It could greatly assist international nuclear disarmament by shaming other nuclear weapons powers into breaking down the walls of secrecy surrounding their nuclear programmes too.'

As the ORG had remarked, the official details of the bombs produced by South Africa only served to emphasize the apparent technological short-comings of the country's nuclear scientists and engineers. The chosen model was a 'gun' or 'cannon' device, similar in principle to the US bomb, known as 'Little Boy', dropped on Hiroshima. It relied on the fact that a quantity of nuclear material would fission and explode when it reached a certain weight, this point being known as the critical mass. With weapons-grade uranium (U-235) this point would be reached with 50 to 55 kg of material, the exact amount depending on the level of enrichment.

In South Africa's gun weapon a lump of uranium weighing approximately 15 kg was fired down a specially designed barrel into a hollowed-out piece of the same material weighing about 40 kg. When the pieces combined, they formed a super-critical mass that exploded with a force of 10 to 18 kilotons. According to the AEC, there was no form of neu-tron initiator to make the fission process more efficient: the design relied on stray neutrons in the atmosphere – from cosmic rays for example.

The gun mechanism had a fail-safe system to prevent detonation if the propellant fired accidentally. The barrel was in two sections which were normally pivoted out of alignment. On readying the bomb for action, a motor rotated one section so that it locked in line with the other. This also prevented another danger: that the smaller lump of uranium might slide down the barrel and mate with the larger piece. In such a circum-stance, they would come together too slowly to create a powerful fission explosion, but the bomb would still 'fizzle' and create a dangerous radioactive outburst.

The gun mechanism and the propellant were developed by a military company called Kentron South, in Somerset West, some 50 km east of Cape Town. In the early 1970s Kentron South came under the National Institute for Defence Research. The company eventually amalgamated with the nearby explosives plant of Somchem, and became part of Armscor when that was formed in 1977.

Richard, a scientist who worked on the programme to design nuclear warheads, disclosed that one of the driving forces behind the programme was Dr André Buys, now senior manager in charge of planning at

Armscor and the man who was so sure red mercury was a hoax when he appeared on television in January 1995 (see Chapter 9). Buys was a ballistics expert who began developing the bomb mechanism at Kentron South in about 1972.

Said Richard: 'Buys had a special area separate from the rest of the plant where tests were done on the gun and its propellant. It was a large room, where firing tests were done on the gun mechanism. We knew he was making a bomb, but it was very secret.'

Richard was also aware that the purpose of the bomb was military – in contrast to the story from the current head of the AEC, Dr Waldo Stumpf, who told Albright that in the early 1970s his organization had only established an internal committee to study the effect of peaceful nuclear explosives for mining – and a scale model of a mechanism, without its uranium, was ready for testing at Kentron South by May 1974.

Our source said work on a complete nuclear weapon was nearing completion by this time: 'I was there. It was very secret, but all the development for the gun mechanism was finished by 1976 and we didn't see much of Buys again. He played a very significant part. He is one of the fathers of the bomb.'

We learned that Buys's work moved to Pelindaba, where a special assembly and test plant had been built in an isolated valley. The buildings are still there – part of a military base. Buildings 5100 and 5200 were laboratories and engineering workshops. The more interesting construction was an isolated block called Building 5000, where the actual atom bombs were assembled.

That building is now deserted. Within the security fence are the dried skeletons of animals that became trapped inside. When we visited it in December 1994, there were old phone books in the entrance hall from the 1976 era. On a desk inside the security post lay a ledger for 1976, recording the visitors who entered this most secret of installations. The names are a roll call of people who contributed to the project: T. Hickey, G. Bekker, G. S. Stoltz, H. C. Crews and M. Trumpelmann. In 1980, when Building 5000 was mainly for storage, appears the signature of Dr Stumpf.

It was in Building 5000 that Buys's first atom bomb was prepared for testing. According to Richard, the slug of uranium that would be fired down the gun when detonated was made up of six slices. The object was to discover how big the slug had to be to create a critical mass when it was fired. 'They found that all they needed was five slices,' he said.

This test was a highly dangerous process known as 'tickling the dragon's tail'. The two pieces of uranium were brought near to one another very slowly, but never close enough to touch, and were monitored to see if nuclear fission was about to begin. Had the two pieces accidentally combined, Building 5000 and its personnel would have been destroyed.

Sources said the first weapon had been finished in 1977, and several others were completed before the buildings fell into disuse in 1981. They confirmed the simplicity of the weapon design but, significantly, placed the manufacture of the six and half devices declared by De Klerk eight years earlier than their official completion date. Richard told us that by 1981 all six and a half weapons had been finished. He added, 'The seventh had a deformed barrel; otherwise it was also deployable.'

Announcing his country's uranium enrichment programme in 1970, Prime Minister Vorster said: 'South Africa will in no way be limited in the promotion of the peaceful application of nuclear energy.' It was a clear enough statement of his intentions, and yet, like many similar pronouncements over the past thirty years, it provoked little international comment and no action.

Equally significant was a scientific study that the AEB produced in this period, and which by some oversight was deposited in several South African public research libraries in 1973.

The document, number PEL224,[1] was an analysis predicting the seismic effects of 'constructive nuclear explosions' at settlements in different parts of South Africa. The author, Dr J. V. Retief, worked at Pelindaba and later played a key role in the bomb development programme. He had gathered together information on population distributions in remote areas where 10-kiloton, 100-kiloton or 1-megaton atomic devices could be detonated without serious seismic damage on the homes of white populations. Retief concluded that sparsely populated areas such as the northern and north-western Cape were the best sites.

1 The document was discovered by Professor Renfrew Christie, dean of research at the University of the Western Cape in Cape Town, who was jailed for ten years in 1980 for passing secret plans to the ANC. He was charged with leaking Retief's report to the banned organization but was acquitted of this charge when he proved the report was available in several libraries. However, he was found guilty of passing to the ANC other information related to nuclear matters. Christie has accused South Africa of having 2-kiloton nuclear shells for use in the G5 and G6 artillery guns, and possibly 10-kiloton bombs for delivery by aircraft. His suspicions about the nuclear programme were first aroused in 1967 when he was a soldier. At an ammunition store at Lenz, south of the township of Soweto near Johannesburg, he spotted a well-guarded bunker with six layers of barbed wire and radioactivity signs. His unit was not supposed to go near, but came upon it when they took a wrong turn. A number of sources said South Africa had acquired a nuclear weapon in that period.

1 South Africa's new Rooivalk attack helicopter can be equipped with ZT3 and
ZT35 missiles (inset), a revolutionary weapon system that can burn its way
through armoured steel up to 1 metre thick. It is said to use a form of red mercury
technology. Near its target, a special chemical in the nose of the missile is ignited,
creating a super-high-temperature blow torch.

2 *Left*: Durban arms dealer Don Lange with former Miss South Africa Sandy McCrystal. Police believe Lange's death was rigged to look like suicide.

3. Arms dealer Dirk Stoffberg and his wife Suzanne. She abandoned her family in Germany and thought her love for him would last forever. He would never let her out of his sight and became annoyed if she looked at another man. They both died in a pool of blood.

4 *Above*: Happier times . . . John Scott, the British company director of Wacker Chemicals in South Africa, enjoys a festive meal with his family. Shortly after this picture was taken the entire family was found slaughtered at their home. Police said he had murdered his family and then killed himself. Others suspect they were all murdered.

5. Alan Kidger, the British international sales director of Thor Chemicals in South Africa. His dismembered body, found in the boot of his car in Soweto, sparked one of the country's biggest murder inquiries.

6   *Left*: This eight-inch-long container was photographed at the home of arms dealer Dirk Stoffberg only a few days before his death. The label indicates it contained red mercury.

7   This Russian-made container purportedly held 20 kilograms of red mercury. Its attempted sale to Israeli buyers led to the death threat against Hounam.

8   Lieutenant-Colonel Charles Landman (with sunglasses), chief investigating officer of the South African police task force set-up to solve the red mercury killings.

9   President Nelson Mandela of South Africa (left) stands for the national anthem at the Dexsa '94 defence exhibition in Johannesburg. At his side are Brigadier Leon Wessels, Chief of Staff Witwatersrand Command of the South African National Defence Force (centre), and Johan Moolman, chairman of Armscor. Mandela later said he was pleased to note Armscor was committed to transparency and accountability: 'This is a challenge facing all South Africans.'

10   *Left*: In 1993, Roelof 'Pik' Botha, then South Africa's Foreign Minister, presented Hans Blix, director-general of the International Atomic Energy Agency, with a miniature plough to symbolize the dismantling of the country's nuclear weapons. The plough was made out of materials from one of the devices.
11   Professor Wynand Mouton, 'The Terminator' of South Africa's declared nuclear weapons stockpile. He said he could not be sure everything was destroyed.

12   A forest of chimneys marks the skyline of Valindaba, whose Y-Plant secretly made South Africa's weapons-grade uranium.

13   One of two operators cycles between the banks of control equipment at the vast Z-Plant where South Africa made low-enriched uranium. It supposedly supplied the Koeberg nuclear power reactor near Cape Town, but there are suspicions that some of the material was used in nuclear weapons.

14 The Skua, a target drone built by Kentron in South Africa. Sources said it can carry a nuclear warhead a distance of 800 kilometres.

15 The mighty G5 in action. Considered to be one of the world's best artillery pieces, this South African howitzer is capable of delivering a nuclear shell.

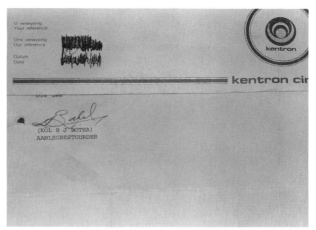

16 *Left*: These vaults contained South Africa's first nuclear weapons. An elaborate security system prevented a complete device from being removed without permission from the head of state. 17 This letter signed by Colonel Hendrik 'Hennie' Botha in 1982 shows that he was the 'aanlegbestuurder', or facility manager, of Kentron Circle. This Armscor plant made South Africa's nuclear weapons. Botha was still manager of this bomb programme in 1984 when he was arrested in London and accused of sanctions busting in what became known as the Coventry Four affair. Later, he was inexplicably released and never stood trial.

18 The Coventry Four pose happily with their wives at a press conference in Pretoria in 1984. They had just announced they would not return to Britain to face sanctions-busting charges. Seated left to right are 'Fanie' de Jager, 'Randy' Metelerkamp, Colonel 'Hennie' Botha and 'Koos' la Grange. Evidence now shows that at the time Botha was head of South Africa's secret nuclear weapons plant. Metelerkamp was head of procuring materials for nuclear warheads from abroad and De Jager was the finance chief.

19 The mission control centre at South Africa's mini 'Cape Kennedy', a high-security missile testing range. South Africa had advanced plans for satellite launchers. However, the United States applied pressure to halt the programme when it realized the real intention was to create intercontinental ballistic missiles.

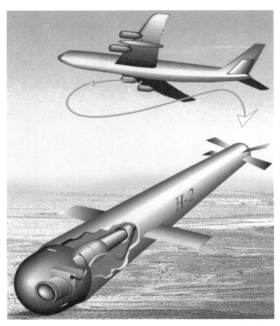

20 An artist's impression of South Africa's 'Hento' glide-bomb, designed to deliver a nuclear weapon. Launched from a Boeing 707, the missile has rectractable fins and a TV guidance system in the nose. It is believed to be the forerunner of the Hakim air-to-surface missile now marketed by the British company GEC.

As a direct result of Dr Retief's search for a safe test range, a site in the Northern Cape near the town of Upington was chosen for an underground explosion. It was an area of the Kalahari desert known as Vastrap. In 1974, an order was given by Prime Minister Vorster for digging to begin in secret, called Operation Ploegskaar (Ploughshare).

A South African mining company began to excavate three shafts with equipment previously used in the attempted rescue of hundreds of miners trapped in the country's worst mining disaster, at Coalbrook in 1960. One shaft flooded because of the geological conditions and was abandoned. The first completed shaft, PG-1, was 385 metres deep and was ready by 1976. PG-2, 216 metres deep, was finished the following year. Both were 90 cm in diameter.

The AEC hoped that no one around the world would be watching such a remote spot, but a Soviet area-survey satellite, Cosmos 922, passed over the Kalahari in June 1977. Almost certainly the signs of construction work were spotted at this point, because a 69A Cosmos 932 satellite was launched the following month with the specific aim of photographing the area. On 22 July and on the following three days it made low-altitude passes.[1] After its re-entry back to earth, it was recovered on 2 August and its film when processed showed the test shafts nearing completion.

In an almost unprecedented move, Leonid Brezhnev, the Soviet President, issued a statement through Itar-Tass, the official news agency, on 21 August saying: 'According to information reaching here, work is now nearing completion in the South African Republic for the creation of the nuclear weapon and preparations are being held for carrying out tests.'[2] On 28 August the *Washington Post* said the data had been confirmed by the Americans. A US official was quoted as saying, 'I'd say we were 99 per cent certain that the construction was preparation for an atomic test.'

There is doubt whether the story would have been disclosed if Brezhnev had remained silent. Evidence points to some of the intelli-

---

[1] The satellite's orbit passed over south-east Zaïre, where, at the time, there was alleged to be a leased enclave used as a test site for rockets and cruise missiles by OTRAG (Orbital Transport and Rockets AG), a West German company.

[2] It appears that Russia knew not only about the test site but of the atom bomb programme too. This may be connected with a spy swap that took place in 1969 between Moscow and Bonn. According to Chinese intelligence sources, several West Germans held in the Soviet Union were swapped with Soviet spy Victor Loginov. The puzzling aspect of this is that Loginov had been caught spying in South Africa and had been secretly handed over to the West Germans.

gence community in Washington already knowing about the test preparations, and turning a blind eye to events in the Kalahari.

In 1982, Commodore Dieter Gerhardt, head of South Africa's main naval base at Simon's Town, near Cape Town, was arrested as a Soviet agent. He later said Moscow had warned Washington of the South African nuclear programme in 1976, a year before Cosmos flew, and there had been a secret meeting between the two powers to discuss it. Apparently, the Soviet representatives sought US co-operation in bringing the programme to an end. Gerhardt said one Soviet suggestion was an air strike on the Y-Plant at Pelindaba, but the US rejected this idea.

Details released by SIPRI, the Stockholm Peace Research Institute, show that the US 56A Big Bird satellite was looking down on the Vastrap area in mid-July 1977, making several passes directly over the test shafts. This was at least a week before the Russian satellite flew over the same spot, and also suggests the United States had decided to remain merely observers.

With test preparations in the public eye, the Western powers were forced to put pressure on South Africa to cease activity at Vastrap. On 22 August the French Foreign Minister, Louis de Guiringaud, told South Africa there would be 'grave consequences' if the test of the bomb went ahead, and hinted that the Koeberg reactor contract might be jeopardized. France had been told that South Africa was about to conduct a 'peaceful nuclear explosion', for earth-moving and mining applications, but clearly Guiringaud did not believe this was the real aim. He said in a radio interview: 'It is not possible to distinguish between a peaceful atomic explosion and an atomic explosion for purposes of military nuclear testing.'

The next day, Defence Minister P. W. Botha replied sternly to the attacks, telling the world that the rumours were 'unbelievable and wholly and totally unfounded'. But the test was cancelled and the test shafts were sealed.[1]

Vorster was undaunted by the international criticism. On 25 August he brought a stamping, cheering crowd to its feet when he said: 'The time will arrive when South Africa will have no option, small as it is, but to say to the world: "So far, and no further."' Owen Horwood, the Finance Minister, was even more specific. He told a party rally on 30

[1] A reporter from the *Sunday Star* in Johannesburg was able to visit the Vastrap nuclear test site in 1993. He interviewed a cook who had worked there in the 1970s. She recalled she had to cook kosher food for the visitors, suggesting there were Israeli nuclear experts in attendance.

August that his country would develop a nuclear weapon if it was deemed necessary. 'If we wish to do things with our nuclear potential, we will jolly well do so according to our own decisions and our own judgement. America cannot pressure us. We will not allow it.'

By this stage the CIA was determined to find out what was happening at Valindaba. The agency brought in a small plane to Pretoria with infrared sensors and cameras slung underneath. It was registered to the ambassador but flown 'for sport' by Colonel Alvin M. Crews, the military attaché, and two other operatives. Crews was instructed to fly over the Y-Plant and measure infra-red radiation from its chimneys. Apparently, for six months Crews made these 'recreational' trips around the skies of Valindaba, until in April 1979 he was spotted by Colonel 'Pine' Pienaar, a security colonel at Pelindaba, and three Mirage fighters were scrambled. The US plane was forced down and Crews and his two assistants were expelled from the country. To mark Pretoria's anger, its ambassador was recalled from Washington for a while.

When Armscor was asked in 1993 about the Vastrap affair, a spokesman gave out the following statement: 'South Africa was preparing for the capability to do a scientific underground nuclear test in 1977. This preparation work was terminated by the head of state when it became known that international opinion turned against him.'

The behaviour of Botha, the statement by the French and that of Armscor all indicate that a nuclear detonation[1] would have gone ahead in 1977 if international pressure had not stopped it. However, it is now officially claimed that the first of South Africa's six and half weapons, itself a crude test device, was not completed until September 1979, some two years later. Pelindaba maintains it planned only a dummy underground test of the bomb mechanism. No functional bomb could be tried out, it is now claimed, because there was simply not enough weapons-grade uranium from the Y-Plant by this stage.

As with previous South African evidence, the world of nuclear diplomacy overlooked the inconsistencies and the Vastrap row quickly subsided. However, there was soon a bigger challenge to South Africa's claims that it had no nuclear ambitions. On 22 September 1979, an American Vela

1 Events at Vastrap may, however, be only part of the real story. The *Nuclear Axis*, by Zdenek Cervenka and Barbara Rogers, published in 1978, claimed that in the 1970s there were a number of officially reported 'tremors' in the northern Cape and Namib desert. Sources involved in the nuclear programme were quoted as saying these were small underground tests, one being in the third quarter of 1976.

early-warning satellite spotted the characteristic double flash[1] of an atomic explosion in the southern Indian Ocean, near South Africa's Prince Edward Island. The implications were serious both for the NPT and for proponents of the Partial Test Ban Treaty which had been signed in 1963. The betting in the press was on a joint Israeli/South African experiment – an alarming scenario for the United States, with its commitment to non-proliferation.

Worries were further raised when P. W. Botha, South Africa's Prime Minister, said three days later that aggressors 'might find out that we have military weapons they do not know about'. President Jimmy Carter ordered an official inquiry into the event by a panel of scientists chaired by Professor Jack Ruina of the Massachusetts Institute of Technology. Initially it was decided that a nuclear explosion had probably occurred, but, on reconsidering, they said the double-flash phenomenon could have been caused by technical malfunction or 'possibly a consequence of the impact of a small meteoroid on the satellite'. It was 'probably not from a nuclear explosion', said Ruina, creating enough doubt to save any further diplomatic upset.

However, the evidence soon piled up against the Ruina panel's conclusions. A radio telescope in Puerto Rico detected a ripple moving outwards through the ionosphere from where the explosion apparently occurred. Sonar detectors measured signals near Prince Edward Island. Personnel at Syowa Base in Antarctica reported a patch of auroral light a few seconds after the Vela event. The Los Alamos National Laboratory in New Mexico – America's nuclear weapons lab – said this could have come from the electromagnetic pulse of a nuclear blast. It emerged that sheep in Australia had swallowed unusually high quantities of iodine, an indicator of radiation. Dr Van Middlesworth of the University of Tennessee had been doing studies on them for the US Department of Energy. He said he had spotted large increases after previous French nuclear tests, and the increase in 1979, although not as big, was 'puzzling'.

In New Zealand, short-life fission products of a nuclear explosion were detected. The Institute of Nuclear Science in Wellington said the readings could be explained only by a recent atom blast of 2 to 4 kilotons. It also turned out that a US Tiros-N meteorological satellite had detected an unusually large burst of electron precipitation. According to

1 When an atom bomb detonates, there is a flash of light followed by a fireball which for a period of about 300 milliseconds ionizes the air and blocks any further light emission.

Los Alamos, this was probably from a 'pre-existing auroral arc', but it also said the readings were 'not inconsistent' with a surface nuclear blast.

In addition, scientists knowledgeable about Vela's detectors (known as bangmeters) came to its defence.[1] The satellite had detected similar double flashes on forty-one previous occasions, and each one had proved to be a nuclear test – on the earlier occasions, by China or France.

There was also evidence of naval shipping activity. Simon's Town base had been under exceptionally high security for several months. It was reported that US intelligence had tracked Israeli naval ships heading for the area; allegedly they had Taiwanese naval officers on board. Also, the alleged nuclear test was in an unusual area of the ocean where the ionosphere comes close to the earth's surface, making explosions difficult to detect, a phenomenon called the Cape Town Anomaly.[2]

As the evidence mounted, two American studies by the Defense Intelligence Agency and the Naval Research Laboratory in the United States concluded that a nuclear explosion of a little less than 3 kilotons had occurred. Abdul Minty, who has campaigned for twenty years against South Africa's nuclear programme on behalf of the Anti-Apartheid Movement, and who is now an adviser to the Mandela government on nuclear proliferation, maintains the Vela satellite had been moved and was not meant to have seen what it did: 'Subsequently the Vela satellite was tested. It was found to be absolutely accurate and all its previous recordings were accurate. So it looked as if it was some kind of cover-up.'

Dieter Gerhardt, the Soviet spy, said Vela had detected a joint Israeli–South African test. On 20 February 1994 he told Des Blow of the South African newspaper *City Press* that the test was called Operation Phoenix: 'The explosion was clean and was not supposed to be detected. But they were not as smart as they thought and the weather changed – so the Americans were able to pick it up.'

1 Vela was not the only thing that apparently went wrong that day. A United States Air Force plane equipped to collect radioactive fallout was ordered to fly to the site from Australia. Apparently, it developed engine trouble and arrived too late to get any clinching evidence.

2 In 1960 the *New York Times* reported that in 1958, under the cloak of International Geophysical Year, the United States conducted secret atomic weapons tests in the area of the Anomaly, aided by South Africa. The tests were called Project Argus and were aimed at analysing the effect of explosions on the ionosphere, which is responsible for the long-distance reception of radio waves.

In his book about the Israeli nuclear programme, *The Samson Option* (Faber and Faber, London, 1991), American author Seymour Hersh says a former Israeli government official had disclosed that the September 1979 event was one of three nuclear tests carried out in that period, for a low-yield nuclear artillery shell. Hersh said Israel had signed an agreement before the 1979 tests for the sale to South Africa of technology and equipment for the manufacture of low-yield 175-mm and 203-mm nuclear artillery shells. This is said to have caused an internal dispute, with senior Israeli officials protesting that South Africa was getting 'the best stuff we got'.[1]

Critical Mass,[2] a book examining nuclear proliferation, quoted an Israeli source who said there were three tests in 1979, all conducted under thick cloud cover. 'There was a storm and we figured it would block Vela, but there was a gap in the weather – a window – and Vela got blinded by the flash.'

Waldo Stumpf, the AEC's chief executive, strenuously denies South Africa's involvement in the Vela incident. He said in 1994: 'There is no explanation' for what the Vela satellite apparently spotted. However, at a coffee-bar in the affluent Hyde Park area of Johannesburg's northern suburbs, we heard a different view. Jan,[3] a senior South African military strategist with the Nationalist government during the 1980s, agreed to talk. He said he had had sleepless nights worrying about whether to meet us, but in the end he had decided there needed to be disclosure.

He said he was informed in secret briefings that the Vela satellite had picked up a small nuclear detonation. 'The test was noticed, but it was condoned,' he said. 'The West perceived us as being friendly, and as long as we didn't flash too much in public we were OK.' Jan disclosed that Israel was heavily involved, and Israeli ships were in the area to observe the results. There had also been a Taiwanese presence.

'My guess is that they shared in the technology and must have got something out of it as well,' Jan continued. 'We were a group of pariah

1 Hersh also disclosed that Israel had formed three nuclear-capable artillery battalions, each with twelve self-propelled 175-mm cannons. These had been created after the 1973 Yom Kippur War, and each weapon had at least three nuclear shells. They could be fired only on direct orders from the Prime Minister as relayed through the Minister of Defence and the army chief of staff to the artillery battalion commander.

2 *Critical Mass* by William E. Burrows and Robert Windrem, Simon and Schuster, London, 1994.

3 Not his real name.

states, known as the "troika", who were very close to each other from a military point of view. There was a lot of co-operation taking place between the Israelis, the South Africans and the Taiwanese. The South Africans were actually involved in combat in Israel, and the Israelis were involved in combat in South Africa.'

According to South Africa's official story, none of its six and a half weapons was low-yield, or small enough to fire from an artillery gun. The sixth and last weapon South Africa has admitted completing is said to have weighed 900 kg, and was 1.8 metres long and 65 cm in diameter. Jan, like Richard, confirmed that these atom bombs were completed in the 1970s, not in the 1980s as his country claimed. He said that in parallel with this there was a secret programme to produce low-yield tactical nuclear weapons of the type tested near Prince Edward Island.

He said the early atom bombs were regarded as 'museum pieces' and were pensioned off soon after they had been built. By this time South Africa had a formidable arsenal of much more advanced nuclear devices for offensive as well as defensive use. 'They just kept the museum pieces so that if the wheels came off we could pull them out and say: "This is all we've got. This is the extent of our nuclear development. We're kind of in the Dark Ages with our nuclear development."

'They were never perceived for domestic consumption [in a potential civil war with the black South Africans]. It was a case of, If push comes to shove, we'll take out Lusaka, Harare and a few other places, and send a message to the Cubans to stay out. Then it was realized that a much better alternative would be a tactical nuclear weapon, like artillery shells.

'Conventional atom bombs would cause huge radioactive damage,' said Jan. 'They tried to get away from that. The attitude was, We're here to stay in this country; we may have to fight a battle here, so we should make something that would cause minimal damage and maximum casualties.'

In 1982 P. W. Botha warned that, if violence was used as a final instrument against his country, something would happen that the instigators of the violence could 'not have dreamed'. He said his country had not begun to resort to the weapons it could use under great pressure. Again, the evidence clashed with De Klerk's account that South Africa had never intended to use nuclear weapons offensively.

Even before the fuss over Vastrap, South Africa was in deep trouble with the United Nations, where a discussion was taking place on a comprehensive international arms embargo. It duly came into force as

Resolution 418 in December 1977, with the Vastrap controversy giving the embargo added impetus.

Anticipating further isolation, the Pretoria government had defiantly formed a new organization in April 1977 to take charge of South Africa's military production. It was called the Armaments Corporation of South Africa Limited, or Armscor, and brought together the nation's major armament plants to spearhead a drive for military self-sufficiency.

In parallel with this move, Prime Minister Vorster asked his senior officials to recommend future plans for the nuclear weapons programme, and his successor, P. W. Botha, formed an action committee in October 1978 to draw up details. In 1978 part of the nuclear weapons programme was therefore transferred from the AEB at Pelindaba to an Armscor subsidiary called Kentron Circle.

The official story is that Pelindaba personnel continued to work on South Africa's first device, known as 'Melba,' which was finished in September 1979, but the remaining bombs were the work of the new Armscor operation during the 1980s – a timetable our sources said was false. Kentron Circle, we were told, played no part in the construction of the 'museum pieces' but embarked on a much more advanced programme to produce tactical and strategic warheads.

De Klerk[1] had said in March 1993 that no advanced thermonuclear explosives had been manufactured, but, said Jan, that was just what Armscor was contracted to produce when Kentron Circle opened, the plan being to create weapons of huge destructive power. He appeared to be indicating that South Africa had mastered the manufacture of boosted nuclear weapons. An ordinary fission bomb can be made much more powerful if its fissioning is enhanced by neutrons from thermonuclear fusion reactions. Such a weapon is not strictly a thermonuclear-type hydrogen bomb, measuring its power in many megatons, but more of an intermediate-technology device. However, with careful design it is possible to achieve yields of hundreds of kilotons.

Jan said South Africa had long been gathering together the expertise to develop such a deadly arsenal: 'The concept of the neutron bomb was not rocket science to these people, and money was no object.'

The new premises at Kentron Circle were tucked away in a valley 15 km east of Pelindaba. From the highway, all that can be seen is a banked racetrack and a cross-country proving-ground for testing military vehi-

1 In an interview only weeks before De Klerk's announcement, the AEC's chief executive, Dr Waldo Stumpf, denied South Africa had a nuclear weapons programme.

cles. However, in a dip beyond the track there are three buildings hidden behind earth mounds. The largest, on the left of the approach road, is the production building, where advanced nuclear bombs were developed and manufactured. A central building, decked with three lightning conductors, contained a manufacturing facility for making explosive lenses, and a third building, to the right, was a service block.

The production building also housed the ten room-sized vaults that had been described to us by Dion, the Kentron Circle manager. This area, the most secure in the entire plant, was approached through two giant steel doors, and each had a fail-safe electronic security system. The vaults were in two rows of five, the upper row approached by a metal staircase. We heard that in 1980 a plaque was unveiled in one of the bomb vaults to commemorate the opening, which was marked with a party for hundreds of people. Present were Defence Minister Magnus Malan, Finance Minister Owen Horwood, Foreign Minister Pik Botha, F. W. de Klerk and Prime Minister P. W. Botha, among others. 'They talked about everything but the bomb,' recalled one of the invited guests.

Dion described how two people had to be present when a vault was opened, and there were strict procedures for keeping the area clean. 'You entered into a white area, then crossed to a blue area where you took off your clothes. Then you moved into the red area where you wore special shoes and overalls. When you came out there was a special machine to check your hands, and a Geiger counter to check your body.

By 1988 the Kentron Circle buildings – by now renamed Advena – were no longer large enough to accommodate all the engineers and scientists working on the nuclear programme. A further complex, known as Advena Central Laboratories, was opened on a neighbouring site at a cost of R36 million ($10 million). Armscor has admitted that by this stage it was working on advanced gun-type and implosion-type nuclear weapons. The implosion programme was a drive towards greater miniaturization but it is claimed that no weapon was built. 'No implosion tests were done up to the time that the nuclear programme was terminated,' said Armscor. 'And no prototypes were constructed.' It said the completion of an implosion weapon was ten years away.

The new Advena Laboratories had over a hundred offices, a clean room for advanced electronics manufacturing, and an integration building for assembling advanced weapons with their delivery systems. The latter had a long central bay, big enough for a ballistic missile, large entry doors at each end, and service rooms where the balancing of rockets for re-entry from space could be undertaken. There were further workshops where highly enriched uranium could be machined into shape. There were also high-security storage vaults to hold 'small' uranium warheads.

An explosion test chamber was capable of withstanding a blast equivalent to 10 kg of TNT, allowing experiments with shaped charges. It was equipped with high-speed instruments including flash X-ray cameras to measure blast phenomena through reinforced windows. Elsewhere on the site were six bunkers and a control building for the storage and testing of explosives.

The extent of the complex was indicative that an even bigger nuclear weapons programme was under way by the late 1980s, and the official line that no devices were produced there was also disputed by our sources. Dion told us that right through to the end of the programme, in 1990, the AEC continued to supply Advena with the fissionable materials needed for weapons.[1] He could not describe the type of weapons being built, except that they were the latest design.

We then met Jeff, a top nuclear weapons expert who had worked on the new range of bombs. 'We did make thermonuclear warheads,' he said, 'We made them for the glide bomb and for missiles. Making an ordinary atom bomb is *Encyclopædia Britannica* stuff. It is a different matter if you have to hang something on an aircraft or fit it into an artillery shell.'

He said the whole programme from 1979 onwards was geared towards making battlefield weapons: 'From a military standpoint you have to carry these things where you want to use them. We produced a total weapons system, including a thermonuclear weapon. It was a battlefield weapon as opposed to the Hiroshima type threatening a civilian target.'

Jeff said the new range of weapons used substantially less than 55 kg of uranium, the weight provided by AEC officials. 'I'm not sure why they would give that figure,' he said. Armscor and the AEC had also said that no South African devices employed a neutron trigger, a mechanism that gives pinpoint detonation in the more advanced type of nuclear weapon. 'That would also be inaccurate,' said Jeff. 'Anyone who designs a weapon like that would say you have to trigger it.'

Both Jeff and Dion said beryllium was used in the bombs being produced, in conflict with the AEC, which claimed that tungsten was employed, giving much inferior results.

1 The AEC also had a high-powered computer department where simulation studies could be done on different types of design, and this was used by Advena until the programme closed in the 1990s.

Jeff said a range of designs for implosion weapons using plutonium was produced and developed to the point where the weapons could easily be built. However, he had been informed by his military superiors that the designs had simply been shelved. 'That is what we were always told, but we all worked in cells and were told things only on a need-to-know basis,' he said. 'After speaking to you, I'm no longer sure.'

He explained that the Angolan crisis in the 1970s played a crucial part in South Africa's thinking. In April 1974 the regime of Marcello Caetano in Portugal collapsed and the country's colonies, including Angola and Mozambique, were soon abandoned. In January 1975 an agreement for a peaceful transition to independence in Angola – the Alvor Accords – broke down and three liberation movements began to fight for control of the country.

South Africa and the CIA feared victory by the MPLA, a Marxist group backed by the Soviet Union. While the CIA provided financial backing for the rival UNITA and FNLA groups, South Africa was persuaded to invade from the south in support. The project was known as Operation Savannah.

At one point SADF forces were said to have fought to within firing range of Luanda, the Angolan capital, but then the United States Senate imposed a total ban on the continuation of the crusade. Daniel Moynihan, US ambassador to the UN, seemed unsure how to describe the now faltering US alliance with South Africa. 'We are doing the same thing, sort of,' he told the press.

In fact South Africa was left isolated and humiliated. Its forces were withdrawn in January 1976, leaving Operation Savannah a code-word for betrayal. The MPLA took over Angola, and more than 10,000 Cuban troops were flown in to support the new strongly anti-South African regime. In Mozambique a Marxist-Leninist group assumed power.

Jeff said the Savannah affair was etched in the memory of the armed forces and many South African politicians, and it had a far-reaching effect on the nuclear programme. He said South Africa's 'betrayal' by the Americans in Operation Savannah gave the generals the determination never to let such a disaster happen again.

It was recognized that the 'museum pieces' being built by Pelindaba were so crude that they could never be used in a battle situation, only as a strategic threat. A crucial decision was therefore taken to build 'a super alternative' – an arsenal of nuclear devices that could be used as tactical weapons. It was seen as a practical solution to South Africa's vulnerable position.

Both Dion and Jeff revealed that the new programme to build hydrogen and neutron bombs was controlled by a secret group composed of some senior Cabinet ministers and top generals. It was known as the 'Witvleiraadt' – 'The White Savannah Committee'.

11 Drinks with the President

First Deputy President Thabo Mbeki knew a can of worms when he saw one. And that's what was on his mind when he glanced through a number of news clippings at his luxury Johannesburg apartment in July 1994.

He was as concerned as anyone else about the trail of death associated with the so-called hoax material red mercury, and that was why he had agreed at short notice to an extraordinary meeting with police chief investigating officer Lieutenant-Colonel Charles Landman.

Mbeki had just returned to Johannesburg after a hectic day in Pretoria. The ANC had been at the South African political helm for only weeks, and the enormity of the task that lay ahead – nothing less than the rebuilding of a nation – was already beginning show on the faces of some of the battle-weary ANC politicians who had campaigned so tirelessly to rid the country of apartheid.

However, Mbeki might have been an exception. He was alert, relaxed and fully in control as he stepped out of his bullet-proof limousine surrounded by bodyguards and advisers. Not even the additional burden of having to act as President because of the temporary absence of Nelson Mandela was slowing him down. It was well after nine in the evening, and he was ready for yet another meeting.

Although Landman had declared himself determined to go the distance with the murder investigations, he was a realist and understood that once his inquiries ventured into areas of military secrets or national security his task would not be easy.

In an effort to pre-empt any problems, he had decided he needed backing from the highest levels if the murder investigation was to succeed. Landman and other officers were about to extend their inquiries to Europe, and he was concerned that, if South African security agencies were indeed involved in the killings or red mercury, his foreign investigation could be stopped by his superior officers – some of them generals who had been in office during the latter years of apartheid South Africa.

And so it was that Landman had asked Steve McQuillan, co-author of this book and then deputy editor of the *Weekend Star*, to arrange a meeting with Mbeki to ask for his backing, bypassing the police hierarchy that could have refused permission. He explained the intricacies of the investigations while sipping a glass of Scotch. Mbeki, having asked a number of questions, satisfied himself that he fully understood the problems and then agreed to help.[1]

It was agreed it was important not to jeopardize the delicate politics surrounding the investigation. McQuillan, and later Hounam, were invited to participate in the discussions provided they remained off the record. That undertaking remains in force, but it is a matter of record that Landman and other detectives expanded their investigations to Europe and had new-found confidence to dig further.

By November 1994, police had realized they could be dealing with a long string of murders – probably many more than they had originally thought. They had already widened their investigations to include all suspicious deaths in the chemical and armaments industries. But the Stoffberg killings had been the final straw. Many aspects of all the cases were troubling them, and Landman was beginning to realize he did not have the resources to cope with the rapidly expanding investigation. It was also becoming difficult to co-ordinate police investigations of deaths in Durban, Cape Town and the Johannesburg area – each centre many hundreds of kilometres from the others.

As well, it was felt the investigation should be isolated from established police structures to minimize any leakage of information as detectives moved into sensitive security areas. It was common knowledge the police force was penetrated by spies from other South African security forces. Some sources were extremely frightened of talking and needed certain guarantees before they could help. The police officers considered the sources' safety a serious issue and believed that if sources realized they were talking to detectives who were outside normal structures they would be more likely to co-operate.

After consultations at the highest levels within the police force and with ministers of the new government, a six-man police task force

1 The meeting arranged by McQuillan was the first of a series of discussions on how best to further the police investigation, whose sensitivity was becoming an area of serious concern so soon after the birth of the democratic South Africa. Later meetings with Mbeki involved Safety and Security Minister Sydney Mufamadi, along with Landman, McQuillan and co-author Peter Hounam.

headed by Landman was now formed to investigate the killings. It was to have its own offices and budget and was to become an isolated unit free of bureaucratic restrictions and reporting to only the highest levels of authority.

The special unit was created on the order of Lieutenant-General Johan le Roux, divisional head of the Crime Combatting and Intelligence Service, and would bring together officers from around the country specializing in fields ranging from computers and forensic science to weaponry. Police announced too that Interpol would be called in to help in the investigation, which was expected to come up against one or more foreign intelligence agencies. Other police generals were ordered to assist.

Detectives were expecting to travel to other African countries, Europe and the Americas. The high-powered task force had been given virtual *carte blanche* to second almost anyone who could be valuable to the investigation from within the ranks of the South African Police Service.[1] It also had been given the authority to extend its investigation in whatever direction it chose.

In announcing the task force, police also made it known that they now believed the Stoffbergs had been murdered because of their red mercury dealings. This was based on new information and came after interviewing and reinterviewing of a range of witnesses, whose stories were told in Chapter 8.

Initially, the investigators would look at the Stoffberg, Kidger, Lange and Van Wyk killings. These were the cases in which most of the groundwork had already been done. Said Landman at the time: 'It's an unusual step to take, but there is so much intrigue and the deals are so sinister that we believe a task force is warranted. And I must stress that it doesn't matter who is involved in these killings – politicians, security services or foreign governments – we intend to press on to the bitter end.

'Every crime we uncover will be investigated. Progress has already been made, and investigations conducted in Europe and Singapore have thrown up a number of interesting leads which are now being followed.' He appealed for people to come forward with information about the deaths or red mercury: 'Their information will be handled in the strictest

1 The South African Police (SAP) had been renamed the South African Police Service (SAPS) in an effort to convey the fact it was providing a service to the community and ward off perceptions held by the black majority that it was an apartheid oppressor.

confidence.' He said the possibility that other security or intelligence services could be involved in the deaths would be investigated: 'We fully understand the sensitivity surrounding this investigation.'

The first thing to be investigated would be how the dead men were linked. Landman said Stoffberg and Lange corresponded on arms deals; Lange knew Kidger for a considerable time and they worked on deals together; and Van Wyk knew both Lange and Kidger. Red mercury was linked to Stoffberg, Lange and Kidger. The task force would have to find out whether Van Wyk was also linked to the substance.

Meanwhile, following the Stoffberg killings, other officials were trying to play down the red mercury connection. Early in 1995 the National Intelligence Service had been recently reorganized and renamed the National Intelligence Agency. It issued a statement saying it had found no evidence to indicate the existence of red mercury and, as for reports that some deaths could be linked to the activities of Mossad, it said it had never succeeded in establishing such a link.

The organization also denied that one of its agents, together with an agent from Military Intelligence, had removed documents from Stoffberg's house. The AEC piped up and rejected reports that its scientists had admitted red mercury existed and that the corporation had manufactured the substance. But the AEC confirmed that one of its scientists had told a reporter for the South African Broadcasting Corporation that it had looked into red mercury from an economic viewpoint. It had tested a chemical sample it had been given, but found it did not comply with claims made about it. The AEC said that at no stage was any developmental work done on red mercury. So far as the AEC was concerned, the substance did not exist.

However the police were keeping their options open, and crucial new information, which surfaced as a result of the media exposure, flowed into the task-force offices. Detectives were now even more certain that a common link in some of the deaths was the men's secret dealings with Middle Eastern countries, including Iraq and Iran, and the black-market demand for red mercury.

A breakthrough on the Alan Kidger murder came soon after the new task force was formed – and it put Thor Chemicals back in the spotlight. Detectives received a tip-off that, just before he was murdered, and while he was employed by Thor, Kidger was secretly dealing with a mysterious military installation that was crucially important to South Africa's chemical and biological weapons programmes. It was the first hint of a link between Thor and the South African military, and partial confirmation of what the security police had told us on previous occasions.

Less than a month before his dismembered body had been packed into the boot of his car, Kidger had arranged the delivery of 2 metric tons of a mercury compound for a company called Delta G. Scientific, based in Midrand, north of Johannesburg. The substance, yellow mercuric oxide, was delivered to the home of one of the directors, a source who worked at the plant said. Nuclear physicist Dr Frank Barnaby confirmed the material could be used as a building block for red mercury.

'We did not know what the substance would be used for, but it was clear the delivery was sensitive,' the former Delta worker told us. 'The delivery was paid for in cash, which was unusual considering the material was not expensive or rare, and the shipping and payment were done secretly. I heard that Kidger wasn't curious as to why Delta wanted this stuff.' He said that, after Kidger's death, staff at Delta were told by executives not to say anything about the Kidger transaction should the police make inquiries.

Although this fell far short of proving official dealings in red mercury, it did shift the focus of the police investigation to the goings-on at Delta and its relationship with Thor. As well, police were highly suspicious of the size, sophistication and scope of Delta, and curious as to why certain dealings, such as the one involving yellow mercuric oxide from Thor, had to be handled in a clandestine manner. Detectives believed they were getting closer to the truth.

However, Delta's former managing director Barry Pithey denied that mercuric oxide was delivered to his home, or the homes of any of the other directors. He said Delta had taken delivery of the mercuric oxide for use in an anti-fungicide for pharmaceutical company Eli Lilly. Delta also had used it as a catalyst in some other procedures for clients in the commercial pharmaceutical industry. 'I never knew or heard of Alan Kidger until his death was reported in the press,' Pithey said. 'Nor, I believe, did any of the other directors.'

About the Kidger transaction, the man who worked at Delta said the company had originally been looking for red mercuric oxide – a well-known and commonly available compound – but supplier Thor had none available. Instead Delta bought from Thor the yellow mercuric oxide, slightly finer than the red but with similar chemical properties.

Pithey denied workers had been told to keep quiet about Kidger and that it was strange for Delta to pay in cash. He said: 'We didn't make the substances we have been accused of making. It's simply not true. Neither I nor any of the chemists know anything about red mercury.'

A Thor spokesman said mercuric oxide was not an unusual substance. It was used extensively in batteries and as a catalyst. The company had no formal record of a 2-tonne sale to Delta.

Soon after the Kidger killing, Delta was accused of leaking toxic chemicals into a nearby river system. There had been other problems too. An explosion at the plant in 1987 had caused substantial damage, and another in 1991 caused more, said workers. Millions of rands had to be spent repairing the complex.

Coincidentally, another plant 500 km away was having equally serious environmental problems. Thor's premises at Cato Ridge, near Durban, was at the centre of a row with environmentalists and others. It had been accused of poisoning the local countryside and its workers.

Eugene, a South African intelligence agent, told us that Mossad had 'a big file' on Thor. It believed many of the chemicals used for the manufacture of red mercury came from the plant, whose owners had many friends in high places, he said. 'Mossad kept Thor under surveillance. Then there was a huge spill. I was told that Mossad had sabotaged some of the chemical taps at the plant to try to bring attention to what it was making.'

The plants of Thor Chemicals and Delta G. Scientific were classified by the South African authorities as 'National Keypoints', said the source. That meant they were controlled by strict legislation in terms of their access and perimeter security and could not be photographed without permission.

Delta was essentially a military operation, and all its staff had high security clearances. Many of its former employees came from the army's Special Forces. 'It was mostly ex-military or security personnel,' said the source.

He also said the type of chemical equipment used was so sophisticated and so well guarded that security was a copycat of that applied to the nuclear industry: 'The plant was geared to handle nuclear substances if necessary. It was a very expensive system. They would never spend that kind of money on a security system that was not needed.'

Thor in South Africa, which wound down its Natal operation after a number of employees died or became seriously ill through overexposure to mercury, was reluctant to speak to the media about Kidger's murder or about its relationship in the dying days of apartheid with Delta,

Armscor or the South African military.[1]

Meanwhile, a growing number of sources were coming forward to relate the strange happenings at Delta before it was taken over by Sentrachem Ltd on 1 August 1993. Their identities had to be protected because they feared reprisals for breaking vows of secrecy. They were concerned that policies that had existed at the plant were effectively undermining a police murder investigation, and some said they had conclusive proof that the intelligence services monitored them outside of work.

Police spokesmen said the new information could help solve the Kidger murder, and detectives planned to question more of Delta's former employees.

Delta G. Scientific (Pty) Ltd was founded in 1982, and its first managing director was a former Special Forces member, Willie Basson. Then, soon after the plant was finished in the same year, Philip Mijburgh, nephew of former Defence Minister General Magnus Malan, took over. Mijburgh was thirty-two and an SF medical doctor.

Employees said the company had originally been set up to make teargas, with Armscor as its principal customer, and it was decided to move the plant to a new complex at Midrand because it was not a clean process and had to be well contained. 'They could make any chemical material at Delta,' said one worker. 'It's the same sort of plant that Saddam has for his chemical/biological weapons. It's one of the best labs in the country, and the people who worked there were doctors and professors – some from the University of Pretoria.

'After Mijburgh took over, the plant started making lots of different chemicals for the armaments industry – biological and chemical warfare

---

[1] Management in South Africa decided in 1993 to wind down all of Thor's mercury-related business by 1996. In February 1994 Thor turned back a routine shipment of waste from the United States and said it would halt all future shipments because of low staff morale and pressure from environmental groups and the African National Congress, which later that year would take political control of South Africa. The ANC and environmentalists alleged that the government was dragging its heels over an ANC report demanding a full commission of inquiry into Thor, including the murder of Kidger. They said the Cato Ridge plant was one of the few in the world where toxic mercury products were being reprocessed. ANC sources claimed the government was blocking the investigation.

The government finally announced it would appoint a commission of inquiry. But in 1995 the environmental group Earthlife Africa decided to legally challenge President Nelson Mandela, as head of state, over the terms of reference of the commission, arguing they were unconstitutional. Earthlife claimed the terms were too narrow and much of the hearing would be held in virtual secrecy, with few of its documents or proceedings being open to the media. Earlier the government had promised an 'open, democratic' inquiry.

stuff as well as tear-gas.[1] It had a large biochemical research department.' It put through a request for special chemical suits in 1991.

Biological weapons are strains of germs or viruses that are refined for delivery as sprays or in liquids and powders. Tiny amounts can kill thousands by introducing new strains of plague, anthrax or virulent strains of common illnesses such as tuberculosis.

All products at Delta were made or bought under a code-name. 'In one purchase, Delta bought fifteen pressure reactors from Hungary – that's 140 tons of reactors,' said an employee. 'The reactors were large cylinders with pipes outside. They put chemicals into these units. Chemicals react under very high pressure. Three were installed there, and two elsewhere. There was a separate security system thrown around these reactors, which probably originated from Poland or Russia.'

Delta's trading company, operating under the name Organochem, was based at Kempton Park, near Johannesburg. When its only listed director, Jerry Brandt, was arrested in the United States in 1989, executives at Delta ordered all paperwork mentioning the Kempton Park company to be shredded. Brandt, who had been caught in possession of secret documents after he had passed through US Customs, was later released after

---

[1] James Adams, the Washington-based correspondent for the *Sunday Times* in London, reported in early 1995 that a secret biological weapons programme used to assassinate opponents of South Africa's apartheid regime was in danger of falling into the hands of the Libyans. Quoting US intelligence sources, he said that efforts by Britain and the United States to persuade South Africa to destroy the weapons and research documents had been made more urgent by intelligence reports that Colonel Muammar Gadaffi of Libya was trying to recruit the scientists who developed them. Although production of the weapons by South Africa had ceased, President Mandela had been unable, despite repeated requests, to persuade his military to relinquish blueprints, which could now fall into the hands of states such as Libya. Intelligence reports that Gadaffi was trying to lure two South African scientists to Tripoli to help him develop his own biological weapons programme had caused deep concern in Washington, said the report. The White House had been spurred into sending an emissary to South Africa to try to persuade the government to take action against the military, which had run the top-secret programme for ten years. According to senior administration officials and sources in the CIA, the programme had been used to assassinate opponents of the apartheid state under the government of former President F. W. de Klerk. 'It was a shocking and disgusting episode,' said one source. 'The fact that a chemical and biological weapons programme was operating is simply incontestable,' said a Pentagon official. 'With BW [biological weapons] it's not enough just to stop making the stuff as you only need a small laboratory. We must know that all the records have been destroyed or there is always the risk it could be started again or the knowledge sold to a willing buyer, like the Libyans.' Not content with the chemical weapons that had been used in Namibia and Angola, South Africa had wanted a new form of terror to use on the opposition or in the event of civil war, said the report. 'It was an extensive effort,' said one senior intelligence official. 'And we still do not know how effective it was as some of the deaths looked as if the people were simply ill with everyday sicknesses.'

mediation by the South African government. He and an accomplice, Grant Wentzel, were accused of trying to export high-tech equipment to the Soviet Union.[1]

Meanwhile, sources said, Delta was buying all kinds of restricted chemicals through Organochem. The company was making a product worth R20,000 ($5,500) a kilogram for doping rhino, 'but this and other sensitive material left the plant after hours, in unmarked trucks.' Before Delta was sold to Sentrachem, all the unmarked end-product chemicals were removed by the Special Forces, said the worker. 'They were taken after-hours to the Valhalla ammo dump.'

Delta was also importing radioactive materials, and had the facilities to handle them. On one occasion strontium peroxide was imported from Sweden. On at least one other occasion false documentation was used to bring an acid from Europe by commercial aircraft.

As the internal situation in South Africa changed and the demand for tear-gas decreased, Delta looked for export markets. Chemists, engineers and biochemists experimented with a number of chemicals 'for defensive purposes' at Delta. There were growing allegations in the media that Delta was involved in the procurement and refinement of chemicals for battlefield use.

As well, a special police department investigating serious economic crime was examining whether there were any irregularities in the running of chemical warfare research projects involving Delta.

Beyond the Delta connection, other clues to the Kidger murder were emerging in Europe by April 1995. We saw two documents leaked to Greenpeace which apparently referred to Thor in South Africa and its murdered executive. The documents detailed chemical specifications for 'red mercury 20:20', described as 'cherry-red' and 'a semi-liquid'; they seemed to form part of a request from an unknown buyer for the supply of '4–10 flasks per month' of the substance.

One of the documents, dated 2 April 1990, was addressed to Wolfgang Dolich at Thor in Speyer, near Mannheim, Germany. Dolich, who was a

1 Brandt and Wentzel were accused of trying to illegally export a Varian 350D ion implanter, used to miniaturize component parts for, among other things, computerized military weaponry, after being caught in a 'sting' operation by US Customs agent Matthew Raffa. They had shown the agent a shopping list of other high-tech items they required 'for a secret unit of the SA military'. They said the Varian equipment was going to the Soviet Union via South Africa. The pair faced charges carrying a maximum of eighty-five years jail and/or a R5 million ($1.4 million) fine. How the South African authorities persuaded the United States to drop the case is not clear.

sales manager at the time and then became the company's German director, told *New Scientist* magazine that he could not remember who had sent him the document, nor could he decipher whose illegible signature appeared on the bottom. But he thought the document was likely to be connected to one of the many requests that he used to receive for mercury products. He said he probably passed it on to his company's sister plant in South Africa, where mercury compounds had been manufactured.

Dolich said that nothing could have come of the request because Thor had never been involved in the manufacture of red mercury. In the light of this, why Dolich even bothered to pass on the documents to South Africa is not clear. One of the documents also contained a handwritten note saying: 'Herewith, all we have on red mercury,' signed 'Alan'. Dolich thinks this is likely to have been Alan Kidger.

Frank Barnaby, who also saw the documents, regarded the specifications as scientifically credible, although they were not always easy to understand. They were similar to others he had seen from Russia, Germany and Austria, and reinforced his view that there was a significant international trade in red mercury. He told *New Scientist* that, in association with two other senior scientists from Italy and the United States, whom he declined to name, he was actively trying to acquire a small sample so its alleged properties could be properly tested in a laboratory. As a proliferation expert, Barnaby is concerned, like other scientists, that if Russia has developed a new type of nuclear weapons technology involving red mercury it would render the Nuclear Non-Proliferation Treaty useless.

New information we uncovered in 1995 suggested Kidger was deeply involved with a secret project within the South African military-industrial complex. An intelligence source told us Kidger was working on 'heavy-duty chemicals' outside Thor. He said, 'The unit he worked for developed chemical weapons – nothing crude like mustard gas – for Iraq.' Kidger had been contracted by Armscor-affiliated companies to work on special projects, he said. This work brought him in touch with the Pretoria-based Mechem chemical and explosives specialists and with EMLC, a technical support department for the army's Security Forces that specialized in, among other things, tailor-made bombs. 'Thor was paid well to allow him to do this research,' said the source.

Kidger worked with various chemicals, but specialized in those that, in cocktail form, made poisonous gases. 'He could also have been working on red mercury.'

The South African intelligence agent said Kidger had a big US-style camper vehicle, packed with research equipment, and had access to a secret laboratory east of Johannesburg. The 'camper lab' indicated that whatever he was doing required him to be mobile. 'He was a top guy in his field – a very knowledgeable scientist.' The source speculated that he was probably directly involved in procuring materials from Europe with other scientists. Together they worked with highly toxic chemicals in various forms. 'He was earning lots of money – but that would have come in cash, and not through bank accounts.'

Corroborating one aspect of this, on 20 August 1994 the *Weekend Star* reported that in 1988 Kidger had telephoned the Council for Scientific and Industrial Research[1] to ask whether its laboratories would be interested in producing red mercury. Simon, a former SF commando who told us red mercury was a component for a new generation of South African weapons, said the CSIR had tested red mercury in the early 1980s. He confirmed that Kidger had been involved with red mercury, and added: 'He was an agent for the South African military.'

Landman had said earlier that Kidger had been highly trained in the use of chemicals that could be used in the manufacture of armaments.

Meanwhile, the police investigation in South Africa was becoming accustomed to interference. The latest incident involved secret police files belonging to the Crime Intelligence Service. Sources told us that these files, concerning the deaths of Kidger, Lange, Van Wyk and the Stoffbergs, had gone missing from police headquarters in Pretoria. The files, written by Landman, had been kept in one folder. Mysteriously, they later turned up at a police station in the remote northern Cape town of Vryburg.

Task-force officers were curious as to why the folder had been sent there. Was there a police investigation involving the killings in that area? If this was the case, why had the task force not been notified? Also, how had the file been removed? Apparently, movement of the CIS files was governed by a detailed procedure of signatures and authorities: they could not be removed simply on a whim. It turned out that there had been an office move and in the process certain files had been misplaced.

There were also suggestions emerging of the involvement of former police officers in the red mercury trade. This was an avenue of investigation feared by most serving police officers. A frightened source had told

1 Before the CSIR was restructured, a division called the National Instutute of Defence Research had worked on military developments, including explosives.

task-force investigators in early 1995 that former police officers had been involved and had had dealings with Kidger in 1991. These dealings had involved discussions with an Arab businessman.

Suggestions of police complicity were not new. An independent researcher had already described to us a network that involved serving police officers in a smuggling operation from Mozambique. The researcher said the officers and others had been involved in removing mercury substances from a Russian ship in Maputo harbour in 1989 – the second time in the investigation that a Russian ship in Maputo had been mentioned. (The first time was in connection with a Don Lange deal.) The deal involved R2 million ($545,000) of red mercury powder and diamonds. The researcher had been told the mercury substances were required for use in bombs and sophisticated weapons-guidance systems.

It was yet another indication that for some reason red mercury was needed in South Africa.

12 Glide Bombs, Missiles and Heavy Water

Evidence from people who had worked at Kentron Circle and at the AEC showed there was a sharp difference between the type of bombs De Klerk had destroyed and the devices built during the 1980s. South Africa had advanced beyond the 'dirty' versions one could 'kick out the back of an aircraft'. The programme was to produce modern tactical weapons giving South Africa the ability to wage a high-tech nuclear war.

The thermonuclear weapons described by Dion and Jeff were high-yield devices measuring their destructive power in hundreds of kilotons – many times more powerful than De Klerk's 'dirty' bombs. We had also discovered they weighed much less than the 900-plus kg given in the official estimate for the six and a half, and there were more than twenty thermonuclear or boosted weapons built.

The sources described how intensive engineering and development work was carried out to standardize the devices so that they could fit a variety of delivery systems, and withstand the stresses of a missile launch. It was this demand that had taxed Jeff, Richard and his colleagues, not the basic technology of producing a modern high-yield device.

While discussing this facet of the bomb programme, we began to hear stories of a unique type of weapon that had been tailor-made to deliver the warheads, called the 'slim bomb' or 'glide bomb'. One version of this had no system of propulsion, relying instead on its aerodynamics to glide silently to its target. It was designed and produced by Kentron Irene, near Pretoria, a sister facility to Kentron Circle and also a subsidiary of Armscor.

To launch a nuclear attack, an aircraft would fly to a height of 50,000 feet and the glide bomb would be released from a housing on one of the wings. After a few seconds, two steerable fins, operated by compressed gas, would be released from two slots at the front end of the device and locked into place, giving it stability in the air.

The mid-section of the glide bomb could carry a thermonuclear weapon. Its range was said to be up to 30 km. Several different types of guidance system were developed, including infra-red and a television-aiming mechanism linked through a telemetry system to a controller in the aircraft.

Dion, a former manager at Kentron Circle, told us the original aim had been to equip South Africa's ageing fleet of Buccaneer bombers to carry the new weapon, but with only three of these left by the mid-1980s there were attempts to adapt South Africa's Mirage aircraft, but technical problems were encountered. Finally it was decided to deploy the weapon on a Boeing 707, the glide bomb being carried beneath one of the wings, with a communications pod on the other.

The SAAF has three Boeings which are equipped as refuelling planes and for early-warning patrols. However, South Africa may have secretly acquired others. Jake, the Armscor agent, disclosed that South Africa bought a number of 707s from Ugandan Airways in the late 1980s via a company in Geneva. 'The idea was that they could masquerade as civil airliners,' he said. 'They even kept the transponders that electronically identified them as being non-military. That's how they would have got through to their target.'

Another informant, an Armscor employee, told us the airframe of the glide bomb was carefully tested but there were often failures in the early days, around 1982, when test ranges near the mine of Copperton, west of Prieska in the northern Cape, were used for field trials. There was an emergency there that shook Prieska and destroyed some of the military buildings. 'The pilot made a mistake and jettisoned the bloody thing. It went head over heels, like a car rolling. We were not sure what it was carrying – probably a dummy warhead made of tungsten – but it made a huge bang. All the guard houses made of brick shook so much that they had to be demolished. It shook the town, and that was 50 km away. '

He said the glide bomb was given the name 'Hento', an Afrikaner name for a family's first-born son. He divulged that military officers from Iraq were present at some of the tests. 'They were going to buy them,' he said. 'They wanted a nice '*skelom*' [Afrikaans for 'undercover'] bomb system. It would have meant a hundred going through the production line.' The order had later been cancelled just before the Gulf War.

His story backed up recent disclosures in the South African press that Armscor did $4.5 million of business with Iraq before the Gulf War. The *Weekly Mail & Guardian* reported: 'The morals of the deal don't seem to have concerned the South African authorities much. Iraq is alleged to have paid for the weapons with oil, desperately needed as the mid-1980s embargo noose tightened.'

Dion also revealed that the glide bomb, with a 1,000-kg conventional weapon, was tested in 1988 during South Africa's battle with Cuban forces in Angola. During the fight for Cuito Cuanavale, the device was launched at a bridge, totally destroying it. In what may be a reference to the same event, the aviation magazine *Flight International* reported in September 1994 that an extended-range South African glide bomb had been used in the Angolan war. Development work had started in the late 1970s, said *Flight*, and the device was known as the H2. A more advanced powered weapon – known as MUPSOW – was now being made by Kentron, it said.

We learned in South Africa that there were indeed powered versions of the Hento, and the programme had depended crucially on US and European technology. Four versions were developed, the largest being known as the H-4 or H-D. This was 4.7 metres long, and capable of carrying a payload of 900 kg – identical to the specification of Israel's Gabriel IV missile.

Jake, the Armscor agent, said the missile programme was in desperate need of gyroscopes for navigation systems in 1988–9. 'We had problems with our own make for the glide bomb,' he said, 'and the fins were also giving trouble. There was also a special gyro brought in for a nuclear ballistic missile. We had to get them from Northrop [the US aviation company]. It was damned difficult, but we managed it.'

South African press reports in November 1989 said gyros from Northrop had been obtained with Israel's help. Three South Africans and two Americans had been indicted for importing them at a cost of R125 million ($34 million).

The Hento range was only one of the delivery systems available to South Africa's nuclear programme. Kentron was also developing a range of devices known as drones or pilotless aircraft. These were marketed for search-and-destroy missions against enemy radar. However, we heard there was another application. With little modification, the drones could be turned into a simple form of cruise missile and carry a nuclear device.

A model called the Lark, or sometimes the Skylark, had a quoted range of 400 km. It could then 'loiter for more than two hours' in the target area before returning to base, landing by a system of parachutes and airbags. An Armscor article said the system came with nine drones per truck and three trucks per system. Each drone was launched with a booster rocket, and then a propeller would take over. 'Once a target has been acquired in the predefined target area, the drone attacks it by diving at a near-vertical angle,' said the article. 'A 22-kg barrel-shaped warhead is mounted in the nose just behind the seeker head.'

There was also a faster 6-metre model called the Skua, also known as the HTD-1, which was powered by a solid-fuel rocket on take-off and then by an Apex TJ 350 turbojet, almost identical in specification to Israel's Bet Shemesh Sorec 4 motor. It had a range of 800 km if it was not required to return to base, and a payload of up to 100 kg – big enough for a compact nuclear device. It could fly at a height of 40,000 feet and, like the Lark, could be launched from a transportable field station.

Very little has been disclosed about a third version called the Flowchart 2, described as a 'stealth drone'. Photographs show that it has a sleek dart-like airframe painted with a black radar-absorbing coating. It was described as a Skua with a stealth airframe surrounding it. Kentron advertised the Flowchart under the slogan: 'Something New Out of Africa'. A brief write-up produced for the South African defence exhibition Dexsa in November 1994 acknowledged it seemed 'a contradiction in terms' but added: 'The point is to develop a target to simulate current and future stealthy aircraft for realistic defence training.'

An Amscor agent told us that all the drones could be adapted for tactical use, and in their most advanced forms they were a type of cruise missile. 'If you can use it for that purpose, you will use it for that purpose,' he said. 'Do you think countries would pay millions for these things just to shoot them down at the first opportunity for fire practice?'

South Africa has never admitted having cruise missiles, but in 1983 the Nigerian government complained that Lagos and Port Harcourt had come within firing range of South African cruise missiles. Nigeria believed they had been jointly developed with Israel.

In July 1986 the head of Armscor, Commandant Piet Marais, announced that land at Overberg, near Cape Agulhas, would be used for the testing of 'long-range missiles to be used in a regional context' with the emphasis on civil applications. The range had been acquired three years earlier and was situated almost as far south as it is possible to go on the African continent. Armscor not only intended testing its own missiles, it emerged, but was providing a launch-pad for its ally Israel, which had great difficulty in launching rockets from its own soil.

In 1988 Israel successfully launched a satellite, Offeq-1, into space, aiming it along the length of the Mediterranean to avoid any problems with countries in the region. However, a failure in mid-flight could have caused major diplomatic problems if the rocket had fallen on foreign soil. The Armscor range presented no such launching problems, and reports indicated that Israel used the Overberg range several times in the mid-1980s. It was reported that seventy-five Israelis were regularly working there on the missile developments.

This collaboration, with South Africa buying in Israeli expertise and supplying uranium for Israel's nuclear weapons plant at Dimona, was said to date from 1979. Iran had been financing part of Israel's new missile programme, but after the Shah's fall South Africa had offered to step in. It was said Taiwan had joined the team to form a 'troika' of similarly shunned countries which were developing cruise missiles as well as neutron shells.

In March 1988 Danie Steyn, South Africa's Minister of Economic Affairs, announced that plans were being made for a South African space industry for 'telecommunication and commercial purposes', but this drew little newspaper attention – perhaps because Overberg was out of bounds to the press. A report in the *Washington Times* said Israel and South Africa were about to test 'a new intermediate-range ballistic missile'. A spokesman for Armscor sidestepped the issue of a military programme: 'We are in the process of firing missiles in order to test the performance of the range,' he said. 'South Africa is strong in the missile field and we have produced several of repute. For obvious reasons we are not prepared to disclose the details of our qualification programme. We will therefore not comment on any speculation ...'

On 5 July 1989 there were reports of a test launch over the Indian Ocean of a South African single-stage booster for a new medium-range missile, nicknamed the Arniston after a fishing village near Overberg. Marais called the event a major milestone and 'another successful launch.' The American network NBC-TV broadcast a story that Israel and South Africa were co-operating on a 'nuclear-capable missile'. It said the Israelis had helped South Africa develop their version, test-flown in July, in exchange for enriched uranium for its nuclear weapons programme.

Margaret Tutwiler, America's State Department spokeswoman, confirmed that the Bush administration had known of the collaboration between the two countries, and said the deal illustrated the difficulties of stemming the spread of such weapons. She declined to comment more because NBC's story was in part based on a CIA document: 'The department does not discuss intelligence matters.'1 However, evidence was

1 In 1987 the Missile Technology Control Regime was agreed by the major powers, setting out guidelines for halting the export of missile-related technology. It was signed by the United States, Canada, Japan, Britain and other Western European nations, but the Soviet Union and China refused to join. The Bush administration wanted to expand the pact, but, according to reports, it was concerned that some who joined might not fully comply.

strengthening that Overberg was being used for more than just civil applications.

A launch of a two-stage booster from Overberg was reported in November 1990. The rumour was that a three-stage missile was being produced, very similar to Israel's 13-metre Shavit, based on its advanced Jericho-II launcher. An Armscor employee who saw the Arniston described it to us as 'a big bastard – a bit bigger than a Scud'.

Another Armscor insider told us the guidance systems were perfected just before De Klerk came to power at the end of 1989. The Israelis were helping, he said, and what was finally produced was similar to their Jericho-II. 'By sharing technology, we ended up with something very similar.'

By now, Overberg had a complete flight-control centre, with banks of TV screens and instrument consoles similar to those used in a Space Shuttle launch. Someone who has seen it said the facilities were 'like a mini Cape Kennedy', although it was essentially a top-secret military base run by Armscor.

In October 1992, press reporters were invited to Rooi Els, at Cape Hangklip, another test site along the coast to the west, to witness a static test of a new rocket motor. It failed to ignite first time, but when the problem was rectified it performed perfectly, frightening the spectators with its ferocity. A spokesman said proudly it had a thrust of 50 tons and could, when combined with a second rocket stage, put a 500-kg payload into space. The next step, he said, was to test the motor in a vacuum, 'to simulate space conditions'. Dawie de Villiers, South Africa's Public Enterprises Minister, was enthusiastic about future prospects, saying his country could soon be a big player in the international space field. 'There is already interest from international companies to place low orbital satellites in space for commercial purposes,' he told journalists. It was announced that a company called Houwteq would now spearhead developments in this field, under the direction of Denel, whose assets included Armscor's former military plants. The pretence continued that this was all South Africa's own work, although when its programme was compared with that of Israel the link-up was obvious.

Israel had gone on from producing its Jericho-I and II rockets to make a more advanced version of the Jericho-II known as the Shavit. This was the three-stage booster that launched its Offeq-1 and later Offeq-2 satellites. Plans had then been laid for a four-stage rocket, known as the 'Next', capable of penetrating well beyond the gravitational pull of the earth.

South Africa in a similar period had produced the RSA-1,2 and 3, the latter being a Shavit clone and capable of launching a payload into low earth orbit. RSA-3, like the Shavit, was said to be up to 18 metres long. The Republic's 'Next' equivalent, the RSA-4, was 23.5 metres long and could lift 550 kg into a 1,400-km orbit. Supposedly, it never flew, but a Houwteq information sheet gave detailed flight-performance data, indicating that at least one launch occurred.

As events unfolded it was clear de Villiers had spoken too soon. The United States had grown increasingly worried about the advances at Overberg, and threatened to veto World Bank loans unless the missile programme was abandoned. Armscor pleaded that Overberg would only be launching satellites for civil purposes, such as its 'Greensat', a 300-kg 'earth observation' module. However, Greensat was itself suspect, as the Americans must have known. It carried a high-tech camera capable of 'near military resolution', and Israel was planning to launch a similar spy-in-the-sky in its Offeq-3 spacecraft.

By July 1993 it was clear the United States was demanding action, and South Africa caved in to the pressure. Denel announced that local plans to manufacture rocket launchers had been abandoned because 'they were not an economic option'.[1] Pik Botha, the Foreign Minister, said he hoped this would enable South Africa to join the Missile Technology Control Regime and that sanctions against Denel would be ended.

It was announced in July 1995 that a top US demolition expert was being sent to South Africa to blow up the missile test sites, at the expense of the State Department in Washington. Overberg was to be kept, but only to launch other country's rockets on a commercial basis.

It was an almost unprecedented act of interference by the Americans, and Jeff, the scientist from Advena, said it came about because South Africa was so close to being able to drop nuclear weapons on any country on earth. He said the object of developing the rockets had always been military, with the aim of giving South Africa's nuclear weapons worldwide range. 'The Houwteq programme is a ballistic missile system,' he said. 'It is designed to deliver nuclear devices. The satellite story is a cover, but it also made a lot of sense to use the missile to put a

1 The rocket programme was said to have cost R15 billion ($4 billion). In comparison, the six and half A-bombs declared by De Klerk were said to have cost just R700 million to R800 million (more than $200 million). The real sums, drawn from South Africa's special defence account, were never open to public scrutiny but are thought to be vast. In 1989, special account spending came to more than R10 billion, which is also the ANC's estimate for the nuclear weapons programme. In 1992, the AEC alone received a subsidy of R685 million.

satellite into orbit. Our thermonuclear devices were tailored to go in an ICBM or the glide bomb. That was the difficult job: getting them engineered to withstand the stresses.'

This was confirmed by a remark to US author Mitchell Reiss by General P. J. 'Tienie' Groenewald, one of the right-wing's most influential figures, a senator for the Freedom Front political party, a former member of the State Security Council and a former head of Military Intelligence. Groenewald said South Africa 'miniaturized nuclear devices for ballistic missiles'.[1]

Jan, the senior military strategist who had given details of the advanced weapons programme at Advena, said there was no doubt South Africa had the capability to put a satellite into orbit – albeit at huge cost – but he added: 'The only difference between a satellite launcher and an ICBM is the payload – i.e. a nuke instead of a satellite.' He said Armscor and the military were interested only in delivering nuclear weapons and perhaps chemical weapons, and to this end long-range missiles had been put into service with the SADF. He said the United States had been permanently watching the Overberg range for some years.

He disclosed there were also a number of fixed launch silos for missiles in the Cape. 'They are at the army battle school in Lohatlha, between Sishen and Postmasburg. It is huge – big enough to shoot a G5 or G6 howitzer across it,' Jan added. 'Israeli military and civilians spent a lot of time there.'

He said there would be three to five silos in each launch site, and there would be a number of these – perhaps ten to twenty. In the early 1980s these already contained medium- to long-range missiles and some were nuclear-armed, though he could not say if the missiles were South African in origin or imports. Silos were dug into the side of a mountain next to an open plain. They carried 'big "dirty" bombs' which would have been targeted on places like Dar es Salaam and Lusaka.

Again, it appeared South Africa was following Israeli practice. Reports show that an Israeli military base west of the town of Zekharyeh has a series of bunkers for nuclear-armed Jericho-II missiles cut out of the Judaean hills.

Jan said missile tests were conducted not only at Overberg, but also at a large restricted test area in Zululand, northern Natal, on the Indian Ocean. 'That's where they were playing games with rockets,' he said.

1 Reiss mentions this in his book *Bridled Ambition*, but consigns it to a footnote because other officials denied it.

The Zululand site had been developed in the 1970s, but problems had arisen with Mozambique. 'There was a lot of spy-versus-spy across the border with the Russians, and huge-scale electronic eavesdropping. When they did that, we could listen back. It was lots of fun and games, but a highly sensitive situation.'

Hennie, a military agent, said Northern Natal was so sensitive that a Russian helicopter which took off in Mozambique was shot down by South African security forces while it was snooping near the missile launch sites. He said he had also heard that David Webster, a Johannesburg anthropologist, was murdered because he saw too much while on field trips near the range. 'I was led to believe he was killed because he saw a nuclear device that was about to be fired, but he was also killed because he had a connection with a foreign government.'

From the comments of the sixteen maverick Denel employees who threatened Armscor over their redundancy terms, we had also learned that mobile launchers were part of the SADF armoury. By coincidence, we saw one of these in Johannesburg in June 1995 when it was brought to a truck depot for servicing. It was an eight-wheel-drive German-made transporter in military camouflage, with a 'rocket command and control' post in the passenger side of the cab. Part of the launcher platform had been extended at the rear of the vehicle on two large hydraulic feet, almost doubling its length. The launcher could be elevated skywards. The cab was low, to allow for the nose of the missile to rest above it. The missile cradle was long enough to hold a 13-metre-long rocket – approximately the length of the RSA-2. It was direct evidence of South Africa's missile advances and of its nuclear capability.[1] It made no sense that such a costly delivery system would be used to deploy conventionally armed warheads.

An anonymous caller urged us to investigate an anti-armour missile produced by Kentron. The caller said he was a scientist who had worked on the South African red mercury programme. The missile was, he said, new and revolutionary, and had been developed for South Africa's Rooivalk (Red Kestrel) helicopter. It used red mercury and, though it was not a nuclear weapon, it had phenomenal performance. He appeared to be referring to red mercury's powerful explosive charac-

1 In March 1993 the *Sunday Times* in London, quoting military sources in Pretoria, said that in the late 1980s South Africa had made a secret $2 billion deal with China for the purchase by Pretoria of long-range missile technology capable of delivering a nuclear warhead more than 2,000 km away.

teristics, but a promised face-to-face meeting never happened.

Then Dion told us about the Kentron's ZT-3 anti-armour missile which was designed for the Rooivalk. He said it had a tapered nose and could burn its way through armoured steel like a blowtorch, creating a hole through which the missile travelled before it exploded inside.

'It goes through 1 metre of armoured steel, not just ordinary steel,' Dion said. 'It uses implosion technology,[1] but it isn't nuclear. You see, the warheads were made at Somchem, down in the Cape. I think it must be a special explosive to get through that much of armoured steel. Do you get it in any other parts of the world? I don't think so.' He said he had heard a special chemical was involved – 'Maybe something like red mercury.'

The story was further confirmed by Jake, an Armscor agent. 'It is a very advanced weapon,' he said, 'and no one has been told what the chemical is in the nose, but I believe it is red mercury. It has one feature that is unique. If you fire it at armour plate at an angle, it doesn't glance off. It just burns its way through and then explodes. Armscor wouldn't waste itself on anything that wasn't world class, or better.'

In July 1990 the organization placed an advertisement in a military journal. It claimed Armscor was taking technology to its limits and beyond: 'Channelling our thinking into weapons that can do their own thinking; seek and identify their own targets through smoke, fog, dust and dark; launch their own missiles from any kind of carrier to penetrate any material of the future – be it 1,000-mm thick steel.' It was another indication that 'special chemicals' were a vital part of Armscor's new product line-up. The ZT-3 is currently a crucial selling-point in South Africa's drive to sell the Rooivalk helicopter overseas.

Dion, the Kentron Circle manager, was insistent that an American called Clyde Ivy had played a vital part in the development of the Kentron missiles and other delivery systems. The name Ivy meant nothing at the time, but we later discovered he had helped to set up Kentron in the late 1970s and then returned to the United States, where he became an executive of ISC, a military hardware company. 'Ivy is important,' said Dion, 'You must check him out. Find out what he was doing in the States.'

We had heard of four nuclear programmes. One had been to acquire a crude weapon in the late 1960s. The second was the production of the

1 This seems a shorthand way of describing the 'ballotechnic effect', described in Chapter 9, by which a chemical is made to release very high amounts of energy by putting it under pressure from an outer layer of ordinary high explosive.

six and a half 'museum pieces' in the 1970s. Following this came the Kentron Circle operation to produce advanced thermonuclear or 'boosted' weapons. Fourth came the deployment of the neutron shell and the 'clean' bomb, apparently incorporating a form of red mercury.

However, one unresolved mystery was whether South Africa ever made atomic and thermonuclear weapons using plutonium rather than highly enriched uranium. Nuclear experts have found it difficult to understand why this was apparently never part of South Africa's nuclear ambitions, as in some ways plutonium is easier to produce than HEU and lends itself to greater miniaturization. But at the end of the 1980s work on plutonium devices was allegedly ten years from realization when de Klerk stopped the nuclear weapons programme.

While HEU has a critical mass of about 55 kg, the critical mass for a sphere of plutonium is between 10 and 12 kg, depending on purity. Plutonium is ideal for an implosion device, in which a ball of plutonium is compressed by the detonation around it of high explosive charges shaped to produce an inward shock wave. In this technique, a quantity of plutonium less than a kilogram and no bigger than a golf ball can be made to fission. An atom bomb using 4 kg is said to be within the technical scope of most countries, as the Israelis proved. Such a device could be easily delivered to a target in a missile, and would have the advantage that it would be symmetrical in shape.

Plutonium is produced in all nuclear reactors after they have gone critical.[1] The weapons-grade variety, plutonium-239, can be extracted in a chemical separation plant using less electricity than an enrichment plant and taking up much less space. This was the reason why Israel chose the plutonium option in the late 1950s.

In 1986 Mordechai Vanunu,[2] an Israeli nuclear technician, divulged how his country was producing nuclear weapons at an underground plant at Dimona in the Negev desert, south of Jerusalem. Vanunu managed to take photographs of the plutonium separation plant, where he

[1] By neutron irradiation, uranium fuel in the reactor is converted to the isotope plutonium-239 (Pu-239) then Pu-240 and then Pu-241 as time passes. It is Pu-239 that is needed to make a nuclear weapon. To get the maximum quantity of this isotope, the fuel rod has to be extracted at the optimum time, before too much Pu-239 has been changed to the higher isotopes.

[2] Sadly, the Israeli was kidnapped by Mossad after he had been debriefed by the *Sunday Times* 'Insight' team, which at the time included Peter Hounam. Vanunu was smuggled back to Israel, where he is serving an eighteen-year sentence for treason. He once told Hounam that scientists at Dimona had talked about visits to South Africa.

had worked, which had been built secretly by the French in the 1960s. The plant occupied seven floors below the surface, but was virtually undetectable from above and appeared to be just a two-storey service block. The French also built a natural uranium/heavy-water reactor at Dimona, a type that is considered optimum for the production of weapons-grade plutonium because it produces low-fission products.

A similar but much smaller heavy-water reactor was built at Pelindaba and, according to the AEB, this was locally designed and constructed.[1]

Begun in 1962, it was called the Pelinduna[2] Project. Drs Ampie Roux and Wally Grant, the twin inspirations behind the nuclear weapons programme, were at the control console when it successfully went critical on 30 November 1967. Extensive research was done on a novel type of nuclear fuel for the reactor. The assessment was that a very large version could be built producing 1,000 megawatts of electricity at a very economic rate.

However, the reactor had been operating for only a few weeks when the project was abandoned. According to official statements, the reactor was dismantled and its 606 kg of uranium fuel[3] and 5.4 metric tons of heavy water were returned to the United States. The AEB said: 'Probably the most significant consideration [in closing Pelinduna] was the phenomenal success of the uranium enrichment project ... To undertake both together would have been more of a burden than the Republic could shoulder and no compromise was possible, it was one or the other.'

If the Pelinduna project had continued, the next logical stage would have been to build a large 1,000-megawatt version. But, said the AEB, such a large reactor was not foreseen as being necessary at the time. The explanation is suspect in the light of the fact that plans were apparently being made at this time for a large-scale nuclear programme to generate 20,000 megawatts of electricity by the year 2000. The plan was eventually made public by Prime Minister John Vorster in 1970, although it was never fully implemented.

The decision to end the Pelinduna project and also to dismantle the

1 However, a source told us the French secretly built a reactor at Pelindaba in this period.

2 'Pelinduna' is an acronym of Pelindaba (Pelin), deuterium (D), uranium (U), and sodium (Na). The original design was a heavy-water-moderated natural uranium reactor using sodium as a coolant, but the prototype used 2 per cent enriched uranium to reduce the number of fuel rods needed.

3 The fuel was returned to the United States in 1971 but, beforehand, it was sent to Britain for reprocessing. This implies that the plutonium in the uranium was extracted, but it is not clear what happened to it after that.

reactor is therefore something of a mystery. The reactor could have been kept running as a research tool for very little extra expense. One suspicion is that the Pelinduna project went underground and became a military-run operation that has never been disclosed.

Wally Grant said of Pelinduna: 'Its flexible design encompassed some of the most advanced and progressive techniques ... From this we learned a lot ... It enabled us to make a tremendous leap forward in nuclear power technology.' His remark is puzzling, as the Pelinduna concept was never developed for producing electricity in South Africa.

In November 1994 a poster appeared on the AEC's stand at the Dexsa military exhibition in Johannesburg, and listed among the products being offered were reactors. We asked Floris Brand, an AEC marketing official, if he could supply a 20-megawatt heavy-water moderated natural uranium model. 'Certainly we can produce one,' he said. 'We have all the expertise necessary.' He also said that the AEC had supplied such designs, similar but larger than Pelinduna, to other customers.

Reactors based on the Pelinduna principle would require either large quantities of carbon as a moderator or heavy water, a material that is internationally controlled to prevent nuclear proliferation.[1] In 1957 a programme was begun in South Africa to establish if a practical heavy-water production plant could be constructed. Engineers were sent to the Heavy Water Group at the Harwell Atomic Energy Research Laboratory in southern England and then to West Germany in search of specialist training.

At the time, the plants run by the South African company Sasol in the eastern Transvaal produced large quantities of hydrogen from its process for making oil, of which South Africa had a serious shortage, from coal, which was plentiful. This hydrogen was being exported to plants producing heavy water overseas, and it seemed feasible that South Africa too could make the strategic material in large quantities.

The project progressed until, like Pelinduna, it was officially scrapped in 1967 – allegedly because heavy water was no longer needed. But again there were stories it was being produced in the Republic in a hidden plant.

In the early 1980s US intelligence discovered that a Swiss company,

1 Heavy water – D_2O or deuterium oxide – is found in minute quantities in ordinary water – H_2O – but it is very difficult to extract. In a reactor, it acts as a 'moderator' – slowing down the neutrons from the uranium and stepping up the fissioning process. It is also a source of deuterium for boosting atomic weapons and facilitating the fusion process in a neutron bomb.

Sulzer Brothers, was on the verge of selling South Africa a heavy-water production plant of the latest design. There is no record of whether the company completed the deal. However, an engineer working for Aserma, a South African munitions company near Durban, disclosed there was a special section there in the early 1980s making a machine tool for use in heavy-water production. He described the device made by the machine tool as a filter, and he had been told it was connected with a trigger mechanism for a nuclear warhead fired from a plane.

'It was very secret,' he said. 'Its code-name was Project Palm Tree. People came from the nuclear place near Pretoria to supervise it. Someone who was working there took a part home to show his friends. He was sacked.' The source said he later heard that the machine had never been used because a foreign system had been obtained that worked better.

Documents at the death scene in Dirk Stoffberg's home indicated he was trying to deal in heavy water. In 1989 a company in San Carlos de Bariloche, southern Argentina, had circulated a letter saying it was interested in an offer of heavy water for use in 'our power station'. It warned: 'This information shall be kept confidential to avoid any misuse of it.' Stoffberg had written a note: 'Above in strictest confidence. Do not disclose our buyer name yet – over to you.' A technical specification sheet for heavy water was attached.

In January 1990 Stoffberg wrote to his partner Malcolm Roelofsz saying: 'I can buy D_2O – heavy water – for peaceful purposes.' A meeting was scheduled in Montreux, Switzerland, with a Spanish company to sell it uranium oxide and heavy water.

As we were writing this book, we heard of large quantities of heavy water being in Brazzaville, in the Congo – part of a consignment that had come from Zaire by train in 1989. The evidence, though not strong, indicated that heavy water was available in Southern Africa and, if this was also the case, it further suggested that the stories of secret reactors could be true – the object being to produce weapons-grade plutonium.

Another potential source was South Africa's two power reactors at Koeberg, near Cape Town, built on contract by the French company Framatome. When the project was tendered in the early 1970s, the Germans were expecting to win. The choice of Framatome caused surprise in the nuclear industry because the French company was not regarded as sufficiently experienced. It marketed a design that had been acquired on licence from Westinghouse, the US company. However, the Germans were out of favour, having complained bitterly about the copying of their uranium-enrichment system.

There were international protests that Koeberg would contribute to a South African bomb programme. The AEC called its accusers 'ignorant' and of 'questionable morality': 'The bigger the lie the more easily it is believed and if it is repeated often enough it will be accepted as the truth.'

But what was the truth? Six months after Koeberg went critical in 1984 it was shut down because of faulty pipes supplied by Framatome. At that point the nuclear fuel rods would have contained an optimum quantity of Pu-239, suitable for the construction of a number of nuclear weapons.

In the late 1970s sources in the French government and Patrick Keatley, a British journalist who was studying South Africa's nuclear development, said the country had built a 'small, working model' pluto-nium processing plant. Keatley further stated that the Republic had already accumulated about 2 or 3 kg of plutonium from its Safari-1 reac-tor at Pelindaba, putting its nuclear capability 'into the big league'. Like the stories of hidden reactors, this implied that South Africa had undis-closed nuclear sites[1] where the main object would have been to obtain enough plutonium for implosion weapons.

Richard, who had worked on the nuclear weapons design pro-gramme, confirmed that work had been completed on this type of war-head: 'We developed an implosion weapon that could also have been

[1] High on the list of suspicious locations was a disused copper mine at Copperton in the northern Cape. The land around the mine, including the former mine village – with squash courts, a swimming-bath, houses and a bar – had been bought by Armscor, according to a manager who worked on the nuclear bomb programme.

He said not far from the mine winding-house a road spiralled downwards to a depth of hundreds of metres before reaching a large cavern. The tunnel was steep and had to be negotiated by four-wheel-drive vehicles. Halfway down there was a passing-place con-trolled by a set of traffic lights.

The manager, who had been inside the mine, said people there used protective clothing which had to be destroyed after use. He and another informant, who was a retired military officer, said they had heard the SADF was running its own reactor in the cavern. The man-ager said the reactor was slightly larger than the Safari reactor at Pelindaba.

A nuclear expert privy to military secrets was more specific: he said there was a heavy-water reactor there that was made in Germany and run by the military. Another source said it had been shut down just before the 1994 election.

High-voltage power lines criss-cross the semi-arid landscape around the mine, in one of the most isolated areas of the Cape, and a large electricity switching station has four cam-ouflaged watch-towers. One man who visited Copperton on military business said that at one stage the community had more than 200 houses, but all were bought by Armscor when they took over the mine. 'You could buy a house there for R1,500 ($450), but had to agree to demolish it within three months. The place is now a wreck. None of the sports facilities are usable. You can bet there is something very big down there.'

miniaturized for a nuclear shell,' he said. The work was being done in the mid-1980s,[1] and a completed design was built. 'It was tested using a tungsten core instead of plutonium at a site near Potchefstroom. A tarpaulin was rigged over it so it could not be spotted by spy satellites.'

Jeff, a weapons scientist, confirmed that fully developed designs were produced on orders from the White Savannah Committee. 'We were always told none were built, but that may not be the case.'

We heard stories of a parallel programme to the one both Jeff and Richard had worked on at Kentron Circle/Advena. It was said that miniature plutonium warheads, including shells, were manufactured with Israeli assistance, although no one could provide a location for the plant.

To deliver nuclear shells, South Africa needed fine artillery, and in the G5 howitzer and its motorized stablemate, the G6, it had some of the best available. The barrel of these weapons was based on original designs by the brilliant Dr Gerald Bull, a maverick Canadian scientist who worked closely with Armscor before his murder in Belgium in 1990.

Bull, who had a PhD by the time he was twenty-two, was fascinated by aeronautical engineering, specifically ballistics. He had worked for the Canadian Armament and Research Development Establishment for ten years, during which time he developed an idea to send projectiles into space from the barrel of a giant gun.

With funding from a number of interested parties, including the US Army, he set up a small research establishment on Barbados, called the High Altitude Research Project. After this money dried up, the project was abandoned and Bull set himself up as a consultant at his Highwater estate, which straddled the border of the United States and Canada. His focus now was conventional artillery.

Off his drawing-board came plans for a 155-mm howitzer that would be more accurate and have a greater range than those already used by the world's armies. Bull designed a shell that could be fired substantially further, even using the existing 155-mm artillery.

Neither the United States nor NATO was interested, but his developments attracted international attention and by 1973, a year after he became a US citizen, he started designing a new-generation 155-mm howitzer which, when built, could out-gun anything built by the Soviet Union. He was invited, with CIA connivance, to help improve the

1 In 1988 Newsweek reported that South Africa had in 1985 been hiring British and American nuclear physicists and technicians to work on its nuclear weapons programme.

artillery of South Africa, then locked in battle with the Cuban-backed forces of Angola. His designs were incorporated into the South African weapons with great success. South Africa then added refinements of its own. The resulting G5 was later considered state of the art.

Bull maintained his association with South Africa over the years, probably grateful to have found a country that appreciated his revolutionary designs. Armscor eventually produced even better 'base-bleed' propellant systems and shells. The result, according to our sources, was that the G5/G6 had a range superior to that of any of its rivals.

Before Bull's death he had taken his ideas a stage further. With his ideas for a supergun, he hoped to be able to send a payload into space. Dion, the Armscor source, said he believed Bull may have built South Africa a supergun, like the one he is known to have been developing for Iraq. 'We did a test at a place called Wallmannstal on this huge barrel,' he said. 'We used pieces of tungsten as a substitute for a warhead. The barrel came from Pelindaba, but it was kept at Armscor's Advena premises, resting on concrete blocks, and went the length of one side of the building.'

It is known that Bull worked with various Armscor subsidiaries. A military agent told us: 'Bull was working on a very special weapon with a special barrel while he was in South Africa. He was also working from South Africa on plans and tests for the supergun. I believe we have one as well. There was a gun used and applied in the Angolan war which had a great range – 120 km.' He said that up to Bull's death, the scientist had been working 'day and night' in South Africa on a special weapon.

On top of this, the agent said: 'I know that South African technicians were also used to help design the supergun that almost reached Saddam. South African technicians were working on that barrel in Britain.'

A 1992 MI5 report produced at the trial of executives of the British machine-tool company Matrix Churchill, which had been bought by the Iraqis, revealed that technology for 210-mm artillery systems was 'being supplied by South Africans'. Lathes for making the shells for these had been supplied by Matrix.

The AEC insists its six and half A-bombs were first devised out of scientific curiosity, a result of the natural tendency for boffins to want to see if their ideas could work. Having satisfied themselves of this, a strategy was then developed to use one 'for demonstration purposes' as a last resort.

It is said that South Africa intended to respond to a threat of invasion with a three-stage plan. In stage 1 it would neither confirm nor deny that it had a nuclear weapon. In stage 2 it would tell the major Western powers of its nuclear capability, in a bid to get them to intervene. If that failed it would move to stage 3 – a demonstration detonation.

The Washington think-tank ISIS was told: 'The weapons were never intended for actual use, and they were never deployed militarily or integrated into the country's military doctrine. In essence the weapons were the last card in a political bluff intended to blackmail the United States or other Western powers.'

Armscor and the AEC illustrate the point with the example of an invasion from Angola or Mozambique by Soviet-backed forces. As a first warning a device would have been detonated in an underground shaft, probably in the Kalahari desert. The object would be to scare world powers so much that they would have to come to the Republic's aid. It was accepted there might have to be two underground tests to achieve this result, and maybe another device would have to be 'tossed' from a Buccaneer bomber as a final show of strength. But, even if this failed to win support, it is said the intention was never to use the weapons against the enemy.

Tielman de Waal, boss of Armscor, told the *Washington Post* in 1993:

> You would say, I am now going to pick up the phone, phone the US President or the British Prime Minister and tell them, look, if you do not apply pressure on the USSR to withdraw these forces, we are going to activate the bomb … The reply would probably be, you have no bomb, so South Africa would explode one or two weapons to demonstrate its nuclear capability, then you would say, we have five more, do you really want to look for trouble.

South Africa's apparent determination not to use the weapons offensively meant that its six and a half devices were never integrated into the SADF for deployment but were kept in the vaults at Advena. It seems the generals were unconcerned that the entire stockpile was therefore vulnerable to a single air strike.

Jan, the military strategist, said it was absurd to think South Africa would make such an error. He said the more advanced weapons were integrated into the SADF/SAAF and were deployed in closely guarded bunkers all over the country. He said he had participated in SADF war games involving the deployment of tactical nuclear weapons.

Jan also said the military came close to a nuclear confrontation in 1988 when South African troops faced overwhelming Cuban forces wielding sophisticated, state-of-the-art Soviet weaponry at Cuito Cuanavale in Angola. He said nuclear weapons were deployed at South African forward bases in Angola: 'They were tactical battlefield nuclear weapons, neutron devices, to be delivered by air.'[1]

Military analysts reported that South African troops lost their air cover in Angola and for some time warplanes had been fighting on the edge of their operational capability, despite the fine reputation of their pilots. Sanctions-hit South Africa was unable to replace lost aircraft, and combined with this was the high risk associated with a strategic withdrawal south. The South African public would not be prepared to accept the possible accompanying loss of life.

Faced with this crisis, military strategists prepared to go nuclear. Another source who spoke to us on condition of strict anonymity was a military Special Forces soldier who guarded the nuclear devices – inside Angola. He said: 'I was told by a general they were neutron devices. He didn't want to go into detail.'

Jan said nuclear weapons would have been used as a last resort if the Cubans had overrun the South African positions. He speculated that an international deal had been agreed as a consequence of which, if South African forces were allowed to withdraw safely, the Namibian problem would be dealt with. This involved the implementation of UN Resolution 435, which covered South Africa's withdrawal from Namibia, which it had occupied since taking over the former German colony, and the holding of elections there. The final settlement was linked to the withdrawal of foreign forces on Angolan soil.[2] It was agreed by South Africa, Angola and Cuba on 22 December 1988.

Before South Africa reached a deal, one of the shafts at Vastrap, which had remained capped with concrete for the previous ten years, was reopened. A hangar-like building was erected above it, and water that accumulated in the shafts was pumped into lorries and taken away. Imitation battle tanks and lorries made of plastic were brought in to make the area look like a military base to spy satellites passing overhead.

Paul, formerly of Military Intelligence, said he was in northern

1 The fact that South Africa deployed these weapons was confirmed by a former agent of the British Secret Intelligence Services and several former Special Forces commandos.

2 The South African military had used Namibia as a buffer zone to prevent their clashes with communist forces spilling across the South African border. With the collapse of old-style communism in the Soviet Union and the removal of foreign forces in the region, strategists considered the military confrontation could be halted and South Africa's borders could remain secure.

Namibia in 1988. 'They mobilized short- to medium-range nuclear missiles,' he said.

Jan said the neutron shell, also deployed in Angola, had been available to the military since 1982. He said South Africa's mobile howitzer, the 155-mm G6, was originally designed to fire them.

Another source, who said he had been with the Civil Co-operation Bureau, the clandestine Special Forces unit, confirmed this: 'We created 155-mm G5 and G6 artillery shells that carry small nuclear warheads. I guarded some at a bunker in a secret base. There were also larger nuclear weapons.' He said that one of these nuclear bunkers was still operational.

The G6 has a published range of 40 km, which is reputed to have been extended to 100 km or more. At first a nuclear shell for these guns used Russian technology, we heard from Jan, but later South Africa developed its own – using a 'special chemical'. 'I know they were very proud of what they had developed. It was better than Russia's. We had hundreds of the shells,' Jan revealed. 'The chemical was something like this material red mercury. It was spoken about with reverence.'

13 Operation Shampoo

The people summoned by President P. W. Botha to an operational meeting of the State Security Council were like-minded securocrats. Their sole interest: the well-being of the Republic of South Africa. Seated around the mahogany conference table were generals from the military and police, ministers, and some of the country's top field operatives. It was a special meeting, convened over a weekend.

The subject under discussion was as serious as the men gathered around the table: the imminent arrival in South Africa of a large, aluminium-hulled yacht carrying contraband worth millions of dollars.

For eight months, through 1987 into 1988, the consignment had been tracked by the security police. They had monitored the progress of the foreign-owned vessel as it forged its way across the Indian Ocean. So far as the police were concerned, its cargo was high-tech weaponry that was being imported into South Africa illegally.

The tale of this yacht was one of the most remarkable of our investigation. We had managed to track down one of the police officers involved and had arranged for him secretly to tell us his extraordinary story. We had met him in a restaurant 100 km from Johannesburg, expecting him to be a little nervous. He wasn't. Rather, he was angry about the myriad lies being told by the establishment.

'It was a big consignment,' he said. 'We knew who had been involved in the shipping, which was from Mauritius, and we knew it was coming to South Africa via Mozambique. We had even established that the owner of the vessel was a member of the yacht club in Durban. We knew what time the yacht was coming in – everything.'

When it was established that the arrival of the yacht was imminent, the case was referred to higher authority to decide on the best course of action. The security police, aided by telephone and radio intercepts, had learned that the consignment was to be off-loaded in the port of Durban, and decisive action was required if the cargo was to be impounded and the smugglers arrested.

However, as the drama unfolded, there was disappointment in store for the police officers who had spent so many months diligently monitoring the yacht. Nothing was what it seemed.

The police officers working on the case had passed on their information to the security committee. The securocrats deliberated behind closed doors – then came their shock decision. The security police would take no further action. All documentation and photographs connected to the case had to be shredded. So far as anyone would know in the future, the eight-month investigation had never occurred. 'We were told the shipment was official,' said the agent.

The yacht arrived as scheduled, and the consignment was off-loaded in great secrecy by Special Forces commandos and taken to Number One Reconnaissance Battalion, whose base overlooks Durban from the Bluff.

We listened intently as the agent described the disappointment and frustration at the wasted investigation that had soaked up so many man-hours and at how the whole incident had been covered up.

He leaned forward, preparing to emphasize a point. 'You see, the yacht was carrying red mercury.' The security police had inadvertently uncovered an arm of South Africa's secret red mercury supply line from Russia, and clearly the less said about it the better. 'They simply didn't want us there,' said the agent.

Amid all the denials of the existence of red mercury, the police officer had decided to meet us partly out of anger. He was incredulous that the official cover-up of red mercury was continuing into the 1990s. 'The fact that it was carrying red mercury was apparently even discussed in front of the President.'

And it was not an incident in isolation.

Our dinner companion also revealed that later another arms deal had attracted the attention of the security police. In this investigation, the police operation had been running for only one month, towards the end of 1989. A top-level security committee meeting was called. The new State President, F. W. de Klerk, was head of the security services at the time.[1] The investigation was immediately chopped, the agent said. Again, the investigation had involved a boat, this time carrying a consignment of red mercury, a plastic explosive called Tovex, diesel and a fertilizer. It arrived in Durban harbour only days after the security committee met.

But there was further evidence of officially sanctioned importation of Russian red mercury. The policeman told us he knew of up to five other

1 De Klerk later refused to be interviewed by the authors about South Africa's nuclear weapons programme. An allegation that South Africa had secretly built more nuclear weapons than the six and a half to which it had admitted was dismissed as 'fantastic' by one of his aides.

cases in which investigations were halted because police officers had inadvertently interfered with red mercury procurement. 'At one stage, I held it in my hand. I saw it through a brown bottle, and it moved like a heavy grease. It was in a sort of lab bottle that had been confiscated in an arms deal.' He said the material was tested and later disappeared – probably stolen. There was no court case.

A number of arms deals were running between 1987 and 1989, and 70 per cent of them included a consignment of red mercury, he said. 'We were told not to touch these deals too. Most came through by boat from Mauritius or Mozambique.'

Another source later confirmed that a blue yacht, registered in Gibraltar, arrived in Durban in May 1988. The source, close to European intelligence operations, said the yacht brought to South Africa a consignment of Russian-made red mercury, top-secret blueprints, microchips and microfiche. The secret cargo was taken from a Russian vessel during a rendezvous off an island close to Mauritius, the intelligence source said.

This was the first long sailing voyage for the vessel. Built in the Netherlands, its ownership was apparently changed in March 1989.

The police officer involved in the abortive investigations said that whatever was going on had the approval of the highest authority. Red mercury was coming into South Africa, and the government did not want it stopped. He recalled what senior officers had called these irregular shipments – they had used the names several times in connection with the deals. The missions were part of a project called Operation Shampoo.

Despite overwhelming official denials, our investigation was uncovering many accounts that contradicted the official line. They showed not only that red mercury existed but, more worryingly, that key politicians and officials would go to great lengths to ensure its existence was covered up.

But now people were talking. The viciousness of the killings combined with a feeling of new-found freedom in South Africa since the 1994 election had slowly encouraged people to emerge and tell their stories. It was during this time that we found an informant who had first-hand knowledge about what had been going on. His dramatic story confirmed our belief that there was indeed an official procurement operation for red mercury, but much more besides.

At first he was unwilling to talk, citing the Official Secrets Act and the dangers of even speaking anonymously about such a sensitive issue. However, he agreed to help after we discussed the possibility of stray nuclear weapons, the killings, and the rights of the victims' families and the public to know what was going on.

Jake was a military sanctions-buster who had operated in the shadowy world of illegal arms deals for his country for many years. He was proud about what South Africa had achieved during the years of sanctions, but concerned about the secret nuclear programmes.

At a meeting in his dusty downtown office in Pretoria he told us that South African agents, operating mostly under cover, were instructed by Armscor in the mid-1980s to procure red mercury and other materials for the country's nuclear weapons programme.

The top-secret project was code-named Shampoo, and fell under the Official Secrets Act. Procurement agents operating in a clandestine cell structure were ordered to find red mercury and bring it back to South Africa. The Armscor agent also revealed how Western countries helped channel to South Africa not only red mercury but also other exotic chemicals urgently required for the country's nuclear weapons programme.

He told us that red mercury was often referred to as PP20/20 or PP50/50 and was crucially important to the weapons designers. Jake prepared written answers to some of our questions.

'Sometime during the mid-1980s external structures were set up for the importation to South Africa of key military parts from manufacturing countries like Britain, the United States, France and Italy. We had "friendlies" in these countries who were willing to meet our military requirements despite heavy penalties if they were caught. We also paid a hefty premium on what we bought from these operatives.

'During the same period we were asked to find RM20/20, osmium 187, rubidium and californium. This was done via certain military operatives in Europe who would help us source the products. After making a few initial contacts in Germany, Italy and the UK, I asked our senior controller here to reassign me to normal procurement of weapons and spares.'

Why? 'I had helped the Israelis, and one Israeli general warned me at the time not to get involved. He said it was "really big shit" and that I should keep my fingers out of it. I took his warning seriously.'

Were you aware of what lay behind red mercury? 'Yes, I knew what it was about. I knew that the code-name for the procurement, processing and storage of RM20/20 was P/S, or Project Shampoo.

'There were four countries directly involved in the technical know-how and funding of the South African project – Britain, France, the United States and Italy. The Israelis were involved as well, providing some of the manpower. They came in as "agricultural researchers and marine biologists on study leave". The Germans were buying red mercury through East Germany, and their operations ran independently of the four other countries.

'These countries would let the substance through to us without hindrance. They knew the ultimate destination was Pretoria. The compound was trans-shipped via black African countries – Zambia, Mozambique and Zimbabwe. Customs there were easily bribed.

'A lot of rubbish came in. I was told that out of every fifty samples submitted on average only one was suitable. Also, there was a protocol of payment – it had to be in US dollars.

'Crime syndicates were heavily involved. This was a technique used during the Second World War to smuggle illicit goods, and it had worked really well. Confusion about what was going on was encouraged by the various security services, to throw people off the scent of what was really happening.

'I also heard that a form of red mercury could be found in certain conventional warheads of Russian origin which were to be found in Angola and Mozambique. South African technicians extracted this and sent it to a local electronics manufacturer, a company which makes detonators for all sorts of weapons.'

What other South African organizations were involved in processing this compound? 'There were technical experts from the AEC and the CSIR[1] who worked on the refinement and testing of the imported material, namely 20/20. EMLC,[2] a technical unit of the Special Forces, was playing an important role here. Thor Chemicals was also linked to the work on red mercury. Alan Kidger was involved in this.

'Ex-senior police officers were involved in the red mercury business, including at least one staunch right-winger with military connections. I heard they were involved in the testing and verification procedures for red mercury.'

How were deals arranged? 'It went like this: they tested the sample,

1 A commodities trader in Johannesburg who had handled several consignments of red mercury said the Council for Scientific and Industrial Research had tested red mercury samples 'in the early years', before all testing had been transferred to the AEC at Pelindaba. The AEC says it has never seen red mercury.

2 An intelligence source said that just before the election, when a decision was made to close down the SF units, EMLC also was closed. But equipment and materials from EMLC were transferred to an underground military base called Silvermine, near Cape Town. Silvermine is a highly secure communications base for the South African navy, built inside a hollowed-out mountain.

and then arranged delivery and payment for the main consignment. The main containers were also tested. This was because in many previous deals people produced a genuine sample but the main containers were filled with shit.'

Who else was involved in these deals? 'Other former police officers and a retired US Navy intelligence officer, who worked closely with EMLC.'

Have you witnessed any red mercury tests? 'Yes, but I should not explain the circumstances.'

Who is behind these numerous killings here which are said to involve the red mercury trade? 'The people who were "taken out" here and in other parts of the world were in one way or another involved in the genuine 20/20 procurement routes. However, I believe they were taken out not by Mossad but by the Iranian or Iraqi equivalent.

'The Americans are very nervous that the truth about red mercury is going to come out as a result of these deaths. They were deeply involved in helping us. In fact, they funded a lot of the development. The CIA was kept in the dark about what was going on, but the Defense Intelligence Agency was heavily involved, and it wanted to make sure no one else knew this. They even tipped us off when the CIA sent someone here to snoop.'

It was an important breakthrough: a first-hand account of how South Africa had been procuring red mercury through official and other channels. It was our first real indication that the nuclear weapons programme involved revolutionary components, and therefore could be far more extensive than first thought. The disturbing disclosure of how it was done – including the dangerously unpredictable use of crime syndicates and the key role played by Western nations – vindicated our persistence in the face of a mountain of denials.

As well, the disclosure was yet another significant indication that South Africa's claim to have dismantled its nuclear weapons arsenal was hogwash – a point that many other sources would expand upon later. So far as we, or indeed the rest of the world, were concerned, the country's six declared nuclear weapons had not used red mercury. So which weapons did?

Many of the claims made by Jake – including the involvement of former police officers and other countries, Operation Shampoo, the verification procedure, and the role played by official or semi-official bodies – were later confirmed by other sources, including scientists, intelligence officers and former government officials.

Meanwhile, another dimension started to emerge. The *Weekend Star* reported in December 1994 that a South African Airways Boeing 747 jetliner, the *Helderberg*, could have been illegally carrying a secret rocket fuel[1] when it crashed into the Indian Ocean off Mauritius in 1987, killing 159 passengers and crew. A key source involved said he was adamant the propellant was red mercury.

The source, a highly placed explosives expert, said the information was so sensitive that if his identity were revealed 'I would need a body-guard.' He was one of a range of sources who, in stories over several weeks, said the *Helderberg* was carrying rocket fuel and that there had been a cover-up. This was denied by Armscor, the airline and the SADF.[2]

An earlier official inquiry had been unable to fully establish what had happened to the aircraft, but the latest claims clearly rattled Armscor. In an unusual step, it took the *Weekend Star* to the Media Council, the press watchdog, which found against the newspaper on a number of key points. It said it found some of its claims unsubstantiated, and the news-paper later apologized to the airline.

The outcome was seen as a slap on the wrist for the newspaper, which promptly abandoned this investigation, although relatives of those killed aboard the airliner had earlier begged the newspaper to press on. Media investigation, they said, was the only chance they would ever have of finding out what had happened to their loved ones.

To this day, it is still not known exactly what happened aboard the *Helderberg*. However, we established that, particularly in the tough sanctions period of the late 1980s, a number of airlines carried potential-ly dangerous materials into South Africa. They ranged from frequency-hopping radio transmitters to missiles and conventional weapons. On one occasion a weapons crate being loaded into the hold of a Johannesburg-bound scheduled flight from Europe had broken open, spilling surface-to-air missiles across the apron. In many cases airlines were not even aware of what they were carrying.

Cargo managers and baggage-handlers were on the payroll of South African security agencies, and South Africa's needs for certain strategic materials – especially in the light of the huge confrontation looming with the Cuban/Russian forces in Angola – were considered more important than aviation safety. Airline sources said pilots had become particularly

1 Red mercury has a range of applications. Apart from being a vital component in some nuclear weapons, it can also be used as a booster for rockets.

2 Now called the South African National Defence Force (SANDF).

jumpy in this period over what was being loaded into their cargo holds.

Eugene, the former South African intelligence agent, told us: 'For years we had imported very sensitive material through airports. The guys handling the cargo were paid by the intelligence agencies. Sometimes even stewardesses were paid agents. At Jan Smuts Airport[1] there were lots of cargo-handlers with two-way radio links to their intelligence bosses who co-ordinated these operations from the sidelines.

'Mauritius, Zaïre, Gabon, Egypt and Iran would help out with end-user certificates, and then the shipments would arrive in South Africa. Sometimes the cargo would be loaded and off-loaded under the command of an airline manager. The manager might have been wearing the uniform of an airline, but really he was there to look after the secret cargoes for the security services. Some cargoes would have couriers, others would not – especially for a small item that might be carried in a captain's safe. But usually one of the crew would know what was being carried.

'The military had been using scheduled flights for years. Israeli ground-to-air missiles had been brought in on scheduled flights, along with highly sophisticated electronic equipment – unofficially and officially. Not everything was dangerous, but some of it was extremely so. Israeli containers had firearms, ammunition, explosives and weapons prototypes. The first Stinger missiles were brought in on scheduled flights, and some of the captains were involved. At Jan Smuts Airport the secret shipments were taken to a security warehouse on the south-western corner. From there the equipment was loaded into other vehicles and nothing went through Customs. Smuts was so easy.'

He said such operations had been running from the early 1980s to the 1990s. The logistics of the secret procurement operations were set up on foreign soil with the help of agents working for the Department of Foreign Affairs, who specialized in intelligence, technical operations and electronics.

Eugene was unable to confirm that red mercury was ever brought into South Africa on commercial airliners, although he did not rule out the possibility: 'They seemed to carry everything else.'

On top of this, our investigation of the Stoffberg killings was paying dividends. After questioning more friends, family members and intelligence sources, a clearer picture was beginning to emerge. The information we had now gathered went a long way to explain why South Africa had

1 Now Johannesburg International Airport.

become a red mercury 'hot spot'.

Of prime interest was information from Eugene, who had been a friend of Dirk Stoffberg. He agreed to talk to us about Stoffberg provided we did not blow his cover. We met him at a small hotel close to the Magaliesberg mountains. He had known Stoffberg for years, and what he was about to tell us would dovetail perfectly with what we already knew of the arms dealer's activities.

Other security sources had disclosed to us that South Africa had progressed beyond having to procure the illicit red mercury on the black market – it was now making its own. Eugene not only confirmed this, he went on to relate a remarkable encounter in 1991 at Stoffberg's Hartbeespoort home in which the arms dealer showed his friends South African-made red mercury.

Describing the evening meeting, Eugene said a number of intelligence and police operatives were present. 'Dirk asked us if we could identify something of great value if we saw it – something of extreme value and sensitivity. He went to his study and asked us to come in and have a look. There we saw a cylindrical, stainless-steel container of a dark colour, greyish blue, and another, smaller, container.

'The larger container weighed about 12 to 15 kg, stood about 45 cm tall, and was about 20 cm across. It was very heavy, but it was impossible to say how much volume was inside: it could have been just a small amount of liquid. It had a screw cap on the top, with handle holes.

'Two containers were sold together as one unit. The small one was about 20 cm high and 10 to 12 cm across the base. It was oval, much like a World War II water bottle. It was the same type of heavy-duty stainless-steel container, dark green or brown I think, and had a cap on the top.

'Stoffberg said when the two substances were combined it would be effective for only a short period – just days. He said this was a revolutionary weapon that could destroy the people of Pretoria but leave the buildings standing. He took off the lid from the large canister and poured a little bit into a glass standing next to it. It was a purple or dark-red thick substance, which was slow-moving. He asked if we knew what it was. "Red mercury," he said. I laughed. It was the first time I had seen the stuff.

'I asked him where he'd got it. "Not far away from here," he replied. [Stoffberg's Hartbeespoort home had a distant view of Pelindaba.]

'The stuff I saw at Stoffberg's home had something missing. You had to take the material to the battlefield and then put two components together – one was non-radioactive, the other radioactive. He said people from the Middle East were buying a lot of useless stuff, but this was the real thing.' Although the South African-made product was different in appearance and colour, its applications were similar to the Russian material, he said.

Other senior intelligence sources confirmed to us that the South African-made substance could be used to make nuclear weapons. One source even suggested that South Africa had made a better product than Russia. It had found a way of storing the chemical for longer periods. The Russian material started to decay after one to three months.[1] To get around this problem, South African technicians had designed a detonator system that kept separate two components of the chemical until the second of detonation, using a membrane to keep them apart inside a small metal container.

Three sources told us that the mixing of two chemicals was a prerequisite of the South African version of red mercury, which was called something else. While the two chemicals were separate, they could be kept for long periods. When mixed, they had a very short shelf-life.

Making such a sensitive chemical was one thing, but what Eugene told us next started to explain the paranoia and life-and-death developments apparently surrounding the material. He disclosed that South Africa was selling the product on the world market – some of it through Dirk Stoffberg. Eugene said Stoffberg had told him that he was the only person officially authorized to sell the South African material, and had been doing so for years.

It is also possible that one of the security agencies was trying to halt the trade. Yet another intelligence source said someone had been photographing visitors to the Stoffberg home and tapping telephones before the double killing. Said Eugene: 'Stoffberg said that if we knew of anyone wanting red mercury, through our overseas contacts, he could supply it – complete with all the official papers.'

Stoffberg showed the small group of men three or four documents, which included specifications. 'He had an English version and what looked like a Russian version of specifications. He had an official South

1 This meant that the Russian military, which used red mercury extensively as detonators, had to frequently 'refresh' the material, apparently a straightforward procedure provided specialized technical equipment was on hand. 'Out-of-date' red mercury that had started to 'separate' or break down into its original constituent parts was still worth up to 60 per cent of its value, according to sources, but was only of use if the owner had access to the equipment that could refresh it. That effectively meant it was of value only to certain governments.

African selling and buying code. He also had documents on how it worked. It was a type of device that had to be used in a certain period of time. He made it clear the Americans didn't have this technology.'

Stoffberg was selling the South African-made red mercury for R43,000 to R46,000 an ounce, or $427,000 to $457,000 a kilogram.

The canisters at his home were going to Belgium. 'Stoffberg contacted us from Brussels on a few occasions. We talked about red mercury again, and he said some of the scientists involved in making it were "outside the field". I said: "Pelindaba?" and he said: "No." The way he said it, I knew he was referring to Advena. Then Dirk faded.'

Eugene said he had met a number of people from various intelligence agencies in Europe who wanted to buy red mercury from South Africa, but he had remained sceptical of its existence until the encounter with Stoffberg.

'I met a Russian intelligence agent in Europe who told me that, although red mercury was made in Russia, its official trade was closely guarded.' Eugene said he believed the agent was probably trying to finance clandestine operations in Europe by buying and selling the South African substance. Much the same kind of dealing in other valuable substances was done by intelligence services the world over, he said.

'Russia had a special arrangement with the United States that this technology would not fall into the wrong hands.[1] There was a strict discipline in Russia. Although Russian nuclear scientists had become a special commodity in Europe, Russia would not sell red mercury officially.'

But, for Stoffberg's friend, final confirmation of what the arms dealer told him came later, towards the end of 1992. During a visit to South Africa's top-secret nuclear weapons laboratory at Advena, he said he saw the material being produced and stored. 'At Advena I saw exactly the same substance I saw in Stoffberg's home. I saw the liquid and the same types of canisters.'

He asked what the material was. 'I was told by an employee that it was a bomb, and it was made at Advena. But this person didn't talk about it being a nuclear weapon.

'I was shown the substance in the laboratory, which is a huge place. There were these long stainless-steel tables, computers, heavy equipment

1 Russian and South African Defence Ministers Pavel Grachev and Joe Modise signed a military co-operation agreement in Moscow in July 1995. Modise visited military bases and industrial complexes. Said Grachev: 'The agreement opens the way for the development of contacts on a number of points between the military structures of our two countries.' Nelson Mandela was scheduled to visit Russia soon after Modise's trip.

and radioactive signs through the length of the building, which stretched as far as the eye could see. And there were emergency containment doors at frequent intervals.

'The red mercury looked as though it was in a sort of cream-separator, an oval thing. There were pipes and other equipment all around it. It was just in the one place. There seemed to be about 5 litres of the stuff in the bowl.'

But sources inside the new Advena laboratories said there was far more than that. By 1993 there were at least forty cylinders of the substance, locked away in a strongroom behind a security screen of various locks and electronic codes. They were stored on metal shelves – five rows of eight.

Eugene said he had been told years earlier that red mercury was a nuclear explosive much in demand in the Middle East. Russia refused to supply its red mercury because of secret agreements with nations that had signed the Nuclear Non-Proliferation Treaty: 'However, South Africa was prepared to do exactly that,' he said. 'And Armscor has a great trade network in the Middle East.' He said South African Military Intelligence had a special procedure for dealing with the Middle East. Operatives would fly to Paris and report to the South African embassy. 'There, MI issues new passports, books hotels, air tickets, and explains a code of conduct for operations in the Middle East. Paris is the main South African embassy for covert operations.'

But individuals were also making money out of the South African substance. Investigations have shown that at least one former police officer and maybe three others were selling red mercury – partly to finance clandestine operations, partly for themselves.

Known in South Africa among arms dealers and intelligence agents as 'rooiwyn', 'roodewyn' or 'rooikwik' – all Afrikaans descriptions – the chemical was still being declared a hoax by Armscor, the AEC and the military as this book was being written.

Meanwhile we established that there were sensitive documents in existence regarding Operation Shampoo that had evaded the security swoop at Stoffberg's home. The documents were signed by both Dirk and Suzanne Stoffberg and concerned the procurement process. Said an intelligence source: 'Everyone dealing with red mercury had to sign the Official Secrets Act.' There were apparently more documents that named other people involved in Operation Shampoo.

Yet other documents showed that the Stoffbergs had not only been selling the South African-made material, they had earlier been involved in purchasing the Russian red mercury too. The papers apparently showed that two former police generals were involved, confirming what other sources had told us.

Further investigation also flushed out another remarkable aspect of the puzzle. A source in the arms industry disclosed that elements of the South African military imported 11 grams of highly radioactive californium in December 1993. If this was the isotope californium-252, it was the most bizarre claim yet concerning South Africa's sophisticated nuclear weaponry, because this material is produced in only fractions of a gram in the West, although Russia apparently produces substantially more.

If the claim was to be believed, 11 grams could represent a substantial portion of the world's total supply. But why bring it to South Africa? Sources would later tell us that californium, which is reportedly a component of a red mercury cocktail for nuclear weapons, could be a key ingredient of the 'clean' bomb.

The source said the purchase of californium, from a company in London, was official and involved military personnel. 'It probably came from Russia and then went to the broker in Britain. It was sent to Pretoria and handled by the military all the way. I've no idea what it was to be used for.'

In what might have been a reference to this, the South African Broadcasting Corporation reported, on 7 June 1995, that Parliament's Public Accounts Committee had heard details of an SADF deal to purchase what was described as 'very sensitive chemicals' from an Eastern European country. Defence Force chief Georg Meiring and other senior defence officials told the committee of a plan in 1992 and 1993 to use covert funds to buy the chemicals.

The deal went wrong and South Africa lost more than $5 million when cash that had been allocated for the transaction was confiscated from a Swiss bank account. General Meiring told the committee he could not provide more details about the chemical substance or the people involved without clearance from the Cabinet.

The report begged a number of questions: What were the chemicals and were they part of Operation Shampoo?

It was clear from Jake's testimony and the story of the yacht that red mercury was being procured and then used to manufacture something very special. We were hearing it was being employed in a revolutionary type of neutron weapon – the 'clean' bomb that would not contaminate the battlefield with high doses of radiaoctivity. Its existence was not just another demonstration of South African technical expertise, it represented a looming nuclear proliferation nightmare.

14 A Little Help from Friends

When the President made his March 1993 announcement about South Africa's disbanded nuclear programme, no words he uttered caused more scepticism than his reference to foreign assistance. De Klerk had told Parliament: 'I wish to emphasize that at no time did South Africa acquire nuclear weapons technology or materials from another country. Nor has it provided any to any other country or co-operated with another country.'

Roger Jardine, then the ANC's co-ordinator on science and technology,[1] said afterwards: 'It is laughable to state that South Africa developed its nuclear weapons capability without outside help ... Throughout the decades, collaboration has been well documented and reported on. We are looking at the role of Israel and West Germany for example.' He added: 'If President de Klerk does not come completely clean on the extent of the nuclear weapons programme, his pronouncement in Parliament must be regarded as a misguided attempt to make party-political gains out of an issue of global importance.'

In 1994, the South African *Weekly Mail & Guardian* called the De Klerk statement 'F. W.'s three lies'. It had evidence, it claimed, of Israeli collaboration. But why would De Klerk, who received the Nobel Peace Prize with Nelson Mandela for helping to bring about democracy in South Africa, be so wrong and remain unchallenged by the Western powers?

The answer appeared to lie in South Africa's former pariah status. Few Western nations would want an inquest into who had helped the apartheid regime, because most had dirty hands. Most embarrassing of all would be the disclosure of who among them had known the secrets of Valindaba, Advena and Houwteq.

South Africa officially had been a pariah state since 1963, when the UN Security Council unanimously approved Resolution 182 for a voluntary embargo on supplying arms. The Asian People's Solidarity

---

1 Now director-general of the Ministry of Arts, Culture, Science and Technology.

Conference and the Pan-Africanist Congress were angry at the United States and European countries who had been supplying arms, and France had come under particular censure.

However, the response to the embargo was less than wholehearted. Sir Alec Douglas Home, the British Foreign Secretary, said his country would oppose the sale of arms for enforcing apartheid but would honour commitments to sell weapons for defence – a very fine distinction. The United States said it would interpret the embargo in the light of requirements for assuring the maintenance of international peace and security. Said the US ambassador to the UN: 'If the interests of the world community require the provision of equipment for use in the common defence effort, we would naturally feel able to do so without violating the spirit and the intent of this resolve.'

One country didn't have to worry about the niceties of UN diplomacy: it was fast becoming a pariah state itself. Israel had the entire Arab world ranged against it – or so it believed. The need for a secret nuclear weapons programme was easy to sell to its top generals, faced with defending the country against apparently impossible odds. Thanks to the information supplied by Mordechai Vanunu, who worked as a technician in Israel's nuclear weapons plant, it is known that nuclear weapons based on plutonium were being produced for military use by the late 1960s. The programme went hand in hand with a mushrooming armaments industry, tightly controlled by the state.

Collaboration with South Africa, therefore, coincided with a period when both countries felt more and more vulnerable. It is said that first discussions on nuclear co-operation began as early as 1953, and that supplies of uranium ore were being shipped by 1963.

This relationship was explained succinctly in 1968 by *Die Burger*, a Cape newspaper loyal to the National Party:

Israel and South Africa have much in common.[1] Both are engaged in a struggle for existence, and both are in constant clash with the decisive majorities in the United Nations ... It is in South Africa's interest that Israel is successful in containing her enemies, who are among our own most vicious enemies; and Israel would have all the world against it if

1 Ironically, the forerunner of the National Party, which came to power in 1948, was the Purified National Party, which was strongly anti-Semitic. John Vorster, later to become South African Prime Minister, was jailed by Britain during the Second Word War for his pro-Nazi sympathies. On the other hand, in 1956 Israel voted with Third World countries for a UN resolution condemning apartheid as 'reprehensible and repugnant'. That the two countries became bedfellows was partly a case of 'the enemy of my enemy is my friend'.

the navigation route around the Cape of Good Hope should be out of operation because South Africa's control is undermined.

These common interests blended even more as international isolation grew. South Africa was said to have sent Mirage fighters to help in the Yom Kippur War of October 1973, and one was allegedly shot down on the Suez front. In 1975 Meir Amit, the former chief of the Israeli secret service, paid a visit to South Africa. He said Israeli officers regularly lectured on modern warfare to their counterparts in South Africa. When asked if military relations were good, he replied: 'That is an understatement.'

There was a two-way growing trade in military hardware, with Israel supplying Mirage parts, field weapons and missiles for seven new South African ships. Dieter Gerhardt, the Soviet spy, said South Africa was also building a new submarine with Israeli help – potentially an ideal delivery platform for nuclear missiles.

Israel had the technology and South Africa had the cash to buy it off the shelf. The country is rich in minerals, diamonds, gold and, of particular relevance here, uranium.

During the early years of Israel's programme, uranium ore had been produced partly from phosphate that occurred near the nuclear research centre at Dimona. To supplement this, supplies had been obtained clandestinely. Numec, a nuclear-waste reprocessing plant in Pennsylvania, was reported to have lost nearly 1,000 pounds of enriched uranium which had found its way to Israel. In 1968 Israeli commandos hijacked 200 tons of uranium ore, or 'yellow-cake', from a ship sailing from Belgium to Italy.[1] However, by the mid-1970s Israel needed regular supplies, and it was her friend protecting the Cape of Good Hope sea route who provided the answer.

The problem was almost certainly raised when Vorster visited Israel in April 1976, to be warmly greeted by Prime Minister Yitzhak Rabin. At a dinner in Vorster's honour, Rabin said both their countries shared the problem of coexisting in the face of 'foreign-inspired instability and recklessness'. He added: 'This is why we here follow with sympathy your own historic efforts to achieve détente on your continent.' The press speculated about military collaboration, but Vorster said this was 'utter non-

1 Commandos stormed the *Scheersburg*, a West German freighter, while it was passing through the Mediterranean. The ship reappeared weeks later with a new crew and a new name. However, it has been claimed that Israel traded technical expertise with West Germany for the ore, and that the hijacking was a set-up to spare West Germany any embarrassment.

sense'. However, during a tour of the Red Sea resort of Sharm-el Sheik, he said co-operation with Israel would be extended in a number of areas, including scientific and technical matters. The press speculated that a nuclear deal was about to be struck. Inevitably, this was denied, but the journalist Seymour Hersh in his book *The Samson Option* claimed that on this trip Moshe Dayan, the Israeli Defence Minister, had won from Vorster a commitment for a series of joint tests in South Africa.

In 1988 the author Benjamin Beit-Hallahmi published a study of his country's covert military links, called *The Israeli Connection*.[1] He wrote:

> The world has been watching Israel, and sometimes South Africa, using the old conventional notions about nuclear weaponry. What some brilliant minds in Israel have developed is an Israeli solution to an Israeli problem. South Africa has been the partner and the beneficiary. Both countries realized in the 1960s that what they needed was tactical nuclear weaponry. This led to the development of the nuclear shell, fired from the 155-mm howitzer or from a naval gun tested in 1979.

It was never more than a suspicion that the Dimona reactor was being fuelled with South African yellow-cake until details of the secret trial of Brigadier Johann Blaauw were leaked in March 1993. Blaauw, who had once served with the SAAF, was accused of attempting to extort mining concessions from Fanie Botha, the former Minister of Mines, by threatening to reveal that Botha was bankrupt. Instead of Blaauw being punished, it was Botha who was pilloried. The court heard he had been perpetually insolvent while he was a minister and leader of the House, and that he was a drunkard. Judge J. Friedman made these comments about the parliamentarian: 'He was prepared to commit perjury, fraud and deceit; he was prepared to become involved in political chicanery of the most despicable kind ... he was prepared to lie deliberately under oath ... no reliance can be placed on his evidence.' He went to jail for a year.

Why the case was kept a national secret under the Nuclear Energy Act is made clear in a summary of the case that was leaked.[2] After Blaauw retired from the SAAF in 1975, he became an unofficial link between Israel and South Africa on military matters. In 1976 he was approached by an Israeli

1 I. B. Tauris & Co. Ltd, London, 1988.

2 The case was eventually reported in South Africa's *Weekly Mail & Guardian* in February 1994, after appearing in the newsletter, *Africa Confidential*. A year earlier the Johannesburg newspaper *City Press* carried similar information without attributing it to the Blaauw case.

member of a council involved in purchasing nuclear materials. Blaauw was quietly asked if he could arrange the supply of South African yellow-cake.

The brigadier approached Vorster, the Prime Minister, and General Hendrik Van den Bergh, the head of the Bureau of State Security (BOSS). Vorster quickly agreed to authorize a shipment, but Piet Koornhof, his Minister of Mines, was strongly opposed to the deal, and attempted to stall it. He was immediately replaced by Fanie Botha, who was clearly regarded as being more compliant.

The court judgement said: 'Blaauw testified that there was at that stage a high degree of confidence developing between the South African and Israeli governments which involved the exchange of military technology, joint aeronautic ventures and the supply of know-how by Israel to South Africa in regard to the manufacture of weaponry.'

Blaauw's first delivery of yellow-cake was a success, and South Africa asked for a favour in return. Van der Bergh asked if Israel could supply tritium, the hydrogen isotope used in thermonuclear weapons, and it was agreed that deliveries of 30 grams would begin. It was a highly classified exercise, given the code-name of Teeblare, the Afrikaans for tea-leaves. There were twelve air shipments, each of a few grams, but every one big enough for a bomb. Senior South African and Israeli officers accompanied each consignment and, reportedly, each head of government was informed of a shipment's safe arrival.[1]

All the tritium consignments had been delivered by 1978, but by then Vorster had been replaced by P. W. Botha.[2] Nevertheless, the trading

[1] The delivery of tritium was divulged to the IAEA after inspections of South Africa's nuclear facilities began in 1991. In a confidential document, the IAEA said the material remained in store until 1987, 'after the withdrawal of a small sample for the verification of its quality'. The AEC now claims that this tritium was then handed over to be used by a commercial company for the manufacture of illuminated signs. The AEC does indeed have a lighting company, called Lumitec, which was formed at the time the IAEA began its inspection visits. There is no guarantee that the tritium, checked by the IAEA, was the same material originally supplied by the Israelis fifteen years earlier. Over that period more than half the tritium would, in any case, have decayed to helium gas and disappeared. So the AEC would only have to produce 13 or 14 grams, which it could have secretly imported or manufactured in a heavy-water reactor. South Africa had apparently also engaged in research on lithium-6, another material used to create thermonuclear weapons, but said it never used it in any weapon.

[2] Vorster was forced to resign in 1978 over what became known as the 'Info-Scandal'. It was revealed that the Department of Information had been secretly funding newspapers, magazines and even feature films, in an expensive bid to manufacture a favourable picture of the Republic and the National Party. The masterminds were Minister of Information Connie Mulder (who gave the scandal its other nickname, 'Muldergate') and his secretary, Dr E. M. 'Eschel' Rhoodie.

continued, as the court records show. Another 50 tons of yellow-cake went on its way to Israel, and then 500 tons was dispatched there to be kept in store. Later, it is said 'this was released for Israel's use'. It is not explained for whose use it was originally intended.

In 1994 De Klerk's office was asked about the reports of tritium imports. 'South Africa did not acquire nuclear weapons technology from another country,' his staff said. 'Although tritium may be used in initiators of nuclear explosive devices ... it has many other commercial uses.' The story had broken in the run-up to the elections for the power-sharing government, and De Klerk himself was out campaigning in the Orange Free State. He called the report 'a rehash of old accusations'.

But in *Bridled Ambition*, a recent book about nuclear proliferation by US author Mitchell Reiss (Woodrow Wilson Press, Washington DC, 1995), there is a telling comment from Errol de Montille, deputy chief of mission at the South African embassy in Washington. He told Reiss in April 1993 that Israel and his country had not only entered into co-operation agreements on nuclear and conventional weapons, but some nuclear agreements were still in force.

If Israel and South Africa were working in close harmony on producing nuclear weapons, the two countries were gripped in a passionate embrace on missile technology, as Chapter 12 showed. By 1987, at least some people in the US Congress were getting worried about this and demanding action. In March that year the Israeli Cabinet had two long sessions to discuss demands that it should sever its military ties with the apartheid regime.

Shimon Peres, Israel's Foreign Minister, announced that no new deals would be struck and a government committee would review other economic, cultural and diplomatic ties with South Africa. The intention was, he said, to bring Israel's policies in line with those of the United States and Western Europe, which had imposed limited trade, diplomatic and travel sanctions on Pretoria.[1] However, the Cabinet

1 Peres made a strong attack on the apartheid system, which he said was 'a policy totally rejected by all human beings', but he said his country was not going to lead a world policy against South Africa.

In July 1986, after Pretoria had imposed a state of emergency, a senior economic team from Israel's Finance Ministry visited South Africa to renew commercial trade agreements and a pact that allowed South African Jews to export millions of dollars to Israel.

In 1986 the US passed legislation allowing military aid to be cut to any country supplying arms to South Africa. Israel was the recipient of $1.8 billion annually, but no action was taken by the State Department when Israel continued to supply to the Republic. It was said that the exports were worth between $50 million and $125 million annually – as much as 10 per cent of Israel's annual arms sales overseas.

had refused to end any existing military pacts.

Officials admitted there had been close links for some time, in defiance of the UN embargo. It was reported that every Israeli defence minister in recent years, including Ariel Sharon, Moshe Arens, Ezer Weizman and Yizhak Rabin, had made secret visits to South Africa to promote defence deals. The Associated Press said Israeli officials would not say how many such agreements there were between the two countries, or when they were due to expire. 'We're not playing games,' said a senior official. 'We have long-term contracts that affect many factories and many workers and their families, and we've decided that when these are going to end we will not renew them. When do they lapse? I have no idea, but it won't happen overnight.'

It didn't happen overnight, and the United States seemed happy with the compromise until 14 December 1990, just a month before the Gulf War began. According to Moshe Arens, the Israeli Minister of Defence, he received a message from the State Department demanding that 'Israel stop immediately all defensive ties with South Africa in the area of nuclear, chemical, and biological weapons technology'. Arens commented: 'That the administration would send Israel this kind of message at this time was to me an indication of utter distrust.' However, as events have shown, it was more an indication that concern had suddenly erupted in Washington that South Africa had been secretly supplying Iraq with military hardware and technological assistance that was partly Israeli in origin.

Before South Africa left the British Commonwealth in 1961, it had close links with the armed forces of the mother country, Britain. The break, following on from bitter opposition to apartheid from the many black states who were Commonwealth members, gave Verwoerd an excuse to strengthen his defence forces, and he lost no time in doing so. In 1965 South Africa started taking deliveries of Mirage IIIEZ fighters, and later variants are now the backbone of the SAAF. That same year, seven Hawker Siddeley Buccaneer bombers were delivered to the SAAF, as part of the Simon's Town agreement by which Britain would supply South Africa with powerful maritime aircraft.

It is now clear why the emphasis in these purchases was on defence, given the decisions by Britain and the United States only partly to implement the UN arms embargo. Perhaps the unworldly mandarins of Whitehall really believed that the Buccaneers were, as South Africa had stated, for use with an aircraft carrier – particularly as all the aircraft had been ordered with folding wings for stowage below decks. However, the Republic had no aircraft carriers in the 1960s, and still has none in the 1990s. South Africa lost no time replacing the folding wings with fixed ones, adding drogue nozzles for long-range refuelling, and transferring them to Twenty-Four Squadron as tactical bombers.

Each could carry four 1,000-pound bombs or missiles, but it must have been in the SAAF's mind that conventional warfare was not the planes' principal purpose. The Buccaneer was specially developed for the British Royal Air Force to deliver nuclear weapons.

South Africa's aircraft were similarly used as the delivery vehicle for the six and a half devices De Klerk disclosed. Britain therefore did a great service in providing South Africa with an A-bomb strike force.[1]

Why would Britain, the United States or other Western countries be seeking to help a racist regime? Historical links must have played a part, but the increasing threat of Soviet-backed regimes in other parts of southern Africa is another factor, according to Jan, the military strategist. 'Look, the perception at the time was that communism was about to overrun the place,' he told us. 'They were worried – the Americans particularly. Don't exclude the Americans – they were the world's biggest hypocrites.'

Collaboration between the United States and South Africa on nuclear matters began in the 1940s, when huge sums were paid to the Republic for uranium ore. South Africa participated in nuclear tests in the area of the Cape Town Anomaly in the late 1950s, and in the 1960s it was a US company that supplied the Safari-1 reactor and arranged regular supplies of highly enriched uranium fuel. Tom Cole, a staff member of Oak Ridge National Laboratory, where the United States made its weapons-grade plutonium and uranium, was seconded to the Safari-1 reactor programme at Pelindaba as a consultant. In addition, four US universities and four research centres helped with its installation.

Between 1955 and 1974 the US Atomic Energy Commission trained eighty-eight South Africans in various aspects of nuclear technology, according to Congressional records. Under the US Freedom of Information Act, it has been established that a dozen South Africans attended classes in the United States on plutonium reprocessing. The classes were barred to

1 Britain also supplied twelve Canberra bombers in the early 1960s. In the late 1970s France supplied 16 Mirage F-1 fighters, and a further thirty-two were assembled under licence by South Africa's Atlas Aircraft Corporation. France also agreed to supply jet fuel and four Airbus A-300 transport tanker planes.

foreigners in 1972, but by then four years had elapsed since South Africa refused to sign the Nuclear Non-Proliferation Treaty.

In this period a number of South Africans were independently studying nuclear technology subjects in the United States. The students later reported that in 1972 the South African government had urged them to apply for jobs in all fields of the US government's nuclear programme. Columbia University helped by passing on to Pretoria the names of all South Africans it had on its rolls.

In the opposite direction, 155 nuclear scientists reportedly visited South Africa between 1957 and 1977. In 1971 Dr Sverre Kongelbeck, described as one of the best nuclear missile scientists in the United States and developer of the world's first fully automated missile launcher, retired as chief engineer of the US Navy's main missile laboratory and was hired by South Africa. He told the local press: 'I believe I could help ... in the field of missiles, radar and satellites ... It is God's own country. I'm not bothered about the racial situation.'

By the mid-1980s about twenty Americans were directly employed by the South African Electricity Supply Commission (ESCOM1) as reactor operators, physicists, safety inspectors and senior technicians at the Koeberg nuclear power station. A further forty-five were working there on behalf of US companies, hired to improve the running of the plant. Thirteen of these firms had official exemption from a US law controlling assistance to any country in the production of plutonium. ESCOM said it had asked its recruits to clarify their status with the US embassy in South Africa. 'The American personnel are not here in contravention of US law,' said a spokesman. 'I am quite sure of it.'

But a diplomat at the embassy was not sure. 'We are in the process of co-ordinating all this with the Commission and the Department of Energy in Washington to work things out in the best way for all concerned,' he said. 'I cannot say we have resolved it all yet.' It was resolved. The Americans carried on working.

With the Y-Plant at Valindaba growing in size through the early 1970s – a visible sign that material for a nuclear weapon would soon be available – the United States was happy to assist in other ways. Two Fox-1 computers, described as the most powerful sensor-based systems available, were supplied by the Foxboro Corporation to automate many of the plant's functions. A team of engineers from the United States carried out the installation.

1 ESKOM's earlier acronym.

Allis Chalmers, the Milwaukee company that supplied Pelindaba's Safari-1 reactor, also came into the controversy. It made compressors, marketed in West Germany by MAN, which, as will be seen later, were a crucial part of the equipment used for the Y-Plant's enrichment process.

There was controversy in the United States in 1976 about plans that later came to nothing to finance two General Electric reactors for Koeberg. Myron Kratzer, the State Department's nuclear technology specialist, pointed out South Africa's key role after the Second World War in supplying the United States with uranium for its defence requirements. Kratzer added: 'It was therefore natural that South Africa should be among the countries with which co-operation in this field would be established.'

He said it was unfortunate the Republic had not signed the NPT, but added: 'We feel the best prospect of bringing that about is to continue the process of co-operation ...'

Dr Ampie Roux was duly grateful. He told the *Washington Post* in February 1977:

> We can ascribe our degree of advancement today in large measure to the training and assistance so willingly provided by the United States of America during the early years of our nuclear programme ... much of the nuclear equipment installed at Pelindaba is of American origin, while even our nuclear philosophy, although unmistakably our own, owes much to the thinking of [American] nuclear scientists.

Jimmy Carter's victory in the US presidential elections of November 1976 heralded an official cooling of relations with the apartheid state. Ken Owen, then a Washington correspondent for *The Star* newspaper in Johannesburg, now editor of South Africa's *Sunday Times,* reported that the US administration feared the Republic was among a potential 'outlaw club' of nations who were beyond the control of the NPT. He said a nightmare was forming in the minds of US policy-makers at this 'potential league of the desperate'.

At the same time, policy-makers in Washington were equally concerned to protect America's own interests. In July 1977 State Department officials were quoted as saying: 'To isolate South Africa when it is a major exporter of uranium is very short-sighted ... the Non-Proliferation Treaty gets nowhere when you isolate the country with 10 to 20 per cent of the world's uranium reserves.'

The United States was also in no hurry to expose the attempted nuclear test at Vastrap in 1977, until Moscow intervened. Carter trustingly told a press conference: 'In response to our own direct inquiry and that of other nations, South Africa has informed us that they do not intend to develop nuclear explosive devices for any purpose, either peaceful or as a weapon, that the Kalahari test site which has been in question is not designed for use to test nuclear explosives, and that no nuclear explosive test will be taken in South Africa now or in the future'.

Vorster was asked about this assurance in an ABC-TV interview a few weeks later. The South African premier said he had given no such assurance. There was no reaction from the US State Department.

This mirrored the response two years later when the Vela satellite registered a double flash and Carter's committee of scientists blamed it on a misreading. Carter may have been reassured, but secretly the CIA was not. In a study labelled 'South Africa: Defense Strategy in an Increasingly Hostile World', which has been only partly declassified, it indicated that South Africa had a clandestine programme to produce and test nuclear weapons.

By 1981 South Africa faced a particular high-profile problem relating to its nearly finished reactors at Koeberg. The low-enriched uranium fuel was stored in the United States and held there because the Republic was refusing to sign the NPT. Pik Botha, South Africa's Foreign Minister, went to see Ronald Reagan, who had ousted Carter, and his Secretary of State, Alexander Haig. Botha recently told the South African *Sunday Times*: 'Haig said the problem was that South Africa was in the process of making a nuclear bomb and I agreed there were suspicions about that. I said we would never explode a device of that nature without first informing the US government, and that changed the whole situation. Reagan looked at Alexander Haig and said "That seems a reasonable attitude, we must help them."' The help was provided in secret, and Koeberg got its fuel.

While the parliaments of Western nations were promoting a policy of active opposition to apartheid, there were even darker forces in action thwarting their wishes. It had happened in Irangate and, we found, it had also been happening with South Africa – notably with nuclear testing.

With high-speed computers, it is said that the simpler types of nuclear weapons can nowadays be perfected without an experimental detonation. However, with nuclear shells and thermonuclear devices there could be no certainty that a design would work without one. We heard that South Africa had secretly conducted tests of nuclear weapons, despite the De Klerk statement that there had never been a South African test of a nuclear explosive.

Jan, the senior military strategist, said tests had been conducted off the coast of South Africa in the early 1980s. 'There were lots,' he said. 'We had the space for these developments and the facilities, but the Western intelligence agencies were fully informed. There was extended eavesdropping. You couldn't fart without somebody knowing about it.'

A former soldier described how he had been on a hunting trip in northern Natal near the military testing range in 1989. He heard a rocket fired out to sea and then a flash. He had never forgotten the impact of it. 'It turned night into day.' It was only an indication that a strange new super-powerful missile was being tried, but later much more specific information emerged. Sources said they knew of two tests off the South African coast – one in 1987 and another in 1989.

Our informant said the first, in 1987, was off the Cape, and fired from land into the sea. 'One purpose was to see if anyone would notice. It landed well outside shipping lanes, but produced a lot of nuclear fallout.[1] From what I know, the preference was for testing at sea.'

The event passed unchallenged, and so a second test was scheduled in 1989, off the northern Natal coast. The source said that, as in the 1987 test, a new type of weapon called the 'clean' bomb was detonated. He added: 'It used red mercury technology, and this time there was little if any fallout ... The US spy satellites were redirected so that the sensors and cameras would not pick up the tests. The Defense Intelligence Agency in Washington co-operated with us. They even sent people here as observers, and a hotline to America was set up. The Americans were deeply involved in helping us. In fact they funded a lot of development.'

He said the CIA was kept in the dark about a lot of what was going on, however. The DIA, part of the Pentagon structure, kept its involvement to itself. The source added: 'The DIA even tipped us off when the CIA sent agents here to snoop. Remember how they were caught in a small plane over Pelindaba, and we confiscated their film? The DIA wanted South Africa to carry out the tests in maximum secrecy.'

1 There were seismic reports from an Indian station on 30 September 1987 that indicated that a nuclear blast had taken place near the border with Mozambique. The reports got widespread publicity, but other stations reckoned the disturbance was centred on an area south of Johannesburg where rock bursts are common. No investigation took place into what the cause was. Rock bursts are frequent events in mining areas in South Africa and can create disturbances of up to 4 on the Richter scale. For this reason it has been suggested that South Africa could easily conduct underground tests without creating any suspicion.

In four countries people knew of the planned detonations: the Americans, the British, the French and the Italians. 'They played it "holier than thou", while we did the dirty work,' he said.

Another source said P. W. Botha, the State President, watched one test from a helicopter, but the pilot flew too close to the shock wave and only just managed to recover control.

We went back to Dion to ask if there was similar clandestine collaboration in the missile programme. 'Britons, Americans, Germans, Israelis, Iraqis, Iranians – we had them all,' he said. 'We even bought a simulator from America to test the complete missile system. We changed the label on it, and to bring it in we had to build a new road. You wouldn't believe it. The road alone cost a million Rand.

'You need to shake, turn and bump the device under precise conditions. Where do you get that stuff? Only in America! Where do you think our computers came from?'

We asked if the visitors from overseas were shown the latest missiles and warheads. Dion replied: 'If you've got a factory selling lipstick and I'm coming from Russia, which range do you show me: the bottom-line ones or the top of the line?'

Jake, an Armscor source, also told how South Africa was dependent on its foreign friends: 'We could get anything we ever wanted – red mercury, giros for missiles, or tritium for nuclear triggers.[1] All the intelligence agencies were aware of this. America, Britain, France and Italy played a central part in obtaining red mercury.' He said Israeli nuclear scientists were working here on the pretence of being agricultural specialists: 'You cannot imagine how far these tentacles went.'

This confirmed the long-held views of Abdul Minty, a campaigner on nuclear issues on behalf of the Anti-Apartheid Movement: 'If you take South Africa's capacity to produce enriched uranium, we calculated in the 1980s it had something like fifteen to twenty bombs of the "dirty" type … We provided information to international seminars and the United Nations in the 1970s showing that Britain, the United States, France, Italy, Portugal and also Israel helped South Africa. South African agents would ignore all the regulations to smuggle items from these countries, and the role of Germany was crucial in providing the technology to enrich uranium.'

He said Waldo Stumpf, now the AEC boss, was sent to Germany for

---

1 We heard that the South African embassy in Paris was a crucial centre for sanctions-busting because of French compliance.

training early in his career. 'In about 1975 a large number of documents were stolen from the South African embassy in Bonn. They contained lots of information about German help for the enrichment programme. There were official documents showing exchange visits with German scientists. Even a German general sitting on a NATO committee visited South Africa under an assumed name and visited nuclear installations.'

Minty said scientists were recruited at international nuclear conferences and the Koeberg power reactors were a useful cover for the military programme. 'I think that Western powers knew that South Africa was embarking on a nuclear weapons programme. I think later some of them were uneasy, but because of their commitment to the apartheid regime they took no action. There was a strong feeling the bomb could have been used in Angola.'

One of the inspirations behind the Western collusion was Henry Kissinger. On becoming US Secretary of State in 1969 he ordered the National Security Council to study policy options for the region, outlining US interests thus:

> Southern Africa is geographically important for the US and its allies, particularly with the closing of the Suez Canal and increased Soviet acitivity in the Indian Ocean. The US uses over-flight and landing facilities for military aircraft in ... South Africa. There are major ship repair and logistic facilities in South Africa with a level of technical competence which cannot be duplicated elsewhere on the continent ... The DoD [Department of Defense] has a missile tracking station in South Africa under a classified agreement and some of the military aircraft traffic involves support of this station.

The conclusion was:

> The whites are here to stay and the only way that constructive change can come about is through them. There is no hope for the the blacks to gain the political rights they seek through violence, which will only lead to chaos and increased opportunities for the communists ... Our tangible interests form a basis for our contacts in the region, and these can be maintained at an acceptable political cost ...

President Richard Nixon's decision was: 'Enforce arms embargo but with liberal treatment of equipment which could serve either military or civilian purposes.' It gave the green light to dual-use exports to the Republic, and a nod to covert operations.

15 A Nod from US Intelligence

For centuries sailors rounding the Cape of Good Hope at the southern tip of Africa have looked in wonder at the rising peaks stretching along the coast from Table Mountain. Whoever commanded them also controlled international trade, and for a long time it was Britain, with its naval superiority, that won the day.

In the twentieth century Britain's colony in southern Africa prospered, and so did the naval port of Simon's Town, 25 km from Cape Town. It had been a valuable haven for the Royal Navy, but South Africa's internal policies after the Second World War had meant it was no longer politically acceptable that warships from the United States, Britain or other European nations use the port. This was a blow, because South Africa was the only country in the region that could conceivably host Western navies.

By the 1970s the area where the southern Indian and Atlantic oceans meet off the coast of South Africa was fast becoming a strategic blind spot for the West as the Cold War progressed. Prowling Soviet submarines patrolling what was once one of the most important shipping routes in the world had become a concern. The Cape sea route – the shipping lanes off the South African coast – was a Western lifeline, carrying vast quantities of oil from the Middle East.

Intelligence officers in London and Washington realized that, should hostilities break out with the Soviet Union, this route could become the West's Achilles' heel. The United States needed the best possible intelligence picture of the activities of the Soviet warships in the area. Despite the politics of apartheid, something had to be done.

Taking up the challenge in the mid-1970s, US intelligence agencies secretly planned a huge transfer of sophisticated espionage equipment to South Africa, including advanced electronic sensors, optics and related goods. The clandestine operation was code-named Project X and was orchestrated by top US intelligence official Admiral Bobby Ray Inman, then director of the Office of Naval Intelligence. In exchange, Pretoria agreed to share with Washington the information it gathered on Soviet ships and submarines.

Today, despite all the United Nations attempts to leave the country technologically isolated, South Africa has one of the most sophisticated electronic eavesdropping stations in the world – at an SA navy base called Silvermine near Cape Town. Built deep inside a mountain that overlooks the Atlantic Ocean, with vast caverns into which numerous offices and floor levels have been built, the base is the most secret and important listening-post in South Africa.

Intelligence sources say the base is able to scan the southern reaches of the Indian and Atlantic oceans and detect all shipping movements, including those of submarines. 'The Americans supplied some of the best electronic eavesdropping equipment available,' said a South African agent, 'including sophisticated radar and satellite communications.' The most astonishing claim made about the base is that it even has an access tunnel for submarines under water.[1]

For Britain, America and the NATO alliance the base has always made a unique intelligence contribution. In the world of high-tech espionage the niceties of United Nations policy have no place.

For one American particularly, Project X was a goldmine. Before it, James Guerin was a small-town electronics manufacturer. Afterwards, he was made for life. Although the Americans were desperate to install the latest technology inside the mountain, and South Africa was equally desperate to receive it, the apartheid issue was getting hot in Congress. The major military electronics manufacturers were increasingly windy of dealing with the South African regime. It was therefore apparent that an intermediate company needed to be found to front the massive deal. Guerin, whose profile was so low it was practically invisible, fitted the role perfectly.

International Signal & Control, Guerin's company, would become one of the most important keys to South Africa's illegal weapons procurement, despite the UN arms embargo. Many details emerged in trials

1 Sources said this submarine pen allowed the vessels to move in and out unnoticed. 'I had heard about this from a number of people over the years, but I wasn't sure whether to believe it,' said one source. 'Then I met someone who had been on board a submarine that travelled through this tunnel into the mountain. He thought it was a fairly open secret and couldn't understand my surprise.' He said the submarine lane was a sensitive area. Scuba divers and fishing boats were warned to stay clear. 'I'm told that fishing boats can be impounded and their owners fined heavily for venturing into this area. This has happened before.' Did South Africa have submarines it did not want the world to see, or did it offer refuelling and other facilities to submarines belonging to countries that could not be seen in SA waters? 'So far as I know, we have only the old Daphne-class diesel submarines,' said the source. Reports appeared in the press in the late 1980s about South Africa acquiring sophisticated submarine designs from the West German government. It is believed these submarines were never built.

in the United States following indictments in 1991. Financed by the South African industrial giant Barlow Rand, ISC would become, some would say, virtually a division of the state-controlled weapons manufacturer, Armscor, and a key player in South Africa's nuclear weapons programme.

Guerin, born in Morristown, New Jersey, had studied agriculture before switching to electrical engineering and taking a graduate degree at the University of Arizona in the 1950s.

He did a stint in the US Navy during the Korean War, and then in 1960 he joined the Lockheed Missile and Space Corporation in Sunnyvale, California, where he was a manager on the Polaris nuclear missile programme. By 1969 he had moved to Lancaster, Pennsylvania, to join a company called Hamilton Watch, then launching a military electronics division. Soon afterwards the division closed, and Guerin decided in 1971 to go it alone with his own electronics company, International Signal & Control, operating from the cellar of his Lancaster home with a loan of $120,000. He put an assembly line into a converted chicken coop, describing his nearby tethered horse as 'the production manager'.

He soon moved ambitiously into purpose-built premises in Lancaster with a staff of twenty, experimenting with a wide range of consumer electronics. But several ventures failed, and Guerin needed yet more cash to stay afloat. In 1974 he flew to South Africa to meet with directors of the government-owned electronics company Barlow Rand. They lent him $2 million against an option to buy ISC. Barlow executive Michael Noyce later recalled that Barlow needed blacklisted goods that ISC could get, despite worries about Guerin's business methods and 'aggressive' accounting practices.

With ISC now so closely linked to the South African military complex, it became an obvious intermediary for the supply of equipment for Project X. Guerin was delighted with these developments. He had been determined to break into the defence business, and the opportunity was being handed to him on a plate. Very soon it was not just eavesdropping equipment that he was sending south-eastwards across the Atlantic but a wide range of high-tech goods. He was doing his own deals with a new silent partner – the South African military machine.

Guerin began to enlist the help of former colleagues at Lockheed, among others. Said one former ISC executive: 'He filled the company's ranks with former military and intelligence officers, and filled their heads with visions of "a billion-dollar technology empire".'

In his drive for success, he was willing to call in favours for acting as a procurement agent – and was prepared to break the law. In 1975 he started to sell defence equipment to South Africa, despite UN attempts to halt all such trade. One way or another, he was determined that ISC would have an export market.

Author Alan Friedman later studied the ISC affair and records how Guerin told an aide that the South Africans were 'fed up' with dealing with European distributors of defence electronics – ISC would now take the lead. Friedman says: 'What he did not tell his employee was the reason he felt able to break American export laws so cavalierly. That year, James Guerin had struck a deal with the government of the United States; he had entered the world of espionage and found a way to ship goods to South Africa.'[1]

Guerin was a secretive man. As president and founder of ISC, he kept his business dealings under wraps, away from the awkward scrutiny that public disclosure, particularly about his South African connections, could bring. The high-tech military electronics company based in Lancaster, Pennsylvania, grew quickly and before long was apparently becoming a significant defence contractor.

During the 1980s his success became obvious to all. The prominent Lancaster businessman built a lavish corporate headquarters and became a major local employer. He had million-dollar homes in Lancaster and Florida, owned a golf course – the Four Seasons Sports Complex in East Hempfield, Pennsylvania – and had opened the Parent Federal Savings Bank in Lancaster. He also had a $150,000 boat. The holding company for his investments, Parent Industries, was drawing $500,000 a year in interest from Swiss and US bank accounts.

In 1982 ISC formed a London-based company and floated the group on the stock exchange there, avoiding the more stringent US disclosure laws. A small ten-man operation, ISC Technologies Ltd, was also set up in Hanworth, west London, through which goods for South Africa were procured.

But Guerin's success was not the reason for his subsequent international profile. That came later, after bombshell disclosures regarding his company's activities. A federal judge in Philadelphia was to brand one of Guerin's business deals 'the largest fraud ever perpetrated in North America'. It crippled a key British defence contractor.

The British military-electronics giant Ferranti International PLC,

1 From Friedman's book *Spider's Web – Bush, Saddam, Thatcher and the Decade of Deceit* (Faber and Faber, London, 1993).

Britain's third-largest defence contractor, had bought out ISC in 1987 for about $670 million. It then almost collapsed because Guerin had padded ISC's books with nearly $1 billion in phoney sales. Several thousand people in Britain and the United States lost their jobs, and what followed was probably the most extraordinary series of US court hearings yet involving arms deals. Executives of the company faced a range of charges, with potential sentences totalling more than 500 years. In sometimes explosive evidence, the hidden hand of US intelligence emerged. ISC executives said US agents turned a blind eye or even guided ISC as it clinched sensitive deals, some strategic in nature, across the globe.

But it was what the court heard about ISC's partnership role with US intelligence on deals with South Africa that was the most startling. It would provide some of the most damning evidence yet on how the Republic was able to secure foreign help on its most sensitive military programmes – including its secret development of nuclear weapons.

It became clear that ISC's business had taken off only after the submarine eavesdropping equipment had been shipped to South Africa. Banned from global markets, desperate for weaponry, South Africa sought and found a convenient front in ISC. In 1977, the newly elected President Jimmy Carter had issued orders to cancel Project X, banning intelligence co-operation, but it seems it just went even more underground until completed.

ISC had begun by selling radios to South Africa's military. Then, former executives testified, came fuses for artillery shells, mortars, bombs and mines. At the same time Guerin had built up lasting and trusted relationships with the Pretoria military establishment and had also become a part-time US intelligence agent. The American courts heard how he had been channelling the information he gathered back to the Gerald Ford administration.

Guerin's former executives said their boss told them the submarine eavesdropping project had been a secret quid pro quo – ISC was secretly permitted to sell weaponry and other strategic materials to South Africa with the blessings of US intelligence, provided the company agreed to spy on South Africa on the CIA's behalf.

The quid pro quo was denied by Inman. 'There was never any authorization for them to ship hardware of any kind at any time to South Africa,' he said, although he admitted his friend had been a useful intelligence source on nuclear matters. But most observers were unconvinced, questioning how Guerin could otherwise have operated unhindered for so long. ISC had continued illegal shipments for a decade without being stopped.

The military hardware destined for South Africa went through an ISC front company called Gamma Systems, set up by Guerin and his brother-in-law Carl Jacobson in New York. Later dismissed by federal prosecutors as nothing more than 'a post-office box to mislead authorities', Gamma was based, conveniently, at Kennedy Airport.

By this time a special high-security area, the special products division, had been created at ISC's headquarters in Lancaster, filled with hand-picked staff whose sole role was to liaise with Washington intelligence contacts and deal with deliveries passing through Gamma to South Africa. In order to get into this area, employees needed a special code, and deliveries to Kennedy airport were hidden in a red piano truck.

'Military technology, missile technology, computer technology – a truck went to JFK every Friday and loaded out on to a South African 747, and there was never a question,' a former ISC executive remembered. 'Guerin repeatedly said: "Gamma is approved by Washington."'

In the court hearings, Inman maintained he was 'absolutely certain' US intelligence had never approved illegal conduct by ISC. CIA spokesman Peter Earnest said their policy was clear: upon learning of violations of US law, the CIA would 'report promptly to the appropriate US law enforcement agencies'. But, though ISC's deliveries to other countries were routinely held up by US Customs officials for minor errors in documentation, the Gamma shipments flowed unchallenged, three ISC veterans recalled. Year after year Guerin kept assuring them that 'Washington' or 'the government' had blessed the deliveries. They believed their boss. Said one manager: 'Everything was sanctioned.'

Other ISC executives said they also met regularly with CIA officials. 'I told them how Gamma Systems worked,' one said. 'I told them exactly what we shipped' to South Africa. 'They told me to maintain my contacts.' Said another: 'The CIA was aware of every ripple that occurred with our business with South Africa.' South Africa was getting US intelligence help during that period despite the ban, said yet another.

Richard M. Moose, the Carter administration's top policy-maker for Africa, became sceptical of the CIA's denial of involvement. 'I didn't trust our own agencies any more than I trusted the South Africans,' said Moose. 'As it turned out, that was not unjustified … Responsible officials of the agency [the CIA] sat in my office and lied to me about what they were doing in Africa.'

Moose wrote a 1977 presidential order banning intelligence co-operation with Pretoria. Despite the ban, the CIA felt their interests were 'best served by a collaborative relationship' with South Africa, he said. He suspected that CIA officers worked to ensure that long-standing contacts they had would continue, along with the transactions and export licences. 'People who believe they are above the law will make those kinds of arrangements.'

On 31 October 1991, seventeen people were indicted for their involvement in the smuggling operation to South Africa co-ordinated by ISC. Guerin, then sixty-one, was accused of helping an arms company owned by the South African government to evade the UN arms embargo. According to the indictment, Guerin and other ISC executives co-ordinated the export of munitions and military data, and seven South Africans, also charged, were responsible for forming front companies to import the materials into their country.

Guerin was also accused of illegally inflating ISC's value by creating more than $1 billion in fraudulent contracts that were placed on ISC's books. To carry out that fraud, the indictment said, Guerin laundered more than $700 million through a network of Swiss and US bank accounts, using thirty-eight Panamanian front companies and other international front companies controlled by ISC.

Guerin had to answer charges of conspiracy, mail fraud, securities fraud, violations of the Arms Export Control Act and the Anti-Apartheid Act, and laundering $958 million, plus two counts of filing false tax returns. Said attorneys representing the state: 'The breadth of the criminal conduct is mind-boggling.' The broader case had involved agents from the FBI, the Customs Bureau, the Department of Defense, the Internal Revenue Service and the CIA.

Guerin was alternately portrayed as a dedicated and religious family man who had done many charitable works and as an arrogant executive who engaged in massive fraud and sold embargoed weapons to a South African-controlled arms company that shipped weapons to twenty-six other countries. 'This man didn't care where these items went as long as he accomplished his goal of corporate growth,' the prosecutor told the court. Guerin tried to contend that the US embargo against South Africa was invalid, as it was implemented 'for reasons related solely to domestic policy (and in spite of sound military or strategic consideration).'

In addition to Guerin and the seven South Africans, others charged included three South African companies – Armscor, the Barlow Rand company Fuchs Electronics (Pty) Ltd and Kentron (Pty) Ltd. Alongside them were seven former ISC executives, a New York freight haulier and a California businessman now residing in South Africa.

One of the US defendants whose role was as significant as Guerin's was Robert Clyde Ivy, then sixty-two, also known as 'Greenleaf'. In 1977 he was working for Teledyne/Brown in Virginia when he was head-hunted by Armscor to help run the former Kentron missile plant. Ivy's employers refused to release him, but then Guerin stepped in, hiring Ivy and dispatching him to Pretoria, where the new plant had been constructed. As group technical manager, Ivy became a revered figure at Kentron, and the bar there is still called 'Clyde's Corner'. In 1980 Ivy returned to ISC, where he continued his work with missiles, and ran the special products division.

Ivy was a sanctions-buster *par excellence*. In partnership with Barlow Rand he set up a company in South Africa called LearnTech to market special interactive computer software for educating South African blacks. It was linked to an ISC subsidiary called Ed Systems, which almost drew Millersville University in Pennsylvania into the scheme. Court evidence showed it was a front for sending advanced US computers and computer parts to the Republic, some of which ended up in Iraq and Iran while the two countries were at war. Federal investigators said South Africa was supplied 'with small sophisticated computers destined for the guidance systems of Israeli-built nuclear-capable ICBMs and other weapons-related components'.

Ironically, it was Ivy who later triggered the disclosures that brought ISC down and laid bare its role as a South African sanction-busting operation. He had sued Ferranti, after it had become the owner of ISC, because it stopped paying him. Federal sources said the allegations filed in Ferranti's resulting counterclaim had formed the basis of the government's investigation into shipments of military hardware to South Africa, prompting Guerin's prosecution.

In the subsequent hearings, ISC links with the intelligence community became much clearer. Three ISC employees testified that US intelligence, ranking military officers, one-time Secretary of State Alexander Haig and a member of the Senate Intelligence Committee all knew about many of ISC's activities that became part of the indictment.

Inman, by now retired,[1] said Guerin provided important intelligence

1 Inman, former deputy director of the CIA under William Casey, retired from that post in 1982. Previously, he had also been a senior official of both the Defense Intelligence Agency and the NSA. When Inman retired, ISC was floating shares on the London Stock Exchange and Guerin was forced to comply with a US law that required any US defence contractor even partly owned outside the United States to form a special 'proxy' board of independent

information on South Africa for the National Security Agency. Guerin's defence attorneys submitted a letter written on his behalf in April 1992 by Inman, who said that the two of them worked together from 1974 to 1978 'on classified US government activities'. He wrote that, at a time when many Americans refused to co-operate with US intelligence, Guerin 'displayed patriotism towards our country and a willingness to provide useful information', despite inherent risks for his company. He told the judge that Guerin voluntarily provided the US government with information obtained during his foreign travels which was of substantial value – 'particularly that related to the potential proliferation of nuclear weapons capability'. As became even clearer later, ISC had been intimately connected with South Africa's programme to deploy such weapons.

Guerin pleaded guilty and was sentenced to fifteen years in jail without parole. He showed no reaction as chief US district judge Louis C. Bechtle announced the sentence in the packed, hushed courtroom. Moments before, he had asked for mercy: 'I ask you to judge me not as a person who intended to conquer the world, not as a person who was motivated by greed, but as a person who lost his way,' said Guerin, who appeared calm but sombre. 'I have nothing left but my God, my family and some special friends.'

He had helped federal authorities untangle the mess which was described by Gary Matthews, district director of the Internal Revenue Service in Philadelphia, as 'an intricate and really enormous tapestry of fraud ... a classic case of incomprehensible fraud'.

For years, federal agents investigating Guerin and the company he started had followed an intricate paper trail of bank accounts from the United States to Europe and had traced the sale of arms components from ISC through various companies to South Africa.

The US government had 'electronically seized' seventy-two bank accounts across the United States, along with real estate and eleven vehicles, from five of the defendants. Prosecutors said the thrust of the ISC smuggling scheme was to take military goods made by US manufacturers

directors. This was to act as a buffer between US companies and foreign investors to prevent leaks of classified information about Pentagon contracts. Inman was the ideal candidate for ISC's board, partly because he already knew the company. The Pentagon approved his appointment to the proxy board, which was responsible for dozens of contracts, without reservation. Inman, a lifetime intelligence professional with a background in cryptography, was nominated for the post of US Defense Secretary in December 1993. Despite predictions of an easy Senate confirmation, he withdrew his nomination on 18 January 1994, after questions about his relationship with Guerin.

and ship them illegally to South Africa. The items, they explained, were necessary 'to make sophisticated weapons work'. Some were for heat-seeking missiles and some ended up in South African-designed 155-mm shells used by the Iraqis against US troops in the Gulf War.

One of those items was a proximity fuse – an electronic device that detonates an artillery round before it hits the ground, thus killing more troops. In 1988 ISC opened negotiations with South African armaments company Fuchs Electronics. US attorney Michael Baylson said ISC officials later developed and made power-supply devices for fuses sent to Fuchs. The prosecutor said 300,000 of these components were sent to South Africa by ISC. After the Gulf War, he said, troops dismantling Iraqi shells discovered 'the power supplies that originated with ISC'.

A later indictment, this time against Fuchs, said ISC intended to supply up to 300,000 FF-1 fuses to Fuchs for delivery to IMEC, a firm with Iraqi links. In return, ISC would receive more than $33 million from Fuchs once it had received payment from Iraq in crude oil. ISC in fact exported more than $4.4 million worth of fuse power supplies to South Africa between 1985 and 1989 'to maintain Fuchs' production line of fuses and to assist Fuchs fulfil its fuse production requirements with Iraq'.

Prosecutors said ISC sold more than $50 million in weapons components to South Africa, much of it via Gamma through Kennedy Airport. Former ISC executive Tom Jasin, who was charged with helping to import South African anti-tank missiles into the United States, gave the most detailed list of contacts with current and former US government officials – including President Ronald Reagan's former Secretary of State, Alexander Haig.[1]

Jasin said in an interview after his indictment that he began working with ISC in 1984 to oversee a programme to import anti-tank missiles from South Africa for US Army covert units at Fort Campbell, Kentucky.[2] ISC had allegedly hired Haig as a consultant, and eventually

1 Haig, who was also White House chief of staff under Presidents Richard Nixon and Gerald Ford and former supreme commander of NATO, received $26,000 from ISC for his 1987 presidential campaign, according to court evidence. A former ISC spokesman reportedly said the company had a keen interest in Haig and thought his presidency would 'be a benefit for us'. A year earlier, Haig had worked as a consultant to ISC and helped negotiate the sale of air-to-ground missiles to Pakistan, Guerin said. New owner Ferranti later said the missile deal with Pakistan had been bogus.

2 Sources in South Africa said that was a likely reference to early versions of Kentron's ZT-3 and ZT-35 tank-buster missiles, which, they said, contained in the nose an extremely powerful chemical – probably red mercury or something similar (see Chapter 12).

paid the former Secretary of State $600,000. Haig had made contact with the Connecticut-based Sikorsky Aircraft, which wanted to use the South African missiles as an attack weapon on helicopters for Fort Campbell. He said Haig and the army knew of their South African origin, although Haig denied this.

Jasin also provided the name of a Philadelphia-based CIA agent and said he met him regularly in 1986. The agent had closely monitored the imports of the South Africa missile components. Separately, Clyde Ivy said he also met the same CIA agent – as well as several other CIA agents who visited ISC. Ivy said he believed sales to South Africa were approved by the US government because none of the weaponry was blocked by any US agency. 'We never had any trouble with any shipment,' he said.

By the time ISC merged with Ferranti in November 1987, it was doing annual business of $600 million, according to its books, designing and making a range of military products including cluster bombs, fuses, missiles and propellants. On paper, it had seemed like a good acquisition.

The marriage went fine until 1989, when Guerin suddenly resigned after trying unsuccessfully to buy back part of his company. Then the bubble burst and Ferranti realized it had been duped. It disclosed that ISC's unlawful shipments to South Africa had included night-vision equipment, infra-red detectors and other components for heat-seeking missiles, navigational systems for fighter planes in the SAAF and sophisticated camera equipment to be used to track and film missiles.

Ferranti was trying to distance itself from the looming scandal, but it had been warned of the political risks before it bought ISC. An internal report to the Ferranti board said: 'It should be noted that a number of ISC's programmes depend on the goodwill and supply of South African elements.' The report also warned that ISC acted as a 'procurement agency' for South Africa.

The report added: 'Whilst it appears that ISC keep very close relations with Washington, one must recognize that some of this is in the covert policy areas.' It also noted that the British Ministry of Defence knew about some of the contracts, and further approval would have to be sought before the take-over which would also put Ivy and Guerin on the board – the latter as deputy chairman.

When the scandal broke, the direct links with the South African arms smuggling operations caused political waves in Britain, embarrassing the Ministry of Defence and implicating British intelligence. Because so much of Ferranti's work was classified as secret by the British government, both Ivy and Guerin would have been vetted by Britain's MI5 internal security agency. How could MI5 have given both directors security clearances when Ferranti took over ISC without knowing of their dealings with South Africa?

For instance, the pair had been dealing with a South African called William Metelerkamp, who was head of procurement for Kentron, the South African missile company, and well known to the British government as a sanctions-buster. US Customs agents had discovered from seized company records that in February 1983 Metelerkamp and his superior, Colonel Hendrik 'Hennie' Botha, had visited ISC headquarters and obtained help from their former Kentron employee Clyde Ivy. He was alleged to have supplied Kentron with a flow of electronic components via a subsidiary of ISC called ESI Manufacturing Inc. through Metelerkamp and other Armscor front men.

To Ferranti's embarrassment, Ivy later admitted his dealings with Metelerkamp and his work with Kentron, but he denied any irregularities. He said he was acting only as a 'travel agent' for Metelerkamp.

Anti-Apartheid Movement chairman and Labour MP Robert Hughes wrote to Margaret Thatcher, the British Prime Minister, demanding an urgent inquiry into links between Ferranti and South Africa. In a four-page letter, Hughes called for a probe into the 'major failures by the security services in relation to Ferranti's South African connections.' He asked how it was possible for people like Ivy and Guerin, with South African links, to become board members of a major British defence contractor.

Shipments to South Africa had continued even after the merger, said US investigators. And Ferranti, which had agreements with ISC going back to 1981, had by 1986 become one of ISC's major subcontractors on a secret contract to develop missiles for the United Arab Emirates, which appeared to have originated in South Africa. Ferranti did not deny that trading with South Africa had taken place, or that illegal shipments may have occurred, but said it had 'not knowingly' engaged in illegal acts.

The heat was also on in the United States. The US Department of Justice and the Pentagon admitted that the United States had supplied ballistic missile technology to South Africa. They said the technology came from ISC between 1984 and 1988 and included telemetry tracking equipment and inertial guidance systems, which were incorporated into the joint South African/Israeli ballistic missile programme

Technology shipped to South Africa through ISC's subsidiary company ISC Educational Systems included gyroscopes for the inertial guidance systems of missiles, telemetry tracking equipment and photo-imaging equipment, used to monitor missile tests. The shipments coincided with the establishment by Armscor of the Overberg missile range in the Cape, hub of its plan to build a nuclear-tipped ICBM which was planned to be South Africa's key deterrent.

ISC was also dealing in South African-designed air-to-ground missiles. Documents in the Guerin case showed he had paid off agents in the United Arab Emirates, in violation of UAE law, to gain $360 million in contracts during the 1980s. ISC's UAE connections are as fascinating as its South African link. It is known that the UAE is a soft touch for end-user certificates, the essential piece of paperwork required by governments before an arms deal can be authorized, and there are fears that the air-to-surface missiles, called the Hakim, were really destined for Iraq.

In court documents, Guerin admitted missiles for the UAE had been built from South African components and assembled at a factory in Wimborne, Dorset. This five-year contract was signed in April 1986. ISC directors in London were alleged to have obtained an export licence from the British government to import missile parts from unnamed suppliers and re-export them to the Middle East, even though they contained South African components. Robert Hughes disclosed that the missiles were of a model designated the Hakim, but its full significance, and its carefully concealed origins in South Africa's nuclear weapons programme, never came to light at the time.

The directory *Jane's Air-Launched Weapons* reported that the Hakim was a family of medium-range laser- or infra-red-guided air-to-ground missiles known as PGMs (Precision Guided Munitions), designated PGM-1, 2, 3 or 4, according to the model. Development first began at ISC in 1984, ostensibly for the UAE. The programme had been given several other names over the years, and the name Hakim was used just for the UAE. Other names for the project included Alpha, GMX, Felix, Pegasus and Little Brother.[1]

1 The programme was first revealed in 1989, when Ferranti disclosed ISC had misrepresented some of its missile contracts. It is believed that the Hakim A/B (PGM-1/2) entered production in 1990 and the PGM-3/4 in 1993. The Hakim B has two externally mounted boosters, giving a range of about 20 km. The PGM-4 Pegasus is believed to be a turbojet-powered 200-km-range variant proposed for British use in 1992. The Hakim A and B (PGM-1/2) are said to have entered service with the UAE in 1992 for use on Mirage 2000 aircraft. The PGM-3s are believed to have gone into production in 1993 and to be scheduled to enter service in 1996. They have several warhead options, including a penetration warhead.

Jane's said an unpowered version, known as the Lancelot, was proposed to meet Britain's requirement for laser-guided bombs in 1993, and there was a glide-bomb version. There had been unconfirmed reports in the mid-1980s linking the Hakim project with Armscor and, through ISC, with China, Pakistan and Iran, but the only known buyer had been the UAE.

Jane's description of the missiles showed there was a 'small' version, the Hakim A/C, which was 3.4 metres long with a diameter of 300 mm and a launch weight of 250 kg. A bigger version, the Hakim B/D, was 4.7 metres long, 380 mm in diameter, and with a wingspan of up to 1.3 metres. It weighed in all 900 kg – indicating a much larger payload for a warhead. Both missiles had a range of 20 km and apparently were available with or without propulsion systems.

The description compared uncannily with that of the 'Hento', South Africa's nuclear-capable glide bomb, which an Armscor employee had told us weighed nearly a ton and had a similar range. The question was, Were they just similar or were they exactly the same missile, being assembled by ISC in Britain and the United States because their South African origin could never be disclosed? Sources in South Africa confirmed that the latter was the case, and that the missiles relied heavily on imported high-tech components.

The *Jane's* report had said the only known user of the Hakim was the UAE, which had reportedly ordered about 1,760 missiles. Did the UAE really need so many of these huge devices? The suspicion must be that the UAE was not the ultimate destination for them.

A scientist now living in London who used to work on South Africa's missile programme said that in about 1992 the Armscor sanctions-busting operation to obtain the necessary components almost went wrong for its allies in the United States. He said twelve gyroscopes had been clandestinely shipped to South Africa after they had been stolen from the aeronautical company Northrop by employees who had been bribed. Suddenly they had to be returned to them in the United States because an investigation had been launched into the possible diversion of sensitive weapons components.

Over the years, South Africa had bought gyros of various types with the help of the Defense Intelligence Agency, said the source. The US agency had been secretly backing the South African military since 1974.

'These were very special gyros,' said the scientist. 'Armscor always wanted them straight away, but it was so sensitive they could not take them all at once, so they had to take them one or two at a time. The money was there – when such items were needed money was always found, even if it had to come from another budget, perhaps from the police – but that wasn't the issue.

'Kentron tried to make their own and failed hopelessly. They tested Russian versions, which were cheap but useless. The French models were very expensive. Northrop produced the best, so it was their officials who were bribed.'

When the investigation began in the United States, the DIA and Armscor's Northrop accomplices were concerned about only twelve larger models – gyros for nuclear missiles.

'They were used in the glide bombs. Something went wrong, and these gyros had to be accounted for,' said the scientist. 'They had been told a stock count was about to be made and there would not have been any end-user certificates to explain their disappearance – that was the problem.'

The gyros had been obtained by Armscor in about 1988 and were passed on to a company near Johannesburg which assembled the missiles. When the panic began over the stock count the gyros had already been installed in missiles and they were in service with the SAAF. 'The missiles went into service on the Cheetahs and Mirages,' said the source.

The aircraft from which the missiles were deployed were effectively grounded. Missile gyros and other high-tech equipment wre removed and routed through the Far East back to the United States via a number of Armscor front companies in several countries.

South Africa had paid about $150,000 each for the football-sized instruments, but demanded double that amount as a guarantee before they were returned. The gyros came back to South Africa three or four months later, after the stock count, and were then refitted to the long-range air-to-ground missiles.

The source said there had been an announcement in South Africa that the Cheetahs had been grounded because of 'technical problems'. He went on: 'Well, I suppose you could call it that. But, if the gyros and other systems aboard the aircraft had not been returned, Armscor's procurement contacts in the United States would have been compromised.' The source said it was unlikely the SAAF would have agreed to such an extraordinary move without the approval of the State Security Council and probably President F. W. de Klerk.

The Guerin court case showed that South Africa's main broker for obtaining gyros for ballistic missiles had been ISC, and this had been confirmed by the Pentagon. It seemed likely that ISC sanctions-busters also were used to procure the gyros fitted to the SAAF missiles. In fact it was possible the 'gyro emergency' at Northrop was connected to the court-directed investigations of US federal agents probing the ISC affair.

South Africa's glide bomb, whether called the Hento or the Hakim, was built to deliver a nuclear weapon. The ISC story suggests direct involvement in its development by ISC in Pennsylvania and by its off-shoots in Britain. In Ferranti's bid to survive after the aftermath of the ISC fraud it sold its ISC missile division to GEC's Marconi subsidiary at Stanmore, Middlesex, north of London. It is currently supplying further versions of the Hakim to the UAE.

ISC was the glittering jewel of Armscor's international procurement net-work, and, according to court evidence, it had been given the nod of approval by US intelligence. Its missile expert, Clyde Ivy, had helped Kentron grow through the 1980s into a highly specialized missile manu-facturer. But never fully disclosed was the pivotal role played by Ivy, Guerin and ISC in South Africa's nuclear warhead programme.

In the ISC court case, Admiral Inman had disclosed that Guerin had been a CIA informant on South Africa's atomic bomb programme, report-ing to US intelligence regularly from 1977 onwards. 'They were happy to hear from him,' and US government officials said Guerin gave them so much information about the programme that a US spy satellite was cor-rectly positioned to observe an ocean test of a nuclear device by Pretoria in the late 1970s – thought to be the Vela satellite incident in 1979.

But the information being funnelled from South Africa was not as startling as the hardware that was being sent back. ISC's shipments to South Africa included seismic detectors for underwater nuclear weapons tests, former ISC executives told the Philadelphia courts. Delivering the seismic detectors in the late 1970s 'put Guerin in a front-row seat' to spy on the regime's nuclear programme, one witness said.

The *Philadelphia Inquirer* said ISC's sales broke US export laws and UN embargoes: 'They began after Guerin helped US intelligence co-oper-ate with South Africa. They continued as Guerin and his executives spied on South Africa for the CIA. And they helped South Africa build a nuclear bomb.' The newspaper asked whether the CIA had 'winked' as ISC dealt with South Africa, clearly believing it had.

As this book went to press, the ISC scandal was not yet over on either side of the Atlantic. South Africa was negotiating with Britain to limit any further embarrassment about the disclosure of illegal defence equipment sales to Pretoria, according to Dr André Buys, planning manager of Armscor.

At a conference for British defence contractors and Whitehall officials in July 1994, Buys disclosed that defence contracts with South Africa still existed, involving both governments and private companies. He admitted that the contracts had been made in defiance of the UN arms embargo. Declining to give details, he said: 'This could be an embarrassment ... and we are discussing at a diplomatic level if they have any objections to these being disclosed.' He hoped all the main contracts could be made public.

A British Foreign Office spokesman confirmed such discussions had taken place, but gave a different explanation: 'We have offered to advise the South African government on export control procedures for defence equipment.' He denied Britain had issued export licences for defence equipment during the embargo.

In the US, charges were still pending against South African executives and their employers for sanctions-busting. Armscor has admitted it was involved in 'sensitive' negotiations with the US government. In its annual report, to April 1995, chairman Johan Moolman said: 'Various efforts have been made to resolve the matter, but no success had been achieved by the end of the financial year.' These efforts had included top-level talks on separate occasions between President Nelson Mandela, his Deputy President Thabo Mbeki, President Bill Clinton and his Vice-President Al Gore. Moolman said Armscor was grateful for representations made by Mandela and Mbeki on his company's behalf: the meetings had created a 'climate that could lead to a reasonable settlement' of the affair. 'However, the matter will have to be resolved in a manner which is legally acceptable to the US Department of Justice.'

In August 1994 it was disclosed that Armscor was offering to pay almost R54 million ($15 million) in an out-of-court settlement to save its officials the embarrassment of being extradited to the United States to stand trial alongside Clyde Ivy. Quoting South African government sources, Johannesburg's *Weekly Mail & Guardian* newspaper said Fuchs Electronics, a Barlow Rand subsidiary when the alleged offences took place, might have to pay a similar amount to escape being arraigned.

By August 1995 it was reported that the admission-of-guilt fine facing Armscor had been reduced to R43 million, and government negotiators were hoping to bring it down further. Fuchs was dragging its heels over whether to join Armscor in the plea-bargain deal, brokered by South Africa's US ambassador Franklin Sonn. The firm was trying to avoid paying more than R35 million ($10 million).

If the plea bargain did not go through, US prosecutors were ready to indict another five South Africans, it was reported. But senior members of the South African group already indicted were exploring deals that could give them the right to stay in the United States, safe from punishment, in return for revealing South African secrets.

Of particular interest to the prosecutors was testimony that procurement agent Metelerkamp and others could give against Ivy. Tielman de Waal, Armscor's chief, said the group had been barred from disclosing anything that could jeopardize South African national security. Judge Pierre Rabie, a former South African chief justice, had ruled that some of the information the group carried had to remain secret. De Waal said the US prosecutors' belief that South Africa had a nuclear weapons pact with Iraq was mistaken.

Metelerkamp himself told reporters: 'Part of the job was to break the law. You knew the risks that went along with it.'

16 The Coventry Four, or Five?

The three South Africans were tired as they checked into the White House, a tourist hotel near London's Regent's Park, in March 1984. They had flown from Johannesburg via Holland for an urgent meeting with Michael Gardiner, a British associate who had recently received an unexpected visit from Her Majesty's Customs & Excise. Fortunately, as Gardiner had reported in a telex, the customs men had not discovered a stash of documents hidden in Gardiner's cellar that would have exposed their massive sanctions-busting operation. But Gardiner was keen to review how he could continue doing business with the apartheid regime: hence his request for a get-together.

After resting overnight, the three planned to meet up with him the following morning. None realized they had walked into a trap, sprung with Gardiner's reluctant help. Long before the three had arrived at the hotel, a Customs investigation team had been expecting the visitors. Their rooms had been selected in advance so that the sting operation would cause as little disruption as possible to other guests. Each room had been comprehensively bugged, although Customs already had sufficient evidence to nail all three. Gardiner had lied in his telex: he had in fact failed to hide his documents in the cellar when the Customs men arrived.

Colonel Hendrik 'Hennie' Botha, William 'Randy' Metelerkamp and Stephanus 'Fanie' de Jager ate in the White House restaurant and then went to their rooms. Metelerkamp was in the shower when two Customs investigators, including team boss Martin Spillane, let themselves in with a pass key. Metelerkamp was furious at the intrusion, and at the indignity of being caught naked: three days earlier he had undergone a vasectomy operation, and he was sensitive about his appearance. Botha and De Jager were also given a nasty surprise as they too were disturbed in various stages of undress.

Botha, Metelerkamp and De Jager were formally cautioned and told they were suspected of involvement in an illegal operation to breach the UN embargo on military sales to South Africa. They were instructed to get dressed and were led shoeless to waiting cars for the two-hour drive northwards to the industrial city of Coventry, where their sanctions-busting had been uncovered.

Meanwhile, at Heathrow airport, a further Customs operation was in progress. Two other South African businessmen, Jacobus 'Koos' la Grange and Professor Johannes Cloete of Stellenbosch University, near Cape Town, were flying home after a successful research trip to a number of British cities. Irritatingly, it had been announced that their flight was delayed by technical problems. Both men were in a bookstore when Customs men took them by the arm and led them to interview rooms. They too had walked into a trap. Their plane was not in fact faulty: Customs had simply refused it permission to take off. Soon la Grange and Cloete were also heading for Coventry minus their shoes.

The sanctions inquiry had begun with a tip-off. A reporter from the *Coventry Evening Telegraph* had rung to warn that packages of military parts were being sent from Birmingham Airport to South Africa. A consignment was intercepted, and twenty-two bronze gears for military gunsights were found. They were being sent by a Coventry Company, D. W. Salt (Engineering) Ltd. Other consignments, including cryostats used for infra-red missile guidance systems, were being sent via Bristol to Heathrow Airport, labelled as tractor equipment.

As inquiries progressed, the Customs team headed by officer Spillane realized that the Coventry firm was deeply involved in manufacturing and sourcing sensitive military equipment for the banned Pretoria regime. The trade had been going on since the mid-1970s.

Five Britons were centrally involved in the traffic. Derek Wilfred Salt (fifty-nine), the managing director of Salt Engineering, and Michael Gardiner (fifty-five), its chairman, were of special interest. Salt was a prominent figure in Coventry and vice-chairman of Coventry Football Club. Gardiner was not only earning a fortune from his illicit dealings with South Africa: he also had two hotels in the Devon seaside resort of Torquay, and he lived in style at a large house in the Devon village of Coleford, where he bred exotic birds.

Also implicated, the Customs men believed, was Michael Swann (thirty-three), described as an export buyer from Royston in Hertfordshire. He seemed to represent a separate network to the one run by Salt and Gardiner. All were dealing directly with Colonel Botha and his team.

Two weeks before the South Africans were pulled, these suspects were visited by the investigation team at their homes. Spillane, assigned to call on Gardiner, was asked to wait for him in a side room but heard a noise in the hall. Going to look, he found Gardiner tiptoeing towards the cellar door, carrying a wire tray of papers and a suitcase full of files. Gardiner admitted sheepishly that he was trying to hide his more sensitive documents. After several hours' questioning, and with the prospect of spending the night at the local police station, he agreed to help Spillane lure Botha and his colleagues back to Britain.

Spillane's prisoners were all taken to the police station at Little Park Street in Coventry and placed in separate cells. It was late in the evening, and it had already been a long day for the Customs men, but they had no intention of giving their suspects time to collect their thoughts. The questioning began immediately, and went on through the night. Botha, the most senior of the party, said he was a personnel manager for the Armscor subsidiary Kentron. Metelerkamp described himself as a consultant, De Jager as a finance manager, and la Grange as an engineer. Professor Cloete was clearly a brilliant scientist.

Then came a sign that this was no ordinary Customs case. At noon the next day Spillane decided to take a break and walked to a café for a bite to eat. When he returned thirty minutes later, he was surprised to see Cloete writing out a statement. Spillane recalled: 'I found he was being released without any consultation with me. I could hardly believe it. We were certain he was directly implicated. I was told there was nothing that could be done about it. Orders had obviously come from a very high level.'

Within minutes, Cloete was being given back his briefcase and belongings and was ushered into a car for Heathrow airport. He flew to Paris, from where, according to sources, his documents were sent to South Africa by diplomatic pouch. The Coventry Five had rapidly become the Coventry Four – the name later given to the case by the British press.

Spillane said Cloete was an expert on missile technology and had been collaborating with a department at Sheffield University which had a top-secret British Ministry of Defence contract to design an electronic radar antenna for guided missiles. He had also been to Ferranti and GEC. Spillane was sure he could charge Cloete with sanctions-busting. 'There was no way he was innocent, but we not only had to let him go, we had to let him take a large amount of technical paperwork he had collected on his British trip.'

Within days the diplomatic hotlines were busy between Pretoria and Whitehall as the implications of the arrests sank home. South African Foreign Minister Pik Botha recalled his ambassador, Marais Steyn, from London for consultations. On Monday 2 April the suspects had to appear in court, facing a variety of charges involving the transfer of

233

military parts in defiance of the UN's embargo. The goods allegedly dispatched included magnetrons, which generate microwaves used to confuse incoming missiles, gas cylinders and cryostats.

The magistrates took a serious view of the charges. The four South Africans were remanded in jail for a week. Swann and Gardiner were each ordered to produce a bail surety of £25,000 ($38,000) and Salt, described as a stockholder in a South African company, had to find two sureties, each of £20,000 ($31,800). All the Britons were ordered to report to police twice a week, surrender their passports, and remain at their current addresses.

Apart from Cloete's disappearance, the case was going normally – except in one respect. Spillane had been assigned a strange chore: he was instructed to write a half-page daily report on the progress of the investigation. He learned it went to his bosses in London, who, after vetting it, passed it on Prime Minister Margaret Thatcher,[1] who was taking a special interest in the case.

For the South African embassy in London, the problem was to find a way to get its nationals back home as quickly as possible. To the Customs & Excise team, this seemed an impossibility. They would certainly oppose any attempt to release the suspects, and no court could be satisfied that the suspects would return to face trial if they were permitted to leave the country.

Seven weeks after the Coventry Four were sent to prison on remand, they appeared in court again and a compromise was agreed. André Pelser, a South African embassy official (now South Africa's ambassador to Turkey), offered to waive his diplomatic immunity to stand surety of £25,000 for each of the prisoners, with a £100,000 surety for himself. Their passports were confiscated by the court, and they were told to live in accommodation to be found by Pelser and to report to a police station every day.

The Customs inquiry delved deeper into voluminous files found in the

---

1 In July 1989 the *Guardian* newspaper in London reported that Patrick Haseldine, a Foreign Office official, had been told to resign because he had criticized Thatcher for adopting double standards over the Coventry Four affair. In an earlier letter to the newspaper, he compared their treatment with the then Prime Minister's 'self-righteous invective' against the Irish and Belgian governments for freeing Father Patrick Ryan, an Irish priest linked to the IRA. Haseldine said Thatcher was keen for the South African embassy to know 'precisely how the legal hurdles governing [their] release and the return of their passports could be swiftly overcome'. He suspected that Thatcher and the South African President P. W. Botha, who had met for the first time in June 1984 in Britain, had a mutual interest in seeing that the four never stood trial.

possession of the defendants, and it was clear the case would take many months finally to come to trial. However, in May 1984 there was another development which further marked out the Coventry Four case as unusual.

In a legal sidestep, the South Africans went before Mr Justice Leonard, a High Court judge, who heard the case in chambers and therefore in secret. Leonard swept aside the decision of the Coventry magistrates. He doubled the total bail money to £400,000 ($600,000), but ordered that the South Africans could have back their passports provided they promised to return for the trial.

All four returned in June for a routine remand hearing, but that was the end of any chance Customs & Excise had of making the Coventry Four face justice. In September 1984 a minor diplomatic problem arose between Britain and South Africa in the coastal city of Durban. Pik Botha, the South African Foreign Minister, accused Britain of failing to act vigorously against a group of black dissidents who had taken refuge from arrest warrants in the British consulate there. Botha announced that the Coventry Four would be instructed not to return to Britain for the committal hearing later in October.

Instead, South Africa was represented by one of Britain's best-known and most ferocious advocates, George Carman QC. He told the court that the Coventry Four had had no say in the decision not to appear: 'They were simply obeying the expressed intention of their own government.' He argued that bail money, which had been deposited with a law firm, should be refunded, because they were literally only obeying orders.

Even Carman's silver tongue failed to have an effect. Helen Freeman, chairman of the magistrates, was outraged. 'Solemn promises and undertakings have been broken by the South African government,' she told Carman, ordering that Pelser's £400,000 bail money be pocketed.

The affair briefly flared up in the House of Commons. Foreign Office Minister Malcolm Rifkind told MPs that relations with Pretoria would be 'significantly affected' if South Africa made no effort to co-operate with the British courts. He called in David Worrall, who had replaced Steyn as the South African ambassador, and gave him a dressing-down, but he rejected a demand from Donald Anderson, a Labour Party opposition spokesman on foreign affairs, that Britain withdraw its no-visa agreement with South Africa. Anderson caused uproar when he described the Tory government's response as 'cool, lame, laid-back and business as usual with the apartheid regime' and concluded that Britain had shown itself 'the best collaborator of the apartheid regime in Europe'.

Were the Coventry Four lying low back in South Africa? Certainly not. At the behest of Armscor, a press conference was arranged in Pretoria for the fugitives to give their own account of the affair. Instructions were issued for the foreign press to be excluded, and there were scuffles outside as British film crews and journalists tried to talk to the four as they arrived. Finally, in front of their chosen audience, the four launched an attack on their treatment by the Customs men from Coventry. They said they had been subjected to seven weeks of degrading treatment while they were held at Birmingham's Winson Green prison earlier in the year, and Metelerkamp complained he had been made to strip in his hotel. He was particularly angry at having to walk around barefoot for two days.

Colonel Botha spoke proudly of the contribution he and his colleagues had made to his country's military programme. He said the loss of the bail money was 'peanuts' compared with what had been saved in purchases of hardware. All four admitted they were either consultants or employees of the Armscor subsidiary Kentron.

In a statement, the four said: 'Normally, a first offence in a British court might have led to a fine and deportation. But there were political dimensions. It is doubtful whether we could have received a fair hearing due to the influence of continuous, politically inspired propaganda on the members of the jury.' The statement added: 'We do not recognize the validity of the arms embargo. We acted in the interests of South Africa. Our contribution has enabled us to develop an advanced weapons system.'

Their defiance led to Worrall getting another tongue-lashing from Rifkind, but that was the end of the diplomatic tiff. One commentator described it as a 'blip in official Anglo-South African relations'. Among the press it seemed the story was almost over, and it was time to follow up some new scandal. However, there was one crucial issue left unexplained. What precisely did the Coventry Four mean when they boasted they had helped to build 'an advanced weapons system?'

The trial of the British defendants came up at Birmingham Crown Court in July 1985, and it helped to explain a little of that mystery. As evidence unfolded, it was clear that very advanced missile technology was being developed in South Africa, with considerable help from Britain and the United States.

Salt, Gardiner and Swann were joined in the dock by Malcolm Bird (forty-eight), Salt's works manager, and Henry Coles (seventy-one), from Bath, described as a business associate. All were charged with various forms of sanctions-busting and were found guilty.

The judge, Sir William Mars-Jones, described Gardiner, who had pleaded guilty, as the mastermind of 'an extensive, profitable and well-organized undercover operation'. He was given a fifteen-month prison sentence and a fine of £100,000 ($150,000), payable within six months. Salt was described by the judge as Gardiner's 'right-hand man'. He was jailed for ten months and fined £25,000 pounds. With Bird, he was found guilty of conspiring to violate the 1977 United Nations embargo on arms shipments to South Africa. Both men had claimed their innocence. Bird was given a three-month sentence with two months suspended. Swann was punished similarly. He and Henry Coles had pleaded guilty to a separate conspiracy to export aircraft parts to South Africa. Coles escaped a prison term only on the grounds he was too frail, but he was fined £2,500.

In the staid, stuffy atmosphere of the courtroom, more of the details of their crimes unfolded. The prosecutor, David Latham, said Salt's engineering firm had supplied South Africa with equipment for making gunsights, detonators and other arms parts, sometimes via West Germany. Some were falsely listed on shipping papers as television camera parts, and a fake drawing of a camera mount had been obtained from South Africa in an attempt to hide what their real purpose was. The men had also exported US-manufactured instruments, including lead-sulphide detectors used in heat-seeking missiles and magnetrons used for jamming radar on missiles. Paperwork indicated they had been falsely described as mining equipment.

Latham said an intricate web of companies had been formed by Gardiner, who was director of a firm called Fosse Way Securities and a number of subsidiaries. He and Salt also had shares in a South African company called Quad Engineering. Metelerkamp had a South African firm called Macnay, which was used by Armscor as a front to purchase high-technology goods in Britain and elsewhere.

The court was told that, after Customs men had questioned Bird, the works manager, he instructed two employees to destroy all material related to the South African companies. Fortunately, one of the employees had disobeyed and kept some of the paperwork for the Customs investigators. The evidence showed that embargoed goods had been traded between all these companies and others in the United States. Customs had uncovered a number of interconnecting networks, including links with Clyde Ivy and James Guerin of ISC.

All five defendants must have reflected that they were lightly treated, considering the magnitude of their trading activities. One estimate put the value of goods they had sent to South Africa at £10 million ($15 million). Salt and Bird in particular were fortunate, as they had been caught before. Their first foray into smuggling military gear was in the early 1970s. Salt was managing director of an engineering group called Redman Heenan (R-H), and Bird was working for him. Among many other items, they were smuggling key parts for the Buccaneer bomber fleet, which South Africa had adapted to carry its early A-bombs.

R-H had discovered the racket and had sacked the pair. However, a 1980 customs investigation discovered that R-H's chairman, Angus Murray, was also implicated. He and R-H were fined, and Salt and Bird were given warnings. Undaunted, they had carried on business through their own companies, bringing in Michael Gardiner to help.

This earlier Customs inquiry also showed that among Salt's main contacts from late 1977 onwards were Colonel 'Hennie' Botha and his team. They had all been operating together since the UN arms embargo came into force. Their activities in Britain mirrored those of the ISC scandal in the United States. On both sides of the Atlantic, a complex web of businesses had been feeding the South African military machine. Clearly, one object had been to develop guided missiles, but the real purpose behind that was never disclosed.

It was Dion, the former manager at Kentron Circle, the nuclear weapons plant, who explained to us the relevance of Botha's arrest and the devastating impact it had back in South Africa. Over several meetings, he often referred to the Coventry Four affair. He had said in passing that we should look into it afresh. Another time, he asked if we knew who Hennie Botha really was. He also said Clyde Ivy was very important.

Finally, in a restaurant in a suburb of Pretoria, Dion explained why we should pursue the matter. 'You see,' said Dion, 'Colonel "Hennie" Botha was my boss. When he was arrested in London, he was facility manager of Kentron Circle and in charge of all the nuclear weapons production there.'

Dion continued: 'Obviously, they must have known about it in Britain. Hennie helped plan Kentron Circle in the 1970s and then took over when it opened in 1980. He is a Broederbonder[1] through and

1 The Afrikaner Broederbond, recently renamed the Afrikaner Bond, is a sixty-year-old secret society. During the years the National Party held power, it was hugely influential in controlling all aspects of South African society. All but two of P. W. Botha's Cabinet were members. It has been likened to the Freemasons, although this would be regarded by its 12,000 carefully selected members as an insult.

through, that guy. Why do you think all the Coventry Four were released? They'd caught the top people in the bomb programme.'

Said Dion: 'Randy Metelerkamp was our procurement boss, the buyer: it was his job to get all the bits we needed from around the world. And Fanie de Jager was the finance guy: he supplied all the cash that was needed for the nuclear design and production. If Botha told him he wanted to buy stuff for six million, he had to authorize it.' Jacobus 'Koos' la Grange was a missile guidance expert working closely with Cloete.

'Hennie Botha made an arse of himself when he was caught,' Dion said. 'He took a book from the library at Kentron which they found when they went through his things at the hotel. It was a bloody book about management, and it had the library's stamp in it. That was what they made us believe. They even made a propaganda training film to show the other guys what fools they made of themselves.'[1]

Dion said that Botha and the others had been caught with gas bottles in London. 'They were for controlling the movement of the fins on the ZT-3 anti-tank missiles, but I didn't believe that story. They would say anything. I don't believe they went there only for the gas bottles – not with their facility manager. Maybe the ZT-3 gas bottles was the cover story.' Several sources said the four were buying tritium.

These were startling disclosures, and they were later confirmed by other sources. Dion felt sure the British authorities knew whom they had caught. He said that even if the high-ups in Customs were fooled, the British secret service were certainly aware.

Was this the explanation for some of the strange events that had marked the Coventry Four case? Spillane had never fully understood why he had to provide daily reports to Downing Street, or what was behind the release of Professor Cloete, or why the remaining South Africans were allowed to return home before they stood trial.

Above all, was the Coventry Four's boast at the Pretoria press conference about an 'advanced weapons system' a reference to South Africa's glide bomb and its thermonuclear weapon payload?

We asked Dion if he could provide documentary proof of Botha's involvement in the programme. After talking in the Pretoria restaurant for two and a half hours, he put his hand in his inside pocket and pro-

1 According to Dion, another glaring example of poor security, also enacted in a training video, was an instance when weapons designer Gerald Bull signed himself into a hotel as 'Mr Poephol', an Afrikaner word meaning 'arsehole'.

duced a letter written to him by Botha. He allowed us to photograph it, after folding it to hide the main contents but showing the letter-heading and the Colonel's signature. It showed Botha was *'Aanlegbestuurder'*, or facility manager, of Kentron Circle. Incontrovertibly, he was at the time the head of the programme to make advanced nuclear weapons.

Dion said that shortly after Botha returned to South Africa he was moved into a post that put him in charge of security for both the missile and bomb programmes. He was replaced at Kentron Circle by Dr André Buys. Summing up the Coventry Four affair, Dion said: 'You know what we called it? "The Broederblunder".'

Shortly after this meeting with Dion in January 1995, *The Star* in Johannesburg carried a short page-1 story. It reported that the British government had dropped all charges against the Coventry Four. Fittingly, the Armscor man who made the announcement was Dr André Buys.

17 The 'Clean' Bomb

It was nine in the evening in a steel-making town south of Johannesburg, and we were waiting in a car park to meet a former soldier who apparently had an astonishing tale to tell. We had been told he once helped to guard some of the world's most advanced nuclear weapons. Would he turn up? Would he talk? And would he be telling the truth? Once more we were trying to shed yet more light on what South Africa had been doing during the apartheid years in a shadow partnership with the most powerful nations in the West.

Koos did turn up. He was polite and modest. He accepted a beer, but didn't want anything to eat. But he said he would tell us what he knew, provided his name was changed. And it was indeed a remarkable story.

Koos had been a member of South Africa's élite Special Forces commando unit. In one of his assignments he had been sent to a military complex in the centre of Pretoria, South Africa's capital city, for special duties as part of a nine-strong team. They would work together in threes, in three shifts of eight hours under conditions of unprecedented security.

Koos was directed through the military complex to the army's bomb-proof bunker in Potgieter Street, next to Pretoria Central Prison.

He had to pass through a cordon of armed troops, but this was just the first line of security. He and his two colleagues were directed through a steel door into a lift that went only downwards to what was called Level Two. Here he was checked again, this time with hand-recognition equipment, photographs and special passes.

On that level, he and his colleagues also stripped off every item of clothing, showered, and were told to put on special antistatic overalls.

The three men then climbed into another lift, heading for Level Three, but this lift was special. It was a glass cylinder just over a metre in diameter. Packed close together, the three just squeezed inside. A door was closed and the compartment rotated twice, slowly, while some kind of electronic screening process was activated, probably again to remove static. Koos said: 'I got the impression that if we had any metal on us the capsule would stop.' After this, the capsule was lowered downwards through the floor.

The men found they were in an octagonal room with metre-thick walls. After they got out of the capsule, it withdrew back into the ceiling, trapping them inside the room. There were no other entrances.

'We couldn't go down there carrying any metal – not even weapons,' said the soldier. 'We were highly trained in hand-to-hand combat, and our orders were that should anyone try to enter the room – generals included – before our shift finished, they should be stopped. They never used the word "kill", but it was clear that's what they meant.'

The soldiers were ordered, in such an event, to break a glass panel that would automatically seal them in. There was no communication to or from the room, and no mains electricity. Power for a light and a TV monitor came from battery packs. The TV, which played a succession of videos, was encased behind glass.

The soldiers were not allowed to take any food or drink with them, but there was a makeshift toilet. Koos said he and his fellow guards underwent medical check-ups every week, and when the shift changed they were checked for radiation

Koos vividly remembered that inside the room there were ten storage racks, each holding what appeared to be eight brown glass containers, which they were ordered not to touch. To one side were toughened plastic containers identical to those used for 155-mm howitzer shells. There were also other devices of different shapes and sizes.

'On one occasion I decided to have a closer look at what we were guarding and took one of the bottles from the packing tray,' he said. 'The bottles were shaped like something from a chemistry lab – a narrow neck opening to a broad base and 12 cm to 15 cm tall. Inside was a thick liquid, just below half-full. In the top was what I later learned was a detonator. I now know it was red mercury. I believe what I was holding was the detonating device for a nuclear shell. The devices with wires at the top of the bottles were the pre-detonators, and sensitive to electricity.'

Koos said he had asked a general what he was guarding. The general said they were neutron devices, and then clammed up.

While guarding the bunker, Koos had also heard his commanding officers talk about 'shampoo' but did not understand what they were referring to, except that it was linked to the small bottles. Koos also said he had carried out a similar assignment inside a similar octagonal bunker in Angola during the Cuito Cuanavale crisis in 1988. He said: 'Exactly the same material went there under exactly the same security.'

The reference to nuclear shells and neutron bombs and how they had been deployed would become a key issue in the disclosures that would follow. Another source, who said he had been with the Civil Co-operation Bureau, the clandestine SF unit, said: 'We've created 155-mm G5 and G6 artillery shells that carry small nuclear warheads.' He too had guarded a secret base where nuclear weapons were stored, he said. One was still operational, but he would not say where.

Koos said he had been told that smaller devices, similar in appearance to those he had seen, could be shot from a hand-held rocket, or even thrown as a grenade. The small but incredibly powerful devices represented 'the best technology available'.

This reference to mini-nukes was backed up by Simon, another former SF commando, who described a tiny bulb-shaped nuclear weapon that could be fired from a rifle-like device. He said he knew these devices had been tested in South Africa's war with Angola. 'We had tiny nuclear devices that could be fired from a hand-held weapon. I knew guys who had fired this thing. The shell had radioactive markings on it and was about the size of a mortar round – it looked like a beer bottle.

'When they fired one, they had to wear a special suit, to protect them from the blast effects, I guess. I was told the device could be fired about half a kilometre. They were stored in octagonal chambers in the operational area. Everyone knew they were nuclear weapons.'

Simon, who had participated in a number of covert operations inside Angola over many years, said four specially camouflaged octagonal-shaped containers had been delivered to the South African military base of Chitado[1] in southern Angola in late 1987 or 1988 – probably airlifted by a Super Frelon helicopter. About 7 metres long and 5 metres wide, the containers could have had steel walls on the outside, but inside the walls appeared to be of a very hard plastic. They were surrounded by the army's 'top brass', and soldiers heard they carried new weapons for 'special ops'. 'We heard they were nuclear weapons,' said Simon. 'All conventional weapons came by road, but these things were flown in. They were creating a lot of attention.'

Simon had not been surprised that new weapons were tested. Earlier, South African experts had participated in the testing in Angola of new Israeli and American equipment too. He said there had been substantial exchanges of technology with other countries, involving many weapons

1 This base had substantial runways and large ammunition dumps. It was one of the key South African staging bases for operations inside Angola.

systems. This had even included secret technical exchanges with the Russians.

He said in 1985/6 SF commandos had tested a 'strim grenade', which had a high-explosive warhead. 'You screwed this thing on the end of an R1 [automatic weapon] and fastened a strap tightly around your arms and waist. I later heard that these same techniques were used to fire the nuclear grenades. The guys who fired these devices had to wear special glasses, and the top parts of their body had to be protected. I knew some of the guys who had fired it. There was no doubt it was nuclear. Even the viewfinders of the new weapons were different to conventional stuff.'

Paul, who had close links to Military Intelligence, said he had heard of such devices and confirmed that they had been tested near the Namibia/Angola border. He too confirmed the existence of such octago-nal-shaped storage bunkers and that soldiers had to wear special protec-tive clothing. 'There was no nuclear fallout. These tests occurred in Military Section 10, which is 15 km across the river inside Angola, near Ruacana Falls.1 There was no threat of radiation. A number of nuclear weapons were tested in Namibia/Angola from June 1988 to December 1988.' He said both South African and the Cuban/Russian forces in Angola had used small neutron bombs or mini-nukes in the conflict. Since then, there have been a number of unconfirmed reports of Angolan troops dying of mysterious ailments.

Laurie, a source close to foreign intelligence operations, said Angola had for years been used as an arena in which new weapons could be test-ed: 'South Africa did have grenades that could be fired from hand-held weapons, and they were used in Angola. The Cubans too were using small tactical devices. Some of the people there are dying like flies. Doctors would find strontium in their throats.' One official South African source would later tell us: 'We produced the best nuclear weapons in the world.'

Revolutionary chemicals were an essential component of new weapon systems that South Africa had designed and built. And the South African equivalent of red mercury was so sophisticated and successful it even hurt Russian production of its secret RM20/20, according to Laurie, the intelligence source.

South Africa's own procurement programme had involved shady arms

1 The South African base at Chitado in Angola is 15 km from the Namibian border and just over 30 km from Ruacana.

dealers, intelligence agents, disinformation, lies, double-dealing and murder. At the centre of this spider's web was arms dealer Dirk Stoffberg.

Colonel Landman, commanding the police task force investigating
deaths in the South African chemical and armaments industries, had, like
us, established that the Stoffbergs had been deeply involved in the trade
in red mercury, code-named Project Shampoo. Asked what Shampoo
was all about, Landman said: 'It's a code-name for red mercury. It
appears that certain chemicals were bought from companies and there
was a procurement programme. I think from there on the manufacturing
process of red mercury started in South Africa.'

This was confirmed by Linda Stoffberg, the arms dealer's sixth wife,
who had been married to him during the Shampoo procurement operations. She said he was an official agent of Armscor – which, of course,
denies this.

She said her ex-husband often talked about Operation Shampoo,
which she said was a procurement project for red mercury. It had started
in the mid-1980s and involved deals with people from East Germany
and Russia, in which he had been involved. She said Operation Shampoo
was linked to the development of a new type of weapon – a 'clean'
bomb. Her ex-husband had told her that red mercury was used in these
new devices.

Dirk Stoffberg's friend Eugene, the former South African intelligence
agent, had heard the same tale. He said he remembered how the arms
dealer had poured red mercury in front of guests at his home. Stoffberg
also told him that the material – part of it radioactive – would make 'the
most dangerous and vital weapon in the world – the "clean" bomb, a
weapon with little or no radioactive fallout that caused minor structural
damage but had frightening killing-power. He said what he was showing
us were components of the "clean" bomb, which could destroy the people of Pretoria but leave the buildings standing.'

Eugene said Stoffberg had concluded a number of weapons deals with
Iraq, where he had strong ties, but he did not know if he had sold the
'clean' bomb, or its components, to any countries in the Middle East.[1]

1 The fact that Stoffberg was apparently selling this material to other countries might
explain why a foreign intelligence operative told the authors that South Africa had 'sold a
nuclear weapon' to Iraq. He believed the sale had gone through just before the election
held on 27 April 1994, and suspected that it brought the Iraqi nuclear arsenal to twenty
warheads. He was unable to show the authors any documentary proof or intelligence
reports concerning the matter, but assured them it was of the 'utmost concern'. He said he
was connected to the Israeli security services, and at one point in the conversation he was
speaking Hebrew to a colleague.

Eugene added: 'One man who I believe worked for the GRU, or Russian military intelligence, wanted to purchase the material from South Africa in exchange for Russian-made equipment. He knew South Africa made red mercury.' He said other military operatives in Greece and Belgium had told him basically the same thing as Stoffberg about the 'clean' bomb and red mercury: 'Red mercury was needed to make a super neutron bomb.'

During a visit to South Africa's top-secret nuclear weapons laboratory at the new Advena Central Laboratories, where he had seen the material being produced and stored, Eugene again heard of the chemical's potency: 'I was told that this was the most dangerous, potent, vital weapon in the world – the "clean bomb", or "skoon bomb". It would kill people but would not destroy buildings.'

Jake, the military sanctions-buster involved in the clandestine Project Shampoo, had earlier revealed that red mercury was indeed needed for South Africa's nuclear weapons programme, and that major Western powers knew exactly what South Africa was developing. He also said the whole project had been geared to make the 'clean' bomb, which he described as the ultimate nuclear weapon. But what did the word 'clean' mean?

'This product was to be used to produce a "clean" explosion: in other words, it killed people without leaving behind any radioactivity,' said Jake. He remembered people joking about the procurement programme Operation Shampoo: '"Hair today, gone tomorrow," they would say.' But he said the weapon was deadly serious.

'Western countries – France, Britain, the United States and Italy – provided technical know-how and funding for the "clean" bomb. They were partners in the project. They were all playing it "holier than thou" about South Africa, but at the same time we were doing their dirty work for them.'

Jake said a prime example of this was the nuclear test that took place off the northern Natal coast in 1989. It had been done in collaboration with the US Defense Intelligence Agency, and was a 'clean'-bomb detonation. 'It was successful,' said Jake. 'There was no radioactive fallout.'

He said that when the foreign powers concluded red mercury could be used to make nuclear weapons, they decided that South Africa – with its high technical ability, non-aggressive media and vast open spaces – would be an ideal testing-ground. 'They thought the "clean" bomb could be developed here without too many people knowing about it. In those days South Africa was virtually a secret society, so secretly buying red mercury – even unofficially – was not a problem. We started to buy it in 1985.'[1]

Jake concluded: 'It's difficult to give a full picture of all this, because, like other security projects, it was set up on a cell structure, so one compartment of the procurement chain did not know what the others were doing. But we did know it was all about the capacity to have a "clean" product. It struck me and others that we, the polecats of the world, were being used by Western powers to develop the "clean" bomb. It was perfect. Who would suspect an African country of having the capability of such a development?'

Jan, a senior military strategist for the former National Party government, told us: 'It was cutting-edge technology. The name "red mercury" is misleading in the South African context, but what you call "red mercury" does exist. All governments put out the story that it is a hoax because they want to hoodwink everyone. We have another name for it here that people use in hushed tones.'

The principle of the 'clean' bomb, as we had learned in Europe, was to kill by neutron irradiation. Such devices would leave no trace of radioactive fission products to contaminate the battlefield, because they were pure fusion devices. The idea that this was technically possible was accepted by former nuclear bomb programme scientists Drs Sam Cohen and Frank Barnaby. Such weapons would be small – 'about the size of a baseball', Cohen had told us. Just how 'clean' the new weapons would be was not clear. But sources in South Africa were adamant that the home-grown device was indeed 'clean' and could be built without the fission component that was present in normal neutron bomb designs.

It was clear that some other nuclear scientists were also becoming extremely suspicious of what might have been developed behind the Iron Curtain during the Cold War. Red mercury, of course, was top secret – possibly the biggest secret in the world – so it was not surprising that few scientists were in a position even to attempt to discuss it. Those who worked with it were probably still bound by security legislation. For scientists schooled in more familiar ideas of nuclear physics, it still seemed absurd. But perhaps if they had been able to accompany Koos into the frightening octagonal bunker in Pretoria to see the eighty bottles of heavy liquid he was so carefully guarding there they might have changed their minds.

1 Another source told us that South Africa had developed red mercury technology by 1987. By then, it had been applied to nuclear weapons and featured in some of the conventional weaponry available for the new South African-made Rooivalk attack helicopter.

In the middle of 1991 the USAF, the Pentagon and US nuclear weapons laboratories initiated several studies on new Precision Low-Yield Weapons Designs, also known as 'mini-nukes,' 'micro-nukes' and 'tiny-nukes', according to a 1995 report in the *Washington Post*.[1] The Pentagon, reported the newspaper, was also involved in work on High-Powered Radio Frequency bombs – nuclear-driven weapons designed to disrupt electronics and communications.[2]

The studies reflected the rising concern about future 'small wars' in which enemies might use weapons of mass destruction against US troops. They did not refer to neutron weapons, but that is what nuclear experts assumed they must have been concerned about.

To persuade the Saddam Husseins of the world never to use nuclear or chemical weapons, US forces might need nuclear weapons small enough to be a plausible deterrent on a regional battlefield, said the *Post*. After watching US warplanes drop bombs down chimneys in Iraq, potential Third World enemies such as North Korea and Libya bought cement and dug deep, hardened bunkers for defence, according to intelligence assessments. Conventional bombs might bust some of those bunkers, but not the deepest ones. In technical terms only, mini-nukes would do the job better.

There needed to be a new strategy for the deployment of US nuclear weapons, partly because of fears that 'loose nukes' could fall into unfriendly hands following the collapse of the Soviet Union. Instead of huge and powerful thermonuclear devices, the United States needed to deploy smaller, less powerful weapons that could be used in small wars.

In 1993 Les Aspin, President Bill Clinton's Defense Secretary, said his country needed to develop new weapons that could penetrate underground bunkers hiding nuclear installations. It also needed to gather better intelligence about emerging nuclear threats. To handle this new initiative, Aspin said he was appointing an assistant secretary of defense for

1 In April 1993 the Joint Chiefs of Staff issued a doctrine for the conduct of nuclear war that said 'a selective capability' of being able to use lower-yield [nuclear] weapons was a 'useful alternative', according to the *Washington Post*. The report said small nuclear weapons might also be valuable in attacking deeply buried enemy targets.

2 When a nuclear weapon explodes, it emits a pulse of electromagnetic energy, called an EMP, that is so powerful it can burn out electrical components. A weapon designed to maximize the power of this pulse would destroy all the semiconductors within its range, immobilizing radios, televisions and the mechanisms of most vehicles and other machinery. In effect it would shut down the target area, rendering it vulnerable to conventional attack. Studies were conducted into these effects at South Africa's University of the Witwatersrand in the early 1980s.

nuclear security and counter-proliferation. The job, he said, was going to Ashton Carter, a thirty-eight-year-old graduate in theoretical physics and medieval history, who had been teaching on national security issues at Harvard.

Carter's new role was to quell fears at the Pentagon that countries like Iraq, Iran, Libya and North Korea not only might acquire nuclear weapons, but would also supply them to terrorist groups. In parallel with this there was a growing black market in nuclear materials, and the weapon stockpiles in the former Soviet Union were no longer under such tight security. Before Aspin's announcement, Clinton had signed a classified Presidential Decision Directive, number PDD-13, giving Carter powers to seek urgent solutions.

Carter quickly discovered that very few people outside the Pentagon wanted to think about the future of nuclear deterrence in regional wars. Even less did they want to miniaturize Washington's nuclear arsenal. In the spring of 1993, nuclear disarmament activist William Arkin disclosed the mini-nuke studies. Several months later a Democrat-controlled Congress, outraged that the Pentagon sought new weapons so soon after the end of the arms race, reacted by banning any further research.

Using a mini-nuke against a terrorist target in the United States or in a friendly country would make sense only if it was truly a 'clean' bomb, a device without radioactive fallout. This point has not been openly discussed by the Pentagon, but no doubt it was part of the studies.

It was reported that a number of war games had been played to see how nuclear terrorism could be confronted. In one example a maverick Russian general had supposedly launched a nuclear attack. Those playing the game found they had to detonate 500 nuclear weapons before this 'limited' war was over. In another exercise, staged by the FBI, agents were told to search for a nuclear bomb hidden by terrorists. They found it only when they were given hints as to where it might be.

In Carter's mind these stories showed that the West was ill-prepared, and that the mini-nuke option should be considered. The *Washington Post* reported that he went to a NATO meeting at the end of 1993 to seek its backing for his plans for a counter-proliferation initiative. He was alarmed at the complacency of the ambassadors. They made it clear they did not want to touch anything that smacked of pre-emptive strikes or new kinds of bomb. They were worried that this would undermine the forthcoming conference to re-examine whether the Nuclear Non-Proliferation Treaty needed updating after twenty-five years. But they agreed to embark on a large-scale classified analysis on new nuclear weapons threats, with Carter and a French colleague as co-chairmen. After that, they would consider whether they needed new weapons to fight the threats. Carter had found, as others would later, that getting countries to act against nuclear proliferation was not easy.

In South Africa, references to the miniaturization of nuclear weapons started to surface in the 1990s. Security sources working in this sensitive area report that they had heard the term 'mini-nuke'. It had been spoken of in reference to the 'clean' bomb, which had devastating power, said a security source. 'The way people spoke of this, it was clear South Africa had it. Everyone knew pieces of the story and could put it all together, but no one spoke about it openly. They called it *"Die Dingetjie"* [the thingy].¹ I knew it was a red mercury device and that it was a "clean" bomb – I was told people could walk back into the blast zone five minutes after detonation.'

But the 'clean' bomb was simply the cherry on the top of the cake. There is now more than enough evidence to show that South Africa was at the forefront of nuclear weapons technology in general, thanks in part to red mercury. Looking at the testimony of the soldier who guarded the underground bunker – he described a stockpile of larger weapons of various shapes and sizes – and what the bomb-makers had told us, South Africa had obviously built a substantial nuclear weapons arsenal.

Other than 'clean' bombs, the nation had a nuclear arsenal that, in the jargon of nuclear confrontation, could wreak mass destruction and render vast areas uninhabitable by nuclear fallout. The existence of such devices meant the country had not simply taken a massive leap forwards in terms of tactical neutron bombs, it must also have had other development programmes that had been quite separate from Operation Shampoo.

And, unfortunately, the chickens were coming home to roost. With the change in government, part of this arsenal, along with other strategic weaponry, was not handed over with the reigns of political power.

Could so many sources all be wrong? If new nuclear weapons had

1 As well, another source who was in close contact with the higher echelons of the South African military had heard senior officers speak about *"Die Dingetjie"*: 'The way they referred to it made me think they were talking about a very powerful weapon.' These references to *"Die Dingetjie"* go back as far as 1985 – the year Operation Shampoo was launched.

indeed been made using red mercury or something similar, could they be small enough to be fired from a hand-held weapon? One thing was sure: if an army had such small tactical nuclear weapons in its arsenal, Angola provided a unique opportunity to try them. It is believed that no army in the world has ever been able to get operational experience with these small weapons, or mini-nukes. The world was simply not watching the war in Angola. If either army involved in the conflict there had them, the temptation to test them would have been irresistible – and publicly undetectable, given the right location.

We now understood what the complex procurement project called Operation Shampoo was all about. South Africa had secretly produced one of the most deadly and advanced nuclear weapons on earth, using a chemical compound similar to the Russian-made red mercury. This meant that, far from being a minnow in the nuclear weapons business, South Africa was one of the sharks. Clearly the country was a substantial nuclear power. If this was the case, it was equally clear that the Western powers, having helped South Africa to go so far down the nuclear weapons road, would have been extremely concerned about what was going to happen to these cutting-edge nuclear weapons amid the South African revolution.

Would the Americans have been happy that a black African state was about to become one of the world's nuclear superpowers? What action would the US government have been prepared to take under such circumstances? They knew, as did the rest of the world, that South Africa had a nuclear arsenal – that had become virtually an open secret. But, if our sources were correct, elements of the US administration also would have had precise knowledge of the sophistication and extent of the South African arsenal. So what was the deal behind the scenes?

18 The Right-Wing Bomb

It was a warm night, but there was a chill blowing through the car as it drove along the straight dirt road, riding high on the corrugations and wallowing slightly as it bounced through the numerous depressions. The beams from the car headlights ranged up and down, picking out the silhouettes of trees, a small farmhouse in the distance, the occasional rabbit.

The apparent switch in temperature inside the vehicle had more to do with what its occupants were about to do than with any sudden rush of cold air. But the conditions seemed good. There was no one else in sight along this lonely stretch of veld 70 km north of Pretoria, and the fenced farmland seemed to stretch for ever. It was close to midnight, so most honest people would be asleep. Perfect.

Sources had told us where a number of nuclear weapons had been stored 'beyond the reach of government'. 'Find a place called Rooilig,' we were told. 'It's a covert military base near a game park.' 'Rooilig' means 'red light' in Afrikaans. One informant had said we should look for the red lights on a hillside in a hidden location north of Pretoria. The weapons were apparently in bunkers guarded by members of a covert military unit dressed as game wardens.

Our first examination of the site, also done in darkness, had ended abruptly. After being given an exact description of what to look for, we had found a location that matched. It was a barracks-like building, with a paved access road and street lights, stuck in the middle of farmland. The entrance gate to this facility had been solidly bolted, and there appeared to be no one around. It had four or five red lights glowing eerily atop steel poles about 5 metres high.

We had stopped at the gate, but then a pick-up truck raced up to us from behind, its lights blinding. It stopped next to our car and a man in shorts and dressed as a game warden jumped out. He raised an R4 automatic rifle and pointed it into our vehicle. 'What are you doing here?' he demanded in Afrikaans. We gave the excuse that we were lost, and he allowed us to leave, following for 10 km until we were out of sight on the main road. But where had he come from so quickly? Was he part of a local farmers' security patrol, or someone who was keeping an eye on this installation?

Inside the car with us on our second visit was a security police officer. He was unable to investigate officially, after being told by higher authority to drop his investigation, but, acting alone, he was about to take a closer look at the facility we had found two weeks earlier.

At a café a few kilometres further back, he had bought two small cans of soda water and then proceeded to pour it over his face, shirt and trousers. We had then stopped while he smeared dirt over the wet patches of his face and clothing. Suitably camouflaged, he was now going to have a closer look at the installation. He asked us to reduce speed to not much more than walking pace, then opened the front door and rolled out of the car and into the bush. We were instructed to return half an hour later.

Since our first visit, the long grass and trees which had obscured the road to anyone observing from the low, barracks-like building had been cleared. Anyone parked on the verge or climbing out of a vehicle could now be clearly seen.

After thirty minutes, we drove slowly back down the road and stopped next to a discarded Coke can which marked the pick-up spot. The officer jumped back inside. He had got into the base and had crawled to near one of the buildings that looked like a dormitory. There were a large number people inside drinking and enjoying themselves. There were also dogs on the loose, and the cop had therefore beaten a quick retreat. The conclusion was that something sensitive was being hidden there, but getting access to any bunkers would have required a private army.

The exercise illustrated vividly how finding any weaponry including 'loose nukes' that might be in the hands of a rebel group was beyond our resources. The answer lay in persuading someone involved with the rebels to talk.

The information we had gathered on the nuclear programme and 'missing' weapons had emerged out of extraordinary circumstances. Like the former Soviet Union before it, South Africa was in a state of political flux, and this had led to the disclosure of many secrets. The lifting of censorship regulations, the new-found rights of individuals under the country's just-ratified interim constitution and a desire to disclose, as if in a rite of absolution, had brought from the shadows a number of former government agents who were revealing from the apartheid past a range of illegal actions – including murder.

As the reigns of political power were handed to the ANC, everyone – including a much-disenchanted SADF – was having to realign long-cherished values and perceptions. This realignment obviously was a difficult process for some of the Republic's whites who had enjoyed political control and were comfortable with state-enforced racial segregation. Now it was a whole new ball game.

There had been much speculation in the media as to how the country's political Right – essentially a white Afrikaner faction – would react in the face of such turmoil. Indeed, there had been doubt that the fully democratic election of April 1994 could be held without problems. But, on the whole, the election had been gloriously successful. The vast majority of South Africans were thrilled, invigorated, by the moment.[1]

Even a right-wing bombing campaign just before the election could not mar this thrilling achievement. But amid the excitement it was easy to forget that emotions were running equally deep, for different reasons, among groups on the right of the political spectrum. After the election, many of these political groups became fragmented and disillusioned, and started to resemble a spent force rather than a mass political movement.

However, the small die-hard right-wing formations remained. These included the Afrikaner Weerstandsbeweging (AWB), the Boere Vryheidsbeweging (BVB), the Boere Krisis Aksie (BKA), the Boere Republikienseleer (Boere Republican Army, BRA), the Church of the Creator, the Transvaal Agricultural Union, and the Orange Free State Agricultural Union. Before the election, the AWB, BKA and BRA were widely considered able to muster paramilitary groups that could be effective – particularly the BKA.[2]

1 From the election, held on 27 and 28 April, South Africa was run by a Government of National Unity, in which political power was shared among key parties despite the huge majority won by the ANC – 62.6 per cent of the vote. The National Party won 20.4 per cent.

2 The AWB had highly organized structures and claimed it could put 10,000 men and women under arms in hours. But its strength and threat potential were virtually dismissed by analysts following a débâcle in the black homeland of Bophuthatswana before the election when it sent hundreds of members to help prop up the discredited puppet regime of President Lucas Mangope. By 1995 its membership was believed to be fewer than 1,000. On several occasions since the election AWB leader Eugene Terre'Blanche had appealed to supporters to disobey the government. The shadowy BRA is based on the Irish Republican Army (IRA), using the same cell structure, and is close to the AWB. The group claimed responsibility for sixteen acts of sabotage just before the election, blowing up communications structures. Like the IRA, it advised minutes in advance that an act of sabotage was to be committed. The BKA was formed when the country's white farmers revolted against the prices of produce in 1989. Operating from the northern Transvaal – the right-wing strong-

Before the election, all had urged their supporters to prepare for a siege by stockpiling weapons, ammunition, food, medicine, firewood, water and other day-to-day necessities. Preparations were widespread, with much of the rest of the white population joining in, prompted by various faxed messages spreading the word. Some of these messages were even sent in the name of senior police and military officers and commando leaders. There was a run on groceries across the country.

For the die-hard white minority, the country's future before and after the election seemed as gloomy as it appeared rosy to the advocates of democracy. Before the election there had been a number of raids on police stations or military bases that had resulted in the loss of large amounts of weaponry. In some cases it looked as though the thieves had been helped by people 'on the inside'. Indeed, elements of the right wing had squirrelled away enough conventional weaponry to start a war, according to intelligence agents monitoring the build-up. Raids by right-wingers on military bases and police stations had started after President F. W. de Klerk cleared the political battlefield by unbanning the ANC and other organizations on 2 February 1990. Since then, huge arms caches had been hidden throughout the northern Transvaal. Several caches of arms shipments from foreign sources had already been uncovered.

It was estimated that the right wing had access to:

- about 100,000 R1 and R4 automatic weapons which could no longer be accounted for by the SADF;
- a Buccaneer bomber, which should have been decommissioned years ago and whose role for the SAAF was to deliver a nuclear bomb;
- an unknown number of drones – unmanned aircraft, used for reconnaissance or for delivering weapons, including nuclear devices;
- six Ratel troop carriers armed with a 20-mm cannon;
- an unknown number of French-designed Eland armoured cars;
- an unknown number of missiles;
- about forty ageing Saracen armoured personnel carriers;
- about twelve G5 howitzer systems, which could deliver a 155-mm

hold – the BKA succeeded in drawing together about 5,000 farmers, who blockaded Pretoria in protest. This led to running battles with the police. After that, the BKA developed its organization and went on to hold sway through a number of the country's rural districts. The Church of the Creator believed in the violent overthrow of the state. The two agricultural unions were at odds with their equivalents in other areas in that they had chosen to challenge the government, with the Transvaal union aligned to the BKA.

shell over a range of more than 40 km;
- about three G6s – the motorized version of the G5, whose sophistication has created a widely held belief that they are the key delivery system for South Africa's nuclear shells;
- an unknown quantity of Rooikat armoured cars.

On top of these local estimates, a British intelligence source told us a squadron of Impala subsonic jet fighters was probably being held at an air-force base sympathetic to the right-wing cause. In fact much of the weaponry in right-wing hands was thought to be in the care of sympathetic military units.

In addition, the SADF was believed to have been sabotaged from within at the time of the election, making it difficult for troops loyal to the new government to respond should they be called upon to do so. The source said South Africa's Lockheed C-130 troop transport aircraft – the Hercules – had been seriously threatened operationally in 1994 because a computer system monitoring spare parts had been sabotaged. Spare parts could therefore not be found, and a number of aircraft were effectively grounded until air-force personnel could untangle the mess.

Police intelligence sources say similar sabotage affected South Africa's helicopter fleet. 'I know for a fact that spare parts for the helicopters were sent to the wrong areas,' said a police agent. 'Our helicopters are twenty, twenty-five years old. They need spare parts, and if you don't have the spare parts on the base what the hell do you do?'

This agent said such sabotage of the capabilities of the helicopters and C-130s would have severely limited the army's ability to move troops rapidly across the country.

This was confirmed by Jan, the senior military strategist with the previous National Party government: 'The air force has indeed been sabotaged, and represents a severely limited threat. There's been a drain of manpower, and lots of funny things happened – deliberate sabotage. I am told that was the situation in December [1994].'

Johannesburg's *Weekend Star* reported in 1994 that sophisticated weaponry – much of it US-made – had been illegally imported into South Africa and was in the hands of right-wing groups. This included the importation in 1993 of 20,000 M-16 and an unknown quantity of LAW rockets and Stinger ground-to-air missiles. It was later revealed that American nationals smuggled into South Africa a cache of sophisticated weaponry found in a shipping container on a Pretoria smallholding. Police said the find, in October 1994, was destined for the Right. It was worth R1.6 million ($437,000).

Police said they believed there were at least three other similar caches as yet undiscovered. In the Pretoria consignment was an unknown quantity of US-made explosive bullets, not seen in South Africa before, designed for assassinations. The container also held more than 47,000 rounds of various calibres, a variety of survival equipment and 321 high-tech weapons: US-made automatic rifles, Czechoslovakian mortars and mortar bombs, improved versions of RPG-7 missiles, Russian-made AK-74s with laser sights, automatic shotguns, handguns, target pistols and knives. There were also three launchers for Stinger missiles, and new M-14 automatic rifles. Security sources said some of the other caches were probably stored in neighbouring countries.

Jan confirmed the movement of foreign high-tech weapons to right-wing elements within South Africa: 'They have state-of-the-art stuff, all diverted from Unita.' He said most of the weapons were stashed in the Natal Midlands.

South Africa had been declared a nuclear-free zone and it was doubtful that Nelson Mandela, with his clear moral position on weapons of mass destruction, would have supported a military that wanted to keep or develop a nuclear weapons programme. It followed that, if there were nuclear devices in South Africa, the government didn't have them. However, against this background, the stories persisted that the right wing did have them. We had briefed senior ministers of the new government on this, but were told they knew nothing of such devices, although they were suspicious of De Klerk's declaration of only six and a half bombs.

We had also tried to glean information from foreign intelligence sources on what was going on in South Africa, but the first attempt ended with an abrupt rebuff. A Johannesburg contact close to the British secret service said he knew nothing about loose nukes but would make inquiries with former colleagues. Their response, relayed to us later, was simply to 'Back off.'

One indication that the Right might have nuclear ambitions came in March 1994, when the sixteen disgruntled nuclear and rocket scientists from Denel threatened to expose military secrets unless they were paid substantial retrenchment benefits. Before they were gagged by a court order, a spokesman for the group, who described himself as a supporter of the right wing, had told the press: 'Some of us and many in the SADF strongly believed that a couple of bombs should have been held back and kept in white hands.'

Six months later we were told that this was more than a belief. Senior security sources, worried that political manoeuvring was spinning out of control, confirmed to us that right-wing elements closely associated with the military had nuclear weapons.

It was a worrying scenario, but there was worse to come. The sources said elements of the new government were being blackmailed by the threat of nuclear weapons to accept a Volkstaat – an autonomous homeland for white South Africans. This was the nuclear nightmare facing President Nelson Mandela.

When we had first approached Jan, the former government military strategist and senior intelligence agent, he said he did not believe it was possible that the right wing had nuclear weapons, although he admitted that South Africa had built many more than it had disclosed. However, when he checked with colleagues in the South African intelligence community, they confirmed the nuclear threat was real. He was shocked, and feared for the safety of himself and his family, but agreed to help because he was appalled at the consequences of what was going on.

He said right-wing forces were extremely serious about their threats. 'They have more than one shell – the standard tactical nuclear shell – and the present government knows about their capability.' These rebels had threatened to use one of South Africa's most formidable artillery pieces against the government. 'The G6, the system designed to deliver a nuclear shell, is the weapon,' he said. 'They have five of them, and a stockpile of shells, all being moved around the country to strategic positions – the majority within easy reach of Gauteng [the Johannesburg area]. The right-wing thinking is that they will fire a shell into a black township if they have to. The G6 is a highly mobile vehicle – they could fire and duck. In minutes it could be on a transporter and out of the area. They are apparently openly talking about their capability.'

He said a committee of right-wing retired senior police, military and Military Intelligence officers – some of them generals – were commanding the weapons. 'They are controlling the weapons very firmly to prevent even renegade elements of the right wing getting hold of them. It will be interesting to see what will be done about it.'

He accused elements within MI of having a hand in the affair. 'They are dangerous, very dangerous. Since I found out about all this, I have been unable to sleep at night.'

He said details of the crisis were known to very few people: 'I think you'll find that maybe a handful of top people know – I'd be very surprised if they don't – because my information is that the highest levels do. They just don't want the public to know, and they don't want the world to know. The threat has already been made: the right wing wants a Volkstaat – but their concept of a Volkstaat could be just a little too much for the government to swallow.'

He said the South African crisis had caused huge concern among the foreign intelligence services, who were 'pouring agents into South Africa' to monitor the crisis. 'The CIA is here in a big way. They are worried the nukes will go somewhere else. The United States is worried particularly that hostile Arab states will get them. They have to find out quickly what is going on here. They have been involved in more intelligence activity in South Africa in the last eighteen months than the last ten years.'

Mossad was also beefing up its presence. 'Suddenly this place is crawling with foreign intelligence agencies. It's like a major spook hunting-ground. The National Intelligence Agency is now running a major investigation into the right-wing capability because they do not trust the police – they don't think they are capable.'

Also, there was great mistrust of the military. 'I don't believe the military is 100 per cent behind the new government.'

On the possibility of foreign military intervention, Jan said: 'I think the Israelis are not exactly married to procedure. If they intervene, the problem is they might wield a few sledgehammers along the way. Maybe they're still in the stage of trying to ascertain whether there really is a threat.' The idea of talking to journalists appalled Jan, but he was worried and wondered whether the security community in South Africa was equipped to deal with such a crisis.

Another source shared Jan's fears, but was actively trying to gather intelligence to counter the threat. Rick, a government agent, had penetrated the right wing. Not only did he confirm that the right wing had nuclear weapons, he said in 1994 he had seen one of them on a farm in the northern Transvaal: 'I have seen part of a warhead and a long missile that was under heavy guard by the Right. So I have one confirmed, but information about four others. I think the threat is imminent.'

He described the missile as an intermediate-range 'Arniston', derived from Israel's Jericho-II. 'It was a missile like a Scud that you can carry over ground – a FROG [Free Rocket Over Ground],' he said. 'It was about 1 metre wide and sat on a trolley device.' Almost certainly he was talking about the RSA-3, equivalent to Israel's Shavit, developed from the Jericho. He put the range of this missile at 3,000 to 5,000 km, but other sources said it was possible to get such a missile into orbit if it carried only a small warhead – and that would make it an ICBM.

Rick said the missile was hidden 4 km from the perimeter of the Louis Trichardt air-force base in the northern Transvaal. It would have been transported there on a truck-launcher. The heavily armed men guarding it were wearing the uniform of the Boere Kommandos. 'It's a pure right-wing group, nothing to do with the boere kommando units of the SADF,' he said.

Rick said the nose had been opened and it was connected to an Apple-type computer, probably in readiness for guidance programming, and a sophisticated cooling system chilled the electronics. The warhead had been opened up, and part of it was being stored in a building 20 metres away. It is not known what type of nuclear device was being carried by the missile. 'They said this was "the big one" – it left no doubt in my mind it was nuclear. Later I was told it was a neutron bomb.'

The missile was hidden in a farmhouse building, protected by a number of US-made Stinger and SAM-7 ground-to-air missiles. The guards carried light machine-guns. 'They were all ex-military people.'

Said Rick: 'I know there is a bomb out there, and it's being controlled by prominent people on the right wing.' Sources in police intelligence believed this group could control up to four other, similar devices. These also were believed to be neutron bombs and were apparently hidden on another farm less than 100 km south of where Rick had seen the missile.

'They are using the threat of nuclear weapons to blackmail the government into accepting a Volkstaat,' said Rick. 'I think it will be in place within two years.'

Rick said he had information that some smaller nuclear weapons could be delivered by drones – remote-controlled aircraft. 'These things can fly about 300 km carrying a small device. They can be controlled from an attache-case-sized command module.'

Hennie, a military agent, was reluctant to talk about what was going on: he said it was better to let sleeping dogs lie. But after hours of persistence he finally opened up. He said there was nothing to worry about if the new government played its cards correctly. If it didn't, that was another matter. He said the Right had a bomber with an old-fashioned atom bomb – one of the South African prototypes – on an air base sympathetic to right-wing aspirations. 'They've got it and they can use it, and will use it if they are threatened. I'm told they have one of the "dirty" bombs and a Buccaneer.'

Rick had heard the same story, but he said this 'dirty' bomb was in fact the most powerful of devices, a thermonuclear weapon.

Laurie, a source close to foreign intelligence operations, said there might be yet another old-fashioned device sitting on a military base in Natal. 'Foreign spy satellites have been realigned to gather as much intelligence as possible,' he said.

The older devices, if used, would cause widespread radioactive fallout. For that reason, said Hennie, it was unlikely that right-wing extremists would consider detonating such a device in South Africa. He said he had been told that if things went wrong one possible target was Harare.

Johan, a retired senior police officer, said: 'There's going to be big shit with the right wing. Be careful. Don't ask me if they've got nuclear weapons – ask the military.'

Other sources came forward with much the same story. Charles, a retired senior military officer, said he had been told by his army sources that the right wing had nuclear weapons. 'There are at least two devices in the northern Transvaal in the hands of the right wing. The place to look for them is between Phalaborwa and Louis Trichardt.'

Police sources said they had information that there was a nuclear weapon in the hands of the Right in the northern Cape. Said Paul, an MI agent: 'The right wing has nuclear weapons and poses a serious threat to South Africa. Ninety per cent of the people involved are military – serving and former. They say within five years they will retake the country.' He said the group involved could not be infiltrated, and two people had been hurt while trying. 'Their weapons have been shown to certain people, including police officers. They have many nuclear shells.'

Meanwhile Eugene, another South African intelligence agent who had penetrated right-wing structures, said he had compiled a report for Nelson Mandela warning of the right wing's nuclear capability. 'He was shocked,' said the agent. 'He extended the briefing from about one hour to the whole morning. The right wing has got up to twelve nuclear warheads stashed at farms across the northern Transvaal.'

The locations of the Right's nuclear weapons sites were passed to the NIS. 'I prepared a long report on the strength of the Right and presented it to the ANC in December 1993,' said Eugene. 'During late 1993 the right wing was preparing for war.' He said a number of the people present at the Mandela meeting, including Mathews Phosa – now premier of the Eastern Transvaal province, renamed Mpumalanga – were shocked at what he reported. Sources in government confirmed that Mandela had received such a report, but were vague about its nuclear component.

The agent said that, at the time, Mandela had discussed revealing the right-wing threat during his visit to Oslo, where he was to receive the Nobel Peace Prize. But ANC advisers counselled against this.

Eugene said he told Mandela that right-wing elements within the existing military would never relinquish control of South Africa's strategic weapons systems – and that included nuclear weapons. 'I was told, without doubt, that South Africa's strategic military potential would never be revealed to the new Government of National Unity. What has happened since, I don't know.'[1]

The strategic capabilities included nuclear weapons and sophisticated missile systems, which were based across the Transvaal. The missiles included surface-to-air and surface-to-surface short-, medium- and long-range systems. Other sources said some of the medium-range missiles were nuclear-armed, though it's not known whether they were still in place by the end of 1993. 'Most had high-explosive warheads, but a number, I believe, had nuclear warheads,' said Eugene. 'I was told all these were strategic weapons and would not be disclosed by the military to the new government.'

Military sources said the missiles were in silos underground or on platforms that could be raised for firing at sites near Ermelo, Hoedspruit, Ellisras, Voortrekkerhoogte, Naboomspruit, Hammanskraal, Warmbaths, Pafuri in the Kruger National Park and in the Waterberg mountain range, among other locations. Some of these stations were manned, others were operated by remote control – armed and controlled by computer. The latter were under sophisticated electronic surveillance.

The missile programme was designed by specialists from the Council for Scientific and Industrial Research, along with specialists from the military, we were told. Several senior intelligence sources said Mandela was threatened with nuclear blackmail by the right wing sometime during 1994.

Said Eugene: 'I had no doubt they could have sent a missile to Lusaka if they wanted to.' This was independently confirmed by Jan, the military strategist: 'These were medium- to long-range missiles, and some were nuclear-armed as long ago as 1982/3. They would have been big, "dirty" nuclear weapons, and would have been targeted on Lusaka, Dar es Salaam, Harare and so on – you could guess where they would be aimed. Israeli military personnel and civilians spent a lot of time at

1 At the time the report was written, some retired generals – particularly former chief of the SADF Constand Viljoen, former MI chief General P. J. 'Tienie' Groenewald and former senior staff officer of strategic defence and tactics Koos Bischoff – still had significant influence within the SADF, and all three were considered supporters of the Right. However, there is no evidence to suggest they were involved in taking nuclear weaponry or that they used their influence.

Lohatla.' He said there were three to five silos in each launch site, and there were a number of different sites.

On the location of nuclear weapons, Eugene said: 'I was told that they were kept on various farms – I had all the names and places involved. I passed all the information I had on the locations to the NIS. Some were on a farm near Ellisras, adjoining one owned by a former NIS agent. Others were in or near Naboomspruit. There were also huge arms caches at Nylstroom and Springbokvlakte.'

For years the strength of the right wing in the northern Transvaal had been slowly growing. And it was due in no small part to a highly influential group of individuals who had come together to marshal strategy.

Acting to preserve the Afrikaner heritage and secure what they considered to be a worthwhile future for whites within the new South Africa, the influential group had formed a think-tank or action group called the Volkseenheidskomitee (Vekom) – the People's Unity Committee. It included senior ex-military and ex-police officers, academics and others still prominent in South African society.

After the election, some political analysts said Vekom's power was on the wane. Others, however, said it remained a significant force in right-wing politics and had within its ranks a small nucleus of top people determined to secure a Volkstaat and able to influence quasi-military forces. It had been under surveillance by the security police since its inception.

The roots of Vekom could be traced back to a split in AWB ranks during 1988. A group of Afrikaner academics, intellectuals and decision-makers led by Dries Alberts, Jan Groenewald and Professor Alkmaar Swart had then formed the Boere Vryheidsbeweging (BVB), out of which was created the Pretoria Boere Kommando Groep, or Committee of Ten, in 1990. This in turn had led to the Eenheidskomitee 25 in 1991 and to Vekom in 1992. The latter two particularly had been involved in military training, using instructors from Belgium, Germany and the United States, among other countries.

Associated with these groupings in periods from mid-1990 were also former police commissioner General Mike Geldenhuys, former chief of the notorious Bureau of State Security (BOSS) General Hendrik van den Bergh, police brigadier Rooi Rus Swanepoel, former chief of the SADF General Constand Viljoen, former intelligence and reconnaissance chief of the SADF's battle-hardened Thirty-Two Battalion Commandant Willem Ratte, Professor Johan Schabort, AWB leader Eugene Terre'Blanche and Jan Groenewald's brother, the former chief of

Military Intelligence, General P. J. 'Tienie' Groenewald. Dr Wally Grant, a driving force behind the AEC's uranium enrichment programme, was appointed chairman of Vekom after it grew from the Eenheidskomitee 25, of which he was also a leader.

Other prominent individuals associated or at least seen by police intelligence agents at Vekom meetings were Conservative Party leader Dr Ferdi Hartzenberg, president of the Transvaal Agricultural Union Dries Bruwer, commandant-general of the Boereweerstandsbeweging Andrew Ford and a leader of the Boere Kommando, Gawie Volschenk. By mid-1993 Vekom had about twenty-five members.

Elements within the Vekom structures had by the end of 1993 become part of the Afrikaner Volksfront (AVF), formed as an umbrella body, a symbol of unity and strength, to represent right-wingers during the negotiations phase of South Africa's political transition. This was steered by the military minds of Constand Viljoen and Tienie Groenewald – considered the 'grand strategist' – among other prominent leaders. Wally Grant, who claimed to have documented the entire history of the nuclear weapons programme to preserve it for future generations, was the AVF's science adviser.

But the AVF was not getting its way in the political negotiations, and subsequently refused to participate in the election. At the eleventh hour, only minutes before the midnight deadline for registration, Viljoen led a breakaway group from the AVF into the election fight. Registering as the Freedom Front (FF), he ensured the Right would have a voice in the new government. Other generals left with him, including Groenewald, the strategist, all of which seriously damaged the AVF.

Viljoen finally cast his ballot at the Voortrekkerhoogte military base near Pretoria in the company of thirty-five former generals, including former police commissioner Geldenhuys and former BOSS chief van den Bergh.

During negotiations that brought the FF into the election process, Viljoen had ensured that the issue of a Volkstaat would not be cast aside by insisting that a Volkstaat Council (VSC) be formed to lobby for the concept. The VSC became an official body, set up under the constitution, although it had no more than advisory powers. Its task, and that of its study groups, was to investigate possible Afrikaner self-determination and to put forward proposals to the Government of National Unity. The VSC wanted 'supreme constitutional sovereignty in a geographical Volkstaat'.

It was against this background that Eugene, the military agent, explained how a shift of power had occurred in the right-wing heartland of the northern Transvaal. He said a group of generals had set up a huge military power base there. Herman Vercueil, the administrator of the Transvaal Agricultural Union and its security adviser, was sitting on joint military operations committees with General Dries van der Merwe and other military leaders. But Vercueil was part of Vekom.

'They recruited widely, and virtually all farms in that region belonged to the Vekom structure,' said the undercover agent. 'Vekom was extremely well placed. Through Vercueil they had access to information. So they recruited helicopter pilots, among others, and many more from within the highly sensitive military areas of the northern Transvaal. They had key people on the inside. A large percentage of all the people living in this area supported Vekom.'

Eugene said that nuclear weapons would have been an integral part of the plans of elements within the Right. 'The talk was that there had been sixty-four nuclear weapons manufactured in South Africa, and they had access to some of them,' he said. 'Certain elements had a blue book on methods of how to take over the country. I was told the nuclear warheads on farms in Naboomspruit and Ellisras could be fired in missiles. I deduced they stole, through their access to nuclear establishments, a number of warheads from secret facilities that were not part of the statements by De Klerk and Pik Botha on the dismantlement programme.'

Asked about the scientists who had aligned themselves to the right-wing cause, Eugene said: 'They have the know-how and design expertise to be working on what they want.' On other right-wing strongholds, the agent said there were about six secret locations in the Louis Trichardt area. 'I knew a number of farms where right-wingers were coming from, but the CIS [Crime Intelligence Service] was well informed.'

He said right-wing plans to act before the election were partly thwarted by the arrest of ten out of twenty key people who were centrally involved in distributing weapons. They were pulled in by police for stealing four tons of weaponry from the air force. 'This seriously disrupted their plans.'[1]

1 Police intelligence reports in 1991 indicated that the South African army was likely to back right-wing demands for a Volkstaat. Right-wing groups, including top politicians, had decided that a commando unit be formed, complete with its own uniform. 'It is already established that the South African Defence Force will lend their support to the commando,' said one report. Associated with the commando group in Pretoria would be at least two military generals and other police generals. 'The main aim of the commando was to establish a strong presence in a particular town or area so that they can say to the government they have taken the place over; in other words, a mini-coup.' The right-wingers believed their plan would be successful because it had the backing of 'the chain of command of the SADF in the specific area', according to the police. However, the result of this strategy was mixed at best.

Said Eugene: 'I don't think the ANC government has got its way on the Volkstaat issue. There is a huge build-up of military power in the northern Transvaal. In the rest of South Africa there's very little. But the northern Transvaal doesn't have a seaport, big airports, fuel or water,' he said, 'so having the Volkstaat there would be difficult.'

However, that might no longer be a problem. On 8 March 1995, well-placed sources told us a deal had been struck on a Volkstaat. It would be in the north-eastern Transvaal, covering a largely undeveloped region adjoining Kruger National Park and encompassing the towns of Phalaborwa and Hoedspruit – home for one of the SAAF's most sophisticated and strategically important air bases.

This 'sovereign state' would include part of the game-rich bushveld and would stretch north towards the Zimbabwean border, but stopping well short of Pietersburg, which had previously been earmarked as a possible Volkstaat capital.[1] It was a 'done deal'. The sources said Mozambique had agreed to the construction of a supply corridor from the coast, probably from the port of Maputo, to the Volkstaat in return for monetary agreements. How it would cross the natural barrier of Kruger National Park was not clear.

We could not verify any of this, and newspapers appeared to have no inkling of any such plan. However, in July 1995, four months after the scenario was described to us, Johannesburg's *Business Day* newspaper reported on its front page that South Africa and Mozambique had almost concluded a 'multi-modal transport agreement' to develop the arterial communications corridor from South Africa to Mozambique's coastal capital, Maputo. The report said that, apart from upgrading the existing road system between Maputo and the Johannesburg area, the plan was also to open up 'a second corridor linking Northern Province, Eastern Transvaal and Mozambique'. It was planned to build a major highway from the centre of the right-wing heartland to the port of Maputo. Every other major highway in the region headed directly for Johannesburg.

The director-general of the South African transport department, Ketso Gordhan, said the first phase of the project would focus on developing Maputo harbour and a twin 'development corridor system' between the two countries. The report said a new highway-based corridor, which was still at the conceptual stage, would link Phalaborwa to Maputo,

1 In August 1995 it was reported that about R6 million ($1.7 million) was to be spent on the 'immediate renovation' of a former air-force base in Pietersburg which would turn it into an international airport.

'possibly via Pietersburg or a new highway'. It was not clear whether this corridor would cut through Kruger National Park.

By August, *Business Day* reported that three South African Cabinet ministers and their directors-general were in Mozambique to finalize details of this 'sizeable' undertaking. Work would begin before the end of the year, said the report. And so it seemed the problem would be solved for the Volkstaat. It would get its life-giving arterial route through to the Indian Ocean and could now be a viable, prosperous state.

Newspapers had reported that Mandela might favour a referendum on the Volkstaat issue to gauge Afrikaner support. Meanwhile, in the eastern Transvaal, the Volkstaat Council had presented its plans for the Volkstaat and was seeking public support.

Finally, in September, the road plan erupted into a major controversy. *The Star*, Johannesburg, splashed on a story that the proposed new highway would, as we suspected, bisect Kruger National Park. Dr Robbie Robinson, head of the National Park's board, said Kruger's integrity would be destroyed: 'We hold Kruger in trust for the rest of the world.' *The Star* said talks had taken place between officials in Mozambique, Phalaborwa's chamber of commerce and the military. Its story did not link the road to a Volkstaat or question the motives of the Mandela government.

Eugene had once told us he had seen the military plan to win a Volkstaat: 'It was frightening. There was a blueprint for war, and within it was a nuclear battle plan.'

Nuclear weapons analyst Nick Badenhorst believed South Africa still had a vast, undeclared nuclear arsenal and delivery systems that included missiles. But they were not under the control of the Government of National Unity, he said. He believed devices were being held at secret locations in the Transvaal. 'It's a rainy-day policy. They are being kept to guarantee the future of the Afrikaner.'

In November 1993 Badenhorst's controversial nuclear scenario, published in the South African magazine *Armed Forces*, had shocked elements of the establishment. He had predicted: 'South Africa's nuclear weapons and delivery systems will not be significantly reduced until the present administration [De Klerk's] gets exactly the governing system and constitution it wants.'

Badenhorst had also elaborated on his theory that 'rogue' elements of the SADF could have seized some of South Africa's long-range missiles, especially the D-25, with a range of 16,000 km, 'on orders from the top'. He stressed that six to twelve such weapons could be carried on mobile launchers and hidden from the government. They would be armed with '500-kiloton warheads that other "rogue" elements developed in secret'.

Why mobile launchers? Because our "rogue" military analysts would have carefully digested the lessons of Operation Desert Storm where – despite thousands of Allied air sorties – Saddam Hussein continued firing his missiles at Israel and Saudi Arabia.

And if they could not find them in the desert, there is no way six to twelve such missiles would be found in a country with mountains, valleys, plantations and forests.

Rest assured, notwithstanding the thousands of IAEA inspections, some of these weapons and missiles will be preserved somewhere.

Later, interviewed about the article, Badenhorst said: 'You should probably look for a small influential group, maybe consisting of members of the previous government, the high echelons of the military, investors, industrialists – people with money to lose. These people could be in this shadowy group that controls SA's nuclear stockpile.'

But where are the weapons? 'They will be hidden away where the International Atomic Energy Agency would never think of looking for them. South Africa has some of the deepest mineshafts in the world and I would venture to suggest you would not get an inspector to go down a mineshaft, especially if it is caved in at one end.

'Alternatively, they could have a stockpile hidden in a friendly neighbouring country. Who are our friends in Africa, South America? Determine that and you have a list of where such a stockpile could be hidden.'

He suggested that the 'final' dismantling of South Africa's nuclear and delivery systems would occur only after the 'final' political settlement had been reached. This in all likelihood would include a Volkstaat, but he said that would not be enough for some right-wing elements. They would want control of the country again.

We were told that South Africa had secretly shipped out of the country most of its vast stock of nuclear weapons in a deal involving the United States and Israel before the Government of National Unity came to power. Confirming this, Jan, the military strategist, said the secret shipments occurred in 1990–91. The weapons were gone before the multi-party Transitional Executive Council was installed to oversee the transition of political power.

This nuclear pact was a central aspect of South Africa's halting steps towards democracy, the highly placed source said. Documents were shredded and secret files were removed. 'All evidence of the secret nuclear programmes was spirited away,' Jan said. 'Before the TEC started, they had sanitized the whole thing. To all intents and purposes these weapons never existed. They were moved out of the country in a deal involving the Americans and Israelis. I have confirmed that these weapons were moved to another country – probably Israel.'

He said the deal would have been that the bombs were handed over in return for substantial financial assistance. But the deal went wrong: the right-wingers involved held back a number of weapons 'for a rainy day'. 'The political integrity of some of the people working on the nuclear weapons programme was highly questionable, so one can understand why some disappeared.'

He said the South African democratic process had been underwritten by nuclear weapons. 'Under the counter they've done a deal. When De Klerk went public with six, behind the scenes he was probably making sure he got the others out so they did not "fall into the wrong hands" during the change in government. However, the plan went wrong.'

Other countries had suspected that South Africa had nuclear weapons, so a public admission of the dismantling was vital, he said. The United States particularly was concerned about 'the black bomb' and would have assisted to prevent the weapons being transferred with political power to the ANC.

Israel, which backed the South African weapons programme from the start, would have been the natural recipient of the devices – particularly considering that Israeli money and expertise went into so many of them in the first place. 'That happened. The stuff moved. It definitely went, but we don't know what got left behind,' said Jan.

Nick Badenhorst had also heard that after De Klerk returned from a 1990 meeting with US President George Bush in Washington a vital document had been left on De Klerk's official aircraft. 'This document reportedly spelt out part of South Africa's political future with regard to the planned handing over of power to a majority government.' Part of that future was a secret stockpile of nuclear weapons, said Badenhorst.

Days before the announcement in March 1993 that South Africa had built nuclear weapons, US officials had said they had collected 'highly sensitive' intelligence on South Africa's nuclear programme from agents and reconnaissance satellites, according to a report in the *Washington Post*. It said US intelligence analysts were concerned that South Africa might have hidden a significant quantity of highly enriched uranium and other components of nuclear warheads.

Washington was worried, said the *Post* report, that HEU might have been stockpiled or hidden by renegade South African officials or perhaps exported to other countries, such as Israel.

US officials with access to intelligence reports said many analysts believed the weapons were meant to be fired from field artillery – as we had been told in South Africa – if major military conflict erupted with neighbouring, communist-led, black-ruled states.

'The United States has serious questions about South Africa's compliance with its Article II and Article III obligations' under the Nuclear Non-Proliferation Treaty, said an intelligence report sent to Congress on 19 January 1993. The unclassified version of the report, which was signed by President George Bush, did not provide details of the US concerns, but Article II of the NPT forbids any manufacture or transfer to another country of 'nuclear weapons explosive devices', while Article III requires international safeguards on all 'special fissionable material' and bars any undeclared export of such material.

A US official with access to classified reports on the South African nuclear programme explained that the biggest concern was how much fissile material had been produced. He said analysts believed South Africa 'declared only a portion' of the material in documents given to the IAEA, prompting concern that the remainder had been hidden or perhaps exported to Israel which, say analysts, has long collaborated with South Africa on nuclear matters.

The US concerns were shared by the Russian Foreign Intelligence Service (FIS), Moscow's counterpart to the CIA. In a report made public in February 1993 by Senator John Glenn of Ohio, the FIS said that while South Africa had in many respects co-operated freely with the IAEA, some experts doubted that the country had declared all of its nuclear materials 'in the form of nuclear explosive devices or weapons'. The report did not say what might have happened to the materials.

In addition to worrying about whether South Africa was still hiding nuclear material, US officials feared some of the bomb-grade enriched uranium already declared by South Africa could be diverted illicitly to other countries or terrorists.

One US official expressed doubt to the *Washington Post* that the intelligence community would ever be satisfied that South Africa's nuclear capability had been eliminated. 'You can never prove a negative,' he said.' You are left at bottom with taking someone's word for it ... The consequence is that maybe the South Africans have a bunch of bombs and maybe they will wind up in the hands of terrorists. That is the best we will ever be able to do.'

We heard other stories – unconfirmed – involving attempts by the military's Special Forces to recover some of the weapons. These devices had purportedly been hidden in mineshafts in the Klerksdorp area, 130 km south-west of Johannesburg, and been recovered after a raid by commandos.

We were also told that SF commandos had been instructed to remove sophisticated detonating capsules – containing a South African-made variant of red mercury – from a number of nuclear weapons just before the election. This rendered the weapons useless. Such stories were impossible to check, but it seemed the country had indeed come close to the brink.

In a revealing interview in Johannesburg's *Saturday Star* newspaper in June 1995, Mandela offered some insight into what had been going on out of the public eye. Asked for his evaluation of his first year in office, he said:

One never expected that the transition itself would be so smooth and peaceful. Without breaching confidentiality, the right wing was ready to start a civil war in this country. We had to work very hard to induce them to abandon those plans, and it could only be done secretly and confidentially without indicating to the public these plans.

We had numerous discussions with Constand Viljoen, Ferdi Hartzenberg, Dries Bruwer ... and when handling such a matter you do not know what is going to happen. Faced with such a situation, you could not have expected that the transition would have been so smooth – that the population would respond so impressively, so remarkably. That is why I say this transition has gone better than my wildest dreams.

19 The Mini-Nuke Conspiracy Widens

Nuclear blackmail, murder, political chicanery – we had watched this real-life techno-drama from ringside seats. The magnitude of deception was awesome, and the powerful nations of the West were deeply implicated.

They knew that President F. W. de Klerk's 1993 statement that South Africa had built only six and half nuclear weapons and had then destroyed them was false, but they stood silently by.

He said that South Africa's bombs were no more advanced than the one dropped on Hiroshima. That too was not true, and the Western powers knew it.

They also covered up the new superbomb programme, linked to technology from Russia, which gave the SADF unprecedented tactical firepower. Using the red mercury technology, the military had hundreds of neutron shells for their G6 and G5 howitzers.

The most brilliant achievement was the development of a pure fusion device – a 'clean' bomb known as the 'mini-nuke' – which could destroy all living things in the blast area, leave buildings intact, and not leave radioactive fallout.

The project, known as Operation Shampoo, enabled South Africa first to obtain the technology from Russia, then to perfect its own superior version. We even found an eyewitness to stockpiles of neutron devices that were kept in specially designed underground bunkers.

All this was meant for the eyes only of South Africa's nuclear élite, its generals and a few politicians. Despite all of them, but with the help of scores of sources, some light has now been shone on one of the biggest deceptions ever.

The picture is troubling for many reasons. If South African renegades have a number of nuclear weapons, then it will be the first time a group unaccountable to any government has obtained this ultimate means of blackmail. On a number of occasions we heard of suggestions that, to demonstrate their nuclear firepower, the rebels should detonate a bomb on the black township of Soweto, or on Harare. These could have been idle threats, but even if the bombs were, or are, under the professional control of the South African military, there could still be real dangers.

It was apparent to us in several discussions with Thabo Mbeki, First Deputy President, that at least some in the Mandela government knew nothing about these weapons. It was extraordinary that people in the highest elected positions might not know their country's true military capability, yet in the corridors of power in Washington, London, Paris, Jerusalem and Bonn the intelligence agency chiefs had long been observing the deadly game being played out on the southern tip of Africa, and smiling with satisfaction. For their own cynical ends, they had helped South Africa's secret White Savannah Committee to build the ultimate weapon. And because some Western countries in the aftermath of détente could no longer dabble in such terrible forms of destruction, it was perhaps convenient to allow South Africa to be a test bed.

Politically, these countries will have to deny involvement – as we have already warned. It is also possible that some South African politicians who never knew what was being done in their name will feel bitter that this book has done their nation an injustice. But the reality is that global strategies and secret alignments with nations are not always the domain of politicians.

The evidence shows that some intelligence agencies, notably the Defense Intelligence Agency in the United States, were working closely with their counterparts in Pretoria to thwart not only the sanctions imposed by the UN but also the non-proliferation policy of Congress and other parliaments.

Irangate, ISC, the Coventry Four scandal – they are all worrying examples of securocrats taking the law into their own hands. But, unlike Irangate, the Mini-Nuke Conspiracy is about weapons of mass destruction, not TOW anti-tank missiles.

We have uncovered a lot about what happened in South Africa's darkest hours, and more will surely be disclosed once the press and politicians get over their honeymoon relationship following South Africa's incredible transition to democracy. Then we suspect that two men will emerge as the cool-headed poker players who have been trying to deal with a potential international catastrophe behind the scenes. They are Nelson Mandela and General Constand Viljoen, each already commanding substantial respect from their own communities, each aware ultimately that violence is not the answer, and each aware of the real threat that underpinned the demands of some influential Afrikaners for their own homeland. We suspect this is what Mandela was referring to when he revealed in 1995 that the right wing had been ready to start a civil war before the election, and he had had secretly to defuse this by seeking the help of Viljoen and others.

Should South Africans have been told what cards were being played? We believe they should. But whether a settlement over a Volkstaat could be reached in the full glare of television lights is another matter.

What of the string of murders? People have died – some in the most horrible ways imaginable – but none of the killers had been caught as we wrote this final chapter. The victims seem to have been involved with red mercury, the secret ingredient of the mini-nuke. Mossad was accused of plotting Alan Kidger's gruesome end, then a police task force was set up to investigate his and other deaths and the red mercury mystery. These stories alone are the stuff of best-selling fiction – but it is all true.

Some cynics predicted the investigation by Lieutenant-Colonel Charles Landman would drift dangerously close to uncovering too many nuclear skeletons, and thereby founder. Under the corrupt and bankrupt political system of the old South Africa such investigations would have been quickly stopped or shelved for ever. But in the new South Africa – a country led by people espousing greater moral responsibility – the outcome should be better.

Landman waited until the new government took charge and then worked night and day to uncover who was behind the slaughter. He persuaded his generals that only a task force could solve the murders. Then, only months after it had been formed in November 1994, it was disbanded. The cynics were right.

As this book went to press, at the Brixton Murder and Robbery Unit in Johannesburg the dust was gathering on the files on Alan Kidger, Wynand van Wyk, Don Lange and Dirk and Suzanne Stoffberg, among others. Landman would comment no more, and repeatedly cancelled arrangements to meet, but a senior police officer who was angered at the decision to disband the task force was more vocal: 'Charlie's murder probe was stopped on orders from the highest level in government,' he said. 'Every lead on red mercury has since fizzled and died.'

Landman has recently been made commander at Brixton and, as such, is now desk-bound. Early in his red mercury investigation a man telephoned the Brixton unit asking how much it would cost to drop the investigation. Now the caller has got what he wanted, and it hasn't cost him a cent.

*

Regrettably, it is not possible to tell in detail the astonishing story of the initial successes of the investigation by the Crime Intelligence Service, because it would compromise the safety of those involved. Their names clearly have to be withheld to prevent possible reprisals from disgruntled right-wingers. But their valiant efforts to investigate the right-wing bomb also have amounted to nothing.

After the attempted collaboration with us, the officers involved – some as senior as colonel – were ordered to end all contact. One colonel eventually left the force for medical reasons, with a severe case of stress-related problems, and another senior officer also left 'because of ill-health'. Yet another officer, who ran a network of sources within the right wing, was redeployed. The moves were attributed to a huge reorganization of the police force, but the fact remains that the CIS's capacity to investigate the right wing in the northern Transvaal – centre of the nuclear crisis – was neutralized. We were told that the Defence Ministry had interfered at a very high level in the police force. The message was clear: Stop the investigation.

But that may not be the whole story. Jan, the military strategist, had assured us that number of foreign intelligence agencies were highly active. They did not fully trust South Africa's NIA to investiage. 'I think there was a turning-point in our relationship with the West where after a while it began to seriously wonder whether we had a bunch of loons down here who had gone out of control. In the late 1980s the wheels generally came off, things were not good. There was genuine concern overseas that we were going to become a serious nuclear state.'

Whatever the intelligence agencies were doing, nothing would ever be revealed to the public. But at least in February 1995 Channel 4 Television in Britain had the resolve to go ahead and transmit a *Dispatches* programme which focused on the possibility that South Africa had not declared all its weapons. It too suffered interference. The South African embassy contacted the TV station and argued that the programme would damage the country's chances of attracting foreign investment. Channel 4 held its ground. Only hours before the documentary was due to be screened, Thabo Mbeki telephoned to ask if he could be interviewed in a television news slot beforehand. Channel 4 turned him down too.

Channel 4 had worked with the *Weekend Star*'s investigation team in Johannesburg with a view to simultaneous disclosure of the story. But, as the TV programme was being edited, the newspaper began to get cold feet. For months editors had understood that sources must remain confidential, but they urged their investigators to continue digging. Then in February 1995 the newspaper was faced head on with the enormity of the story told in thousands of words of copy. Editors fretted over the fact that sources could not be named.

It was indeed the Watergate problem. But surely the newspaper would recognize that informants directly involved in the nuclear programme could never safely speak on the record about such a sensitive topic. Rightly, these contacts feared for their lives, or a criminal charge that could lead to a twenty-year jail term for leaking secrets. They were taking a risk only because they believed they were acting in the national interest. Sadly, the *Weekend Star* took the easy option. Not only was the story axed, the investigation itself was terminated.

We are not alone in alleging a cover-up by South Africa of its programmes to build mini-nukes and thermonuclear weapons. Anti-apartheid campaigners have never been satisfied that every bomb was dismantled and destroyed. Roger Jardine, who was the ANC's spokesman on nuclear issues, said: 'When De Klerk made his announcement, reactions were mixed. On the one hand, we had a feeling of having achieved something. On the other hand there was a feeling of anger and sadness at the extent to which the apartheid state was willing to go to preserve white supremacy.

'Two to three months before his statement, they were still denying the nuclear weapons programme ... in fact the Atomic Energy Corporation accused us of making trouble and being ill-informed.'[1]

'One has no way of assessing whether De Klerk's statement was the whole truth and nothing but the truth.' He said some analysts believed there were twenty-five nuclear weapons in the South African arsenal: 'The question arises, If there were more, where are they? That is one of the lingering, troubling questions.'

Jardine said he was confident that more officials from the past would come forward to talk about what happened as they became more confident about South Africa's new democracy.

Then there were the remarks of Abdul Minty, who campaigned on behalf of the Anti-Apartheid Movement for twenty years. 'I think that Western powers knew that South Africa was embarking on a nuclear weapons programme. I think later some of them were uneasy, but

[1] In an interview only weeks before De Klerk's announcement, the AEC's chief executive, Waldo Stumpf, had denied that South Africa had a nuclear weapons programme.

because of their commitment to the apartheid regime they took no action.'

Indeed it was the looming end of the De Klerk government and the take-over by Mandela that seems finally to have got the West worried enough to intervene.

In April 1995, representatives of 178 nations gathered in New York to review the working of the Nuclear Non-Proliferation Treaty. It was a unique opportunity for the failings of the treaty to be rectified and to take account of new developments, such as mini-nukes.

When the conference began, one might have expected an open discussion, with delegates debating the pros and cons of a subclause here or a composited amendment there. In fact it was a fruitless jamboree.

Before the delegates had even unpacked their suitcases, a clique of nuclear countries had decided the conference was a damaging threat to their plans. The United States, Russia, China, France and Britain had been lobbying for weeks. In the case of the United States it was more like arm-twisting, and the US had been doing that for several years.

The 'Big Five' were the only countries allowed nuclear weapons under the 1968 treaty, and they were determined it should remain unchanged, despite its obvious flaws. Their publicly expressed argument was that even a small amendment would require all members to ratify it, and, given that opportunity, there were fears some signatories would simply withdraw.

The fear was probably well-founded, as some countries had observed that quite a few non-treaty members, such as Israel, had developed a sophisticated nuclear armoury and no one seemed inclined to do anything about it. But was the treaty worth keeping in those circumstances? That was the big debate.

Countries within the Non-Aligned Movement suggested the treaty should be extended for a limited period to pressure the Big Five to implement its provisions fully. Led by Indonesia, the NAM called for them to disarm, share peaceful nuclear technology, and give non-nuclear countries binding assurances about their security.

Before the conference, South Africa was seen as a strong potential ally of this grouping, as it was widely respected as the first country unilaterally to dismantle its own nuclear weapons. The vote was touch and go, but, with the Republic's help, the nuclear 'have-not' countries could cock a snook at the nuclear 'haves'.

The address by South African Foreign Minister Alfred Nzo started well. He acknowledged that the NAM countries' criticisms of the treaty were valid. He urged that the NPT be strengthened to ensure nuclear powers did more to meet NPT obligations, and suggested proposals for doing so. But then he said the proposals should not be made a condition of the NPT's indefinite extension, otherwise the treaty would be weakened. He added that South Africa was acting in the interests of the greatest possible consensus. But many in the hall, including political observers from around the world, wondered how the Big Five had suddenly become the Big Six. With South Africa's help, the nuclear club won the vote.[1]

Peter Vale, a foreign policy analyst and professor of southern African studies at the University of the Western Cape, was nonplussed. He told Johannesburg's *Weekly Mail & Guardian* in April 1995 that South Africa had 'buckled under pressure from the United States', and warned there would be 'a great deal of disquiet within the Non-Aligned Movement'. Vale added: 'This foreign policy decision will be seen to be one made by whites in the interests of a world in which white interests are protected and defended. It does not reflect what the majority of people feel about the issue – South Africa's people have not been consulted at all.'

David Fig, director of South Africa's Group for Environmental Monitoring, said the independence and integrity of his country's foreign policy was now in doubt and he agreed with Vale's analysis: 'We are submitting to extreme pressure exerted by the United States to conform to its desires.' Fig said South Africa had failed to use the moral ground it had acquired when it became the world's first country to unilaterally and voluntarily dismantle its own nuclear weapons arsenal. It was 'a severe set-back' for alliances being built between South Africa, its southern African partners and the NAM.

'The position plays into the hands of the existing nuclear weapons states, particularly the United States, which knows the extension of the treaty makes no significant demands on the weapons states to reduce their existing arsenals.'

Fig added: 'The non-aligned countries need strong evidence of good

1 An important talking-point at the conference centred on whether certain chemicals such as tritium should come under the NPT's provisions. Like red mercury, there are a number of special substances which are much sought after by weapons designers and which, if controlled, would slow progress towards making a workable device. As the treaty remains unchanged, there is of course still no bar to trade in these materials unless individual countries decide to take action.

faith in the willingness of nuclear weapons states to disarm before they can agree to participate in such an unequal non-proliferation regime.' This, he said, was why South African officials had originally proposed a compromise position of a rolling extension at a preparatory conference in January. 'This compromise would have opened the way for the resolution of the inequalities in the spirit of global non-proliferation ... Our new leaders are becoming indistinguishable from the old in their adherence to the foreign policy prescriptions of the rich and privileged countries.'

These were harsh words to direct at the ANC, which for almost all its existence had supported the underdog countries of the world. It was almost as if the new South Africa was acting like a nuclear superpower itself. But why?

A clue to the volte-face was disclosed by the *Washington Post* a few weeks before the conference opened. It reported that Princeton Lyman, the US ambassador to South Africa, had delivered a *démarche*, or formal note of protest, to Alfred Nzo on 10 March warning that a vote against the treaty's indefinite extension, which Nzo was canvassing, would undermine 'mutual interests' and affect Washington's view of South Africa's non-proliferation credentials. It wasn't clear what Lyman had meant about US and South African 'mutual interests', but it was obviously important.

Coen Snyman, a South African foreign affairs spokesman, could not confirm the *démarche*, but said the issue had a long history with 'lots of communication' between South Africa and the United States. President Clinton had even written to President Mandela about it.

The *Post* said the *démarche* also noted that the United States had supported South Africa's membership of the Nuclear Suppliers Group – an exclusive cartel of nuclear nations that controlled nuclear technology sales. The United States clearly expected South Africa to do it a favour in return, and it seems the NPT vote was that favour.

In the aftermath of the Cold War, the possibility of nuclear confrontation no longer terrifies people as it did. The NPT conference and the failure to update it should have been front-page news: instead, it was consigned to the foreign pages of most newspapers.

The delegates went home and, as had long been its role, the IAEA was left alone again to act as the world's nuclear policeman.

Being a UN body, the IAEA has immense authority to stop the spread of nuclear technologies and the illicit sale of nuclear materials. But if the NPT is a flop – as many nuclear analysts believe – the IAEA is an even bigger one. The story told in this book is evidence of that.

After the De Klerk announcement in 1993, South Africa made maximum capital of its new innocence. Pik Botha, then Foreign Minister, went to Vienna and presented Hans Blix, the IAEA's director-general, with a model of a plough made from parts of a destroyed warhead. Photographs show Blix smiling with delight while a serious-looking Botha stands beside him. Or was Blix smiling with embarrassment?

The IAEA had made more than 150 inspections in South Africa from 1991 to 1995 without apparently uncovering anything untoward. Blix is not a nuclear scientist but a Swedish-trained lawyer. He is also accused of being naïve in his optimism that his organization can stem the spread of nuclear weapons.

The case for his naïvety was most forcefully made by the *Washington Post* in April 1995. It said the IAEA boss still worked long hours at the age of sixty-eight, and was passionately committed to nuclear disarmament. But, it said, 'Blix knew that while some officials in Washington saw his agency as part of the solution to emerging nuclear threats, others regarded the IAEA as part of the problem.'

Such attitudes arose from the IAEA's performance in Iraq. The newspaper reminded its readers that, after the Gulf War had ended in 1991, the United Nations discovered that Saddam Hussein had pursued a $10 billion secret nuclear weapons programme under the noses of the IAEA's inspectors. 'Blix and his agency took a lot of heat in Washington,' continued the *Post*.

Based on confidential interviews with returning inspectors, a 1993 study by the Pentagon's Defense Nuclear Agency concluded: 'Iraq often successfully manipulated the inspections. The lesson here is that any potential violator in the future may be able to out-wait the inspection process through delays and denials.'

Said the *Post*: 'Several Americans who had worked at the IAEA publicly attacked Blix's inspectors as weak-kneed, Milquetoast UN types. Some US nuclear weapons scientists returned from IAEA-supervised missions to Iraq grumbling that Blix wouldn't know a nuclear bomb if he tripped over one.'

Jay Davis of the Lawrence Livermore US atomic weapons laboratory said: 'Blix, an attorney, would argue with me as a scientist that we weren't understanding what we were seeing. He was not perturbed by transparent Iraqi deceptions.'

The paper disclosed that Blix had been given secret briefings by the CIA, with sight of satellite evidence, to show him the extent of the preparations some countries were making to build nuclear weapons. But he faced the problem that IAEA rules limited how thorough inspections could be. Inspectors had become like 'bank auditors', the newspaper said: they 'depended heavily on the good faith of their clients, so they were vulnerable to a devious embezzler'.

This might explain why the IAEA confirmed the quantities of weapons-grade uranium declared by South Africa, despite the evidence that it has been deliberately understated.

This is a bleak story, and a salutary one for counter-proliferation policy-makers. But the scientific principles behind the mini-nuke and, ironically, the new technologies in the secret nuclear programmes of South Africa, the former Soviet Union and probably some Western countries could in another way be of enormous benefit to mankind.

We learned that nuclear fusion, the principle behind the 'clean' bomb, if properly harnessed can also provide cheap and limitless electrical energy – the Holy Grail sought by physicists all over the world. Pik Botha, now South Africa's Minister for Mineral and Energy Affairs, seemed to acknowledge this in the conference speech he gave in January 1995, when he speculated that it may be possible to convert red mercury into electrical power. He was perhaps the first politician to recognize openly the long-term potential of this controversial material.

But even this prospect would not be universally welcomed by nations and mulitnationals whose fortunes depend on oil and nuclear power. It was put to us that this was also part of the mini-nuke conspiracy – that there is a secret pact between certain nations to slow down the pace of these developments.

Meanwhile the killings continue. As this book went to press in September 1995, it was announced by police that Major Juanita du Plessis, a military intelligence officer, and her husband André, had been found with their throats cut in their Pretoria apartment. Police said it was a professional job with a stiletto knife and the deaths might be linked to red mercury.

In Greece it was reported that a military plane from Kiev had crashed near the port city of Thessaloniki, killing a number of military officers from Mali and a French secret agent who had allegedly helped in the capture of Carlos the Jackal. Rescuers also found on board the plane three Deutsche Bank cheques, each for $6 million; a photograph of Pavel Grachev, the Russian defence minister; forged dollars with a printing plate for making them; and six canisters of red mercury 'used to make nuclear weapons'.

And on the borders between the Ukraine and Belarus the smuggling of the material continued. Guards were reported to have confiscated about 1 kg of red mercury found hidden under the front mudguard of a Ford Sierra car. They also seized approximately 14 kg of palladium and gallium, and 1 kg of arsenic.

However much the big powers might want to douse speculation about new nuclear technologies, such stories will continue to fuel suspicion that an enormous conspiracy is being perpetrated. And one thing is certain: such concern will not be quelled until the scientific facts are independently investigated and made public. This might show that red mercury is the world's biggest ever hoax, and put an end to it. But if it is not a hoax, as this book seeks to show, then the world has a right to know what perils it faces from a new and frightening generation of secret weaponry.

APPENDICES

Appendix 1: List of Documents Concerning Export of Red Mercury 20/20

This is a translation of a Russian list of red mercury transactions compiled by the KGB and leaked to the authors in Moscow. It demonstrates that many highly placed organizations and politicians have been involved in granting permission for the material to be exported. Most noteworthy is the name of the Russian President, Boris Yeltsin, who granted a license to a firm called Promecology (see 06.03.92).

DATE	ORGANIZATION OF ORIGIN	ADDRESS AND SENDER	DECISION	VOLUME IN KG	BROKER	CLIENT	PRODUCER	PRICE IN US $M
10.02.90	USSR Council of Ministers	–	–	300	NTZ DVMPO (Dalvent)	Massandra (Liechten)	–	48
02.90	Firm 'NTT' Far-East Dept. Assoc. Dalvent	–	Contract	300	'NTT'	Massandro (Liechtenst) Unknown Firm	–	48
02.90	Scientific Technologic Association of Moscow Sverdlovsk area 'Technology'	–	Telex deal between area dept. and director	30 per month for 5 years	NTTM	'Network' UK capital £100.00 bankrupt in 1989	–	£6.00 per month
08.90	Electro Technology Firm ZSE (Czechekosl.)	–	Protocol of intent signed abroad	300 + 2	'Sevkabel' Leningrad	ZSE	–	0.28 for 1kg
12.12.90	Post GMBH & CO (West Germany) Wilfrid Post GMBH und CO, KG	GTU Ministry Foreign Economic Relations Mr Lapshev, Wilfrid Post	–	–	Wilfrid Post	–	–	–
08.91	'Kuzin Group'	So-called contract	–	207	–	Firm unknown	–	–

DATE	ORGANIZATION OF ORIGIN	ADDRESS AND SENDER	DECISION	VOLUME IN KG	BROKER	CLIENT	PRODUCER	PRICE IN US $M
09.91	'F.K. Intern'	Contract	–	25 tonnes	Altay Chemical Industry	–	–	1 per kg
09.91	'Foreign N.O.T investors bureau' USA	Protocol of Intent	–	10	'Russian Court'	–	–	3
09.91	Mashin Technology	Agency Datas	–	–	'Kazakintorg'	–	–	–
30.09.91	Moscow Lizensentorg (Licence Buro)	Mr Kurushnic V.I. Mr Ignashev V.V.	–	10 tonnes	'Lizensentorg' There is a licence	–	'M.P. North-Sever' 'M.P. Reagent'	–
10.10.91 IP. 001/91	TOO 'Simatek' Moscow	Mr Lobov O.I. Mr Gribakin S.I. Mr Gaidar E.T. Mr Titkin Mr Piskunov	–	500 per month	TOO 'Simatek'	International Group of investors R. Kasulke	Organisation of production in 4–5 months	–
No date	State Foreign Economy Company for export and import of arms	Mr Burbulis G.Z. Mr Krasnov S.N.	GB-5-41404 11.11.91	–	State Foreign Economy Company	–	–	–
25.11.91	Government Russian Federation	–	GB-5-39738	–	Documents	–	–	–
09.12.91 6	Ural Regional Economic Committee — Ekaterinburg	Mr Burbulis G.Z. Mr Vozdviznensky S.B.	G.Z. Mr Aven P.D. GB-5-41404	3,000 per year	AO 'Zitron'	AO 'Tungsram' (Hungary) & US	Company Ural Region	–

Date/Ref	Organization	Requestor	Officials	No.	Code/Firm	Moscow	Other
11.12.91	Intraco & I.A.T.) (Bulgaria)	Mr Silaev I.S.		–	–	–	–
28.12.91 65ss	Independent Association 'Yupiter'	Mr Yeltsin B.N. Mr Nozdrachev V.D.	Mr Gaidar E.T. Mr Aven P.O. Mr Zakharov Mr Petrov Y.V. Mr Karabelshikov Mr Barannikov	–	–	Ind. Ass. Yupiter Moscow	Deutsche Bank- German Government
12.91	Seems request comes from – 'A.T. Ventures Inc.'			624	'Simako' Unknown US firm	–	0.3... 1
20.01.92	Building production Commercial Association 'Videonas' (Moscow)	Mr Smelov Mr Koyedyaev Mr Mazur V.D.		–	–	–	–
23.01.92 1-4	'Interpromtorg' (Moscow) Company does not exist	Mr Burbulis G.Z. Mr Nikolaev A.M.	Mr Gaidar E.T. Mr Olkmovnikov Mr Titekin Mr Nikipelov Mr Aven Mr Olkmovnikov-Semenzov	–	Interpromtorg	–	–
23.01.92 566/3/386	Department head chemical troops of sup. Gov. CIS (Moscow)	No address Mr Orlev V.N.		–	'Symbol'	–	–
23.01.92 80005-15	Ministry of Foreign Economic Relations – GIU (Moscow)	No address Tretyak V.D.		100 – 400	'Symbol'	'IBC' - (Tallin)	–

DATE	ORGANIZATION OF ORIGIN	ADDRESS AND SENDER	DECISION	VOLUME IN KG	BROKER	CLIENT	PRODUCER	PRICE IN US $M
24.01.92 18-01	Scientific Technical Production Association 'Symbol' Ural Section (Ekaterinburg)	Mr Gaidar E.T. Mr Syskov V.V.	–	–	–	–	There are links– with NI ... and firms' producers ...	–
28.01.92 PK-05-01	Sverdlovsk Regional Government	Mr Gaidar E.T. Mr Anisin A.S.	–	–	'Symbol'	'IBC' (Tallin)	Companies of – Ural Region	–
07.02.92 B/N	Hi-tech International Moscow	Mr Necmaev A.A. Mr Akhmed S.K.	Mr Nechaev Mr Olkmovnikov Mr Olkmovnikov-Semenbov	400	'Promecology'	'HTI'	–	–
19.02.92 14329/2-046	Socmi Scientific Research Centre (SOCMI)	Mr Amirkhanov M.	Of letter by Orlov V. Sup. Sov. CIS & GIU KVZS Ministry of Foreign Affairs V. Tretyak	–	Sverdiovsk Region			
19.02.92 2/19	'Videonas' Moscow	Mr Voronin Y.M. Mr Tunikas V.A.	Mr Smeboldaev V.B. Mr Voronin Mr Lebedev Mr Barannikov	–	–	–		–
05.03.92 12/3	PKF 'Oykumena' (Kaliningrad)	Mr Gaidar E.T. Mr Baranov O.V.	Mr Smokin A.N. Mr Mikhailov Mr Vishnevsky	50 per month	'Oykumena' (Licence Buro) N.O.T.	Lizensentorg	–	–

Date / No.	Organization	Signatories / Proposal	Recipient / Details		Amount	Association	Licence	Value
05.03.92 119/10	'Lizensentorg' (Moscow) (Licence Buro) N.O.T.	Mr Gaidar Mr Kushev	Mr Titikin Mr Aven Mr Kruglov ASH-PZ-10179 Mr Olkhovikov-Semenzov	(as above)	200–300 per month	'Oykumena'	Lizensentog There is licence	0.3
06.03.92 003-0136	Association 'Promecology' (Ekaterinburg)	Sadykov Commercial proposal, looking for suppliers	Authorisation B.N. Yeltsin 75-RPS 21.02.92		10,000	Ass. 'Promecology'	–	–
11.03.92 95	Moscow Ass. Organization of Veterans of Afghan war	Mr Gaidar E.T. Mr Lagunov A.P.	Mr Gaidar Mr Materov Mr Aven Mr Materov-Semenzov		1,000	MOOVVA	–	–
16.03.92 003-0165	Association 'Promecology' Ekaterinburg	Proposal to Foreign Companies to sell Red Mercury	–		–	–	–	–

Appendix 2: Specification of Liquid Red Mercury

This specification for 'RM 20/20' or 'red mercury' is a translation of a Russian document given to the authors by a government official in the city of Ekaterinburg. It is typical of many that circulate on the black market. Some of the scientific details baffle scientists, notably its density and its being a liquid. In its normal state $Hg_2Sb_2O_7$ is a powder.

Product:	Red Mercury, R 20/20
Density:	20/20
Chemical Formula:	Hg2SB2O7
Molecular Mass:	756.61
Purity:	99.99%
Colour:	Cherry Red
Form:	Liquid, in case of Ro = 1.01325 bar
Melting Temperature:	−37.87°C
Flare Temperature:	170. 026°C
Boiling Temperature:	350.72°C
Isotope Temperature:	160.87°C
Natural Radioelements:	SF & SIC Circa in Number 0.784
Gamma FS:	0.440
Reaction K:	0.00015
Reaction R:	9,000–8,000
Reaction Absolute Temperature:	0.062
Reaction VIT Temperature:	1.024
Reaction VDSA:	0.30–0.29
Reaction Ren:	0.794
Warning:	The substance is mildly radioactive, handling is safe.
Package: Possibility No.1:	Retort NY 22
	Gross Weight: 39.5 kg
	Net Weight: 34.5 kg/retort
Possibility No.2:	Wooden box package with 3 standard ceramic carboys, 4 litres capacity, hermetically closed by lead seals with registration number, supplied with ampoules with samples and placed in aluminium vessels.
	Net Weight: 90.89 kg
	Gross Weight: 110 kg
Preparation date:	No more than 15 days
Special analysis:	With samples of 7.5 grammes

Special analysis. Metal content (%):

Co 2 x 10^{-7}	Sn 1 x 10^{-8}	Ag 3 x 10^{-8}
Cr 1 x 10^{-7}	Al 1 x 10^{-7}	Mg 1 x 10^{-7}
Ni 1 x 10^{-7}	Cu 1 x 10^{-7}	Pb 3 x 10^{-7}

Transuranic – Actinide: Lawrencium (Lr – 103)
Isotopic Structures (%):

O 16:	99.76	Hg 196:	0.18
O 17:	0.037	Hg 198:	10.20
O 18:	0.20	Hg 199:	16.80
		Hg 200:	23.10
		Hg 201:	13.22
		Hg 202:	29.80
		Hg 204:	6.80

Appendix 3: Red Mercury Nuclear Devices

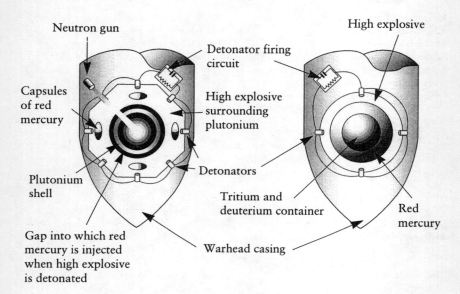

Neutron gun

High explosive

Detonator firing circuit

Capsules of red mercury

High explosive surrounding plutonium

Plutonium shell

Detonators

Tritium and deuterium container

Red mercury

Gap into which red mercury is injected when high explosive is detonated

Warhead casing

The diagrams above illustrate the supposed principles of two types of red mercury nuclear weapon. They were published by *International Defense Review* in 1994 in an article by the nuclear analyst Dr Frank Barnaby.

On the left is a fission device: an advanced type of atom bomb. Capsules of red mercury are embedded in high explosive surrounding a spherical shell of plutonium. When the explosive is detonated, the red mercury is injected into a gap around the plutonium. It acts as a neutron reflector, increasing the efficiency of the nuclear fission process, and as a tamper, preventing the plutonium from disintegrating too quickly. Neutron rich elements known as actinides (e.g. Californium 252) in the red mercury also give a boost to the fission process, increasing the yield of the bomb for a given quantity of plutonium.

On the right is a pure fusion neutron bomb. An outer layer of high explosive is detonated causing the inner layer of red mercury to release an enormous amount of stored energy. The energy implodes the tritium and deuterium at the centre of the device, producing enough heat to create a fusion reaction and a massive release of high-energy neutrons.

Index

Mechem 126, 162
Media Council 191
Meiring, Bridget 38
Meiring, Georg 28, 197
Mercury (Switzeralnd) 63
Mercury Printers 12
Messerschmidt Boelkow Blohm 64
Metelerkamp, William 'Randy' 224, 230, 231, 233, 236, 237, 239
Meyer, Roelf 28
MI5 10, 16, 181, 224
MI6 8, 10, 11, 97
Middlesworth, Dr Van 144
Mijburgh, Philip 159
Mikerin, Yevgeny 61
Mikhailov, Viktor 61-2
Military Intelligence (MI) 16n, 17, 21, 41, 97, 102, 106, 107, 110, 115, 135, 156, 196, 244, 258
Mintek 38, 39
Minty, Abdul 145, 211-12, 276-7
Missile Technology Control Regime (MTCR) 54, 55, 69, 169n, 171
Mitchell, David 102
Modise, Joe 6, 7, 195n
Moolman, Johan 229
Moose, Richard M. 218-19
Mossad 5-8, 13, 14, 22, 24, 25, 30, 35, 40, 41, 92, 156, 158, 175n, 190, 259, 274
Mouton, Professor Wynand 46-50, 69, 135
Moynihan, Daniel 151
Mozambique National Resistance (MNR; Renamo) 89n
MPLA (Popular Movement for the Liberation of Angola) 151
Mufamadi, Sydney 7, 154n
Mulder, Connie 203n
Murray, Angus 238

National Institute for Defence Research 138, 163n
National Intelligence Agency (NIA) 16n, 41, 156, 259
National Intelligence Co-ordinating Committee 16n
National Intelligence Service (NIS) 16n, 21, 82, 100, 107, 110, 115, 156, 261, 263
National Investigation Services 16n
National Party 28, 46, 52, 67, 75, 101,

200, 203n, 238n, 254n
National Security Agency 220
NATO 180, 212, 214, 249
Naval Research Laboratory (US) 145
NBC-TV (US) 169
Negin, General Yevgeny 62
Newby-Fraser, A.R. 70n
Newsnight (BBC TV programme) 33
Non-Aligned Movement (NAM) 277, 278
North, Colonel Oliver 101
Northrop 167, 226, 227, 228
Noyce, Michael 215
Nuclear Non-Proliferation Treaty (NPT) (1968) 44, 54, 68, 78, 80, 83, 84, 121, 137, 144, 162, 196, 207, 208, 249, 270, 277, 278, 279
Nuclear Suppliers Group 279
Numec nuclear-waste reprocessing plant 201
Nzo, Alfred 7, 277-8, 279

Oak Ridge National Laboratory (US) 206
October Surprise affair 101
Office of Non-Proliferation Support, US Department of Energy 117
Office of Threat Assessment, US Department of Energy 117
Omar, Dullah 16n
Operation Desert Storm 267
Operation Kertoring (Operation Church Tower) 71
Operation Phoenix 145
Operation Ploegskaar (Ploughshare) 141
Operation Savannah 151
Operation Shampoo xix, 23, 24, 185-98, 187, 245, 246, 250, 251, 272
Orange Free State Agricultural Union 254, 255n
Orbital Transport and Rockets AG (OTRAG) 141n
Ordine Nuovo 120
Organization of African Unity (OAU) 74-5
Organochem 160, 161
Osiraq Research Reactor, Baghdad 8
Overberg missile range 168-9, 170, 171, 172, 225
Owen, Ken 125, 208
Oxford Research Group (ORG) 137, 138
Oxley, Vicki 105-6

Pan-Africanist Congress 16n, 200

297